Challenging Behavior in Young Children

Understanding, Preventing, and Responding Effectively

Barbara Kaiser
Judy Sklar Rasminsky

Boston • New York • San Francisco
Mexico City • Montreal • Toronto • London • Madrid • Munich • Paris
Hong Kong • Singapore • Tokyo • Cape Town • Sydney

Series Editor: *Traci Mueller*
Editorial Assistant: *Erica Tromblay*
Marketing Manager: *Elizabeth Fogarty*
Production Editor: *Christine Tridente*
Composition Buyer: *Linda Cox*
Editorial Production Services: *TKM Productions*
Electronic Composition: *TKM Productions*
Manufacturing Buyer: *JoAnne Sweeney*
Cover Administrator: *Kristina Mose-Libon*

For related titles and support materials, visit our online catalog at www.ablongman.com.

This book has been adapted from *Meeting the Challenge: Effective Strategies for Challenging Behaviours in Early Childhood Environments* by Barbara Kaiser and Judy Sklar Rasminsky. © 1999, Canadian Child Care Federation, 201-383 Parkdale Avenue, Ottawa, Ontario, Canada, K1Y 4R4. The authors wish to express their gratitude to the Canadian Child Care Federation for granting permission for its use.

To obtain permission(s) to use material from this work, please submit a written request to Allyn and Bacon, Permissions Department, 75 Arlington Street, Boston, MA 02116 or fax your request to 617-848-7320.

Between the time Website information is gathered and published, some sites may have closed. Also, the transcription of URLs can result in unintended typographical errors. The publisher would appreciate notification where these errors occur so that they may be corrected in subsequent editions.

Library of Congress Cataloging-in-Publication Data

Kaiser, Barbara.
  Challenging behavior in young children : understanding, preventing, and responding effectively/Barbara Kaiser and Judy Sklar Rasminsky.
      p. cm.
  Includes bibliographical references and index.
   ISBN 0-205-34226-4
   1. Behavior modification. 2. Early childhood education. 3. Classroom management. I. Rasminsky, Judy Sklar. II. Title.
  LB1060.2 .K35 2003
  371.39'3--dc21   2002074799

Printed in the United States of America

10 9 8 7 6 5 4 3 2 1   08 07 06 05 04 03 02

Photo Credits: p. 13: Tom McCarthy/PhotoEdit; **p. 16:** Shirley Zeiberg; **p. 31** Health Canada; **p. 39:** Edouard Berne/ Getty Images, Inc.; **p. 54:** SW Productions/Getty Images, Inc.; **p. 55:** Robert Harbison; **p. 64:** Will Hart; **p. 75:** Will Hart; **p. 83:** Don Smetzer/Getty Images, Inc.; **p. 84:** Will Hart; **p. 89:** Shelley Rotner/Omni-Photo Communications, Inc.; **p. 91:** Brian Smith; **p. 112:** David Young-Wolff/PhotoEdit; **p. 115:** Robert Harbison; **p. 119:** Laima Druskis/Pearson Education/ PH College; **p. 121:** Michael Newman/PhotoEdit; **p. 131:** Will Hart; **p. 138:** K and K Ammann/Getty Images, Inc.; **p. 148:** Cindy Charles/PhotoEdit; **p. 160:** Will Hart; **p. 165:** Will Faller; **p. 185:** Richard Hutchings/PhotoEdit; **p. 187:** Dennis MacDonald/PhotoEdit; **p. 199:** Bob Daemmrich/Bob Daemmrich Photography, Inc.; **p. 207:** Will Hart; **p. 221:** Bob Daemmrich/Bob Daemmrich Photography, Inc.; **p. 227:** Michael Newman/PhotoEdit; **p. 233:** Richard Hutchings/PhotoEdit; **p. 241:** Mary Kate Denny/PhotoEdit; **p. 247:** Laima Druskis/Pearson Education/PH College.

To all the Andrews, Michaels, and Jessicas—
past, present, and future

Contents

Foreword by Sue Bredekamp   xi

Acknowledgments   xiii

Introduction   **1**

1 *What Is Challenging Behavior?*   **9**

    Isn't challenging behavior sometimes appropriate for very young children?   10
    Do children outgrow challenging behavior?   11
    What is aggression?   13
    Does culture play a role in aggressive behavior?   17
    What do you think?   18
    Suggested reading   19
    References   19

2 *Risk Factors*   **22**

    What causes challenging behavior?   23

Biological Risk Factors   **23**
    Genes   23
    Temperament   24
    Attention deficit disorder and attention deficit hyperactivity disorder   28
    Complications of pregnancy and birth   29
    Substance abuse during pregnancy   30
    Malnutrition   32
    Language and cognition disorders   32
    Gender   34

Environmental Risk Factors   **35**
    Family factors and parenting style   35
    Poverty and the conditions surrounding it   37

Exposure to violence   38
Turbulent times   40
Violent media   42
Child care   43
Understanding risk   44
What do you think?   45
Suggested reading   45
References   45

3 *Protective Factors*   **50**

Who is the resilient child?   51
What makes a resilient child bounce back?   52
How does the family contribute to resilience?   53
What is the community's role in resilience?   54
What do you think?   56
Suggested reading   56
References   57

4 *Behavior and the Brain*   **58**

How do babies' brains develop?   59
How does experience spur nerve cells to connect?   60
Is there a critical period for social or emotional behavior?   61
What does caregiving have to do with it?   62
What about neurotransmitters?   65
Which parts of the brain are involved in aggressive behavior?   66
What does all this mean?   68
What do you think?   68
Suggested reading   68
References   68

5 *Understanding Yourself*   **70**

The caring connection   70
"Who are you?" said the caterpillar   71
What influences the way you relate to a child with challenging behavior?   72
What is self-reflection?   74
How do you reflect?   74

When do you reflect?   75
What do you reflect about?   76
Are there any techniques to help you reflect?   76
What do you think?   77
Suggested reading   77
References   78

6   *Understanding the Child's Family and Culture*   **79**

Collaborating with Families   **79**
Getting to know you   80

Opening the Culture Door   **82**
What is culture?   82
What does culture have to do with identity?   83
Are cultures really so different?   85
How can you see your culture?   87
The culture of child care and school   88
What happens when children move from one culture to another?   90
How does culture influence behavior?   91
Why all this matters   100
What do you think?   101
Suggested reading   101
References   101

7   *Preventing Challenging Behavior with the Right Physical
Space and Program*   **105**

How does prevention work?   106
Meeting children's needs   107
We're all the same, yet we're all different   107

The Physical Space   **109**
Wide open spaces   110
What will go inside each area?   110
What about the people?   111
Does the level of stimulation make a difference?   113
Consider the results   114

The Program   **114**
Offering choices   114
Choosing materials   116

Are some activities harder for children with challenging behavior?   118
How do you get from A to B?   120
When circumstances change   123
What do you think?   126
Suggested reading   127
References   127

8   *Preventing Challenging Behavior with the Right Social Context*   129

***Creating the Social Context*   129**
What kind of social context fosters prosocial behavior and discourages aggressive behavior?   130
What is the teacher's role in the social context?   130
How can you create a cooperative and inclusive community?   132

***Teaching Social Skills*   136**
Why are social skills important?   136
How do children learn social skills?   137
Why should we include children with challenging behaviors?   139
How do you teach social skills?   139
What skills do children need to learn?   140
What do you think?   152
Suggested reading and resources   152
References   153

9   *Guidance and Punishment*   157
What information will you need?   158
How useful is positive reinforcement?   159
Which is better: Praise or encouragement?   162
What if positive reinforcement provokes challenging behavior?   163
What about natural and logical consequences?   165
Is it good practice to use time-out?   167
What's wrong with using punishment?   170
What do you think?   171
Suggested reading   172
References   172

10 *The WEVAS Strategy*   **174**

Calibration: Zeroing in on the child's state of mind   175
The anxious state: The early warning system   177
The agitated state: Reactions intensify   179
The aggressive state: The fire inside   186
The assaultive state: Involving the community   190
What about using restraint?   191
The open state: A time to debrief and learn   191
Returning to the group   192
What do you think?   194
Suggested reading and resources   194
References   194

11 *Functional Assessment*   **195**

What do you need to know to figure out the function of a behavior?   196
What about appropriate behavior?   198
How do you get the information you need for a functional assessment?   198
How do you observe?   201
What do you do with all this information?   203
What do you think?   211
Suggested reading   211
References   211

12 *Working with Families and Other Experts*   **213**

How do families react to news of challenging behavior?   214
How do you feel?   216
How can colleagues help?   217
How do you arrange a meeting?   218
What should happen in a meeting with the family?   220
How do you close a meeting?   223
What if you and the family disagree?   224
How do you handle challenging behavior when the parent is present?   225
What should you say to the parents of the other children?   225
What about getting expert advice?   226
What if the child needs more help?   226
What about asking a child with challenging behavior to leave?   229
What do you think?   229

Suggested reading   230
References   230

13 *Bullying*   **231**

What is bullying?   231
How common is bullying?   233
Who are the children who bully others?   234
Who are the targets of bullying?   236
Who are the bystanders?   238
How can teachers combat bullying?   241
What helps children cope with bullying?   245
How do you respond to bullying?   247
What do you do if you don't see the bullying?   251
How can you work with the parents of children involved in bullying?   252
What do you think?   255
Suggested reading and resources   255
References   255

Appendix A   The Functional Assessment Observation Form   259

Appendix B   The Functional Assessment A-B-C Chart   264

Appendix C   The Division for Early Childhood of the Council for Exceptional Children: Position Statement on Interventions for Challenging Behavior   265

Index   267

Foreword

Anyone who has ever been a teacher has taught at least one child (and often more) whose behavior was so disruptive that he (and it was usually a he, let's admit it) made it almost impossible to provide a good learning experience for the other children. If you are a truly caring teacher, no matter how many years you've taught, you always remember those children. They're the ones who got away. You can't help feeling that you failed them and that in doing so, failed the others as well.

I have my own memories of Jeffrey and Scott. I encountered 4-year-old Jeffrey during my first year of teaching in a child-care center. He was extremely intelligent, was socially and physically awkward, and, in retrospect, obviously had attention deficit hyperactivity disorder (ADHD). Totally unprepared as a teacher, I struggled terribly throughout the year in a class with many other children I found challenging as well.

I wanted to continue teaching but couldn't face such failure, so during my second year I took a course in guiding behavior. It was also during that year that I had 3-year-old Scott in my class—the "bad boy" whom the other children blamed for misdeeds even on days when he wasn't there! Fortunately, in my college class I had learned some of the key content that is presented in this book. I learned to evaluate and reorganize the physical facility to help Scott to do his best. I learned to reflect on my own behavior and started to give him attention for his good deeds, instead of only when he misbehaved. When I started "catching him doing something right," as Kaiser and Rasminsky recommend, he started doing right more often. Having changed the physical environment and changed my own behaviors, I found that there were fewer of his challenging behaviors that I needed to address directly. Using strategies such as those recommended in Chapters 9 to 13 of this book, I established an excellent relationship with Scott, and his second year in my class as a 4-year-old was a great learning experience for us both. So I know from my own experience that what you'll learn from reading this book will have a significant positive effect on you as a teacher and on the hundreds of children you will eventually touch.

Most people don't read books straight through from cover to cover, but some people do read forewords and prefaces first. If you are reading this book, then it is highly likely that you are or will be facing a situation with one or more children who have challenging behaviors. You will be tempted to skip directly to Chapters 9 to 13, hoping to find quick solutions to your problems. Please resist that temptation. There are no quick and easy answers to children's challenging behaviors. Be sure to read Chapters 7 and 8 before 9 to 13, because prevention is always easier and more effective than later intervention. And don't miss Chapter 5, because to deal with children with challenging behaviors, you must understand yourself. Oh, yes, and you must read Chapters 6 and

12 because so much of this work depends on establishing productive relationships with families, and such relationships are so complicated by the reality of cultural and linguistic diversity in North America. At some point, you're going to want to understand the bigger context for these vital developmental issues; Kaiser and Rasminsky provide clear, concise summaries of the research and theoretical base in the first four chapters.

You *must* read the authors' introduction. It will help you understand why this is such a wise but eminently practical book. Barbara Kaiser and Judy Sklar Rasminsky have walked in your shoes. They understand how you feel as a teacher when a child is completely out of control, threatening you and the other children. They know what it's like to feel angry or impotent, to attribute motives to the child that he doesn't really have, and to question whether teaching is right for you. And they want more than anything to help you apply the research-based knowledge that will not only help the child with challenging behaviors develop more social competence and emotional control but will also support social-emotional and cognitive development among all the children.

Young children today are growing up in a changed world and those changes are manifest in their behavior. Teachers of young children today report that more children have challenging behaviors and that the behavior itself is more challenging than ever. This book is timely in providing guidance for teachers working with a generation of children post-September 11, 2001, and also in providing strategies for bullying behavior, which seems to have become an ever-increasing problem.

The content and teaching strategies recommended in *Challenging Behavior in Young Children* are thoroughly based in current research and theory. But the authors' straightforward, honest, clear writing style makes this important knowledge easily accessible for the reader. Some phrases embed themselves in memory. I just wish that I knew to "concentrate on the soles of my feet" the time that Richard spit in my face. I know the outcome would have been better for both of us.

At the end of each chapter are questions that ask What Do You Think? Engage yourself deeply with these questions, because these are the kind of hard questions you must ask yourself if you are to work successfully with children with challenging behaviors. And don't kid yourself—every group you teach will include at least one child with a challenging behavior and he or she will have almost perfect attendance. Oh, and don't think that if you get through that year and pass the child on to someone else, everything will be just fine. As you'll learn from reading this book, children with challenging behaviors in preschool are much more likely to have difficulties in school and later in life. Those children who cannot control aggression at age 4 are likely to have significant social and behavioral problems in adolescence and adulthood, and the entire social welfare and justice system is likely to fail to remediate them. The behavior of these children is likely to have long-term negative consequences for themselves and society as a whole, so passing them on without intervention is not an acceptable option.

Preventing challenging behavior, addressing it effectively when it occurs, and teaching appropriate alternatives in preschool are the responsibilities of every early childhood educator. They are also the aims of this book. Read it and use it; not only will you survive as a teacher but you will have perhaps the most important impact on the future that any teacher could.

Sue Bredekamp, Ph.D.

Acknowledgments

George Sklar, a playwright and novelist and the father of one of the authors of this book (Judy), used to say that the secret to writing is putting the seat of the pants to the seat of the chair. Like any book, this one has demanded its fair share of solitary sitting. But it has also required two and a half decades of work in the field of early care and education and the help of a great many colleagues, friends, and family members.

Our heartfelt thanks go to Neil Butchard and Bob Spencler for their commitment to children and their willingness to share their wonderful WEVAS program; to Eleanor Chornoboy, Kate Andersen, Carol Patterson, Alida Jansen, and Abby Kleinberg-Bassel for passing along their vast experience and expertise in working with children and their families; to Carol Copple of the NAEYC and to Joan Duffell of the Committee for Children for their unflagging belief in us from the beginning of *Meeting the Challenge*; and to Sue Bredekamp for making us feel as if our work made a difference and was worth telling others about. We'd also like to thank our reviewers for their valuable feedback: Saun Floyd (River Valley Child Development Centers, Proctorville, Ohio), Sue Grossman (Eastern Michigan University, Ypsilanti), Dorothy Hewes (San Diego State University), Diane Levin (Wheelock College, Boston), and Diane Strangis (University of Florida, Gainesville).

For their help in understanding the many cultures that make this continent so rich and interesting a place for children to grow up, we are grateful to Amna Al Futaisi, Bibiana Burton, Peggy Clements, Eva Echenberg, Ed Greene, Thao Huynh Thanh, and Dixie Van Raalte. We are also grateful to Ed for advice and support above and beyond the call of duty.

For giving this book a special spirit, we owe thanks to our young artists, Guillaume and Solene Bernier; Bobby, Julia, Krissy, and Michael Keech; Christine Kilmer, Abigail Rasminsky, and Hallie Walsh, as well as to their families.

Traci Mueller has been a dream editor, giving us lots of positive reinforcement and setting firm limits, ably aided by Erica Tromblay, who hit the ground running. Pat McNees has earned our eternal gratitude by scrutinizing our manuscript with her keen writer's eye and painlessly delivering incisive comments.

Joan Rosen Karp, the sister of the other author (Barbara), is a terrific prekindergarten teacher who shared her classroom experiences and offered many helpful suggestions. Barbara's friends Nicole and Bibiana, and Judy's brothers, Daniel and Zachary Sklar, provided outstanding support throughout the writing process, furnishing us with wise words, chicken soup, and chocolates when we were down.

Barbara would like to thank her children, Jessika and Maita, for being so challenging and teaching her so much. Judy would like to thank hers, Sonya, Oren, and Abby, for being so understanding of her obliviousness to their lives since this book began.

We are especially thankful that our husbands, Martin Hallett and Michael Rasminsky, have managed to love and support us, each in his own way, despite the stress. We couldn't have written Chapter 4 without Michael's expertise and forbearance. Meals, books, graphs, and journal articles miraculously appeared, while computer glitches and dirty teacups miraculously disappeared. Their patience, encouragement, and willingness to roll up their sleeves have made this book possible.

Introduction

This book has two authors with two different strengths. Barbara was the director of a nonprofit community child-care center for over 20 years and taught early care and education courses to college and university students; Judy is a professional writer with a long-time interest in child-care and family issues. This book couldn't exist without both of us. But it began with one child.

Barbara had been working in the field for 14 years when a 2½-year-old named Andrew turned her world upside down. The staff at her center were all experienced and qualified early childhood teachers, but during the three years this child spent with them, he brought out every flaw in the program and taxed every skill they'd developed.

The staff had encountered children with difficult behaviors before, but this was the first time they lacked the skills to help a child understand and regulate his own behavior. Because they couldn't keep Andrew from hurting them or the other children, many of the children no longer felt safe, and several became anxious, copied his behavior, or were just too scared to do much of anything. Three or four children managed to cope when the activity went as planned but became very nervous and agitated when Andrew lost control and the adults didn't know how to respond. These "borderline" children, as the staff called them, sometimes tried to provoke Andrew when things were calm. If they could make him angry and get him to scream, hit, or throw things, they knew what to expect. When they were in need of attention themselves, they saw what worked for Andrew and followed his example. As a result, the group soon contained four or five children with challenging behavior.

The teachers spent their days putting out fires, consoling children, and saying no. They knew they weren't helping Andrew and, worse, they found themselves liking him and some of the other children less—a feeling that made them profoundly uncomfortable. As the year wore on, the staff began to feel resentful, burned out, inadequate, and full of self-doubt. They sometimes wondered whether they even wanted to continue working with children.

As Andrew got older, his problems, and theirs, got bigger. Because he had no diagnosed medical problem or medication, there were no treatment guidelines or extra money for staff to help care for him. Large for his age, he had poor gross-motor skills—and, aside from puzzles, he wasn't particularly interested in fine-motor activities either. Although he was extremely articulate, he had difficulty relating to other children, and the only way he could play or communicate was to kick, hit, or push. During transitions and free-play, he systematically worked the room, moving from one target to the next, pushing over block structures, grabbing toys, or getting too close for comfort. At snack and lunchtime, he ignored the empty chairs, selected one that was occupied, and sat on the occupant. After a while, the children waited until Andrew was seated, then chose a place to sit as far away as possible. Needless to say, this did little for Andrew's self-esteem. If he got angry, he emptied the shelves onto the floor and flung chairs around the room. When the teachers tried to discipline him, he kicked and head-butted them.

Because Andrew's facial expressions and body language seldom reflected his feelings or intentions, his behavior seemed to come out of nowhere. One of his 4-year-old classmates said it best: "Andrew is like a volcano; he's calm on the outside and ready to explode on the inside."

The staff tried to encourage him when he was behaving appropriately, but positive reinforcement made Andrew nervous. If a teacher showed interest while Andrew was concentrating on a puzzle, he shoved it to the ground or threw the pieces at her. Eventually, the teachers found themselves viewing his positive behavior as a chance to take a breath or be with the other children, who were receiving less and less care. They were teaching Andrew that the best way to get their attention was to do something that made them angry.

On the rare occasions that Andrew was absent, everyone felt the difference. The atmosphere was more relaxed, and the children enjoyed playing with one another without looking over their shoulders. On those days, Barbara asked herself if it would be better to ask Andrew to leave the center. Some of the staff thought he shouldn't be there. They felt ill equipped and unwilling to have a child like Andrew in their group. Not only did he jeopardize the safety of the other children, but his presence compromised their ability to provide the program the children deserved. He consumed so much of their time and energy that they had almost nothing left to give.

There were also some very angry parents. Each day their children came home with stories about what Andrew had done, sometimes sporting bruises he had inflicted.

The parents simply didn't understand why he was allowed to remain at the center. Barbara empathized with them, but she couldn't help wondering what would happen to Andrew if she asked him to leave. Would another center tolerate his behavior better? Or would he just bounce from one center to another?

Barbara also felt a sense of responsibility, and she wasn't ready to give up. Once it became clear that none of them had the techniques required to address Andrew's behavior effectively, she brought in experts to advise them. But she had waited too long to ask for help, and the teachers were so stressed and defensive that they couldn't hear the consultants' advice or follow their recommendations. They focused more on punishment than on teaching, and they felt so overwhelmed that they didn't recognize that any challenging behavior that persists over time is working for the child. Although they tried, they didn't help Andrew learn the skills he needed to manage his own behavior and succeed in school. When he finally went to kindergarten, they felt they had failed, and they knew it was only a matter of time before another child with challenging behavior appeared in their midst.

Andrew's legacy

Barbara vowed that she would never let this happen again, and she and the staff committed themselves to being prepared. She set out in search of methods that work with a child who presents challenging behaviors, and she discovered a series of research-based strategies that she brought back to the center. In addition, she and the teachers attended workshops, read books and articles about challenging behavior, and devoted a portion of each staff meeting to discussing what they were learning and how to implement it.

It wasn't all smooth sailing. There were nine people on staff, and they didn't always see things the same way. Some teachers were enthusiastic and eager to try everything. Others were still convinced that children with challenging behavior don't belong in regular child-care centers. Their emphatic responses reflected their diverse personalities, life experiences, cultures, philosophies, and attitudes toward children. Because teaching isn't simply what one does but also who one is, it was important to pay attention to what everyone felt, so they took it slowly, considered each opinion valid, and looked for solutions that felt comfortable to all of them.

The staff came to realize that Andrew hadn't actually been out to ruin everyone's day. His behavior had much more to do with the way he saw the world and the fact that he didn't know how to respond appropriately. More than anybody, he probably wished that things had been different. Once the teachers recognized that their job was to teach, not to police, they were on the right track. They were able to focus on their goals, to help children feel confident and competent, and to enable them to grow, make friends, and have fun.

The new approach

Three years later, 3½-year-old Michael started at the center. During the two-hour orientation session for new children and their parents, a teacher came to get Barbara from another room. Michael was running around screaming and grabbing toys from the other children. The horrified parents were backed up against the walls while the children, immobilized, watched. The staff were trying to act normally in order to help everyone feel safe on the first day in child care.

With an audience of parents in attendance, the teachers looked to Barbara for direction. In her head, she reviewed everything they'd learned. Then she sat on the floor next to Michael. This seemed to throw him off guard. He couldn't figure out what she was doing there. Since she and Michael didn't know each other at all, Barbara didn't talk. Michael was playing with a truck, so Barbara began playing with a truck. As they played, he started to calm down and relax. She talked about how much fun she was having and asked if he wanted to trade trucks.

After a while, another child asked if he could play, too. Barbara consulted Michael, who was thrilled to be asked and equally thrilled that another child wanted to play with him. She stayed by his side for several more minutes, then moved a short distance away and checked in with him periodically. He felt that he had made a buddy, and when it was time to clean up, Michael helped Barbara put away the trucks. They washed their hands and went to snack together. She kept an eye on him, smiled, and encouraged him. Snack went well, and luckily the orientation ended a few minutes later.

As soon as the children and parents left, the staff decided to hold an emergency meeting. They talked about what Andrew had taught them and how they could help Michael to develop social skills, impulse control, and self-esteem. Prevention was uppermost in their minds. To keep him from losing control, they decided that he would become the partner of one of the teachers, they would place his cubby next to hers, they would give him focused and limited choices during free-play, and they would assign everyone tasks at clean-up and seats at snack and lunchtime. Because they didn't yet know what would make Michael feel good about himself, they decided to reinforce his appropriate behavior by smiling, giving him thumbs up throughout the day, and letting him choose a song if he was doing well at circle time.

The teachers also talked about their feelings: their attitudes toward Michael's presence, his behavior, their different levels of tolerance, their verbal and nonverbal messages, and their level of confidence as individuals and as members of a team. They knew it was important to be consistent, so they had to agree about which behaviors were acceptable and what they would do when Michael's behavior was unacceptable. As the meeting went on, it became clear that they all felt much more confident than they had with Andrew. They weren't helpless; they had strategies and plans. They could handle it.

It didn't take long for them to discover that Michael loved to have his back rubbed and that he grinned infectiously when they gave him a thumbs up. Within six weeks all the strategies they'd worked on were in place, the staff were feeling competent and comfortable about having him at the center, and he was able to play with others, share, and make friends. Instead of being anxious or frightened, the other children were learning to recognize Michael's strengths and weaknesses, and they enthusiastically encouraged his efforts to behave appropriately. Their support helped him enormously.

It wasn't all perfect, of course. Any change in routine—for example, if his teacher was absent—derailed him. And no matter how much progress he made during the day, his challenging behavior reemerged when his mother arrived. You could see her hesitation and feel her apprehension as she walked down the corridor to pick him up.

To help her see how well Michael was doing before she reached his classroom, the staff made a point of greeting Michael's mother with a smile and telling her about something positive he'd done that day. As time passed, they encouraged her to spend a few minutes in the room with him before bundling him up for the trip home. Michael was delighted to have her sit beside him and meet his friends. He couldn't wait to tell her about the painting he'd made or the game he'd played in the gym. Eventually, even the hassles at the end of the day turned into easy routines. As his mother became more confident about herself and Michael's behavior, Barbara and the teachers met with her to talk about what they were doing at the center and what she was doing at home. Perhaps because of her new confidence, Michael's behavior began to improve at home, as well.

After two years in the child-care center, Michael went off to school. Although he's had some testy moments, he has made friends and is adjusting well.

Sharing the knowledge

Even before Michael came on the scene, we had decided to write a book together. The need for it was all too evident. Because we had been coauthors for many years and Judy had been the first chair of the child-care center's board of directors, the two of us talked endlessly about child-care issues and the center's struggles and triumphs. Judy went along when the staff attended workshops on challenging behavior and read everything she could get her hands on, and we pushed each other to search out new ideas, constantly trying to understand more.

We felt it was imperative to share what we had learned. In 1999, the Canadian Child Care Federation in Ottawa and the National Association for the Education of Young Children in Washington, DC, published *Meeting the Challenge*, our 40-page booklet for front-line staff. But in 40 pages, we couldn't tell the whole story. Virtually every topic we covered demanded more explanation, and we believed it was vital to reach out to students, too.

A recent study by the Early Child Care Research Network of the National Institute for Child Health and Human Development (2001) has made it clear that the time children spend in child care affects their behavior, regardless of the quality of that care. A ranking of high quality doesn't mean that a center's staff has the know-how required to effectively manage children with challenging behavior. Classrooms in today's child-care centers and schools are filled with Andrews and Michaels, and all too often their teachers are completely unprepared to help them. Teachers have been taught that if they respond to children warmly and consistently, know the material, and prepare activities that are interesting, culturally sensitive, and age appropriate, they will succeed in winning children's hearts and minds. If by chance children push, grab toys, or ignore instructions, gentle guidance and positive reinforcement will quickly transform them into cooperative members of the group. The first time a 4-year-old throws a four-letter word or a chair at them, teachers are shocked and stunned.

Events at Columbine High School and the after-effects of September 11, 2001, have changed our world forever. It has become increasingly apparent that the people who work with young children must have the knowledge, strategies, and skills required to help children with challenging behavior as early as possible. Although research shows that aggressive behavior in early childhood tends to persist throughout later childhood, adolescence, and even adulthood (Coie and Dodge, 1998; Tremblay, Pihl, Vitaro, and Dobkin, 1994), it also shows that children with challenging behaviors can learn appropriate ways to behave. If teachers know what they're doing and why they're doing it, they can make an enormous difference in the lives of these children (Eron and Slaby, 1994; Slaby, Roedell, Arrezo, and Hendrix, 1995; Yoshikawa, 1994).

Who should read this book?

This book is intended for all students and teachers who work with young children, because it's likely that each of you will eventually encounter a child with challenging behavior. It can also be useful to administrators, who set the tone in schools and child-care centers. Their backing for teachers as they deal with children with challenging behavior can make an enormous contribution to their success. In fact, the most successful approach to challenging behavior is what's called a *whole-school policy*—or a *whole-child-care-center policy*—where everyone from the principal to the maintenance staff works together to teach and reinforce appropriate behavior, and everyone responds to inappropriate behavior in the same way, using the same rules and vocabulary. But individual teachers can also prevent and manage challenging behavior effectively if they have the knowledge and skills they need.

What is in this book?

This book is a kind of survival manual. Its aim is to give you the basic facts and skills you need in order to understand and prevent challenging behavior, to address it effectively when it occurs, and to teach appropriate alternatives. It brings together information and techniques drawn from neuroscience, psychology, psychiatry, special education, early care and education, child development, cross-cultural research, and proactive social skills programs.

Because it isn't a special education text, this book doesn't describe special education techniques in great detail, and because teachers aren't physicians or psychologists, it won't tell you how to diagnose or treat problems such as attention deficit disorder or fetal alcohol syndrome. Neither does it provide recipes or formulas, because each child is unique and every situation requires a unique solution. And it certainly doesn't come with a money-back guarantee. But this book does offer ideas and strategies that have been proven to work time and again—and that *will* work if you give them a chance. Many weeks may elapse between the moment you first realize that you need help with a child with challenging behavior and the day that a consultation can finally be organized. These weeks are the time when you are most liable to burn out—and a time when the strategies here will be useful. But don't wait until then to try them. They can benefit every child in your class, not just those with challenging behaviors.

By helping the Andrews and the Michaels, you are also helping the other children, who, in the presence of the Andrews and Michaels, are learning to become bystanders, accepting the role of victim, or joining in the aggressive behavior if they become frightened or excited (Slaby et al., 1995). When you are prepared—when you know how to handle Andrew's and Michael's behavior appropriately, or better still, how to prevent it—all the children will feel safe, and the challenging behavior will be less severe, less frequent, and less contagious. Then it becomes possible to make the commitment that everyone who works with young children wants to be able to make: to welcome and help each child in your class.

Nuts and bolts

This book falls into two parts. The first four chapters explain the background—some of the theory and research that underlie effective practice. They contain information about aggression, risk factors, protective factors, and the brain's role in challenging behavior. The nine remaining chapters are more practical. They describe strategies for preventing and managing challenging behavior. Each of these methods can be used alone, but they work extemely well together. The last chapter deals with a special kind of challenging behavior, bullying, and it comes at the end because it is a kind of summary: Addressing bullying effectively requires the use of virtually all of the techniques presented in this book.

We believe that culture is a basic part of who children are, and we have tried very hard to make our book culturally sensitive. However, we are both European American, and in the end, we probably can't disguise that fact. It is important for you, as readers, to be aware of our bias.

Although challenging behavior is more prevalent among boys, it is increasingly common among girls. In recognition of this situation—and to avoid the awkwardness of "he or she"—we have called a child *he* in the odd-numbered chapters and *she* in the even-numbered chapters.

Many children inhabit these pages, but three are more prominent than the rest: Andrew, Michael, and Jessica. Their stories illuminate the behavior and strategies that are at the heart of this book.

Hang in there

Here are a few hints to keep in mind as you read:

• Have confidence in your own abilities—you can handle this.

• View inappropriate behavior as an opportunity to teach. That will help with everything you do.

• Take it slowly, one behavior at a time, one child at a time. Build in success by setting realistic goals.

• At the end of the day, reflect on what went wrong and what went right. Make notes in your agenda or on post-its so you can figure out what to do next time.

• Train yourself to look for, measure, and record minute improvements—they are important signs of progress. Remember that you can't eliminate challenging behavior overnight.

• When you try a new approach, things may get worse before they get better. But if you don't see gains within a reasonable time, try another tack.

• If you work with other people, set common goals. Laugh together; support and compliment each other. If you work alone, seek out your peers. Visit your neighborhood resource program or join a support group. Everyone needs someone to talk to.

• Give yourself a reward, not a guilt trip. Eat that brownie, take that walk, rent that video. Do whatever will keep you going.

References

Coie, J. D., & Dodge, K. A. (1998) Aggression and antisocial behavior. In N. Eisenberg (Ed.), *Handbook of child psychology: Vol 3, Social, emotional and personality development* (5th ed., pp 779–862). New York: Wiley.

Eron, L. D., & Slaby, R. G. (1994). Introduction. In L. D. Eron, J. H. Gentry, & P. Schlegel (Eds.), *Reason to hope: A psychosocial perspective on violence & youth*. Washington, DC: American Psychological Association.

National Institute for Child Health and Human Development, Early Child Care Research Network. (2001, April). *Early care and children's development prior to school entry*. Presentation at the meeting of the Society for Research in Child Development, Minneapolis, MN.

Slaby, R. G., Roedell, W. C., Arezzo, D., & Hendrix, K. (1995). *Early violence prevention: Tools for teachers of young children*. Washington, DC: National Association for the Education of Young Children.

Tremblay, R. E., Pihl, R. O., Vitaro, F., & Dobkin, P. L. (1994). Predicting early onset of male antisocial behavior from preschool behavior. *Archives of General Psychiatry, 51*, 732–739.

Yoshikawa, H. (1994). Prevention as cumulative protection: Effects of early family support and education on chronic delinquency and its risks. *Psychological Bulletin, 115*, 28–54.

1

What Is Challenging Behavior?

Challenging behavior is any behavior that

- interferes with children's learning, development, and success at play

- is harmful to the child, other children, or adults

- puts a child at high risk for later social problems or school failure (Chandler and Dahlquist, 1997; Klass, Guskin, and Thomas, 1995; Ritchie and Pohl, 1995).

We do not call this behavior challenging because it summons you to a duel or battle but because it is threatening, provocative, and stimulating, all at the same time.

First of all, this behavior is challenging for the child. It puts him in danger by preventing him from learning what he needs to know to succeed in school and get along well with his peers. It is also challenging for him because he probably doesn't have much control over it. Even if he knows what to do instead—and chances are he doesn't—his ability to regulate his feelings and actions just isn't up to the job yet. Improving matters will be an enormous challenge for him.

Perhaps more to the point, challenging behavior is challenging for *us*, the people around him, his family and teachers. In the face of this behavior, we often find ourselves at a loss. We don't know how to turn things around, how to make the situation tenable, how to help the child get back on track, behaving appropriately and feeling good about himself.

Yet it is essential for us to rise to this challenge. The child's future can depend on it—to say nothing of our own sanity and the well-being of the other children in the classroom. By its very nature, a challenge is difficult, but once conquered it brings incredible rewards. This is a challenge that is worthy of your very best efforts.

Any child can exhibit challenging behavior. To begin with, it is developmentally appropriate early in life, and all children continue to use it as they grow—once in a while, when they're angry or having a bad day. Some even use it for an extended period when parents separate or divorce, a new baby arrives, a parent loses a job or falls ill, or the family moves to a different place. Children find such events confusing and difficult, and they often react with challenging behavior. Although most children eventually manage to cope with these experiences, they usually need extra support and understanding from their families and teachers for quite some time.

Then there are the children whose problems are more difficult, the children who have come to rely on challenging behavior as the best way to respond to a situation. Their behavior is challenging in all three aspects of the definition and demands very special care and handling. With the appropriate information and strategies, the adults in their lives can play a pivotal role, helping these children avoid serious risk and blossom into the fully functioning people all children deserve to become.

This book focuses on aggressive, antisocial, and disruptive behaviors because their impact is so dramatic and so vast. But many of the ideas here will work equally well with children who display timid and withdrawn behaviors, which certainly also qualify as challenging.

Isn't challenging behavior sometimes appropriate for very young children?

Many children discover the use of physical aggression before their first birthday, as they become interested in controlling their own possessions and activities (Coie and Dodge, 1998). In one study, most mothers reported that their children grabbed, pushed, bit, hit, attacked, bullied, or were "cruel" by the time they turned 2 years old. Children with siblings exhibit more aggressive behavior than only children, and when there's a brother or sister in the family, boys and girls behave equally aggressively (Pepler and Craig, 1999; Tremblay et al., 1999).

In the National Longitudinal Survey of Children and Youth, a random sample of more than 20,000 children living in Canada, researchers found that the use of physical aggression peaks between the ages of 27 and 29 months, when 53.3 percent of boys and 41.1 percent of girls are trying it out (Tremblay et al., 1996). As Richard E. Tremblay of the University of Montreal points out, "The question . . . we've been trying to answer for the past 30 years is how do children learn to aggress. [But] this is the wrong question. The right question is how do they learn not to aggress?" (Holden, 2000).

A Rose by Any Other Name

Challenging is not the only label that adults have affixed to problem behaviors or the children who use them. Here are some others:

- High maintenance
- Antisocial
- High needs
- Bad
- Out of control
- Hard to manage

- At risk
- Disruptive
- Aggressive
- Violent
- Impulsive
- Spirited

- Oppositional
- Noncompliant
- Mean
- A problem
- Attention-seeking
- Willful

Labels are extremely powerful, which is why it's wiser not to use them—or if you do, to apply them to the behavior rather than the child. Employing language carefully makes a big difference in the way you see a child and think about who he is and what he can and cannot do. Negative labels can all too easily become self-fulfilling prophecies. They prevent you from seeing the child's positive qualities and may even cause you to lower your expectations of him. A child you've thought of as stubborn could just as easily be tenacious or persistent, important characteristics for success in school.

When you can see a child in a positive light, it helps him to see himself that way, and to act more positively, too.

Do children outgrow challenging behavior?

Sometimes yes, sometimes no. From about the age of 30 months on, physically aggressive behavior gradually decreases as children learn to regulate their feelings and understand one another's point of view. With the aid of families and teachers, they steadily get better at using assertive and prosocial strategies to communicate their needs and achieve their goals. They are also increasingly able to delay gratification and increasingly intolerant of one another's aggressive acts (Coie and Dodge, 1998). By the time they enter kindergarten, most children are relatively pacific (Tremblay, Masse, Pagani, and Vitaro, 1996).

But for an estimated 3 to 15 percent of preschool-age children, aggressive and antisocial behavior continues well beyond the age of 3 (Vitaro, De Civita, and Pagani, 1995), and about half of these children (Campbell and Ewing, 1990) are starting down a road that will eventually lead to a delinquent adolescence and a criminal adulthood (Coie, 1996; Webster-Stratton, 1997). The longer a child continues to use aggressive behavior, the more worrisome its fallout becomes and the more difficult it is to change his direction. It is therefore important to intervene as early as possible (Slaby, Roedell, Arezzo, and Hendrix, 1995).

Children with behavior problems often find themselves rejected by their peers—disliked, ridiculed, not invited to birthday parties or to other children's homes to play. These experiences wound their self-esteem and self-confidence, leave them isolated and depressed, and deprive them of opportunities to develop and practice the social skills they desperately need. Instead they learn to expect rejection and may even discover that the best defense is a strong offense and strike out preemptively to protect themselves (Moffitt, 1997). Once rejected by a group, a child will probably continue to be rejected and will have an equally hard time joining a new group (Campbell, 1990).

Behavior problems can lead to trouble at school, too. Because of their problems with social skills, emotional control, and language development, many children with challenging behavior come to school unprepared for the most basic task of their early school years—learning to read (Coie, 1996). As a result, they struggle with virtually everything academic. It doesn't help that they are also often hyperactive, inattentive, disruptive, and unable to concentrate.

Teachers sometimes exacerbate the problem. One study showed that they are more likely to punish children with challenging behavior and less likely to encourage them when they behave appropriately (Webster-Stratton and Herbert, 1994). Teachers also call on children with aggressive behavior less frequently, ask them fewer questions, and provide them with less information (Shonkoff and Phillips, 2000). As a result, children with challenging behavior soon fall behind, and they're likely to be held back or placed in a special class (Kazdin, 1987; Pepler and Rubin, 1991).

All of this primes them to band together with their like-minded peers, raising their risk for school dropout, delinquency, gang membership, substance abuse, and psychiatric illness. As adults, they are less likely to hold jobs or earn good wages and more likely to commit violent crimes (National Crime Prevention Council Canada, 1996). Their marriages are also more likely to be rocky. The boys may become batterers, and new research is finding that the girls, who are at higher risk for early pregnancy and single parenthood, lack parenting skills and may be mothering the next generation of children with challenging behaviors (National Crime Prevention Council Canada, 1996; Serbin, Moskowitz, Schwartzman, and Ledingham, 1991; Tremblay, 1991).

Brotherly Love

Because they spend so much time together, siblings in mainstream North American culture fight a lot (Dunn and Brown, 1991). As early as 16 to 18 months, they know exactly what will upset and annoy their brother or sister. Observers in one study saw children remove a sibling's comfort object during a fight, leave a fight to destroy a sibling's cherished possession, hold a desired object just out of reach, and pull a sibling's thumb out of his mouth (Dunn and Slomkowski, 1992).

Some experts believe that sibling interactions teach children how to handle relationships with their peers; others believe that sibling interactions are different because there is a built-in imbalance in power—and because terminating a relationship with a sibling isn't really an option (Katz, Kramer, and Gottman, 1992).

Children who are rejected by their peers learn to expect rejection and may even discover that the best defense is a strong offense and strike out preemptively to protect themselves.

What is aggression?

Psychologists often define *aggression* as behavior that is aimed at harming or injuring others (Coie and Dodge, 1998). Challenging behavior isn't always aggressive—sometimes it is disruptive or antisocial or annoying. But aggressive behavior is always challenging.

It can assume many forms. It can be *direct* (like hitting, pushing, biting, pinching, kicking, spitting, or hair-pulling) or *indirect* (like bullying, teasing, ignoring or defying rules or instructions, spreading rumors, excluding others, name-calling, or destroying

Sooner or Later?

Many researchers divide teenagers who run into trouble with the law into "early onset" or "late onset"—meaning that their aggressive behavior started either in early childhood or in adolescence. Although both groups get involved in serious offenses, gangs, substance abuse, unsafe sex, and dangerous driving at about the same rate, those who begin young are at much greater risk of violent and criminal behavior in their adult years and represent a far greater problem for society (Berk, 2000; Coie, 1996).

objects). Indirect aggressive behavior ("You're not my friend") is also called *relational aggression* because it endangers the relationship between the two people (Berk, 2000).

Because the question goes straight to the heart of who we are as human beings, philosophers have been arguing about the nature of aggression since the time of the Greeks. Some, like Seneca and the Stoics in ancient times and Thomas Hobbes in the seventeenth century, assert that aggression and anger are uncontrollable biological instincts that must be restrained by external force. Others, like the English philosopher John Locke, believe that a child comes into the world as a blank slate—*tabula rasa*—and experience makes him who he is (Dodge, 1991).

Both views still exist today. The *frustration-aggression theory* holds that when people are frustrated—when they can't reach their goals—they become angry and hostile and act aggressively (Dodge, 1991; Reiss and Roth, 1993). *Social learning theory* takes the Lockean perspective, and it has dominated thinking on the subject of aggression for the last three decades. Based on principles of conditioning and reinforcement, it says that people learn aggressive behavior from the environment and use it to achieve their goals. Of course, these distinctions are difficult to make in practice. When you get right down to it, it's impossible to attribute all aggression to frustration, and the way you respond to frustration probably depends on what you've learned (Pepler and Slaby, 1994).

The father of social learning theory is Stanford University psychologist Albert Bandura, who contends that children learn aggressive behavior primarily by observing it. Children are great imitators, and they copy the models around them—family, teachers, peers, neighbors, television. At the same time, they observe and experience the rewards, punishments, and emotional states associated with aggressive behavior. When they see that a behavior is reinforced, they're likely to try it for themselves; when they experience the reinforcement directly, they're likely to repeat it. That is, when Zack hits Ben and gets the red fire engine, he will almost certainly try hitting the next time he wants something.

Social learning theory has spawned several sister theories that place more emphasis on cognition. According to the *cognitive script model*, proposed by L. Rowell Huesmann and Leonard D. Eron, children learn scripts for aggressive behavior—when to expect it, what to do, what it will feel like, what its results will be—and store them in their memory banks. The more they rehearse these scripts through observation, fantasy, and behavior, the more readily they spring to mind and govern behavior when the occasion arises (Coie and Dodge, 1998; Pepler and Slaby, 1994; Reiss and Roth, 1993).

Vanderbilt University psychologist Kenneth A. Dodge has proposed a *social information processing model* for aggressive behavior. In every single social interaction, there is lots of information to be instantly processed and turned into a response. The social cues coming in must be properly encoded and interpreted, and the possible responses need to be thought of, evaluated, and enacted. Children with very challenging behavior often lack one or more of the skills required to process this information properly. Even as preschoolers, they tend to see the world with a jaundiced eye. When another child bumps into them, for example, they think he did it on purpose, attributing hostile intent in situations most children would regard as neutral. They don't look around for new facts that might help solve a problem, don't think of many alternative solutions, don't anticipate what will happen if they respond aggressively, and end up choosing passive or aggressive solutions that don't work (Dodge, 1980; Dodge and Frame, 1982).

Seeing Straight

Researchers Kenneth Dodge, John E. Bates, and Gregory S. Pettit (1990) wanted to find out if physical abuse affects the way a child processes social information. They showed roughly 300 5-year-olds, some of whom had experienced abuse, a series of cartoon vignettes depicting unpleasant events—a child's blocks get knocked over, a child tries to enter a group and fails, and so on. In some of the stories the event is an accident, in some it is intentional, and in still others it is hard to tell.

When the researchers asked the children to answer questions about the vignettes, they found that the children who were physically abused gave different answers from the children who were unharmed. The children who had been abused were significantly less attentive to social cues, more likely to attribute hostile intent to someone in the stories, and less likely to think up competent solutions to the problems the stories posed. Their teachers also rated their behavior as more aggressive.

The researchers concluded that the experience of being physically abused leads children to see the world as a hostile place and impairs their ability to process social information accurately.

Like the philosophers, Dodge makes a distinction between two kinds of aggression. Children use *proactive aggression* (also called *instrumental aggression*) as a tool to achieve a goal, such as obtaining a desired object (the red fire engine) or dominating a peer (Alexa scratches Melanie to remind her that she is the boss of the game). Proactive aggression is more common among very young children because they don't yet have the words to ask for the ball, the seat next to David, or the teacher's attention. They aren't angry or emotional; they're just using the means at their disposal to get what they want and to make themselves understood. Interestingly, young children who engage in the use of proactive aggression don't necessarily earn the rejection of their peers. In fact, they often show leadership qualities. But by the time they reach the primary grades, the other children are no longer willing to tolerate this behavior and will reject a child who uses it (Dodge, 1991).

Reactive aggression (also known as *hostile* or *affective aggression*) appears in the heat of the moment in reaction to some frustration or perceived provocation. Angry, volatile, and not at all controlled, it is often aimed at hurting someone. The children who use it are invariably disliked. Dodge and his colleagues have found that children who are prone to reactive aggression make errors in social information processing—they attribute hostile intent to others in ambiguous or neutral situations (Dodge and Frame, 1982).

Other psychologists have also noticed distinctive thought patterns. For example, children who use aggressive behavior believe that aggression is perfectly acceptable. In their minds, it can enhance a reputation and raise self-esteem, and it doesn't even hurt the guy on the receiving end of it. Morever, children with challenging behavior believe that aggression pays off, and in their experience, it often does (Slaby, 1997). In one study, preschoolers who used aggression got what they wanted three-quarters of the time, and because they were so successful, they were more likely to try this method again (Maccoby, 1980). Television and life in the inner city tend to perpetuate such beliefs.

Children who behave aggressively may also lag behind in moral understanding. They are more liable to view aggressive responses as morally acceptable, and they may be unable to see things from another person's perspective. They may insist on having their own way, blame others when things go wrong, and continue to attack even when the other child is in pain (Coie and Dodge, 1998; Perry, Perry, and Kennedy, 1992). They may also overestimate their own competence (Asher, Parkhurst, Hymel, and Williams, 1990). In a recent study, children rated as aggressive by their teachers rated themselves as perfect on a test of self-esteem (Berk, 2000)!

Preschoolers with aggressive behavior who are also rejected by their peers experience more stress. When researchers tested the children's stress hormones, those with aggressive behavior had much higher levels than other children in the classroom (Shonkoff and Phillips, 2000).

Aggression is not the same as *conflict,* which occurs when people have opposing goals or interests. Conflict can be resolved in many ways—by negotiating, taking turns, persuading, and so on—and skill in conflict resolution is important in helping children learn to be assertive about their own needs, regulate their negative feelings, and understand others (Cords and Killen, 1998; Katz et al., 1992). Aggressive behavior is just one tactic for dealing with conflict—in fact, some researchers consider it a mismanagement

Children with challenging behavior believe that aggression pays off, and in their experience it often does.

of conflict (Perry et al., 1992; Shantz and Hartup, 1992). But most conflicts don't involve aggression. One study found that physical aggression takes place in only 17 percent of the conflicts among 24-month-olds (Ross and Conant, 1992).

Aggressive behavior is more likely to occur when the environment considers it normal and acceptable and when children have encoded it in their repertoire of responses (Guerra, 1997). When the environment devalues aggressive behavior and children have competent, effective, nonaggressive responses in their repertoire, they have a far better chance of solving their problems amicably.

Does culture play a role in aggressive behavior?

Cultures vary in the way they view aggressive behavior, highlighting the importance of learning. When the adults actively discourage aggressive behavior, the result is a peaceful society, such as that of the Amish or the Zuni Indian (Delgado, 1979). When they encourage it, the result is an aggressive society. Anthropologist D. P. Fry (1988) studied two neighboring villages in southern Mexico. In La Paz, the inhabitants frown on aggressive behavior, and there is very little of it. In nearby San Andres, the residents think aggressive behavior is normal, and when children throw rocks at each other, their parents don't intervene. The result? The homicide rate is five times higher in San Andres than in La Paz.

A study of the behavior of children in six cultures—India, Okinawa, Kenya, Mexico, the Philippines, and the United States—found that, relatively speaking, U.S. parents tolerate a fair amount of aggressive behavior among children (Segall, Dasen, Berry, and Poortinga, 1990). The noted legal scholar Lawrence Friedman has remarked that violence is "as American as apple pie" (1993), and criminologist Joan McCord declares that "America is the most violent of countries—more violent, in fact, than other industrialized countries" (1997). Just look at the homicide statistics: In the year 2000, the United States averaged 5.5 homicides per 100,000 residents, compared with 1.8 for Canada (Gannon, 2001). Homicide rates among U.S. youth have fallen recently, but they are still alarmingly high. In 1997, homicides claimed 2,144 victims and 1,700 perpetrators under the age of 18 (Thornton, Craft, Dahlberg, Lynch, and Baer, 2000).

The 1999 Youth Risk Behavior Survey (Thornton et al., 2000), a nationally representative sample of students in grades 9 to 12, reported that almost 36 percent of students had been in at least one physical fight in the last year, and almost 5 percent carried a firearm within the last month. Each year there are about 50 deaths in schools, and murderers are getting younger. The arrest rate for children ages 14 to 17 who were charged with homicide rose 41 percent from 1989 to 1994 (National Center for Injury Prevention and Control, 2000).

Although there are higher rates of violence among African Americans, Latino Americans, Native Americans, and Asian Pacific Americans than among European Americans (Hill, Soriano, Chen, and LaFromboise, 1994), "ethnicity in and of itself should not be considered a causal or risk factor for violence," says the American Psychological Association's Commission on Violence and Youth (Eron, Gentry, and Schlegel, 1994, p. 101). In these communities there is much more poverty, which is a significant risk factor for violence. When socioeconomic status is taken into account—

Teacher's Choice

In *Preschool in Three Cultures*, authors Joseph Tobin, David Wu, and Dana Davidson vividly describe a 4-year-old in a Japanese preschool who spends his day wrestling and fighting with the other children, ruining games by throwing cards over a balcony, and loudly singing, joking, and commenting on the group's activities. For the most part, his teacher ignores his behavior.

This is a deliberate choice. The Japanese teacher doesn't believe in confronting, isolating, censuring, excluding, or punishing. She believes that the best way for a child to learn to control his behavior is by interacting with his peers. She also believes that fighting among boys is inevitable and age-appropriate behavior that allows children to learn how to deal with conflict and become more complete human beings.

The Chinese have a completely different perspective on aggressive behavior: They believe the teacher must intervene at once. "If you let a child behave that way in preschool," says one Chinese teacher, "he will think it is acceptable to be that way, and he will develop a bad character that may last his whole life." The responsibility for teaching appropriate behavior falls squarely on the teacher.

In the United States there is a third—and yet again different—approach. Here, words will solve the problem of aggressive behavior. Together, teacher and children talk about the rules and what each child wants, and little by little they negotiate a solution to their dilemma (Tobin, Wu, and Davidson, 1989).

along with community disorganization, joblessness, racism, and discrimination—the differences in violence rates are small.

There are no real differences in the rates of aggression between African American and European American elementary school children—or among young people ages 18 to 20 who are employed or living with a partner or married (Coie and Dodge, 1998). This is an eloquent statement about intervention.

Regardless of their culture, race, or ethnicity, children need to feel safe, respected, and cared for to be able to learn. It's much more difficult to create the conditions that make learning possible when there's a child with challenging behavior in the classroom. The information in the chapters that follow will help you understand challenging behavior as well as the children who use it. It will also enable you to develop the skills you need to prevent and manage challenging behavior effectively so that every child you teach can have the opportunity to learn and reach his potential.

What Do You Think?

1. What does the following quote by Richard E. Tremblay mean to you? "The question . . . we've been trying to answer for the past 30 years is how do children learn to aggress. [But] this is the wrong question. The right question is how do they learn not to aggress?" How would you explain it to someone else? Why is this such a difficult question? Why is it so surprising to think that people are naturally aggressive? If they are naturally aggressive, how would that affect their ability to control their aggression?

2. In the text of this chapter, we say, "Negative labels can all too easily become self-fulfilling prophecies. They prevent you from seeing the child's positive qualities and may even cause you to lower your expectations of him. A child you've thought of as stubborn could just as easily be tenacious or persistent—important characteristics for success in school." How does labeling affect your attitude? Have you ever been labeled? How did the label affect your behavior and your relationships? Can you think of situations when you have labeled someone else?

3. Why is it hard for children with aggressive behavior to succeed in school? What other problems can aggressive behavior create for them?

4. "There are no real differences in the rates of aggression between African American and European American elementary school children—or among young people ages 18 to 20 who are employed or living with a partner or married." Why do we refer to this as an eloquent statement about intervention?

5. How does social information processing affect a child's behavior?

Suggested Reading

Garbarino, J. (2000). *Lost boys: Why our sons turn violent and how we can save them.* Garden City, NY: Anchor.

Harris, J. R. (1998). *The nurture assumption: Why children turn out the way they do.* New York: Simon & Schuster.

Kagan, J. (1971). *Understanding children: Behavior, motives, and thought.* New York: Harcourt Brace Jovanovich.

References

Asher, S. R., Parkhurst, J. T., Hymel, S., & Williams, G. A. (1990). Peer rejection and loneliness in childhood. In S. R. Asher & J. D. Coie (Eds.), *Peer rejection in childhood* (pp. 253–273). New York: Cambridge University Press.

Berk, L. E. (2000). *Child development* (5th ed.). Boston: Allyn and Bacon.

Campbell, S. B. (1990). *Behavior problems in preschool children: Clinical and developmental issues.* New York: Guilford.

Campbell, S. B., & Ewing, L. J. (1990). Follow-up of hard-to-manage preschoolers: Adjustment at age 9 and predictors of continuing symptoms. *Journal of Child Psychology and Psychiatry, 31,* 871–889.

Chandler, L. K., & Dahlquist, C. M. (1997, April). *Confronting the challenge: Using team-based functional assessment and effective intervention strategies to reduce and prevent challenging behavior in young children.* Workshop presented at SpecialLink Institute on Children's Challenging Behaviours in Child Care, Sydney, Nova Scotia.

Coie, J. D. (1996). Prevention of violence and antisocial behavior. In R. DeV. Peters & R. J. McMahon (Eds.), *Preventing childhood disorders, substance abuse, and delinquency* (pp. 1–18). Thousand Oaks, CA: Sage.

Coie, J. D., & Dodge, K. A. (1998). Aggression and antisocial behavior. In N. Eisenberg (Ed.), *Handbook of child psychology: Vol. 3, Social, emotional, and personality development* (5th ed., pp. 779–862). New York: Wiley.

Cords, M., & Killen, M. (1998). Conflict resolution in human and nonhuman primates. In J. Langer & M. Killen (Eds.), *Piaget, evolution, and development* (pp. 193–218). Mahwah, NJ: Erlbaum.

Delgado, J. M. R. (1979). Neurophysiological mechanisms of aggressive behavior. In S. Feshbach & A. Fraczek (Eds.), *Aggression and behavior change: Biological and social processes* (pp. 54–65). New York: Praeger.

Dodge, K. A. (1980). Social cognition and children's aggressive behavior. *Child Development, 51,* 162–170.

Dodge, K. A. (1991). The structure and function of reactive and proactive aggression. In D. J. Pepler & K. H. Rubin (Eds.), *The development and treatment of childhood aggression* (pp. 201–218). Hillsdale, NJ: Erlbaum.

Dodge, K. A., Bates, J. E., & Pettit, G. S. (1990). Mechanisms in the cycle of violence. *Science, 250,* 1678–1683.

Dodge, K. A., & Frame, C. L. (1982). Social cognition biases and deficits in aggressive boys. *Child Development, 53,* 620–635.

Dunn, J., & Brown, J. (1991). Relationships, talk about feelings, and the development of affect regulation in early childhood. In J. Garber & K. A. Dodge (Eds.), *The development of emotional regulation and dysregulation* (pp. 89–108). New York: Cambridge University Press.

Dunn, J., & Slomkowski, C. (1992). Conflict and the development of understanding. In C. U. Shantz & W. W. Hartup (Eds.), *Conflict in child and adolescent development* (pp. 71–92). New York: Cambridge University Press.

Eron, L. D., Gentry, J. H., & Schlegel, P. (Eds.). (1994). Introduction: Experience of violence: Ethnic groups. In *Reason to hope: A psychosocial perspective on violence & youth* (pp. 101–103). Washington, DC: American Psychological Association.

Friedman, L. M. (1993). *Crime and punishment in American history.* New York: Basic Books.

Fry, D. P. (1988). Intercommunity differences in aggression among Zapotec children. *Child Development, 59,* 1008–1019.

Gannon, M. (2001). *Crime comparisons between Canada and the United States* (Catalogue No. 85-002-X1E-Vol.21, No.11). Ottawa, Ontario: Canadian Centre for Justice Statistics.

Guerra, N. (1997). Intervening to prevent childhood aggression in the inner city. In J. McCord (Ed.), *Violence and childhood in the inner city* (pp. 256–312). New York: Cambridge University Press.

Hill, H. M., Soriano, F. I., Chen, S. A., & LaFromboise, T. D. (1994). Sociocultural factors in the etiology and prevention of violence among ethnic minority youth. In L. D. Eron, J. H. Gentry, & P. Schlegel (Eds.), *Reason to hope: A psychosocial perspective on violence & youth* (pp. 59–97). Washington, DC: American Psychological Association.

Holden, C. (2000). The violence of the lambs. *Science, 289,* 580–581.

Katz, L. F., Kramer, L., & Gottman, J. M. (1992). Conflict and emotions in marital, sibling, and peer relationships. In C. U. Shantz & W. W. Hartup (Eds.), *Conflict in child and adolescent development*

(pp. 122–149). New York: Cambridge University Press.

Kazdin, A. E. (1987). Treatment of antisocial behavior in children: Current status and future directions. *Psychological Bulletin, 102,* 187–203.

Klass, C. S., Guskin, K. A., & Thomas, M. (1995). The early childhood program: Promoting children's development through and within relationships. *Zero to Three, 16,* 9–17.

Maccoby, E. E. (1980). *Social development.* New York: Harcourt Brace Jovanovich.

McCord, J. (1997). Placing American urban violence in context. In J. McCord (Ed.), *Violence and childhood in the inner city* (pp. 78–115). New York: Cambridge University Press.

Moffitt, T. E. (1997). Neuropsychology, antisocial behavior, and neighborhood context. In J. McCord (Ed.), *Violence and childhood in the inner city* (pp. 116–170). New York: Cambridge University Press.

National Center for Injury Prevention and Control. (2000). *Fact book for the year 2000: Working to prevent and control injury in the United States.* Atlanta: Centers for Disease Control and Prevention. Retrieved January 18, 2002, from http://www.cdc.gov/ncipc/pub-res/FactBook/default.htm.

National Crime Prevention Council Canada. (1996). *Preventing crime by investing in families.* Ottawa, Ontario: Author.

Pepler, D. J., & Craig, W. (1999). *Aggressive girls: Development of disorder and outcomes.* Toronto: LaMarsh Research Centre on Violence and Conflict, York University.

Pepler, D. J., & Rubin, K. H. (1991). Introduction: Current challenges in the development and treatment of childhood aggression. In D. J. Pepler & K. H. Rubin (Eds.), *The development and treatment of childhood aggression* (pp. xiii–xvii). Hillsdale, NJ: Erlbaum.

Pepler, D. J., & Slaby, R. G. (1994). Theoretical and developmental perspectives on youth and violence. In L. D. Eron, J. H. Gentry, & P. Schlegel (Eds.), *Reason to hope: A psychosocial perspective on violence & youth* (pp. 27–58). Washington, DC: American Psychological Association.

Perry, D. G., Perry, L. C., & Kennedy, E. (1992). Conflict and the development of antisocial behavior. In C. U. Shantz & W. W. Hartup (Eds.), *Conflict in child and adolescent development* (pp. 301–329). New York: Cambridge University Press.

Reiss, A. J., Jr., & Roth, J. A. (Eds.). (1993). *Understanding and preventing violence.* Washington, DC: National Academy Press.

Ritchie, J., & Pohl, C. (1995). Rules of thumb workshop. *The Early Childhood Educator, 10,* 11–12.

Ross, H. S., & Conant, C. L. (1992). The social structure of early conflict: Interaction, relationships, and alliances. In C. U. Shantz & W. W. Hartup (Eds.), *Conflict in child and adolescent development* (pp. 153–185). New York: Cambridge University Press.

Segall, M. H., Dasen, P. R., Berry, J. W., & Poortinga, Y. H. (1990). *Human behavior in global perspective: An introduction to cross-cultural psychology.* New York: Pergamon.

Serbin, L. A., Moskowitz, D. S., Schwartzman, A. E., & Ledingham, J. E. (1991). Aggressive, withdrawn, and aggressive/withdrawn children in adolescence: Into the next generation. In D. J. Pepler & K. H. Rubin (Eds.), *The development and treatment of childhood aggression* (pp. 55–70). Hillsdale, NJ: Erlbaum.

Shantz, C. U., & Hartup, W. W. (1992). Conflict and development: An introduction. In C. U. Shantz & W. W. Hartup (Eds.), *Conflict in child and adolescent development* (pp. 1–11). New York: Cambridge University Press.

Shonkoff, J. P., & Phillips, D. A. (Eds.). (2000). *From neurons to neighborhoods: The science of early childhood development.* National Research Council and Institute of Medicine, Committee on Integrating the Science of Early Childhood Development, Board on Children, Youth, and Families, Commission on Behavioral and Social Sciences and Education. Washington, DC: National Academy Press.

Slaby, R. G. (1997). Psychological mediators of violence in urban youth. In J. McCord (Ed.), *Violence and childhood in the inner city* (pp. 171–206). New York: Cambridge University Press.

Slaby, R. G., Roedell, W. C., Arezzo, D., & Hendrix, K. (1995). *Early violence prevention: Tools for teachers of young children.* Washington, DC: National Association for the Education of Young Children.

Thornton, T. N., Craft, C. A., Dahlberg, L. L., Lynch, B. S., & Baer, K. (2000). *Best practices of youth violence prevention: A sourcebook for community action.*

Atlanta: Centers for Disease Control and Prevention, National Center for Injury Prevention and Control. Retrieved January 18, 2002, from http://www.cdc.gov/ncipc/dvp/bestpractices.htm.

Tobin, J. J., Wu, D. Y. H., & Davidson, D. (1989). *Preschool in three cultures: Japan, China, and the United States.* New Haven, CT: Yale University Press.

Tremblay, R. E. (1991). Aggression, prosocial behavior, and gender. In D. J. Pepler & K. H. Rubin (Eds.), *The development and treatment of childhood aggression* (pp. 71–78). Hillsdale, NJ: Erlbaum.

Tremblay, R. E., Boulerice, B., Harden, P. W., McDuff, P., Perusse, D., Pihl, R. O., et al. (1996). Do children in Canada become more aggressive as they approach adolescence? In *Growing up in Canada: National longitudinal survey of children and youth* (pp. 127–137). Ottawa, Ontario: Human Resources Development Canada and Statistics Canada.

Tremblay, R. E., Japel, C., Perusse, D., McDuff, P., Boivin, M., Zoccolillo, M., et al. (1999). The search for the age of "onset" of physical aggression. *Criminal Behaviour and Mental Health, 9,* 8–23.

Tremblay, R. E., Masse, L. C., Pagani, L., & Vitaro, F. (1996). From childhood physical aggression to adolescent maladjustment. In R. DeV. Peters & R. J. McMahon (Eds.), *Preventing childhood disorders, substance abuse, and delinquency* (pp. 268–298). Thousand Oaks, CA: Sage.

Vitaro, F., De Civita, M., & Pagani, L. (1995). The impact of research-based prevention programs on children's disruptive behaviour. *Exceptionality Education Canada, 5,* 105–135.

Webster-Stratton, C. (1997). Early intervention for families of preschool children with conduct problems. In M. J. Guralnick (Ed.), *The effectiveness of early intervention: Second generation research* (pp. 429–454). Baltimore: Paul H. Brookes.

Webster-Stratton, C., & Herbert, M. (1994). *Troubled families—Problem children: Working with parents: A collaborative process.* Chichester, England: Wiley.

2

Risk Factors

When a child with challenging behaviors enters the world of your classroom, even if you are the most experienced and confident of teachers, you can find yourself filled with self-doubt. As feelings of insecurity, inadequacy, and defensiveness come flooding in, your first instinct is often to blame someone—yourself, the child's parents, the child herself. When you feel this way, a wall goes up, and it's hard to ask for help and even harder to accept it. One way to break down that wall is to understand something about the causes of challenging behavior.

Good teaching begins where the child is. Children with challenging behavior have real needs that must be met before they can begin to succeed. Understanding why a child behaves in a particular way makes it much easier to meet those needs and to manage her behavior effectively. When you can recognize that her behavior is governed largely by biological or environmental factors and not by the desire to ruin your day, it becomes possible for you to figure out what she can do, what she can't do, and what she needs to learn in order to succeed.

What causes challenging behavior?

The vast outpouring of research in both neuroscience and child development in recent years has made this interesting question more difficult than ever to answer. People used to ask, "Which is more important, nature or nurture?" But experts now tell us that this debate has become "scientifically obsolete" (Shonkoff and Phillips, 2000, p. 6). They have discovered that nature and nurture are inextricably entangled and work together in every aspect of human development. We will try to tease a few threads out of this intricately woven fabric so that we can examine them more closely, but we must warn you that they won't come out neatly.

These threads are called "risk factors," and they have a cumulative effect. A child who has one risk factor faces no more risk of developing challenging behavior than a child who has none. But a child who has two risk factors faces a risk *four times as great* (Rutter, 2000; Yoshikawa, 1994). Where risk factors are concerned, one plus one equals more than two.

These risk factors aren't usually visible, and parents may or may not even know they're there. You can ask about them if it seems appropriate, but it's entirely possible that no hard information will ever come to light. That is a fact you just have to accept. But don't let it stop you from using your skills to observe a child with challenging behavior closely, and don't let it stop you from talking to the family about what's going on. As you do, keep these risk factors in mind. They will give you insight, empathy, and ideas about how to proceed.

The risk factors for challenging behavior fall into two broad categories: biological and environmental. We've defined *biological* as anything that impinges on a child starting from conception to birth; we've considered anything that influences her after birth as *environmental*, whether it acts on her directly (such as physical punishment or lead in her drinking water) or indirectly (such as poverty). As we'll explain in Chapter 4, in the end everything comes together in the brain.

Biological Risk Factors

Genes

Is a tendency toward aggressive behavior inherited? This question—which is extremely controversial because it raises the specters of eugenics and "designer people"—also has a complicated answer. Recent research has revealed the startling finding of genes associated wih aggressive behavior in fruit flies and mice (Chen, Lee, Bowens, Huber, and Kavitz, 2002; Young, Berry, Mahaffey, Saionz, Hawes, Chang, et al., 2002), but so far scientists have found no genes directly linked to criminal or aggressive behavior in human beings. Although one of the best predictors of antisocial behavior in boys is having a parent with a criminal record (Frick et al., 1991; Reiss and Roth, 1993), it is more likely that genes influence the traits *associated with* aggressive behavior: impulsivity, novelty seeking, difficult temperament, lack of empathy, low IQ, attention deficit disorder, and others (Holden, 1996; Reiss and Roth, 1993).

Double Dose

A study of children adopted in Iowa compared the biological children of parents who were in trouble with alcohol or the law with the biological children of parents who did not have these problems. It turned out that the children who had both the problem genes and a problematic environment in their adopted home were much more prone to aggressive and antisocial behavior than the children who had only the problem genes or only the difficult environment. Their genes made them vulnerable to the environment or, to view it from another angle, their environment made them vulnerable to their genes (Hamer and Copeland, 1999; Rutter, 2000).

Even inheriting the genes for these traits doesn't guarantee that a child will have them. Each trait is probably governed by many genes, and the environment plays a powerful and complex role in whether and how they'll be expressed. A child may inherit her father's gene for tallness, for example, but if she doesn't have adequate nutrition, she may not grow to her full height (Raine, 1993).

The physical, cultural, and social environment all sway the expression of genes. Even the body's own internal environment is an important influence. Factors such as "the flux of hormones during development, whether you were lying on your right or left side in the womb, and a whole parade of other things" affect how genes are expressed, according to Dean Hamer of the National Cancer Institute (Mann, 1994).

Temperament

In 1956, New York University psychiatrists Alexander Thomas and Stella Chess and their colleague, pediatrician Herbert G. Birch of the Albert Einstein College of Medicine, began a pioneering longitudinal study of temperament. By collecting data on a homogeneous sample of 133 children from infancy through young adulthood, they discovered that children are born with distinct temperaments—a particular behavioral or emotional style, a characteristic way of doing things and interacting with the world around them.

Thomas, Chess, and Birch (1968) identified nine traits that make up temperament and appear in different people in different combinations and quantities. These traits, along with others identified by subsequent researchers, emerge early and can become relatively stable as early as 4 months of age (Shonkoff and Phillips, 2000).

Thomas, Chess, and Birch (1968) made another interesting observation: They found three distinct types of children, whom they classified as easy, slow to warm up, or difficult. Most children fall into one of these types.

The children in the easy group, who made up about 40 percent of the New York Longitudinal Study sample, delighted their parents and teachers. They had a sunny outlook on life, adapted easily to change, and ate and slept on schedule. Over the years, a mere 7.5 percent of them developed behavior problems (Chess and Thomas, 1984).

Batteries Included?

According to Thomas, Chess, and Birch (1968; Thomas and Chess, 1977), children come endowed with a mixture of nine character traits, all of which offer advantages and disadvantages, depending on one's point of view. Several books—most notably *The Difficult Child* by Stanley Turecki (2000) and *Raising Your Spirited Child* by Mary Sheedy Kurcinka (1992)—have popularized this work. They, too, use temperament scales, though they sometimes name and order these traits in a different way.

• *Activity level.* A child's activity level can range from slow and quiet (a baby who wakes up in the same spot where she fell asleep) to high energy (a child who's always on the go).

• *Rhythmicity or regularity.* At one end of the scale, a child can be absolutely regular in her sleep, eating, and bowel habits; at the other end, a child can appear to have no biological pattern whatsoever.

• *Approach or withdrawal.* This trait has to do with a child's initial response to new situations, people, places, foods, and so on, and can range from wading right in to categorical rejection.

• *Adaptability.* This trait is concerned not with an initial response but with how readily a child can modify her first reaction and settle into a situation. The scale ranges from great willingness to great reluctance and inability to deal with change.

• *Intensity of reaction.* One child may have very mild reactions (you have to pay close attention to know what she's feeling); another may react with great force and power, whether she's ecstatic or furious. Thomas, Chess, and Birch (1968) write about a child who loves the bath so much that she tries to climb into the tub fully dressed.

• *Threshold of responsiveness.* This trait indicates sensitivity to smells, sounds, sights, touch, taste, and pain. Some children simply don't notice sensory stimulation and need lots of it—loud voices, big bumps—to respond. Others, like the princess and the pea, can't bear to feel the labels in their shirts or tend to fly off the handle in crowded or noisy rooms.

• *Quality of mood.* Mood can range from finding pleasure everywhere to seeing the world as a serious place indeed.

• *Distractibility.* Some children can't be derailed no matter what; others notice and pay attention to absolutely everything that crosses their path.

• *Attention span and persistence.* These two traits are related. Some children tune in for just a few minutes, then need a break; others stick with something that interests them through countless obstacles and attempts to interrupt them.

There is no correlation between temperament and intelligence, gender, birth order, or social and economic status (Turecki, 2000; Kurcinka, 1992).

The children who were slow to warm up, about 15 percent of the sample, took a long time to get used to new things, but with patient care they became interested and involved. About half of them had some problems with behavior (Chess and Thomas, 1984).

The difficult group of children demanded much more of their families and teachers. They cried loudly and often, had tantrums, resisted new things and changes in routine, ate and slept unpredictably, and always seemed to be in a bad mood. Although they made up just 10 percent of the study sample, about 70 percent of them developed problem behaviors (Thomas, Chess, and Birch, 1968).

In trying to figure out why 30 percent of the children with difficult temperaments managed *not* to develop problems, Thomas, Chess, and Birch (1968) evolved the concept of "goodness of fit." Serious disturbances are more likely to arise, they found, when the temperament of the child and the expectations of the family or teacher are out of sync. Traits of temperament are neither good nor bad in themselves; what matters is how the environment responds to them.

Families and teachers who understand and accommodate temperamental traits will manage more successfully, gradually extending the child's capacity to cope (Carey and McDevitt, 1995; Thomas and Chess, 1977; Turecki, 2000). For example, Jerome Kagan (1998), a Harvard University developmental psychologist who's studied the temperamental trait of shyness in hundreds of babies, has found that over one-third of those who are timid at 4 months of age are no longer especially fearful by the age of 2 years. To help new mothers learn to adapt to the temperament of their irritable babies, researchers in the Netherlands (van den Boom, 1994) taught them to imitate the infant's behavior, repeat their own verbal expressions, and stay quiet when the baby looked away. A few months later, their babies showed more prosocial behavior, less fussing and crying, and more willingness to explore their surroundings than babies whose mothers hadn't learned these techniques. Daily experience helped the babies in both Boston and Holland learn to control their fear and irritability—or not (Kagan,

What Comes in the Package

By studying the resemblances between large numbers of identical twins and large numbers of fraternal twins, behavioral geneticists can figure out how much of a temperamental trait is caused by genes. This is called *heritability*. Researchers have found that, on average, traits of temperament are about 50 percent heritable (Plomin, Owen, and McGuffin, 1994), although of course the heritability of each trait is different.

Fifty percent may not sound impressive, but it is (Plomin, 1990). Genes account for an enormous amount of who we are. The environment plays a significant role in how the genes express themselves, but they in turn exert considerable influence on the environment. In fact, they help to create it by eliciting responses from the people around us, by determining how we experience it, and by influencing with whom and what we elect to surround ourselves (Caspi and Silva, 1995; Plomin et al. 1994).

1994). Babies with more extreme temperamental traits find such learning much more difficult, which makes it harder to care for them. If their needs aren't being met, their behavior is more likely to become challenging.

These examples show how the environment can influence temperament, but it is important to remember that the biology comes first. Even though the environment can influence them, temperamental traits tend to be stable over time and are often still apparent in adults in one guise or another (Berk, 2000; Caspi and Silva, 1995). They may look entirely different from the outside, but the temperamental traits remain—which explains why a self-assured young woman who talks easily to strangers at a party may still regard herself as a shy person.

The theorists who've followed Thomas and Chess—such as Jerome Kagan, Mary Rothbart, John Bates, and others—have built on Thomas and Chess's model and begun to describe and measure some different dimensions, including shyness-sociability, novelty seeking, and harm avoidance.

Kagan (1994) is also interested in the physiological basis of temperament, which so far remains little understood. He has found several physiological differences in inhibited and uninhibited children, most notably that the heart rate of uninhibited children is less likely to accelerate when they are stressed. Researchers have also seen a lower heart rate in older children with aggressive conduct disorders (Reiss and Roth, 1993). Some investigators believe that the extreme version of an uninhibited temperament in childhood may be a risk factor for later aggressive behavior if the child also has trouble with self-control (Shonkoff and Phillips, 2000; Reiss and Roth, 1993).

Survival of the Fittest

In 1974, medical student Marten deVries went to Kenya and Tanzania to collect information about the temperament of the children of the Masai, a semi-nomadic tribe on the Serengeti Plain. Using temperament scales based on Thomas and Chess's criteria, he identified 10 infants with easy temperaments and 10 with difficult temperaments.

The area was in the midst of a severe drought, and when de Vries returned five months later, conditions had worsened. Most of the Masai's cattle and many of their people had died, and they were searching for better land. Though deVries couldn't locate all of the babies, he found seven with easy temperaments and six with difficult temperaments. Of the seven with easy temperaments, five had died; all but one of those with difficult temperaments had survived.

What accounted for the unexpected survival of the children with difficult temperaments? DeVries credited several factors. First, the Masai admire their warriors and encourage aggressiveness and assertiveness in their children. Second, shared caregiving in the Masai's large extended families makes it easier to deal with children who are difficult. Third, Masai mothers breast-feed on demand, and children who are fussy ask for—and receive—more nourishment.

The qualities that European American middle-class families regard as difficult—loud and frequent crying, for instance—are an advantage in an environment of scarcity (Chess and Thomas, 1989; deVries, 1984).

Influenced by both biology and child-rearing values, temperament varies from culture to culture (Kagan, 1994, 1998; Kagan et al., 1994). Chinese and Japanese mothers spend a lot of time holding and gently soothing their babies, who tend to be calm and quiet. These practices reflect the high value their culture places on early mastery of self-control (Ho, 1994) and on interdependence, where being a member of the family group is most important. European American mothers use a more active and verbal parenting style because their culture values individuality, independence, and verbal facility.

Interestingly, third-generation Japanese American infants are just as talkative and physically active as their European American peers (Ho, 1994). This demonstrates how temperament can change under the influence of changing cultural values.

Attention deficit disorder and attention deficit hyperactivity disorder

Children with challenging behavior are often diagnosed with attention deficit disorder (ADD) or attention deficit hyperactivity disorder (ADHD). Neurological syndromes with a genetic base, ADD and ADHD feature these hallmark symptoms:

• *Distractibility or inattention.* Because children with ADD or ADHD can't block out unimportant stimuli, they see and hear things others don't, like the lawnmower on the next block. As a result, they find it hard to focus and stay on track. Interestingly, they sometimes also have the ability to hyperfocus (Hallowell and Ratey, 1995; Schettler, Stein, Reich, and Valenti, 2000).

• *Impulsivity.* Children with ADD or ADHD have a tendency to say and do whatever comes into their minds, including lashing out when they're frustrated. "If you think of ADD as a basic problem with inhibition," write Edward J. Hallowell and John J. Ratey in *Driven to Distraction*, "it helps to explain how ADD people get angry quicker. They don't inhibit their impulses as well as other people" (1995, p. 15).

The Young and the Restless

Attention deficit disorder is not nearly as common in Britain as it is in the United States. In *Driven to Distraction* (1995), psychiatrists Edward J. Hallowell and John J. Ratey analyze the phenomenon this way:

One possible explanation . . . is that our gene pool is heavily loaded for ADD. The people who founded our country, and continued to populate it over time, were just the types of people who might have had ADD. They did not like to sit still. They had to be willing to take an enormous risk in boarding a ship and crossing the ocean, leaving their homes behind; they were action-oriented, independent, wanting to get away from the old ways and strike out on their own, ready to lose everything in search of a new life. The higher prevalence of ADD in our current society may be due to its higher prevalence among those who settled America. (p. 191)

• *Hyperactivity.* Hyperactivity, which Hallowell and Ratey call "excess energy," differentiates ADD from ADHD, and it may or may not be present. It is absolutely noticeable when it is. Children with hyperactivity are constantly on the go.

These symptoms may appear early, but the diagnosis—which a doctor must make—isn't usually confirmed until a child reaches 5 or 6 years of age. More prevalent among boys than girls, ADD and ADHD affect 3 to 5 percent of school-age children in the United States and they are often accompanied by learning disabilities (Marshall, 2000; Schettler et al., 2000). It is important to know that ADD or ADHD is sometimes mistakenly diagnosed when a child has been exposed to violence and is suffering from posttraumatic stress disorder.

Complications of pregnancy and birth

Studies of rhesus monkeys have shown that the stress mothers experience during pregnancy can change the physiology and psychology of their babies. As adolescents, these offspring cling to their mothers, don't hang out much with their peers, and tend to behave aggressively (Clarke, Soto, Bergholz, and Schneider, 1996).

There is also beginning to be some human evidence of these neuropsychological effects of stress and health in pregnancy. In a study in upstate New York (Olds et al., 1998), researchers arranged for nurses to visit poor, young, or unmarried women at home at least once a month during their pregnancies. When they followed up 15 years later, the researchers found that the children of these women had fewer arrests and ran away from home less often than the children of unvisited mothers. That is, the intervention during their mothers' pregnancy lowered the risk for these children, even though the nurses had never visited them after they were born. The researchers believe that improving prenatal care and promoting maternal health probably reduce the risk of neuropsychological damage to the baby.

Some studies have shown that mothers who are depressed during pregnancy have newborns who are fussier and more difficult to soothe (Dawson, Hessl, and Frey, 1994). The babies of mothers who are stressed may have a smaller head circumference, which indicates less brain growth (Nelson, 1999).

Neuropsychological damage may also lie at the root of the problems of children who are born prematurely or who experience delivery complications (Brennan, Mednick, and Kandel, 1991). Prematurity predisposes an infant to brain injury and deprives the developing brain of the sustenance it needs (Shonkoff and Phillips, 2000). Premature babies and those of low birthweight are more likely to suffer from speech and language disorders and problems with balance, coordination, and perception, all of which are associated with the development of aggression (Reiss and Roth, 1993).

Researchers speculate that obstetrical problems damage the brain mechanisms that inhibit aggressive behavior or cause hyperactivity, impulsivity, and cognitive deficits that can trigger aggressive behavior (Reiss and Roth, 1993). Several studies have linked serious delinquency and criminal offenses to perinatal trauma, and there is even a study connecting children's temper tantrums to a difficult delivery (Raine, 1993).

Early Birds

Like dinner guests who arrive early, premature babies and those with low birthweights can easily throw their unprepared parents for a loop.

When their babies have to stay in a hospital's neonatal intensive care unit, it's hard for parents to connect with them, and once they come home, they are more difficult to care for than full-term infants. Their cry is more disturbing and irritating, parents find them less satisfying to feed and hold, and parents' expectations of them are often unrealistic (Brady, Posner, Lang, and Rosati, 1994; Moffitt, 1997).

Substance abuse during pregnancy

During the prenatal period, the baby's developing nervous system is extremely vulnerable to assaults from the outside world, as episodes involving German measles and thalidomide have dramatically demonstrated. Alcohol, drugs, and chemicals ingested during pregnancy can do considerable harm. How much harm depends on the fetus's stage of development, as well as how much, how long, and how often exposure takes place. The resilience of the fetus and the mother's health and prenatal care have an impact (Shonkoff and Phillips, 2000), and so does the parents' behavior after the baby's birth. If parents of newborns continue to abuse drugs or alcohol, their children may face the added danger of neglect, abuse, or chaotic, inconsistent, and unresponsive caregiving (Griffith, 1992; Leslie and DeMarchi, 1996).

Alcohol

Alcohol, a legal substance, is responsible for much more damage to unborn babies than any illegal drug. Drinking during pregnancy—especially heavy or binge drinking—causes lifelong damage to the developing brain, and consuming even small amounts of alcohol can cause neurological deficits. A 1995 survey put the percentage of pregnant women who drink at 15.3 (Secretary of Health and Human Services, 2000).

First identified in France in 1968, the set of birth defects known as *fetal alcohol syndrome (FAS)* occurs at a rate of roughly 0.5 to 3 per 1,000 live births—more often in some African American and Native American communities (Shonkoff and Phillips, 2000; Secretary of Health and Human Services, 2000). But not all children show the characteristic facial defects and growth deficiency of FAS. A much larger number—perhaps ten times as many (Shonkoff and Phillips, 2000)—have mental impairments just as serious, hidden behind perfectly normal faces and bodies. This condition, formerly called *fetal alcohol effects (FAE)*, has been renamed *alcohol-related neurodevelopmental disorder (ARND)*. Children with FAS or ARND have lower IQs as well as difficulties with learning, memory, attention, problem solving, and social interactions. Their motor control and executive functions may be affected, and hyperactivity is a common symptom. Because they often act impulsively and become easily frustrated, they are at risk for challenging behavior.

All Canadian cigarette packages carry health alerts. This one warns of the dangers for the fetus of smoking during pregnancy. Smoking during pregnancy is a risk factor for behavior problems.
Photo courtesy of Health Canada.

Tobacco and nicotine

The warnings on cigarette packages are there for good reason: Smoking during pregnancy causes babies to be born prematurely and to have low birthweights. Because it probably reduces the flow of oxygen and nutrients to the fetus, smoking is a risk factor for behavior problems, attention difficulties, impulsiveness, hyperactivity, problems regulating emotions, and lower IQ (Olds, 1997; Olds, Henderson, and Tatelbaum, 1994; Schettler et al., 2000).

Cocaine and crack

Recent research suggests that cocaine—which passes through the placenta—may damage areas of the fetal brain that regulate arousal and attention (National Institute on Drug Abuse, 1999). Babies exposed to crack or cocaine *in utero* may have more trouble regulating their responses, concentrating, and focusing their attention (Eyler, Behnke, Conlon, Woods, and Wobie, 1998). They may also have language delays and poor organizational skills. In addition, cocaine use during pregnancy increases complications during pregnancy and delivery (Brady et al., 1994; Leslie and DeMarchi, 1996).

Heroin and methadone

Injected during pregnancy, opiates such as heroin cause prematurity and low birthweight in babies and put them at risk for attention and developmental problems. They are born addicted and must go through the withdrawal process, and if they are living with substance-abusing parents, their home environment may hold as many risks for them as their prenatal drug exposure (Brady et al., 1994; Leslie and DeMarchi, 1996).

Marijuana

Marijuana is the most widely used illicit drug—some estimate that up to 20 percent of newborns have been exposed to it prenatally. Children whose mothers smoke marijuana during pregnancy perform poorly on attention, memory, and verbal tests, and they are also more likely to be impulsive and hyperactive (Brady et al., 1994; Leslie and DeMarchi, 1996).

Malnutrition

For optimal development of the human brain, a child needs adequate nutrition both before birth and during the first two or three years of life. Malnutrition seems to hit hardest in the social and emotional realms (Shonkoff and Phillips, 2000). Babies who are malnourished *in utero* are irritable and unresponsive, and their high-pitched cry makes them difficult to care for (Lozoff, 1989). They also have trouble handling stress and focusing their attention (Carey and McDevitt, 1995). Iron deficiency, which often accompanies malnutrition, also causes shortened attention, irritability, and cognitive impairment (Shonkoff and Marshall, 2000).

Language and cognition disorders

Problems with brain function—with language, memory, and attention in particular—are very common in children with challenging behavior (Reiss and Roth, 1993).

Language

Studies report a 50 percent overlap between language delays and behavior problems (Campbell, 1990). Psychologists often find unsuspected language disorders among the children referred to them with challenging behavior (Campbell, 1990), and language specialists find behavior problems among children referred to them with language delays (Coie and Dodge, 1998). According to psychologist Terrie E. Moffitt of the University of Wisconsin, "The link between verbal impairment and antisocial outcomes is one of

Using Your Words

Language and verbal skills are utterly essential, and it is easy to see how children without them might turn to challenging behavior. In his book *The Explosive Child* (1998), child psychologist Ross W. Greene of the Massachusetts General Hospital describes some of the barriers that such children encounter.

- *Understanding.* When a child doesn't understand the words of the people around her, she becomes confused and frustrated and finds it hard to respond appropriately.

- *Categorizing, labeling, and storing emotions and previous experiences in language.* If a child can't use language to classify and store her feelings and experience, she doesn't really know how she feels or what she did the last time she felt this way.

- *Thinking things through in language.* When a child can't use words to think things through, she can't figure out what to do, even when she knows what she's feeling.

- *Expressing complicated feelings, thoughts, and ideas.* A child may have trouble going beyond simple language to articulate what's bothering her.

Any of these problems easily leads to frustration and botched communication with both peers and adults.

the largest and most robust effects in the study of antisocial behavior. The verbal deficits of antisocial children are pervasive, affecting their memory for verbal material and their ability to listen and read, to solve problems, and to speak and write" (1997, p. 132).

Children need language to convert the reassurances and instructions they get from adults into tools for self-control. If they don't really understand the words or principles involved, they may try out many varieties of misbehavior, eliciting punishment instead of positive responses from their parents and teachers. They can all too easily end up being hard to manage and even hard to love (Moffitt, 1997).

These neuropsychological problems—which are also called *mild cognitive impairments* or *language or motor delays*—are often so subtle that they manifest themselves as problems of temperament (Kazdin, 1995; Moffitt, 1997). Researchers studying low-birthweight infants from two-parent, middle-class families found that the babies' neurological problems and difficult temperament were significantly related (Moffitt, 1997).

Nonverbal learning disabilities

Children who do not have language problems may have nonverbal learning disabilities. Problems in the motor, visual spatial, and social realms are reflected in poor skills in problem solving, a lack of flexibility and adaptability, and difficulties with social perception, social judgment, and social interaction (Greene, 1998; Andersen, 2001).

Problems in sensory integration

Some children are unable to sort out and integrate all the sensory information that comes their way. Difficulties that include poor motor coordination, hypersensitivity to sensation, distractibility, hyperactivity, and slow speech may be linked to challenging behaviors (Ayres, 1979). Some of these children hardly seem to notice sensory input; others overreact and develop strong preferences for such items as seamless socks and bland, lukewarm foods that don't overwhelm their extra-sensitive systems (Greene, 1998). Their subtle gross- and fine-motor problems often make them seem clumsy and uncoordinated, forever tripping and bumping their way through life (Kazdin, 1995; Moffitt, 1997).

Executive functions

Children with challenging behavior often have another related, subtle brain problem: Their *executive functions* do not work properly. This catch-all phrase encompasses a series of interdependent skills that children need to perform any goal-directed activity, from taking a sip of juice without spilling it to entering a game of hospital in the dramatic play corner. The executive functions include:

• Planning and organizing behavior, including anticipating problems and figuring out strategies to cope with them

• Sequencing behavior

• Sustaining attention and concentration

• Being flexible and able to shift from one mindset to another

• Inhibiting responses

- Self-monitoring

- Taking the perspective of others (Moffitt, 1997; Shonkoff and Phillips, 2000)

Executive functions have a lot to do with emotional regulation and self-control. When they're out of kilter, children can't control their behavior very well and will act impulsively, without considering the impact on others (Moffitt, 1997).

Gender

In 1974, psychologists Eleanor Maccoby and Carol Jacklin analyzed thousands of research studies and concluded that physical aggression is one of the few areas where there's a difference between girls and boys.

In European American culture, parents discourage aggressive behavior in children of both sexes (Pepler and Slaby, 1994), and in nonviolent households, boys and girls show about the same level of aggression (Gulbenkian Foundation, 1995). Nonetheless, boys are at greater risk for aggressive behavior than girls, perhaps because of the male sex hormones they are exposed to before birth and the fact that many families tolerate their aggressive behavior more easily (Berk, 2000). In the 1996 National Longitudinal Survey of Children and Youth in Canada, boys scored higher than girls on physical aggression in every age group (Offord and Lipman, 1996; Tremblay et al., 1996). Boys hit and insult each other more, respond to hits and insults more quickly, spend more time in rough-and-tumble play, and accept aggressive behavior more readily than girls.

Now that they are finally studying aggressive behavior in girls, researchers are redefining it to include indirect aggression, where girls score higher (Offord and Lipman, 1996; Tremblay et al., 1996). By the age of 4 or 5, girls who use physical aggression find themselves disliked by their peers, who prefer the indirect means of exclusion, backstabbing, gossiping, belittling, and the like (Pepler and Craig, 1999; Pepler and Slaby, 1994).

However, recent research shows that physical aggression is becoming more normative and acceptable among girls (Pepler and Slaby, 1994). The arrest rate for girls 17 years old and under increased 103 percent from 1981 to 1997, whereas the rate for boys rose only 27 percent (Children's Defense Fund, 2000). It seems that the environment also figures prominently in girls' aggressive behavior (Pepler and Slaby).

Like boys who don't renounce physical aggression before they enter school, girls who continue to act aggressively face the prospect of school failure and rejection by their peers. They often join groups of boys and get into fights with boys, and eventually they date—and marry—boys who act aggressively. As the boys grow bigger and stronger, these girls may find themselves in considerable danger because they haven't acquired the social and problem-solving skills they need to sustain an intimate relationship (Pepler and Craig, 1999).

Girls may also continue to use aggression within their families. They behave more aggressively with their parents than their brothers do, and their mothers respond by behaving aggressively in return. Again, this pattern of behavior puts them at high risk in future relationships (Pepler and Craig, 1999).

Girls who behave aggressively are also more likely to become single teenage mothers (Pepler and Craig, 1999). Psychologist Lisa Serbin and her colleagues at Concordia University in Montreal, who have been following a large group of girls with aggressive behavior from elementary school into adolescence and adulthood, are finding that these young women aren't well prepared for their adult roles. They don't provide their children with many appropriate play materials, and they aren't very emotionally or verbally responsive. Their children show early signs of psychosocial difficulties and make frequent visits to hospital emergency rooms—which has made the researchers worry about possible physical abuse (Pepler and Craig, 1999; Pepler and Slaby, 1994; Serbin, Moskowitz, Schwartzman, and Ledingham, 1991).

Environmental Risk Factors

Family factors and parenting style

Because parents play so vital a role in their children's development, they are an easy target whenever challenging behavior appears on the scene. Parenting is difficult and complicated work that requires a vast amount of time and energy—items that are in short supply in young families. It is important for teachers to understand the parents' role in challenging behavior, but it is equally important not to blame them. It is far better to become their partners.

Any life circumstance that hinders a parent's well-being can put children at risk, including:

- A mother who had her first child when she was very young (Haapasalo and Tremblay, 1994)

- Parents with little education (Coie and Dodge, 1998)

- A parent with mental illness, especially a mother who's depressed (Shonkoff and Phillips, 2000)

- A parent who is abusing alcohol or drugs (Farrington, 1991)

- A parent with antisocial or criminal behavior (Farrington, 1991; Frick et al., 1991)

- A large number of children in the family (Farrington, 1991; Raine, 1993)

Indirectly, all of these factors influence the parent-child relationship, the first line of defense against later aggressive behavior. A secure attachment to a primary caregiver is the foundation of a child's emotional development, enabling her to learn to control and express her feelings, to cope with stress, to accept limits, and to have a sense of herself as a competent and effective person. Some studies have shown that an insecure attachment is correlated with aggressive behavior (Coie and Dodge, 1998; Moffitt, 1997). The parent-child relationship also acts as a prototype for future relationships (Coie, 1990).

Inappropriate parenting increases the risk of challenging behavior. When parents aren't involved with their children, don't respond warmly to them, and use harsh and inconsistent discipline, the children may react with defiant, aggressive, impulsive behaviors (Coie, 1996; Eron, Huesmann, and Zelli, 1991; Haapasalo and Tremblay, 1994). Poor supervision also has an impact, probably because it indicates that parents aren't spending much time with their children (Raine, 1993).

Some families inadvertently teach their children to use aggression. Rather than clearly saying what they expect, they use inappropriate and ineffectual tactics, communicating their feelings of anger, impatience, and irritation, and they ignore or even punish their child's prosocial behavior (Webster-Stratton, 1997). Gerald R. Patterson of the Oregon Social Learning Center has carefully documented a cycle of interaction between parent and child that he calls "coercive" (1982, 1995). It can begin with a relatively trivial demand, such as a parent asking a child to do, or not do, something. The child ignores the request or refuses to comply. Then the parent responds more aggressively, scolding, nagging, or pleading; the child again refuses, whining or talking back. The exchanges escalate to yelling, threats, hitting, and temper tantrums, until the parent finally gives up and gives in—or explodes into violence—and then the child stops, too.

When the parents give in, which is most of the time, they are actually rewarding their child's negative behavior and increasing the chances that she'll behave the same way again. At the same time, the child is reinforcing the parents by ceasing her own negative behavior (Coie and Dodge, 1998).

When the parents explode, they are modeling the use of aggression as a way to solve problems. The child may do as they ask, but she is more likely to feel hostility toward them and to become aggressive with both parents and peers in the future, especially if they don't have a warm relationship (Coie and Dodge, 1998). Each time the parents use this method, it will be less effective, and they will probably use greater force, which may eventually lead to abuse (American Academy of Pediatrics, 1998). Whether they give in or resort to violence, the parents become demoralized and interact with

Wanted Children

Economists John Donahue of Stanford University Law School and Steven Levitt of the University of Chicago (2001) have an interesting explanation for the dramatic drop in crime across the United States during the 1990s. They attribute half of it to *Roe* v. *Wade*, the 1973 Supreme Court decision legalizing abortion.

Donahue and Levitt conclude that children who are wanted are less likely to commit crimes. The peak years for criminal activity are 18 to 24 years, and when the children born in the era of legalized abortion started to turn 18 years of age, crime rates began to fall. The rates decreased first in the states that first made abortion legal.

Although the study took into account factors such as rates of imprisonment, number of police, and the state of the economy, the findings have stirred up considerable controversy.

their child less and less, missing opportunities to help her gain the emotional control, social skills, and cognitive skills she needs to make friends and succeed at school.

It is important to remember, however, that parent-child interaction is definitely a two-way street. Every child is different, and so is every parent. The child's temperament strongly influences the way the people in her life treat her and react to her. If she rarely smiles, if she whines when she talks, if she finds it hard to adapt to new foods, clothes, and people, her family will have a harder time figuring out how to make her happy and she will have a harder time engaging them in positive relationships (Webster-Stratton and Herbert, 1994). Each parent will respond according to his or her own temperament. If the fit between them isn't a good one, poor parenting may be the result.

Poverty and the conditions surroundings it

Poverty has an enormous impact on children's lives and puts them at risk for challenging behavior even before they are born. More than 35 percent of children who live in poor families have seven or more risk factors—versus 7 percent of those who live in wealthy families (Sameroff and Fiese, 2000).

Good prenatal care is often not available to low-income families. One study found that in New York City's poor health districts, for example, the infant mortality rate was as high as 43.5 per 1,000 live births, versus 6.6 per 1,000 live births in the city's wealthier sections (Sampson, 1997). Babies in poor families also confront a higher risk of prematurity, low birthweight, and neurological damage (Sampson, 1997), all possible factors in challenging behavior.

Poverty brings a high level of stress to families' lives—nonstop anxiety about food, housing, jobs, health care, safety and more. In high-poverty urban neighborhoods, families often have little or no social support, formal or informal. It is hard to make and keep friends when you're living in a gigantic housing project, when people move all the time and you don't know your neighbors, when one person carries the full responsibility for the family, when people are afraid to go to church, the local store, even to school. As a result, there is no one to keep an eye on anyone else's children or

Hidden Threat

Lead, which is found in old lead-based paint, water pipes, improperly glazed dishes, and lead-based gasoline embedded in the soil, poses an especially potent threat to pregnant women and children living in old housing and poor inner-city neighborhoods (Shonkoff and Phillips, 2000).

Even at very low levels, lead affects the developing nervous system. It interferes with the ability to restrain impulses and leads to aggressive and delinquent behavior (Needleman, Riess, Tobin, Biesecker, and Greenhouse, 1996; Wasserman, Staghezza-Jaramillo, Shrout, Popovac, and Graziano, 1998). It is also linked to attention deficits, learning disabilities, and lowered IQ (Raine, 1993). About one million children in the United States have excessive levels of lead in their blood (Schettler et al., 2000).

Please Won't You Be My Neighbor?

A neighborhood can make a difference, especially for children at high risk.

Although research in this field is still far from conclusive, data from a few large-scale quasi-experimental studies in Chicago, Boston, and Baltimore suggest that moving from a high-poverty area to a low-poverty area can lower school dropout rates; increase college enrollment; decrease accidents, injuries, and asthma attacks; lower the rate of challenging behavior among school-age boys; and reduce the arrest rate for violent offenses among adolescents (Shonkoff and Phillips, 2000).

property, it's nearly impossible to supervise adolescents, and, as children grow, the neighborhood offers them little in the way of access to resources, health and recreational services, and mainstream role models and opportunities. This "social disorganization" (Sampson, 1997), as the sociologists call it, is becoming more and more common in U.S. inner cities (Garbarino, 1999).

About 27 percent of poor African American children and 20 percent of poor Latino American children live in the inner city, compared with 3 percent of poor European American children (Shonkoff and Phillips, 2000). A family who belongs to a minority group faces the additional stress of racial discrimination, which damages self-esteem and provokes feelings of rage and shame (Garbarino, 1999).

All of this makes parenting extremely arduous. Whether or not they live in the inner city, stressed parents find it hard to attend to their children's needs, and as a result they may be less apt to provide warmth, emotional support, stimulation, and supervision. They may depend instead on coercive parenting techniques, harsh discipline, punishment, and even physical abuse (Dodge, Pettit, and Bates, 1994; Fick, Osofsky, and Lewis, 1997), increasing their children's risk of challenging behavior.

Exposure to violence

Violence is endemic in American life and culture. Children run into it everywhere—in the news, in games and sports, in adult conversation, in Saturday morning cartoons.

Children who encounter violence at close range find that it has a deep and powerful effect, even when they aren't its direct victims (Jenkins and Bell, 1997). It "changes the way children view the world and may change the value they place on life itself," according to Betsy Groves and Barry Zuckerman of the Boston Medical Center School of Medicine. "It affects their ability to learn, to establish relationships with others, and to cope with stress" (p. 183).

In a study in Washington, DC, researchers Esther Jenkins and Carl Bell (1997) found that 31 percent of the fifth- and sixth-graders in their sample had witnessed a shooting, 17 percent had seen a stabbing, and the majority knew either the victim or the perpetrator. Even the very young are not exempt: 10 percent of the children under the age of 6 who visited a pediatric clinic at Boston City Hospital in 1991 reported witnessing a shooting or a stabbing (Groves and Zuckerman, 1997).

Violence is endemic in American life and culture.

Children are all too aware of these events (Jaffe, Wolfe, and Wilson, 1990). Besides feeling frightened, vulnerable, anxious, depressed, and confused, some exhibit symptoms of posttraumatic stress disorder. They cling to their parents and teachers, and their eating, sleeping, and toileting may be disrupted. They have trouble paying attention, remembering things, and relating to others. They may have flashbacks where they replay the violent incident over and over in their minds; they may try to avoid thinking about it, experience emotional numbing, or become hyperalert. Many have trouble controlling their aggressive impulses (Jenkins and Bell, 1997; Osofsky, 1997). Parents, who have the most power to help, may also be traumatized and fail to recognize and respond to their children's distress (Osofsky, 1997).

When violence takes place within the child's family, it is even more devastating (Jenkins and Bell, 1997). Over 3 million children are at risk of witnessing physical assaults between their parents each year (National Center for Children Exposed to Violence, 2001). Even verbal conflict upsets children, and when it's combined with physical conflict it contributes to both emotional problems and challenging behavior (Zeanah and Scheeringa, 1997; Yoshikawa, 1994). Psychologist Hirokazu Yoshikawa (1994) of New York University notes that conflict between parents has a greater negative influence on a child than the loss of a parent by death or divorce, and some studies consider it as harmful as physical abuse of the child (Widom, 1989).

Abuse and neglect are also shockingly common—nearly 3 million cases of child abuse and neglect were reported in the United States in 1998 (U.S. Department of

Health and Human Services, 2000). Poor families are especially at risk (Bethea, 1999). Children who are abused are often insecurely attached to their caregivers (Shonkoff and Phillips, 2000), with whom they are angry, frustrated, and noncompliant. They also behave aggressively with their peers, and instead of trying to comfort a friend in distress, they respond with fear, lash out with attacks and anger, or act totally unconcerned. They also have fewer words for their feelings (Coie and Dodge, 1998; Zeanah and Scheeringa, 1997).

In addition to their psychological injuries, children who are abused have physical injuries. In infants, abuse accounts for most of the head injuries, which are particularly dangerous. Shaking or hitting a child on the head is probably much more common than most people think because these injuries can't be seen and the effects are often cumulative rather than immediate. Head injuries affect coping skills, judgment, self-control, empathy, social skills, and problem-solving skills (Raine, 1993), and research connects head injuries firmly to violent and aggressive behavior later on. Dramatically, one study of 15 young murderers on death row found that all of them had had severe head injuries (Raine, 1993).

Turbulent times

Violence in the lives of children takes on a new meaning during a national crisis. On September 11, 2001, life in the United States changed forever. The extraordinary events of that day and the days that followed shattered everyone's sense of safety and security. Glued to their television sets, people watched time and time again two hijacked planes crash into the World Trade Center in New York. Young children, with their limited understanding of the world, believed that each replay was a different event, a different plane, and yet another building. Some felt as if there were no safe place left on earth. If their parents worked in tall buildings or traveled in planes, they worried that they would never see them again.

Catastrophic events such as terrorist attacks, riots, hurricanes, and earthquakes create a sense of helplessness and make everyone feel frightened and defenseless, especially when they happen close to home. Children are particularly vulnerable, because they depend on the adults around them to make them feel safe. Their ability to recover is intimately connected to the ability of their families and teachers to comfort and reassure them.

Each child responds differently to an event like September 11. Some react right away; others take weeks to show their fear, anger, and sadness; some bounce back relatively quickly; others may experience problems over a long period. Several factors influence a child's reaction: her age (both chronological and developmental), her temperament, her family's response to the event, and how physically and emotionally close she is to the disaster. Children who've lost a friend or relative or witnessed the event in person will be the hardest hit (Greenman, 2001). Boys take longer to recover and are more prone to act aggressively; girls express their feelings in words and ask more questions (American Academy of Pediatrics, n.d.).

Children age 5 and under may express their anxiety by crying, whining, throwing tantrums, or becoming afraid of strangers. They may also be more frightened of the

"For the people of New York City. I am sorry." By Christine Kilmer, age 3, Bowling Green, Ohio, September 13, 2001.

world and new situations, cling to their parents and/or favorite objects, and become afraid to leave home. They may have difficulty sleeping and regress to behaviors that they used when they were younger. School-age children may also experience these symptoms, as well as others. Their behavior may be aggressive or disruptive; they may get more angry and combative; they may be irritable and have trouble paying attention. Or they may withdraw and become depressed, anxious, or emotionally numb (National Institute of Mental Health, 2001).

Extremely sensitive children and those already struggling with stress will have a particularly hard time. Children who've experienced previous losses, children whose families are too upset and fearful to provide the reassurance they need, and children who were barely coping in the period before the disaster may be overwhelmed. Children whose behavior was already out of control may deteriorate further. Children who are surrounded by angry people looking for revenge may respond with anger that comes to the fore in their interactions with their peers. In all of these cases, challenging behavior is often the result.

Violent media

Some experts believe that when it comes to involvement with violence, the media exert as much influence as family and peers (Levin, 1998; Slaby, 1997). Eric Harris and Dylan Klebold provide vivid anecdotal evidence for this opinion: The teenagers who killed 13 students and teachers at Columbine High School in Littleton, Colorado, in 1999 played the video game Doom obsessively every afternoon (Bai, 1999).

Children spend an average of 35 hours a week watching television and videos or playing video games—more time than they spend doing anything but sleeping (Levin, 1998). African American children watch more television than European American children, and children in poor families watch more television than children in affluent families (Slaby, 1997).

In 1972, the Surgeon General's Scientific Advisory Committee on Television and Social Behavior concluded that there is a direct, causal link between seeing violence on television and aggressive behavior. Recent meta-reviews of the most rigorous studies in the field indicate that the effects of television violence are very strong (Coie and Dodge, 1998). In the last decade, television and video games have become even more violent (Levin, 1998).

Children are the most susceptible viewers because they are the least able to evaluate what they see (Slaby, 1997). Researchers (Coie and Dodge, 1998; Donnerstein, Slaby, and Eron, 1994; Slaby, 1997) have documented at least four main effects:

- *Aggressor effect.* Children who watch violent media are more likely to engage in aggressive behavior, especially if they identify with aggressive characters or find the violence realistic and relevant to their own lives. They may come to think that aggression is an acceptable and justifiable way to resolve conflict. The more violence a child watches, the more aggressive the child's behavior is likely to become.

- *Victim effect.* Watching television violence makes some children more fearful.

Most vulnerable are those who identify with the victim and perceive the violence as realistic. Heavy viewers of violence can acquire "mean-world syndrome," mistrusting people and seeing the world as much more dangerous and violent than it really is. Youth and adults with this perspective may carry guns to protect themselves—which actually makes them more likely to become victims.

• *Bystander effect.* Watching media violence desensitizes children and leads them to think that violence is normal, especially when programs present it as acceptable, normal, and without consequences. Instead of responding to real-life pain and suffering with sympathy, child viewers of violence remain indifferent. In one experiment, children who had watched a violent program were far less likely to intervene or call for help when fighting broke out among the children they were "babysitting" (Thomas and Drabman, 1975).

• *Increased appetite effect.* When television violence is fun and exciting, children crave more of it. Children who behave aggressively watch more violent television in order to justify their behavior.

Prosocial television has prosocial effects, but there is relatively little of it to be seen (Donnerstein et al., 1994; Murray, 1997).

Whether violence enters their lives via their own families, their peers, their neighbors, or the media, children who are exposed to it are learning that it is an acceptable—and effective—way to resolve conflict and gain power. They become more ready to accept aggressive behavior both in themselves and in others, and they are at high risk for criminal behavior and for aggressive behavior in their own dating and marital relationships (Suderman and Jaffe, 1997).

Child care

In 1997, 76 percent of children under age 5 in the United States went to child care (Capizzano, Adams, and Sonenstein, 2000), including large numbers of infants born to single mothers who are required to work by the 1996 welfare reform (Shonkoff and Phillips, 2000).

Children don't choose to attend child care; they have to go. When they're there for many hours a week, they have very little control over their own lives. Their individual needs often take a backseat to the needs of the group and the teachers (children often nap so that teachers can have a lunch break, for example). Children who are inflexible or easily frustrated and children who are very active or very timid find this extremely difficult, and it's more difficult when they spend the entire day in child care. Challenging behavior is their way of letting us know what they feel.

Research over the years has shown that stimulating and emotionally supportive care is associated with positive developmental outcomes for children. But a longitudinal study of 1,300 children by the Early Child Care Research Network of the National Institute for Child Health and Human Development (NICHD) (in press) has found a link between the number of hours that 4½-year-olds and kindergartners spend in child care and their social competence and problem behavior. As the children's time in child care increased, so did their problem behavior and aggression. The study takes into account the quality of care, along with other factors, including gender, ethnicity, mother's education, and family income.

When these results were first presented at a meeting of the Society for Research in Child Development in 2001, they raised alarm among parents and outrage and disbelief in the child-care community. People rushed to point out that this is observational research, not a controlled experiment, so it does not prove that more hours of care *cause* aggressive behavior; and they offered several possible reasons that more time in child care might be associated with more problem behavior. One is that parents enroll children with behavior problems in child care earlier and longer because they're hard to handle at home; another is that the economic stress that makes families put their children into child care in the first place spills over to those children, causing problem behavior. In addition, the percentage of children with behavior problems in child care is about the same as the percentage in the general population.

Even though it's disturbing, it's important to take this research seriously. It is a rigorous study, the largest of its kind ever conducted, and the researchers are respected experts. Because it seems to show that time spent in child care affects problem behavior and quality doesn't, it suggests that even trained, qualified, and experienced teachers working in high-quality centers often do not have the skills that are required to work effectively with children with challenging behavior. Such skills simply haven't been part of their education.

When the teacher can't cope with one child with challenging behavior, other children in the classroom who can regulate their behavior under normal conditions tend to become very anxious, frightened, or excited, and they frequently follow the lead of the child with challenging behavior. The result is that suddenly there are several children with challenging behavior in the group. The more time that children spend in such a situation, the more opportunities they have to learn and practice challenging behavior. This state of affairs has less to do with the quality of care in the center (as it is usually measured) and more to do with the special skills of individual teachers.

The NICHD Early Child Care Research Network is continuing to follow the same group of children. Future reports will probably reveal whether the link between problem behavior and quantity of time in child care remains—or disappears—as the children get older.

Understanding risk

This chapter presents a long list of risk factors, and after reading it you might feel that it's a miracle if any child manages to emerge from early childhood without challenging behavior. But remember that these risks have a cumulative effect. Each one you can counteract or help a child to avoid will made a substantial difference in her ability to cope. The simple fact that you understand more about who she is should increase your empathy and enhance the quality of your relationship—and the strength of your influence. The next chapter will aid you in this undertaking by telling you about some of the factors that actually protect children from risk.

What Do You Think?

1. In this chapter we've separated biological and environmental risk factors, but in reality they are inextricably intertwined. Can you think of some examples of how they're intertwined?

2. A child's temperament becomes a problem only when it clashes with the temperament of those around her, especially her family and teachers. How would you describe your temperament? Was there a "good fit" between you and your family? How has your temperament affected your life?

3. What kinds of stress do families who live in poverty encounter? How does family stress make parenting a more difficult job?

4. Some experts think the media play an extremely important role in increasing aggressive behavior. What do you think? How have the news and films that you've seen shaped your attitudes toward other people and the world?

5. Why do you think the NICHD Early Child Care Study indicated that the amount of time spent in child care is more important than the quality of child care when it comes to problem behavior?

Suggested Reading

Flick, G. L. (1998). *ADD/ADHD behavior-change resource kit: Ready-to-use strategies & activities for helping children with attention deficit disorder.* West Nyack, NY: Center for Applied Research in Education.

Kleinfeld, J., & Wescott, S. (1993). *Fantastic Antone succeeds! Experiences in educating children with fetal alcohol syndrome.* Fairbanks: University of Alaska Press.

Kranowitz, C. S. (1998). *The out-of-sync child: Recognizing and coping with sensory integrative dysfunction.* New York: Berkley.

Levin, D. (1998). *Remote control childhood? Combating the hazards of media culture.* Washington, DC: National Association for the Education of Young Children.

McCord, J. (Ed.). (1997). *Violence and childhood in the inner city.* New York: Cambridge University Press.

Turecki, S., with Tonner, L. (2000). *The difficult child.* New York: Bantam Books.

References

American Academy of Pediatrics. (1998). Guidance for effective discipline (RE 9740). *Pediatrics, 101,* 723–728.

American Academy of Pediatrics, Work Group on Disasters. (n.d.). *Psychosocial issues for children and families in disasters: A guide for the primary care physician.* Elk Grove, IL: American Academy of Pediatrics. Retrieved September 24, 2001, from http://www.mentalhealth.org/publications/allpubs/SMA95-3022/SMA3022.htm.

Andersen, K. (2001, January). Non-verbal learning disability. *BDINews — A Newsletter about Caring for the HighMaintenance Child, 3*(6). Retrieved from http://www.b-di.com.

Ayres, A. J. (1979). *Sensory integration and the child.* Los Angeles: Western Psychological Services.

Bai, M. (1999, May 3). Anatomy of a massacre. *Newsweek, 133,* 24–31.

Berk, L. E. (2000). *Child development* (5th ed.). Boston: Allyn and Bacon.

Bethea, L. (1999). Primary prevention of child abuse. *American Family Physician, 59,* 1577–1598.

Brady, J. P., Posner, M., Lang, C., & Rosati, M. J. (1994). *Risk and reality: The implications of prenatal exposure to alcohol and other drugs.* Washington, DC: U.S. Department of Health and Human Services and U.S. Department of Education.

Retrieved February 4, 2002, from http://www.com-over.to/FAS/Research.htm.

Brennan, P., Mednick, S., & Kandel, E. (1991). Congenital determinants of violent and property offending. In D. J. Pepler & K. H. Rubin (Eds.), *The development and treatment of childhood aggression* (pp. 81–92). Hillsdale, NJ: Erlbaum.

Campbell, S. B. (1990). *Behavior problems in preschool children.* New York: Guilford.

Capizzano, J., Adams, G., & Sonenstein, F. (2000). Child care arrangements for children under five: Variation across states, No. B–7. In *Assessing the new federalism.* Washington, DC: The Urban Institute. Retrieved February 19, 2002, from http://newfederalism.urban.org/html/series_b/b8/b8.html#about.

Carey, W. B., & McDevitt, S. C. (1995). *Coping with children's temperament.* New York: Basic Books.

Caspi, A., & Silva, P. A. (1995). Temperamental qualities at age three predict personality traits in young adulthood: Longitudinal evidence from a birth cohort. *Child Development, 66,* 486–498.

Chen, S., Lee, A. Y., Bowens, N. M., Huber, R., & Kravitz, E. A. (2002). Fighting fruit flies: A model system for the study of aggression. *Proceedings of the National Academy of Sciences, 99,* 5664–5668.

Chess, S., & Thomas, A. (1984). *Origins and evolution of behavior disorders from infancy to early adult life.* New York: Brunner/Mazel.

Chess, S., & Thomas, A. (1989). Temperament and its functional significance. In S. I. Greenspan & G. H. Pollock (Eds.), *The course of life: Vol. 2, Early childhood* (pp. 163–228). Madison, CT: International Universities Press.

Children's Defense Fund. (2000). *The state of America's children.* Boston: Beacon Press.

Clarke, A. S., Soto, A., Bergholz, T., & Schneider, M. (1996). Maternal gestational stress alters adaptive and social behavior in adolescent rhesus monkey offspring. *Infant Behavioral Development, 19,* 453–463.

Coie, J. D. (1990). Toward a theory of peer rejection. In S. R. Asher & J. D. Coie (Eds.), *Peer rejection in childhood* (pp. 365–401). New York: Cambridge University Press.

Coie, J. D. (1996). Prevention of violence and antisocial behavior. In R. DeV. Peters & R. J. McMahon (Eds.), *Preventing childhood disorders, substance abuse, and delinquency* (pp. 1–18). Thousand Oaks, CA: Sage.

Coie, J. D., & Dodge, K. A. (1998). Aggression and antisocial behavior. In N. Eisenberg (Ed.), *Handbook of child psychology: Vol. 3, Social, emotional, and personality development* (5th ed., pp. 779–862). New York: Wiley.

Dawson, G., Hessl, D., & Frey, K. (1994). Social influences on early developing biological and behavioral systems related to risk for affective disorder. *Development and Psychopathology, 6,* 759–779.

deVries, M. W. (1984). Temperament and infant mortality among the Masai of East Africa. *American Journal of Psychiatry, 141,* 1189–1194.

Dodge, K. A., Pettit, G. S., & Bates, J. E. (1994). Socialization mediation of the relationship between socioeconomic status and child conduct problems. *Child Development, 65,* 649–665.

Donahue, J. J., & Levitt, S. D. (2001, May). The impact of legalized abortion on crime. *The Quarterly Journal of Economics, 116,* 379–420.

Donnerstein, E., Slaby, R. G., & Eron, L. D. (1994). The mass media and youth aggression. In L. D. Eron, J. H. Gentry, & P. Schlegel (Eds.), *Reason to hope: A psychosocial perspective on violence & youth* (pp. 219–250). Washington, DC: American Psychological Association.

Eron, L. D., Huesmann, L. R., & Zelli, A. (1991). The role of parental variables in the learning of aggression. In D. J. Pepler & K. H. Rubin (Eds.), *The development and treatment of childhood aggression* (pp. 169–188). Hillsdale, NJ: Erlbaum.

Eyler, F. D., Behnke, M., Conlon, M., Woods, N. S., & Wobie, K. (1998). Birth outcome from a prospective, matched study of prenatal crack/cocaine use: II. Interactive and dose effects on neurobehavioral assessment. *Pediatrics, 101,* 237–241.

Farrington, D. P. (1991). Childhood aggression and adult violence: Early precursors and later life outcomes. In D. J. Pepler & K. H. Rubin (Eds.), *The development and treatment of childhood aggression* (pp. 5–30). Hillsdale, NJ: Erlbaum.

Fick, A. C., Osofsky, J. D., & Lewis, M. L. (1997). Perceptions of violence: Children, parents, and police officers. In J. D. Osofsky (Ed.), *Children in a violent society* (pp. 261–276). New York: Guilford.

Frick, P. J., Lahey, B. B., Kamphaus, R. W., Loeber, R., Christ, M. G., Hart, E. L., et al. (1991). Academic underachievement and the disruptive behavior disorders. *Journal of Consulting and Clinical Psychology, 59,* 301–315.

Garbarino, J. (1999). *Lost boys: Why our sons turn violent and how we can save them.* New York: Free Press.

Greene, R. W. (1998). *The explosive child: A new approach for understanding and parenting easily frustrated, "chronically inflexible" children*. New York: HarperCollins.

Greenman, J. (2001). *What happened to the world? Helping children cope in turbulent times*. Retrieved February 1, 2002, from www.brighthorizons.com/talktochildren/whathapp.pdf.

Griffith, D. R. (1992). Prenatal exposure to cocaine and other drugs: Developmental and educational prognoses. *Phi Delta Kappan, 74*, 30–34.

Groves, B. M., & Zuckerman, B. (1997). Intervention with parents and caregivers of children who are exposed to violence. In J. D. Osofsky (Ed.), *Children in a violent society* (pp. 183–201). New York: Guilford.

Gulbenkian Foundation. (1995). *Children and violence*. London: Author.

Haapasalo, J., & Tremblay, R. E. (1994). Physically aggressive boys from ages 6 to 12: Family background, parenting behavior, and prediction of delinquency. *Journal of Consulting and Clinical Psychology, 62*, 1044–1052.

Hallowell, E. M., & Ratey, J. J. (1995). *Driven to distraction: Recognizing and coping with attention deficit disorder from childhood through adulthood*. New York: Touchstone.

Hamer, D., & Copeland, P. (1999). *Living with our genes: Why they matter more than you think*. New York: Anchor Books.

Ho, D. Y. F. (1994). Cognitive socialization in Confucian heritage cultures. In P. M. Greenfield & R. R. Cocking (Eds.), *Cross-cultural roots of minority child development* (pp. 285–313). Hillsdale, NJ: Erlbaum.

Holden, C. (1996). Child development: Small refugees suffer the effects of early neglect. *Science, 274*, 1076–1077.

Jaffe, P., Wolfe, D., & Wilson, S. K. (1990). *Children of battered women*. Thousand Oaks, CA: Sage.

Jenkins, E. J., & Bell, C. C. (1997). Exposure and response to community violence among children and adolescents. In J. D. Osofsky (Ed.), *Children in a violent society* (pp. 9–31). New York: Guilford.

Kagan, J. (1994). *Galen's prophecy: Temperament in human nature*. New York: Basic Books.

Kagan, J. (1998). Biology and the child. In N. Eisenberg (Ed.), *Handbook of child psychology: Vol. 3, Social, emotional, and personality development* (5th ed., pp. 177–235). New York: Wiley.

Kagan, J., Arcus, D., Snidman, N., Feng, W. Y., Hendler, J., & Greene, S. (1994). Reactivity in infants: A cross-national comparison. *Developmental Psychology, 30*, 342–345.

Kazdin, A. E. (1995). *Conduct disorders in childhood and adolescence* (2nd ed.). Thousand Oaks, CA: Sage.

Kurcinka, M. S. (1992). *Raising your spirited child: A guide for parents whose child is more intense, sensitive, perceptive, persistent, energetic*. New York: Harper Perennial.

Leslie, M., & DeMarchi, G. (1996). Understanding the needs of substance-involved families and children in a child care setting. *Ideas, 3*(2), 12–16.

Levin, D. E. (1998). *Remote control childhood? Combating the hazards of media culture*. Washington, DC: National Association for the Education of Young Children.

Lozoff, B. (1989). Nutrition and behavior. *American Psychologist, 44*, 231–236.

Maccoby, E., & Jacklin, C. (1974). *The psychology of sex differences*. Stanford, CA: Stanford University Press.

Mann, C. C. (1994). Behavioral genetics in transition. *Science, 264*, 1686–1689.

Marshall, E. (2000). Duke study faults overuse of stimulants for children. *Science, 289*, 721.

Moffitt, T. E. (1997). Neuropsychology, antisocial behavior, and neighborhood context. In J. McCord (Ed.), *Violence and childhood in the inner city* (pp. 116–170). New York: Cambridge University Press.

Murray, J. P. (1997). Media violence and youth. In J. D. Osofsky (Ed.), *Children in a violent society* (pp. 72–96). New York: Guilford.

National Center for Children Exposed to Violence (2001). Statistics: Domestic violence. New Haven, CT: Author. Retrieved February 4, 2001, from http://www.nccev.org/resources/statistics/statistics-domestic.html.

National Institute for Child Health and Human Development, Early Child Care Research Network. (in press). Early child care and children's development prior to school entry: Results from the NICHD Study of Early Child Care. *American Educational Research Journal*.

National Institute of Mental Health. (2001). Helping children and adolescents cope with violence and disasters (NIH Publication No. 01-3518). Bethesda, MD: Author. Retrieved November 28, 2001, from http://www.nimh.nih.gov/publicat/violence.cfm.

National Institute on Drug Abuse. (1999). *Drug abuse and addiction research: The 6th triennial report to Congress* [Electronic version]. Bethesda, MD: National Institutes of Health.

Needleman, H. L., Riess, J. A., Tobin, M. J., Biesecker, G. E., & Greenhouse, J. B. (1996). Bone lead levels and delinquent behavior. *Journal of the American Medical Association, 275,* 363–369.

Nelson, C. A. (1999). Neural plasticity and human development. *Current Directions in Psychological Science, 8,* 42–45.

Offord, D. R., & Lipman, E. L. (1996). Emotional and behavioural problems. In *Growing up in Canada: National longitudinal survey of children and youth* (pp. 119–126). Ottawa, Ontario: Human Resources Development Canada and Statistics Canada.

Olds, D. (1997). Tobacco exposure and impaired development: A review of the evidence. *Mental Retardation and Developmental Disabilities Research Review, 3,* 257–269.

Olds, D., Henderson, C. R., Jr., Cole, R., Eckenrode, J., Kitzman, H., Luckey, D., et al. (1998). Long-term effects of nurse home visitation on children's criminal and antisocial behavior: 15-year follow-up of a randomized controlled trial. *Journal of the American Medical Association, 280,* 1238–1244.

Olds, D. L., Henderson, C. R., Jr., & Tatelbaum, R. (1994). Intellectual impairment in children of women who smoke cigarettes during pregnancy. *Pediatrics, 93,* 221–227.

Osofsky, J. D. (1997). Children and youth violence: An overview of the issues. In J. D. Osofsky (Ed.), *Children in a violent society* (pp. 3–8). New York: Guilford.

Patterson, G. R. (1982). *Coercive family process.* Eugene, OR: Castalia.

Patterson, G. R. (1995). Coercion — A basis for early age of onset for arrest. In J. McCord (Ed.), *Coercion and punishment in long-term perspective* (pp. 81–105). New York: Cambridge University Press.

Pepler, D. J., & Craig, W. (1999). *Aggressive girls: Development of disorder and outcomes* (Report No. 57). Toronto, Ontario: LaMarsh Research Centre for Violence and Conflict Resolution, York University.

Pepler, D. J., & Slaby, R. G. (1994). Theoretical and developmental perspectives on youth and violence. In L. D. Eron, J. H. Gentry, & P. Schlegel (Eds.), *Reason to hope: A psychosocial perspective on violence & youth* (pp. 27–58). Washington, DC: American Psychological Association.

Plomin, R. (1990). The role of inheritance in behavior. *Science, 248,* 183–188.

Plomin, R., Owen, M. J., & McGuffin, P. (1994). The genetic basis of complex human behaviors. *Science, 264,* 1733–1739.

Raine, A. (1993). *The psychopathology of crime: Criminal behavior as a clinical disorder.* San Diego: Academic Press.

Reiss, A. J., Jr., & Roth, J. A. (Eds.). (1993). *Understanding and preventing violence.* Washington, DC: National Academy Press.

Rutter, M. (2000). Resilience reconsidered: Conceptual considerations. In J. P. Shonkoff & S. J. Meisels (Eds.), *Handbook of early childhood intervention* (2nd ed., pp. 651–682). New York: Cambridge University Press.

Sameroff, A. J., & Fiese, B. H. (2000). Transactional regulation: The developmental ecology of early intervention. In J. P. Shonkoff & S. J. Meisels (Eds.), *Handbook of early childhood intervention* (2nd ed., pp. 135–159). New York: Cambridge University Press.

Sampson, R. J. (1997). The embeddedness of child and adolescent development: A community-level perspective on urban violence. In J. McCord (Ed.), *Violence and childhood in the inner city* (pp. 31–77). New York: Cambridge University Press.

Schettler, T., Stein, J., Reich, R., & Valenti, M. (2000). *In harm's way: Toxic threats to child development.* Boston: Greater Boston Physicians for Social Responsibility. Retrieved February 6, 2002, from http://www.igc.org/psr/.

Secretary of Health and Human Services. (2000). *Tenth special report to the U.S. Congress on alcohol and health: Highlights from current research.* Washington, DC: U.S. Department of Health and Human Services. Retrieved February 6, 2002, from http://www.niaaa.nih.gov/publications/10report/intro.pdf.

Serbin, L. A., Moskowitz, D. S., Schwartzman, A. E., & Ledingham, J. E. (1991). Aggressive, withdrawn, and aggressive/withdrawn children in adolescence: Into the next generation. In D. J. Pepler & K. H. Rubin (Eds.), *The development and treatment of childhood aggression* (pp. 55–78). Hillsdale, NJ: Erlbaum.

Shonkoff, J. P., & Marshall, P. C. (2000). The biology of developmental vulnerability. In J. P. Shonkoff & S. J. Meisels (Eds.), *Handbook of early childhood intervention* (2nd ed., pp. 35–53). New York: Cambridge University Press.

Shonkoff, J. P., & Phillips, D. A. (Eds.). (2000). *From neurons to neighborhoods: The science of early childhood development.* National Research Council and Institute of Medicine, Committee on Integrating the Science of Early Childhood Development, Board on Children, Youth, and Families, Commission on Behavioral and Social Sciences and Education. Washington, DC: National Academy Press.

Slaby, R. G. (1997). Psychological mediators of violence in urban youth. In J. McCord (Ed.), *Violence and childhood in the inner city* (pp. 171–206). New York: Cambridge University Press.

Suderman, M., & Jaffe, P. G. (1997). Children and adolescents who witness violence: New directions in intervention and prevention. In R. DeV. Peters, R. McMahon, & D. A. Wolfe (Eds.), *Child abuse: New directions in prevention and treatment across a lifespan* (pp. 55–78). Thousand Oaks, CA: Sage.

Surgeon General's Scientific Advisory Committee on Television and Social Behavior. (1972). *Television and growing up: The impact of televised violence.* Washington, DC: U.S. Government Printing Office.

Thomas, A., & Chess, S. (1977). *Temperament and development.* New York: Brunner/Mazel.

Thomas, A., Chess, S., & Birch, H. G. (1968). *Temperament and behavior disorders in children.* New York: New York University Press.

Thomas, M. H., & Drabman, R. S. (1975). Toleration of real-life aggression as a function of exposure to television violence. *Merrill-Palmer Quarterly, 21,* 227–232.

Tremblay, R. E., Boulerice, B., Harden, P. W., McDuff, P., Perusse, D., Pihl, R. O., et al. (1996). Do children in Canada become more aggressive as they approach adolescence? In *Growing up in Canada: National longitudinal survey of children and youth* (pp. 127–137). Ottawa, Ontario: Human Resources Development Canada and Statistics Canada.

Turecki, S., with Tonner, L. (2000). *The difficult child* (2nd rev. ed.). New York: Bantam.

U.S. Department of Health and Human Services. (2000). Child abuse and neglect national statistics (Fact sheet). From *Child maltreatment 1998: Reports from the states to the National Child Abuse and Neglect Data System.* Washington, DC: U.S.

Government Printing Office. Retrieved February 5, 2002, from http://www.calib.com/nccanch/pubs/factsheets/canstats.cfm.

van den Boom, D. C. (1994). The influence of temperament and mothering on attachment and exploration: An experimental manipulation of sensitive responsiveness among lower-class mothers with irritable infants. *Child Development, 65,* 1457–1477.

Wasserman, G. A., Staghezza-Jaramillo, B., Shrout, P., Popovac, D., & Graziano, J. H. (1998). The effect of lead exposure on behavior problems in preschool children. *American Journal of Public Health, 88,* 481–486.

Webster-Stratton, C. (1997). Early intervention for families of preschool children with conduct problems. In M. J. Guralnick (Ed.), *The effectiveness of early intervention: Second generation research* (pp. 429–454). Baltimore: Paul H. Brookes.

Webster-Stratton, C., & Herbert, M. (1994). *Troubled families — Problem children: Working with parents: A collaborative process.* Chichester, England: Wiley.

Widom, C. S. (1989). Does violence beget violence? A critical examination of the literature. *Psychological Bulletin, 106,* 3–28.

Yoshikawa, H. (1994). Prevention as cumulative protection: Effects of early family support and education on chronic delinquency and its risks. *Psychological Bulletin, 115,* 28–54.

Young, K. A., Berry, M. L., Mahaffey, C. L., Saionz, J. R., Hawes, N. L., Chang, B., et al., (2002). Fierce: A new mouse deletion of *Nr2e1;* violent behaviour and ocular abnormalities are background-dependent. *Behavioural Brain Research, 132,* 145–158.

Zeanah, C. H., & Scheeringa, M. S. (1997). The experience and effects of violence in infancy. In J. D. Osofsky (Ed.), *Children in a violent society* (pp. 97–123). New York: Guilford.

3

Protective Factors

Challenging behavior is not inevitable, even when a child is at high risk.

After decades of trying to figure out why things go wrong, researchers came up with the idea of trying to figure out why things go *right*, even in adversity. Child development specialists, pediatricians, psychiatrists, psychologists, and sociologists set to work studying children who were growing up in difficult circumstances—in war, in poverty, in families where there is violence or mental illness—to determine why some of them have the ability to cope successfully no matter what hurdles they encounter. The researchers named this ability *resilience* (Masten and Coatsworth, 1998; Rutter, 2000; Werner, 2000).

They found a series of *protective* or *opportunity* factors that buffer the impact of the risk factors in a child's life. The more opportunity factors there are, the better the child's developmental outcome is likely to be (Dunst, 1993). The researchers discovered that it isn't necessary to eliminate the risk factors; it's possible to upgrade resilience by either decreasing the risk factors or increasing the protective factors. When there are enough protective factors to balance the risk factors, children aren't overwhelmed by the stress in their lives, and chances are they'll turn out to be competent and caring adults (Werner, 2000).

A child's age and gender—as well as the timing, duration, and severity of the risk factors—make a difference in the outcome (Rutter, 2000). Some children thrive under stress, and as long as it doesn't swamp them, it can actually stimulate growth (Anthony, 1974). But risk factors have a tendency to pile up, each one bringing others in its wake. A child who can't read in third grade, for example, automatically becomes a high risk for school failure, to say nothing of peer rejection and low self-esteem, which in turn put him at risk for aggressive behavior, gang membership, substance abuse, and delinquency. We may not be able to protect a child completely, but if we bolster his protective factors early on, we can stop some of those risk factors in their tracks and send him into an entirely different developmental trajectory (Masten and Coatsworth, 1998; Rutter, 1987).

Many of the risk factors described in Chapter 2 may seem far too large for an individual teacher to tackle alone—we couldn't possibly change the fact that a family lives in poverty or a child's mother abused drugs when she was pregnant. But we can definitely help the child (and maybe even his family) to cope with those risk factors more effectively. And that may be enough to ward off a whole slew of risk factors later on.

Who is the resilient child?

Research on resiliency has created a striking portrait of the naturally resilient child, who seems to emerge unscathed from beneath a stack of risk factors that's as tall as he is. His family and teachers describe him as "very active, affectionate, cuddly, good-natured, and easy to deal with," with few distressing eating or sleeping habits (Werner, 2000, p. 120). He is extremely responsive to everyone and everything around him, and he has a wonderful ability to seek out and relate to other people (Osofsky and Thompson, 2000).

Obviously, such a child will receive any help he needs; almost anyone he meets will happily bend over backwards for him. In their book *Vulnerable but Invincible* (1982), resiliency pioneers Emmy Werner and Ruth S. Smith put it this way: "To the extent that children [are] able to elicit predominantly positive responses from their environ-

Juggler

James Garbarino, professor of human development at Cornell University, has been studying violence and its impact on children and youth for 25 years. In his book *Lost Boys* (1999), he emphasizes the importance of protective factors:

> It is the accumulation of threats that does the damage. And trouble really sets in when these threats accumulate without a parallel accumulation of compensatory "opportunity" factors. Once overwhelmed, defenses are weakened. . . . I look at it this way: Give me one tennis ball, and I can toss it up and down with ease. Give me two, and I can still manage easily. Add a third, and it takes special skill to juggle them. Make it four, and I will drop them all. So it is with threats to development. (pp. 75–76)

ment, they [are] found to be stress-resistant or 'resilient,' even when growing up in chronic poverty or in a family with a psychotic parent" (p. 158).

Such children have no need for challenging behavior. Let us focus instead on the children Werner and Smith describe next, the ones this book is about: the children who elicit negative responses from their environment. They are correspondingly vulnerable, regardless of their socioeconomic status and physical and mental health (Werner and Smith, 1982). They are much more likely to have challenging behaviors and require those extra ounces of protection.

The question is, How can teachers accept the vulnerable children for who they are and at the same time help them to become more like the naturally resilient children? What secrets of success do the resilient children hold, and how can we bottle them for everyone's use?

What makes a resilient child bounce back?

Protective factors fall into three categories: factors within the individual child, factors within the family, and factors within the community. Let us look first at factors within the child.

In addition to their outgoing personalities, resilient children have at least an average level of intelligence, which enhances their coping ability (Garbarino, 1999; Masten and Coatsworth, 1998). They have also learned some very important skills, which Bonnie Benard (1995), a specialist in prevention theory and practice, classifies this way:

• *Social competence.* Resilient children are sociable. They have the ability to engage the people around them in a positive way. Because they get lots of practice, they have good communication skills, and they tend to be flexible and empathetic. They also have a good sense of humor (Rutter, 1987).

Overcoming the Odds

In 1955, developmental psychologists Emmy E. Werner and Ruth S. Smith (1982) began a landmark longitudinal study of 698 newborns on the island of Kauai in Hawaii. The fathers of the children were mostly semiskilled or unskilled laborers, many of their mothers didn't graduate from high school, and about half of the families lived in chronic poverty.

Despite these risk factors, two-thirds of the children became healthy young people and adults. Among them was a group of 72 children who faced enormous obstacles—four or more risk factors before the age of 2—who nonetheless developed into "competent, confident, and caring adults" (Werner, 2000, p. 119).

Though only about 10 percent of the children were naturally resilient, children who are more vulnerable can become more resilient if the adults around them boost their protective factors.

- *Problem-solving skills.* Resilient children are able to plan, to think critically and creatively, and to foresee consequences (Rutter, 1987). They know how to ask for help, too.

- *Autonomy and self-esteem.* Resilient children seem to believe in themselves and to take charge of their own lives. They are independent, competent, self-confident, and self-reliant. They can control their impulses and do what needs to be done, even in difficult surroundings. They have varied talents, interests, activities, and coping strategies that aren't narrowly gender-stereotyped. In Werner's (2000) words, resilient children "pick . . . their own niches" (p. 128). They choose or build environments that reinforce their dispositions and reward their competencies. And they ascribe their success to their own efforts and abilities, not sheer luck (Brooks, 1994).

- *Sense of purpose and future.* Resilient children are optimists. They have goals and aspirations; they believe in achievement and are motivated to persevere and succeed. They may also have a spiritual side that adds meaning to their lives (Benard, 1995; Garbarino, 1999).

Any child with challenging behavior is likely to have some of these qualities and skills in a more embryonic form—we just have to look for them. One of the keys to enhancing resilience is to search out these strengths—what psychologist Robert B. Brooks calls "islands of competence" (1994, p. 549)—and use them to build skills and self-esteem.

How does the family contribute to resilience?

Families are on the front lines in shoring up a child's resilience. The most important protective factor of all is a competent, caring person who is absolutely committed to the child, whom the child can love and trust in return. If the parents can't provide this bond, someone else can. What matters is that at least one loving and available person—a grandparent, an older sibling, an aunt, an uncle, or cousin—supports and accepts the child unconditionally (Benard, 1995; Rutter, 1987; Werner, 2000; Werner and Smith, 1992).

It also helps when parents have high expectations and give children the support they need to fulfill those expectations. Boys flourish in a structured environment where there are rules and supervision. Girls thrive when they aren't overprotected but are encouraged to take risks and be independent. For the preschool girls in the Kauai study and for African American and Chicana girls in other studies, having an employed mother as a role model is a particularly powerful protective factor (Werner, 2000; Werner, 1984). Both boys and girls do better in a small family where the children are spaced at least two years apart.

Families also provide protection by expecting their children to become helpful, responsible members of the household. When they babysit or do chores, children acquire a sense of pride, accomplishment, and competence that sticks with them (Benard, 1995; Werner, 2000).

The most important protective factor is a loving and available person who supports and accepts the child unconditionally.

Again, religious faith and observance seem to have a protective effect, offering coherence, stability, and a belief that things will work out in the end (Benard, 1995; Werner, 2000).

What is the community's role in resilience?

According to Garbarino (1999), the community can play a powerful part in fostering resilience. When children receive support from outside the family, they have a chance to feel connected to other people and the core values of the community. Community support comes to the child in the form of relationships. Like a parent, caring and competent teachers, neighbors, coaches, or friends can act as positive role models and make a child feel loved and valued. Over and over again, the children of Kauai pointed to favorite teachers as important influences in their lives (Werner, 2000).

By believing in the child, expecting a lot of him, and supporting him as he extends his reach, a caring adult can help him to believe in himself and to develop competence and confidence (National Crime Prevention Council Canada, 1995). A caring adult can

Teachers, coaches, or friends can act as positive role models and make a child feel loved and valued.

also help a child expand his ability to cope with stress by creating a supportive environment and gradually enlarging the challenges he must face. As the prominent child psychiatrist Sir Michael Rutter says, protection "resides not in the evasion of risk but in successful engagement with it" (1987, p. 318).

Friends also provide protection against risk. Resilient children make them easily and rely on their emotional support for years. Their friends' parents can act as protective factors, too. Spending time with another family gives a child some perspective on his own (Werner, 2000).

Life Is Beautiful

In 1945, the Jewish community in Britain managed to bring 24 orphans who had spent the Second World War in hiding, concentration camps, or orphanages to a new home in England. The oldest child was 11 years old; most were the only member of their family to survive.

Until they were adopted or old enough to live independently, they lived together under the care of a remarkable woman who provided them with warmth and security and taught them to behave compassionately, despite all they had been through. When they were interviewed some 35 years later, they were unanimous in characterizing their teacher-caregiver as a powerful force in their lives. As one of them put it, she "was there for us night or day.... I think that's what home is" (Moskovitz, 1983, p. 135).

It is also helpful if the child's school or child-care center is a warm, safe, and predictable place, with consistent teachers, peers, schedules, and limit-setting. When a child knows where to go, what to do, and who will take care of him, he is free to be himself and to focus on learning (Garbarino, 1999; Werner 2000).

Shifting the Balance

In an article in *Young Children*, Emmy Werner makes these suggestions for teachers, neighbors, coaches, social workers, community workers, police, and others who spend time with children:

- Accept children's temperamental idiosyncracies and allow them experiences that challenge, but do not overwhelm, their coping abilities.

- Convey to children a sense of responsibility and caring, and in turn reward them for helpfulness and cooperation.

- Encourage a child to develop a special interest, hobby, or an activity that can serve as a source of gratification and self esteem.

- Model, by example, a conviction that life makes sense despite the inevitable adversities . . . each of us encounters.

- Encourage children to reach out beyond their nuclear family to a beloved relative or friend. (Werner, 1984, p. 71)

What Do You Think?

1. Think about your own risk factors and protective factors. Is there an activity or a person in your life who made a difference—a parent, a friend's parent, a teacher, or a neighbor who helped you to recover from a trauma or sustained you through a stressful period? How?

2. There are advantages and disadvantages to knowing about a child's risk and protective factors. How could this knowledge change your attitude and your behavior toward a child or her family?

Suggested Reading

Werner, E. E., & Smith, R. (1992). *Overcoming the odds: High risk children from birth to adulthood.* Ithaca, NY: Cornell University Press.

Werner, E. E. (1984). Resilient children. *Young Children, 40,* 68–72.

References

Anthony, E. J. (1974). The syndrome of the psychologically invulnerable child. In E. J. Anthony & C. Koupernik (Eds.), *The child in his family 3: Children at psychiatric risk* (pp. 529–544). New York: Wiley.

Benard, B. (1991). *Fostering resilience in kids: Protective factors in the family, school, and community.* San Francisco: Far West Laboratory for Educational Research and Development.

Benard, B. (1995). Fostering resilience in children [Electronic version]. Urbana IL: ERIC Clearinghouse on Elementary and Early Childhood Education. (ERIC Digest ED386327).

Brooks, R. B. (1994). Children at risk: Fostering resilience and hope. *American Journal of Orthopsychiatry, 64,* 545–553.

Dunst, C. J. (1993). Implications of risk and opportunity for assessment and intervention practices. *Topics in Early Childhood Special Education, 13,* 143–153.

Garbarino, J. (1999). *Lost boys: Why our sons turn violent and how we can save them.* New York: Free Press.

Masten, A. S., & Coatsworth, J. D. (1998). The development of competence in favorable and unfavorable environments: Lessons from research on successful children. *American Psychologist, 53,* 205–220.

Moskovitz, S. (1983). *Love despite hate: Child survivors of the holocaust and their adult lives.* New York: Schocken.

National Crime Prevention Council Canada. (1995, November). *Resiliency in young children.* Ottawa, Ontario: Author.

Osofsky, J. D., & Thompson, M. D. (2000). Adaptive and maladaptive parenting: Perspectives on risk and protective factors. In J. P. Shonkoff & S. J. Meisels (Eds.), *Handbook of early childhood intervention* (2nd ed., pp. 54–75). New York: Cambridge University Press.

Rutter, M. (1987). Psychosocial resilience and protective mechanisms. *American Journal of Orthopsychiatry, 57,* 316–331.

Rutter, M. (2000). Resilience reconsidered: Conceptual considerations. In J. P. Shonkoff & S. J. Meisels (Eds.), *Handbook of early childhood intervention* (2nd ed., pp. 651–682). New York: Cambridge University Press.

Werner, E. E. (1984). Resilient children. *Young Children, 40,* 68–72.

Werner, E. E. (2000). Protective factors and individual resilience. In J. P. Shonkoff & S. J. Meisels (Eds.), *Handbook of early childhood intervention* (2nd ed., pp. 115–132). New York: Cambridge University Press.

Werner, E. E., & Smith, R. S. (1982). *Vulnerable but invincible: A longitudinal study of resilient children and youth.* New York: McGraw-Hill.

Werner, E. E., & Smith, R. S. (1992). *Overcoming the odds: High risk children from birth to adulthood.* New York: Cornell University Press.

4

Behavior and the Brain

It is only natural to wonder about the brain's role in challenging behavior.

Some clues are beginning to emerge, but for the moment the question must remain open. The development of the brain is perhaps the most complex phenomenon in all of biology (Nelson and Bloom, 1997), and even though there has been astonishing progress in the last 20 years, work that uses the techniques of neuroanatomy, molecular biology, neurochemistry, neurophysiology, brain imaging, and the like does not easily translate into statements about complex human behavior such as aggression in either adults or children (Kandel, Jessell, and Sanes, 2000; Shonkoff and Phillips, 2000).

Some of neuroscience's wonderful tools, such as electroencephalographic (EEG) techniques, which record the brain's electrical activity from electrodes attached to the scalp, have adapted well for use in research with young children. But others that show the brain at work on specific tasks, such as functional magnetic resonance imaging (fMRI) and positron emission tomography (PET), are not yet suitable or may never be used specifically for research with young children, although PET is now being used for diagnostic purposes. As a result, there are very few studies of this age group that involve imaging of the brain at work, and those that have been done so far haven't focused on the regions of the brain involved in complex developmental tasks such as emotion and cognition (Shonkoff and Phillips, 2000).

In fact, most of what is known about how the brain is wired and developed comes from studies of animals, which can provide extraordinary insights, but may apply somewhat differently or not at all where human beings are concerned. Much of the most important work on brain development has been done in the visual system of animals such as cats, monkeys, rodents, and even frogs. It's tempting to extrapolate those findings, but other systems may operate in quite different ways (Greenough, Black, and Wallace, 1987).

As we rush to understand the brain, it's useful to remember that quite a lot of our knowledge comes from research on behavior. It's exciting to have new and more direct evidence of how the brain works at a cellular and molecular level, but carefully observing what children do has allowed specialists in child development to amass a considerable amount of valuable information about the brain as well (DiPietro, 2000; Nelson and Bloom, 1997).

How do babies' brains develop?

Not too long ago, people believed that genes completely controlled brain development (Shonkoff and Phillips, 2000). Now it's clear that the environment also plays a large part, both before and after birth, and is even involved in turning genes on (Shonkoff and Phillips; Nelson, 2000). This is where biology and environment, nature and nurture, merge. Genes provide the grand plan, but experience is necessary to organize and structure the brain's circuitry (Shonkoff and Phillips; Nelson and Bloom, 1997).

Babies are born with 100 billion brain cells, but only a small proportion of them are connected. As babies interact with their environment, their brain cells send and receive signals, making 1,000 trillion connections, or synapses, by the time they turn 3 years old. This number—twice as many as adults have—remains constant throughout the first 10 years of life (Shore, 1997). During childhood and adolescence, frequently

All Roads Lead to Rome

How can we link behavior with brain processes? One hopeful example of convergence comes from psychiatry. Researchers recently demonstrated that two different treatments for obsessive-compulsive disorder—one that used behavior therapy and another that used drug therapy—had identical outcomes. The patients' behavior changed in the same way with both treatments.

The patients' PET scans showed that their brains had also changed in the same way, confirming that researchers are beginning to see how the brain and behavior relate to one another. What's happening on the outside mirrors what's happening on the inside (Baxter et al., 1992; Nelson and Bloom, 1997; Schwartz, Stoessel, Baxter, Martin, and Phelps, 1996).

used connections become stronger, and those that aren't used are eliminated in order to streamline the system (Shonkoff and Phillips, 2000). The number of synapses reaches adult levels in the third decade of life (De Bellis, Keshavan et al., 1999).

How does experience spur nerve cells to connect?

William Greenough and his colleagues at the University of Illinois (Greenough et al., 1987) have identified two major mechanisms at work. They call the first *experience-expectant*. Some experiences occur everywhere in the environment and are readily available to all members of a species—experiences such as hearing speech sounds and seeing light and patterns, for example. As the brain develops, it "expects" to encounter and use these ubiquitous experiences to form and reinforce the connections it needs (Nelson and Bloom, 1997). When experiences occur as expected, brain cells connect and systems organize themselves in the normal way; if the experiences don't occur as expected, neural organization is abnormal.

Nobel Prize winners David Hubel and Torsten Wiesel provided the classical evidence for this pattern in the 1960s. They noticed that if children with cataracts weren't treated promptly, they remained blind in the obstructed eye even after the cataracts were removed. To explore this phenomenon, Hubel and Wiesel performed experiments where they closed one eyelid of newborn kittens. Although the eye itself functioned normally, when it was reopened three months later, the kitten could not see because its nerve cells hadn't made the appropriate connections in the brain (Bruer, 1999; Shatz, 1992). The brain needed the normal experience of exposure to light and patterns in order to connect properly with the eye and interpret the information coming from it. In the meantime, connections from the open eye co-opted the closed eye's targets in the brain, leaving the closed eye unconnected.

Hubel and Wiesel had discovered what scientists call a *critical* or *sensitive period* for the visual system. If the nerve cells in the kitten's eye failed to make the appropriate connections in the brain during that sensitive time, the kitten lost sight permanently in that eye (Kandel et al., 2000). There is also a critical period for vision in humans. This is why it's so important to detect and treat all vision problems early. (Because their visual systems are already developed, adults can wait years to have their cataracts removed without putting their vision in jeopardy, but a child must have her cataracts removed promptly in order to see properly.) Although the auditory system and other sensory systems are more difficult to study, it's likely that something similar occurs during their development, so it's important to catch problems with them early, too. Chronic ear infections, for example, can affect hearing and language development (Bruer, 1999; Shonkoff and Phillips, 2000).

Critical periods for the appropriate development of different brain systems vary enormously. Indeed, they are probably only important for systems that develop in the same stereotyped way for all members of a species (Bruer, 1999; Nelson, 2000). For example, all human beings have a visual system, so there is a critical period for vision. But not everyone reads, so there is no critical period for reading; one can learn at any age (Bruer, 1999).

Sight for Sore Eyes

Hubel and Wiesel and their colleague Simon LeVay also studied the development of the visual system in monkeys. In experiments similar to those they'd performed on kittens, they discovered that monkeys who had both of their eyes closed for the first six months of life had entirely normal vision in both eyes. Spontaneous neural activity in the visual system before birth actually provided enough stimulation for the nerve cells to make the right connections in the brain (Bruer, 1999).

On the other hand, when they closed one of the monkey's eyes at birth, opened it later, and closed the other eye, the money had normal vision in each eye if the procedures took place early. But the monkey did not develop binocular vision—and the ability to perceive depth—because that requires both eyes to be open at the same time.

Children with strabismus—commonly called *crossed eyes* or *lazy eyes*—often have their eyes alternately patched so that the brain will make the connections necessary for seeing with both eyes. But they still may not have depth perception.

The brain needs balanced and simultaneous stimulation to develop normal vision (Bruer, 1999).

Greenough and his colleagues (1987) noticed that experience guides brain development in a second way, which they call *experience-dependent*. Much of the information that humans must acquire is unique to their own environment—how to navigate in their physical surroundings and relate to the individuals around them, for example. Again, experience triggers nerve cells to make connections, but this process isn't subject to critical periods. The brain is constantly restructuring and refining itself to reflect its new experience. In this way, a child actually participates in the development of her own brain (Gopnik, Meltzoff, and Kuhl, 2001). This experience-dependent learning goes on throughout life. Because the brain is so plastic, human beings are incredibly adaptable and attuned to their environment.

Is there a critical period for social or emotional behavior?

Scientists have known since the 1940s that babies and children brought up in orphanages under conditions of severe deprivation develop serious behavioral problems (Bruer, 1999; Kandel et al., 2000). Henry and Margaret Harlow (1962) saw similar effects in the 1950s in their landmark studies of rhesus monkeys reared with surrogate mothers of wire and terrycloth. Extremely fearful, agitated, or aggressive, they were never really able to form relationships with other monkeys. Although these studies are based on behavior, they have led scientists to deduce that there is a critical period for the development of social and emotional traits and behavior (Bruer, 1999).

Research on Romanian orphans raised in institutions and later adopted is providing more information about this critical period. "The longer a child has spent in an orphanage, the more behavior problems he or she had three years later," says psychologist Elinor Ames of Simon Fraser University in British Columbia, who heads a study of some of the Canadian adoptees (Holden, 1996). Children who are adopted early—before the age of 6 months—are virtually indistinguishable from peers living with their own parents and peers adopted in the usual way within their own country (Holden, 1996; Rutter, 1998). According to Michael Rutter, who is studying the British adoptees, those who were adopted later had made a "spectacular" recovery in language, physical growth, and the ability to make a secure attachment when they were tested at ages 4 and 6. But they were still behind in IQ and social behavior: They had trouble with their tempers, fighting, and picking up social cues (Holden, 1996).

Although the critical period for forming attachments seems to extend at least through the early childhood years and some late adoptees have become attached to their adoptive parents, a substantial minority of the Romanian orphans seem unable to form deep relationships (Shonkoff and Phillips, 2000). Without these relationships, they've had problems with concentration, attention, and inhibitory control (Shonkoff and Phillips, 2000). The implication seems to be that at least one close relationship with a caregiver in the first few years is essential for normal brain development (Berk, 2000; Shonkoff and Phillips, 2000).

What does caregiving have to do with it?

Why does early caregiving have this powerful effect? One answer may lie in the stress system, which can have a dramatic impact on brain development (Shonkoff and Phillips, 2000). When human beings are threatened or frightened, the stress system roars into action. A whole cascade of changes takes place in the brain and body, getting them ready to flee or fight. Any process that isn't essential at the moment—including growth—gets put on hold, and the steroid hormone cortisol floods the brain (Shonkoff and Phillips, 2000).

Models of Love

In *The Scientist in the Crib* (2001), Alison Gopnik, Andrew N. Meltzoff, and Patricia K. Kuhl describe how new experience can change the way children view relationships.

> The new idea about attachment, or bonding, is that babies and young children develop "internalized working models" that are systematic pictures of how people relate to one another—theories of love. Of course, these models are heavily influenced by children's observations of the people around them. . . . If you see that the people you rely on for warmth and comfort turn away from you when you're in distress, that may influence your expectations about how other people will act and your interpretations of what they actually do. But rather than being fixed, these internalized working models are actually flexible. . . . As children get new information about how people work together in intimate ways, they modify their own views. Even abused children often seem to escape long-lasting damage if there is somebody around who doesn't turn away. A relatively brief experience of a friend or an aunt or a teacher can provide children with an alternative picture of how love can work. (p. 49)

When the threat recedes, cortisol levels ordinarily return to normal. But if a threat continues over a long period of time, the stress system may be reset so that it's easier to activate. The result is an animal or human who is quick to experience fear, anxiety, and stress, and may have a very hard time turning those feelings off (Gunnar, 2000). An animal or human in this state also becomes vulnerable to the toxic effects of cortisol itself, which in large amounts in adult animals tends to destroy nerve cells in brain areas concerned with memory and emotional regulation (Gunnar, 1998).

Caregiving has a remarkable influence on this system. Researchers have found that rat mothers maintain the correct level of the rat equivalent of cortisol in their pups by licking and grooming them and nursing in an arched-back position. In the first few weeks of life, when researchers remove either the mother or the pups for a few minutes every day—which is probably about how long they'd be apart in the wild while the mother searches for food—the mother's behavior becomes more organized, and she licks, grooms, and nurses more effectively. In turn, her pups develop more cortisol receptors in their brains and have more control over cortisol production. They become less fearful and anxious, it takes a greater threat to unnerve them, and their stress systems turn on and off quickly. But if the mother and her pups are separated for several hours rather than several minutes, the mother becomes disturbed and disorganized, and the pups react very easily to stress (Gunnar, 2000).

These early experiences influence how the stress system will react to stressful stimuli for the rest of the animal's life (Liu et al., 1997). Rats that are handled at a later age don't change their response to stress (McCain and Mustard, 1999).

Although so far there is no direct evidence that cortisol levels influence brain development in human children, these animal studies certainly suggest that it may. Megan R. Gunnar, a specialist in child development and psychobiology at the University of Minnesota, has been examining cortisol and the stress system for many years, and she and her colleagues have found these connections between cortisol and caregiving (Gunnar, 1998):

• Preschoolers who have the most trouble with self-regulation and effortful control (that is, they can't inhibit a response they're all set to perform; they run before the starter gives the signal for the race to begin) have the highest cortisol levels in their class.

• Quality of attachment seems to make a difference in the way children react to stress. When a clown approaches, an 18-month-old who has a secure attachment will have normal cortisol levels, but one who's insecurely attached will have significantly higher levels. Children whose attachment is classified as disorganized/disoriented—which is typical of children who've been abused or neglected or who have a depressed parent—also have higher cortisol levels.

• Children seem able to use a substitute caregiver to buffer their stress reaction. Nine-month-old babies who spend 30 minutes with a strange babysitter who is sensitive, friendly, and playful don't show a rise in cortisol. But those left with a cold and distant sitter have elevated cortisol.

A caring teacher can have a remarkable influence on the stress system.

• Quality of care probably makes a difference. Toddlers in child-care centers with larger groups and poorer teacher-child ratios have higher cortisol levels.

• Temperament also plays a role. Children with more negative and reactive temperaments have higher cortisol levels, tend to be most upset by stress, and benefit more from sensitive, responsive substitute care.

Other researchers are studying what happens to the stress system when care falls below acceptable standards. A study of children suffering from posttraumatic stress disorder after experiencing abuse found that years later they had high cortisol levels that correlated with the duration of the abuse (De Bellis, Baum et al., 1999).

Two-year-olds who've spent all their lives in Romanian orphanages don't have a normal daily cortisol pattern—instead of rising and falling, the lines on their charts are flat. Researchers have also found this flatness in rhesus monkeys reared with cloth surrogate mothers, in severely neglected infants, and in psychosocial dwarfs—children who don't grow because they are so deprived of emotional nurturing (Gunnar, 2000).

There is some evidence that this flat pattern across the day is linked to real confusion of the stress system, but scientists don't yet know how changeable the system is or how early they must intervene to make a difference. What does seem clear is that sensitive, responsive, secure caregiving plays an important role.

What about neurotransmitters?

Neurotransmitters are the chemicals that carry messages between brain cells. Several of them are involved every single time information is passed within the nervous system.

Neuroscientists strongly suspect that neurotransmitters are involved in both emotional regulation and aggression. They've zeroed in on serotonin, a neurotransmitter that is active throughout the body but is most famous for its association with Prozac and other antidepressant drugs. Although researchers disagree about how antidepressants work, many think that they raise spirits by raising serotonin levels in certain parts of the brain (Hamer and Copeland, 1998).

Serotonin is believed to inhibit impulsive aggression. Several studies have shown that aggressive animals—including humans—have lower levels of serotonin in their cerebrospinal fluid, which implies that they have lower serotonin levels in their brain (Davidson, Putnam, and Larson, 2000; Enserink, 2000). Both genes and environment seem to be involved in adjusting the level of serotonin. Mother rats can increase it in their pups with more licking and grooming in the same way that they can lower the level of stress hormones (Shonkoff and Phillips, 2000).

Other neurotransmitters—such as norepinephrine, dopamine, and vasopressin—may also influence aggressive behavior (Davidson et al., 2000; Enserink, 2000).

Caregiver Love

A strain of overly impulsive and sometimes aggressive rhesus monkeys metabolize serotonin more slowly than normal monkeys, Stephen Suomi at the National Institute of Child Health and Human Development has discovered (Hayden, 2000; Suomi, 1997). He also found that they have a short form of a serotonin-transporter gene that helps to regulate the amount of serotonin in the nerve cells. Animals with the long form are much more calm and rational.

Irascible by nature, these overly impulsive monkeys court trouble by baiting dominant males and leaping to branches that are too far away. When an average mother takes care of them, they end up being virtual social outcasts.

But when Suomi and his colleagues placed them in foster care with extra-nurturing mothers, the overly impulsive monkeys learned to regulate their emotions by seeking help and avoiding stressful situations, and they handily won the acceptance of their peers and rose to top positions in the group's hierarchy. Their serotonin metabolism changed, too. The extra-sensitive care actually brought their serotonin levels back to normal.

First-rate mothering trumped both genes and chemistry, providing a perfect example of nature and nurture working together.

Which parts of the brain are involved in aggressive behavior?

Research on adults reveals that many areas in the brain are involved in aggressive and violent behavior, but neuroscientists are starting to look hard at the frontal lobe (see Figure 4.1), one of the newest and most advanced parts of the brain from the point of view of evolution. It is also an area that is full of cortisol receptors, at least in animals (Gunnar, 1998).

Researchers are especially interested in a region of the frontal lobe called the prefrontal cortex, which is concerned with cognitive function, planning, impulse inhibition, and regulation of emotion and affect. The prefrontal cortex is important in the control of social behavior (Raine, 1993). Positron emission tomography studies of adults with impulsive aggression show prefrontal abnormalities, and one PET study of murderers who acted impulsively (as opposed to murderers who planned their crimes) found that impulsive murderers had less activity in the prefrontal cortex (Davidson et al., 2000).

The prefrontal cortex also has a high density of serotonin receptors, and serotonin helps to inhibit aggression. Some scientists suspect that damage in this area might alter serotonin metabolism and play a role in making aggressive behavior more likely (Davidson et al., 2000).

The orbitofrontal cortex, downstairs from the prefrontal cortex, is even more closely connected with antisocial and violent behavior. Through its connections to oth-

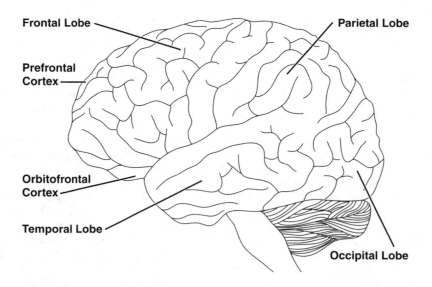

FIGURE 4.1   *The prefrontal cortex, a region of the frontal lobe of the brain, is important in the control of social behavior.*

Inhibition Disbarred

The case of Phineas Gage was one of the first to link antisocial behavior with the frontal lobe of the brain. Gage worked as a dynamiter for the Rutland and Burlington Railroad in Vermont. Considered an efficient, reliable, and capable man, he was the foreman of a construction gang and had no history of violent or antisocial behavior.

In 1848, an explosion rammed an iron rod through Gage's head, damaging his left frontal lobe. He survived, but he became an entirely different person—impulsive, irreverent, profane, obstinate, and antisocial (Raine, 1993; Phineas Gage's Story, n.d.).

er brain regions, it regulates emotion—especially negative emotion—and plays a crucial role in suppressing impulsive outbursts (Davidson et al., 2000). Researchers have found that damage to this area produces aggressive behavior, impulsivity, emotional explosions, and a lack of concern, emotion, and guilt (Raine, 1993).

By using electroencephalography (EEG) to study the infants of depressed mothers, psychologist Geraldine Dawson and her colleagues at the University of Washington are finding other links between behavior, the frontal lobe, and the early social environment (Dawson et al., 1999).

Because their mothers don't interact with them as sensitively or positively as nondepressed mothers, these children have difficulty regulating their emotions, and they are at risk of developing behavior problems and problems with their peers. Dawson and her colleagues found that 13- to 15-month-old babies of depressed mothers were less affectionate and more aggressive, negative, and hostile in interactions with their mothers. At the same time, their EEGs showed more generalized activity in the frontal lobes and less activity in the left frontal lobe, which specializes in the expression of behavior and emotions such as joy and interest. Babies whose mothers had been depressed for a longer time were more likely to behave this way.

Researchers are now trying to figure out whether these patterns—in both the brain and behavior—can be changed.

Hold That Feeling

In a series of experiments at the University of Wisconsin, adult subjects looked at neutral or unpleasant pictures. The researchers asked them to consciously regulate the emotion the pictures evoked—they were to suppress it, enhance it, or maintain it after the picture disappeared.

The researchers found large and measurable differences in individuals' ability to suppress their negative emotions. These differences coincided with differences in orbitofrontal activity that they saw on fMRI scans. The scientists concluded that differences in emotion regulation skills may enable researchers to figure out who is vulnerable to aggressive and violent behavior (Davidson et al., 2000).

What does all this mean?

Although there is clear evidence that people and their brains continue to develop throughout their lives, when it comes to social and emotional development, early experience seems to play an important part in shaping the brain's circuitry (Davidson et al., 2000). Research on both the brain and behavior shows that nurturing and stable relationships with adults are essential for young children. This means that teachers may have an unparalleled opportunity to make a difference in children's lives. It may not be too far-fetched to say that consistently offering high-quality care may help to change children's brains and make children more resilient. How teachers respond to children with challenging behavior and difficult temperaments, who need extra help in learning skills to regulate and cope with their feelings, is especially critical.

What Do You Think? _____

1. What do Hubel and Wiesel's experiments show about the connection between the brain and experience? What is a "critical period"? What is known about a critical period for social or emotional behavior?

2. Can you think of some examples of learning that are "experience-expectant"? Can you think of some examples of learning that are "experience-dependent"? For example, what about learning a language, learning to swim, or learning to ride a bike?

3. Do you know anyone who had a corrective eye operation when he or she was a child? What is different about that person's vision? Why?

4. What physical and psychological effects does stress have on a young child? What role does caregiving play in managing stress? How does the quality of care, parental or nonparental, influence brain development?

Suggested Reading _____

Bruer, J. T. (1999). *The myth of the first three years: A new understanding of early brain development and life-long learning.* New York: Free Press.

Shonkoff, J. P., & Phillips, D. A. (Eds.). (2000). *From neurons to neighborhoods: The science of early childhood development.* National Research Council and Institute of Medicine, Committee on Integrating the Science of Early Childhood Development, Board on Children, Youth, and Families, Commission on Behavioral and Social Sciences and Education. Washington, DC: National Academy Press.

Shore, R. (1997). *Rethinking the brain: New insights into early development.* New York: Families and Work Institute.

References _____

Baxter, L. R., Schwartz, M. M., Bergman, K. S., Szuba, M. P., Guze, B. H., Mazziotta, J. C., et al. (1992). Caudate glucose metabolic rate changes with both drug and behavior therapy for obsessive-compulsive disorder. *Archives of General Psychiatry, 49,* 681–689.

Berk, L. E. (2000). *Child development* (5th ed.). Boston: Allyn and Bacon.

Bruer, J. T. (1999). *The myth of the first three years: A new understanding of early brain development and life-long learning.* New York: Free Press.

Davidson, R. J., Putnam, K. M., & Larson, C. L. (2000). Dysfunction in the neural circuitry of emotion regulation—A possible prelude to violence. *Science, 289*, 591–594.

Dawson, G., Frey, K., Self, J., Panagiotides, H., Hessl, D., Yamada, E., et al. (1999). Frontal brain electrical activity in infants of depressed and nondepressed mothers: Relation to variations in infant behavior. *Development and Psychopathology, 11*, 589–605.

De Bellis, M. D., Baum, A. S., Birmaher, B., Keshavan, M. S., Eccard, C. H., et al. (1999). Developmental traumatology part I: Biological stress systems. *Biological Psychiatry, 45*, 1259-1270.

De Bellis, M. D., Keshavan, M. S., Clark, D. B., Casey, B. J., Giedd, J. N., et al. (1999). Developmental traumatology part II: Brain development. *Biological Psychiatry, 45*, 1271–1284.

DiPietro, J. A. (2000). Baby and the brain: Advances in child development. *Annual Review Public Health, 21*, 455–271.

Enserink, M. (2000). Searching for the mark of Cain. *Science, 289*, 575–579.

Gopnik, A., Meltzoff, A. N., & Kuhl, P. K. (2001). *The scientist in the crib: What early learning tells us about the mind.* New York: Perennial.

Greenough, W. T., Black, J. E., & Wallace, C. S. (1987). Experience and brain development. *Child Development, 58*, 539–559.

Gunnar, M. R. (1998). Quality of early care and buffering of neuroendocrine stress reactions: Potential effects on the developing human brain. *Preventive Medicine, 27*, 208–211.

Gunnar, M. R. (2000, July). *Brain-behavior interface: Studies of early experience and the physiology of stress.* Paper presented at the meeting of the World Association for Infant Mental Health, Montreal, Quebec.

Hamer, D., & Copeland, P. (1999). *Living with our genes: Why they matter more than you think.* New York: Anchor Books.

Harlow, H., & Harlow, M. (1962). Social deprivation in monkeys. *Scientific American, 207*, 137–146.

Hayden, T. (2000, Fall–Winter). A sense of life. *Your Child* [Special issue], *Newsweek*, 58–62.

Holden, C. (1996). Child development: Small refugees suffer the effects of early neglect. *Science, 274*, 1076-1077.

Kandel, E. R., Jessell, T. M., & Sanes, J. R. (2000). Sensory experience and the fine-tuning of synaptic connections. In E. R. Kandel, J. H. Schwartz, & T. M. Jessell (Eds.), *Principles of Neural Science* (4th ed., pp. 1115–1130). New York: McGraw-Hill.

Liu, D., Diorio, J., Tannenbaum, B., Caldji, C., Francis, D., et al. (1997). Maternal care, hippocampal glucocorticoid receptors, and hypothalamic-pituitary-adrenal responses to stress. *Science, 277*, 1659–1662.

McCain, M. N., & Mustard, J. F. (1999). *Early years study: Reversing the real brain drain.* Toronto: Publications Ontario.

Nelson, C. A. (2000). The neurobiological bases of early intervention. In J. P. Shonkoff & S. J. Meisels (Eds.), *Handbook of early childhood intervention* (2nd ed., pp. 204–227). New York: Cambridge University Press.

Nelson, C. A., & Bloom, F. E. (1997). Child development and neuroscience. *Child Development, 68*, 970–987.

Phineas Gage's Story. (n.d.). Retrieved January 17, 2002, from http://www.hbs.deakin.edu.au/gagepage/PGSTORY.HTM.

Raine, A. (1993). *The psychopathology of crime: Criminal behavior as a clinical disorder.* San Diego: Academic Press.

Rutter, M., & the English and Romanian Adoptees Study Team. (1998). Developmental catch-up, and deficit, following adoption after severe global early privation. *Child Psychology and Psychiatry, 39*, 465–476.

Schwartz, J. M., Stoessel, P. W., Baxter, L. R., Martin, K. M., & Phelps, M. E. (1996). Systematic changes in cerebral glucose metabolic rate after successful behavior modification treatment of obsessive-compulsive disorder. *Archives of General Psychiatry, 53*, 109–113.

Shatz, C. J. (1992). The developing brain. *Scientific American, 267*, 60–67.

Shore, R. (1997). *Rethinking the brain: New insights into early development.* New York: Families and Work Institute.

Shonkoff, J. P., & Phillips, D. A. (Eds.). (2000). *From neurons to neighborhoods: The science of early childhood development.* National Research Council and Institute of Medicine, Committee on Integrating the Science of Early Childhood Development, Board on Children, Youth, and Families, Commission on Behavioral and Social Sciences and Education. Washington, DC: National Academy Press.

Suomi, S. J. (1997). Early determinants of behaviour: Evidence from primate studies. *British Medical Bulletin, 53*, 170–184.

5

Understanding Yourself

Research about the brain and resiliency reveals that consistent, nurturing relationships are a child's best protection against risk—including the risk of challenging behavior. Families usually provide such relationships, but they don't have exclusive rights in this domain: Anyone is welcome, especially teachers. Because teachers spend so much time with a child, teachers can play a vital role in his life. They are particularly important when family relationships are wobbly.

The caring connection

This caring connection with a child is the most powerful tool you have as a teacher. In a safe, loving relationship with an adult, a child finds a secure base for emotional devel-

This chapter has been adapted from *Partners in Quality, vol. 2/ Relationships* © CCCF 1999, written by Barbara Kaiser and Judy Sklar Rasminsky based on the research papers of the Partners in Quality Project. With permission from Canadian Child Care Federation, 201-383 Parkdale Avenue, Ottawa, Ontario, K1Y 4R4.

opment. He learns to value himself and believe in his own personal power. He learns that he can send messages that influence the other people in his world and that they can help him fulfill his needs. With a caring, respectful adult as a guide and a model, he can learn to understand and control his own feelings and behavior, and he can learn to care about other people, see things from their perspective, and understand their feelings, too (Emde and Robinson, 2000; Greenspan, 1996).

When challenging behavior enters the picture, this crucial relationship may falter. The behavior gets in the way, blocking your view of the child and making it much more difficult to establish a connection with him. Yet it remains utterly essential to create that bond—because the relationship is the key to success. When you and a child care about each other, he has a desire to learn and a model to emulate, and you have the possibility of real understanding. All of this enormously augments your ability to help him learn to behave appropriately.

"Who are you?" said the caterpillar

So how do you forge a relationship with a child with challenging behavior? How can you come to accept him for who he is and care about him no matter how he behaves?

Knowing where he comes from will certainly help. But before you can appreciate where the child is coming from, you have to understand where you are coming from yourself. The reason for this is simple: How you relate to the child depends on what you see when you look at him—and what you see depends on who you are. Whether you're aware of it or not, everything about your teaching—how you respond to the children, set up your room, plan your day, choose and present activities, even your knowledge of child development and theory—filters through the prism of your own beliefs, values, and culture as well as your own temperament, emotions, and experiences (Bowman, 1989). A teacher, says William Ayers in *The Good Preschool Teacher* (1989), is "the perceiver, the selector, and the interpreter of a child's behavior" (p. 137).

That is why it's important for you to discover who you are, to know what matters to you, to understand your reasons for doing this work, to figure out your philosophy of child care and education, to know what kind of people you want the children you care for and teach to become. Knowing about yourself allows you to see the child much more clearly.

There is another reason to look inward. When you're with a child with challenging behavior, it's critical to stay cool and collected. If you're defensive and stressed, it's hard to think clearly and act rationally. At the same time, it's vitally important to show the

Loving to Learn

In *The Scientist in the Crib*, Alison Gopnik, Andrew N. Meltzoff, and Patricia K. Kuhl (2001) tell us that social factors can dramatically alter how animals learn: "Babies who are caught up in flirtatious dialogues with people they love . . . seem very involved and attentive, and happy, too, and this could be part of why they learn so quickly" (pp. 194–195).

child that you can accept, control, and express your feelings in direct and nonaggressive ways. And he needs to see that you aren't afraid of his intense emotions and won't punish, threaten, or withdraw from him (Furman, 1986; Gartrell, 1997; Marion, 1997).

Knowing yourself won't give you magic powers, but it can bring you more control, and it will allow you to accept and talk about your feelings, to be honest with yourself and the children, to see the child and the environment more clearly, and to empathize more fully. As you come to know yourself better, you open the door to new possibilities, new perspectives, and new choices for yourself and for the child.

What influences the way you relate to a child with challenging behavior?

Without question, feelings are the most prominent barrier between you and the children. A child with challenging behavior evokes plenty of them, often negative. Fear, anger, guilt, anxiety, frustration, inadequacy, blame—they seem to have a life of their own, gushing out to manipulate your reactions whenever challenging behavior appears.

Initially, these feelings come from the present situation—the fear that a child will get hurt, the frustration that you can't do the activity you'd planned, the anxiety that you won't be able to manage the child's behavior. Then older feelings join in. The child may remind you of qualities you don't particularly admire in yourself, such as a tendency to act without thinking, or he may bring back unwelcome memories, such as the terror you felt in the presence of that boy who bullied you in the second grade. Although they usually intensify reactions, feelings can also be strong enough to render you numb, unable to respond at all.

Past experiences also make a substantial contribution to the way you respond to a child. Without realizing it, you may react the way your mother reacted to you when you

Seeing Is Believing?

In "Seeing the Child, Knowing the Person," Nancy Balaban (1995) gives this striking example of how feelings can distort a teacher's view of a child's capabilities:

> A teacher of seven-year-olds disliked the way Tim followed her and whined "teacher, teacher" many times during the day. The teacher was particularly repelled when Tim picked his nose and rolled the mucus into balls.
>
> One day the teacher brought in some sand and fine-, medium-, and large-mesh screens for the children to explore. She recorded the activities of a small group, including Tim, as an exercise for a course she was taking. The record contained Tim's words: "Hey, the sand comes out faster when the holes are larger!" Reading the record aloud at the course, the teacher disregarded this statement until several members of the course called her attention to Tim's discovery. The teacher's prior judgment about Tim had prevented her from seeing the child's achievement. (p. 50)

Source: Nancy Balaban, Infant and Parent Development and Early Intervention program, Bank Street Graduate School of Education. Reprinted by permission.

Barriers, Obstacles, and Filters

When a child with challenging behavior comes on the scene, it is normal for all kinds of feelings, attitudes, and assumptions to emerge. Here are some common reactions:

- He shouldn't be in this classroom.
- I'm not trained to work with children like this.
- I can't keep the other children safe.
- The other children aren't getting what they deserve.
- That child is out to get me.
- I can't help him—look at his parents.
- Children have no respect any more.
- His parents spank him so he doesn't pay any attention to me.

Having these feelings doesn't mean that you're doing a bad job. On the contrary, they provide you with a learning opportunity, warning you to become aware of what pushes your buttons.

dropped her favorite dish ("You're so clumsy and stupid!"). Or you may be following the example of the kindergarten teacher who took you by the hand and dragged you inside when you didn't want to come in from recess. As Carl Rogers and Jerome Freiberg say in *Freedom to Learn* (1994), "We tend to teach the way we've been taught [and] discipline the way we've been disciplined" (p. 241).

When a child with challenging behavior is involved, your temperament tends to get into the act, too. If you like to slow things down to make sure that every child has an opportunity to talk, children who need more activity may respond by creating extra stimulation for themselves. If you're a person with strong moods and reactions, some children may get frightened in your presence and act unpredictably.

Values and beliefs are also powerful influences. Because they're usually part and parcel of the culture you live in and the way you've been brought up, you may not even be aware of them. When a child refuses to look you in the eye, it's easy to jump to the conclusion that he's rude if you don't realize that in his culture eye contact with an adult can be a sign of disrespect, contempt, or aggression. Or if you believe that children should do what adults tell them to do, you may be offended by a child who wants to know why you've asked him to do something like come in from the playground.

Left to their own devices, these barriers work full time, influencing the way you see the children, skewing your expectations of them, affecting the way they see themselves—and the way they behave. Fortunately, such obstacles aren't necessarily permanent fixtures. When you take the time to think about who you are and what you believe, it becomes possible to remove or alter them.

The Inside View

"Greatness in teaching...requires a serious encounter with autobiography: Who are you? How did you come to take on your views and outlooks? What forces helped to shape you? What have you made of yourself? Where are you heading? An encounter with these kinds of questions is critical to outstanding teaching....Of all the knowledge teachers need to draw on, self-knowledge is the most important (and least attended to)," William Ayers writes in *To Teach: The Journey of a Teacher* (1993, p. 129).

What is self-reflection?

In the past few years, you have probably done quite a lot of thinking about what's important to you. You've faced the gigantic question of choosing the work you want to do, which meant figuring out where and what you'd study as well. To make those decisions, you had to take a close look at your interests and talents and weigh them alongside family and financial considerations. At different times in your life you may have had to grapple with the beliefs—religious, political, cultural, personal—you grew up with. In new relationships with friends and partners, you've doubtless had to confront your personal values. You've probably spent time figuring out whether to drink or smoke, whether to eat meat, and how to take care of your body. Even deciding what to wear requires an encounter with values. As Rogers and Freiberg say, "We are [all] engaged in a struggle to discover our identity, the person we are and choose to be. This is a very pervasive search; it involves our clothes, our hair, our appearance. At a more significant level it involves our choice of values, our stance in relation to parents and others, the relationship we choose to have to society, our whole philosophy of life" (p. 52).

All of this thinking is called *self-reflection*. It is both a method and an attitude—a strategy for increasing your skill and a willingness to look hard at yourself and your work and to act on what you find. *Why* is at the heart of the matter: Why am I doing what I'm doing the way that I'm doing it?

When you think about your feelings, values, and beliefs and how they affect your actions, each task and each interaction with a child becomes more meaningful. You have more self-respect because you know why you are doing what you do, you have control over it, and you have ownership of it. You are working from a position of strength inside yourself.

How do you reflect?

The process of reflection is a messy mixture of the rational and the intuitive, of melding knowledge of yourself with knowledge from your training and experience and information gleaned from families, colleagues, and written sources.

In *How We Think* (1933, pp. 30–32), the philosopher and educator John Dewey, the father of reflective thinking, recommends cultivating three attitudes:

• *Open-mindedness*, which is the "active desire to hear more than one side; to give heed to facts from whatever source they come; to give full attention to alternative possibilities; to recognize the possibility of error even in the beliefs that are dearest to us"

• *Whole-heartedness*, which is a willingness to throw yourself totally into the endeavor

• *Responsibility*, which is a form of integrity; a willingness to consider the consequences of possible changes and to go forward if they're consistent with your beliefs

When do you reflect?

You should always be thinking about what you're doing and why you're doing it. At the same time, it's important to think about what your feelings are and where they're coming from. This is particularly critical when you're confronted with a child with challenging behavior because your feelings affect both your behavior, and the behavior of the child.

Robert Tremmel (1993) likens the process of listening to your feelings to the practice of Zen Buddhism—paying attention to the here and now and investing the present moment with your full awareness and concentration. In *Multicultural Issues in*

When you think about your feelings, values, and beliefs and how they affect your actions, each task and each interaction with a child becomes more meaningful.

Child Care (1997), Janet Gonzalez-Mena advises: "Tune in on those times when something bothers you instead of just ignoring it and hoping it will go away. Work to identify what specific behaviors of others make you uncomfortable. Try to discover exactly what in yourself creates this discomfort" (p. 33).

There are certainly times when this is out of the question—when a child is throwing chairs around the room, you may have to concentrate on the soles of your feet just to maintain your equilibrium. But that evening or the next day, some reflection is in order. If you can figure out what your feelings were and where they came from, you can see how they affect your work and what you can do to make things better.

What do you reflect about?

In addition to focusing on specific incidents and feelings, you can reflect on anything that has to do with a particular child, the group in general, and your program. But it's also a good idea to spend some time becoming aware of your own personal history and culture. Where you come from can explain a lot about who you are now and help you to understand your feelings and regulate your behavior. Think of yourself as an anthropologist setting out to explore that most fascinating person of all: yourself.

Talk to your family about why they or their ancestors came to North America. Where did they come from? What language did they speak? Where did they settle? What was life like when they were growing up? Were they ever involved in politics? Was religion very important in their lives? And how central was family (Lynch, 1998)?

Think about your childhood. What was your parents' philosophy of child rearing? Did your mother work, or did she stay home to take care of you? How did your mother and father respond when you cried? Did they feed you on a schedule or on demand, and did you eat alone or with the whole family? Did you spend a lot of time together? How did they discipline you? Did your parents treat you the same way they treated your brother or sister? Did they encourage you and make you feel special, or did you promise yourself that you'd never use their methods with your own child? If there are things about your upbringing that you don't remember or understand, talk to your parents, siblings, grandparents, aunts, uncles, and cousins.

Take a look at your education, too. Which teachers did you like, and which couldn't you stand? Why? How did they make you feel?

Can you see the child you used to be in the person you are today? It's likely that he or she is nearby when you are interacting with the children in your classroom, affecting your perceptions, interpretations, and behavior.

Are there any techniques to help you reflect?

Several tools can assist you in the process of reflection. One traditional way is to keep a journal. It is both a record and "an instrument for thinking about teaching and children in a critical, sustained way" (Ayers, 1993, p. 39). It allows you to return to a situation, to construct a whole out of many bits, and to increase your self-awareness by forcing you to put your thoughts in writing. When you write for yourself, without worrying about what others will say, feelings and ideas have a way of spilling out unbidden, bringing insights in their wake.

Write in a notebook, type on a computer, or talk into a tape recorder. You can concentrate on daily events, memorable incidents, one child or several, one topic or many. If you're using a notebook, try dedicating one side of the page to record keeping and the other to reflection. Carry it with you or keep it in a handy spot in the classroom. If you set aside a regular time each day to write in it, you're more likely to be faithful to the task. When you have a child with challenging behavior in your class, writing in a journal can help you to identify what's working, what isn't, and why.

Though some people consider reflection a personal matter and believe they can be more honest when they reflect in private, others like to have a sounding board. When you're reflecting, questions inevitably arise, and it's useful to have a safe, supportive environment for sharing your doubts, your insights, your experiences. One way to arrange this is to make a regular date to get together—in person, on the phone, via e-mail—with a friend or colleague. Staff meetings, case consultation, and feedback from supervisors also provoke useful reflection (Bowman and Stott, 1994).

We tend to pay attention to problems, but remember to give equal time to your successes. Positive reinforcement works just as well for teachers as it does for children, and your triumphs can tell you just as much about your practice as any difficulty.

Be patient with yourself. As you become more comfortable with the process, you can expand into more sensitive and difficult arenas. The goal is to turn reflection into a reflex, an instinct that sits quietly at the back of your mind weighing pros and cons and whispering, "Why should I do that?"

What Do You Think?

1. On page 72, in the box entitled "Seeing Is Believing?" Nancy Balaban provides a dramatic example of how feelings can distort perceptions. Have you ever noticed how your own feelings alter what you see or how you act? Can you give one or two examples? Were you able to correct or clarify the situation later?

2. Have you ever kept a diary or journal? How did it help you to see the things around you differently? Try keeping a journal of your experience in this class. How does it influence what you perceive and learn?

3. Interview your parents, grandparents, or other family members about your childhood and your family's early experiences in the United States. You can use some of these questions in the text (page 76) or make up your own.

Suggested Reading

Ayers, W. (1993). *To teach: The journey of a teacher*. New York: Teachers College Press.

Ayers, W. (Ed.) (1995). *To become a teacher: Making a difference in children's lives*. New York: Teachers College Press.

References

Ayers, W. (1989). *The good preschool teacher: Six teachers reflect on their lives.* New York: Teachers College Press.

Ayers, W. (1993). *To teach: The journey of a teacher.* New York: Teachers College Press.

Balaban, N. (1995). Seeing the child, knowing the person. In W. Ayers (Ed.), *To become a teacher: Making a difference in children's lives* (pp. 49–57). New York: Teachers College Press.

Bowman, B. T. (1989). Self-reflection as an element of professionalism. *Teachers College Record, 90,* 444–451.

Bowman, B. T., & Stott, F. M. (1994). Understanding development in a cultural context: The challenge for teachers. In B. L. Mallory & R. S. New (Eds.), *Diversity and developmentally appropriate practices: Challenges for early childhood education* (pp. 119–133). New York: Teachers College Press.

Dewey, J. (1933). *How we think.* Boston: Heath.

Emde, R. N., & Robinson, J. (2000). Guiding principles for a theory of early intervention: A developmental-psychoanalytic perspective. In J. P. Shonkoff & S. J. Meisels (Eds.), *Handbook of early childhood intervention* (2nd ed., pp. 160–178). New York: Cambridge University Press.

Furman, E. (1986). Stress in the nursery school. In E. Furman (Ed.), *What nursery school teachers ask us about: Psychoanalytic consultations in preschools.* Madison, CT: International Universities Press.

Gartrell, D. (1997). Beyond discipline to guidance. *Young Children, 52,* 34–42.

Gonzalez-Mena, J. (1997). *Multicultural issues in child care* (2nd ed.). Mountain View, CA: Mayfield.

Gonzalez-Mena, J. (2002). *The child in the family and the community* (3rd ed.). Upper Saddle River, NJ: Merrill Prentice-Hall.

Gopnik, A., Meltzoff, A. N., & Kuhl, P. K. (2001). *The scientist in the crib: What early learning tells us about the mind.* New York: Perennial.

Greenspan, S. I. (1996). *The challenging child: Understanding, raising, and enjoying the five "difficult" types of children.* Reading, MA: Addison-Wesley.

Lynch, E. W. (1998). Developing cross-cultural competence. In E. W. Lynch & M. J. Hanson (Eds.), *Developing cross-cultural competence: A guide for working with children and their families* (2nd ed., pp. 47–89). Baltimore: Paul H. Brookes.

Marion, M. (1997). Guiding young children's understanding and management of anger. *Young Children, 53,* 62–67.

Rogers, C., & Freiberg, J. (1994). *Freedom to learn* (3rd ed.). New York: Merrill.

Tremmel, R. (1993). Zen and the art of reflective practice in teacher education. *Harvard Educational Review, 63,* 434–458.

6

Understanding the Child's Family and Culture

Collaborating with Families

Creating a good relationship with a family is another important part of creating a good relationship with a child. That means coming to understand something about her family and her culture. Research shows that the more that teachers and families communicate, the more interaction there is between teacher and child and the higher the quality of care and education (Endsley, Minish, and Zhou, 1993; Hogan, 1991; Smith and Hubbard, 1988). This relationship is especially important when a child with challenging behavior is involved—everyone needs all the help that's available.

This chapter has been adapted from *Partners in Quality, vol. 2/ Relationships* © CCCF 1999, written by Barbara Kaiser and Judy Sklar Rasminsky based on the research papers of the Partners in Quality Project. With permission from Canadian Child Care Federation, 201-383 Parkdale Avenue, Ottawa, Ontario, K1Y 4R4.

Thanks to the ecological theory of Urie Bronfenbrenner (1979) (which urges us to look at the child in the context of family, community, and society) and family-systems theory (which reminds us that family members are all connected to one another), we now know that child and family are one big package, an integral whole. By supporting families, teachers are also supporting children's well-being and development.

Here are some of the basic ideas behind this family-centered approach (Chud and Fahlman, 1995):

- Family is central to children's lives—their first and main teachers.

- Each family has its own strengths, competencies, resources, and ways of coping.

- Every family must be respected and accepted on its own terms, without judgments or preconceptions.

- Each family's race, culture, ethnicity, religion, language, and socioeconomic status must be respected.

- Services and programs are effective to the degree that they support the family in meeting the needs it has identified itself.

When we work together, we are all much stronger.

Getting to know you

How can you establish a positive, productive relationship with families? Research provides some useful clues. One study indicates that the more the child-care center staff communicate formally with parents (via meetings, conferences, orientations, newsletters, notes, phone calls, potluck dinners, and so on), the more likely the parents are to become involved (Endsley et al., 1993). A school-based study shows that parents are more likely to become involved in a child's education if they believe that they can help her to succeed. They are also more likely to get involved if they believe that the teacher's invitation is serious and sincere and that their child wants them there (Hoover-Dempsey and Sandler, 1997).

These findings emphasize the importance of the teacher's role. Some parents will be involved no matter what you do; some have neither the time nor the inclination and will never be involved. But some may respond if you approach them the right way. What's required is a strong, clear message that their involvement can really help their child and that you truly value and respect their views.

Although it's important to start getting to know families as soon as possible, it's also a process that takes time. One way to begin is to develop your own welcome letter and enrollment form with questions that will help you become acquainted with the child and the family. Ask about other members of the family, where they come from, what languages they speak, what the child likes to do, and some specific questions about their culture and child-rearing practices, such as the child's eating and sleeping habits. Be sure to ask whether there's anything else they want you to know about their child. Supplying this information will make the parents feel more confident about their child's care and education, and having it will help you to understand the child. (It will also give you tips for encouraging families to become involved in your classroom as experts, resources, and helpers.) In your letter, tell them something about yourself, too—your name, your cultural background, what languages you speak, whether you're married and have children—whatever information you'd like to share. This friendly exchange provides a good base for establishing a relationship.

Talk with family members as often as you can. Each contact helps to build trust, and in many cultures polite greetings and conversation are absolutely essential to communication. It's hard to talk to people when they arrive all at once or you're comforting an unhappy child, so it's important to keep track of your daily contact. If you haven't managed to connect with a family all week, make a mental note to chat with them early the following week or, if you feel comfortable, to phone.

This is virtually impossible in a school setting, where you may not meet until parent-teacher night. To make families feel at home on that occasion, set aside time to talk informally, perhaps around coffee and cookies. In the meantime, keep in touch by sending home notes and information about what you're doing in class.

Make a point of treating each parent as a distinct person in her or his own right, not just as Kevin's mother or Yolanda's father. Parents often want to keep their private lives private (Larner, 1994; Powell, 1989), but, paradoxically, they may also want teachers to be interested in them as people (Powell, 1998). Like their children, they have their own temperaments, needs, and preferences.

If possible, try to arrange to visit the family in their home at some point during the year. Though such a visit may seem fraught with difficulty, it is definitely worth the effort, especially if the family is from a different culture. You'll get to know them better as people and gain valuable insights into their child-rearing practices and the child's

Going Home

Worried that their students weren't mastering the skills the state of New Mexico expected at their level, kindergarten and first-grade teachers Maralee S. Gorter-Reu and Jean Marie Anderson (1998) decided to give them a boost. They developed kits to help parents teach their children, and they visited their homes to meet the families. The children gained skills, and their home visits changed the teachers' lives.

> We came away from our children's homes with respect and admiration for families doing the best they could, sometimes under dire circumstances. We realized that all parents want a good education for their children even when parents work all night and can't get their child to school on time. . . .
>
> In the past it was easy to blame parents for a child's lack of school success by saying, "I wish someone at home cared about this child." We discovered instead that of course parents do care!
>
> . . . We found ourselves relating more often, verbally and emotionally, with the children . . . [and] we began to view all of the children in our classes more compassionately and with greater understanding. (p. 74)

development. The child will feel proud to have you in her home with her family, and the family will feel honored to have you as a guest. Be sure to make arrangements in advance, keep your stay to under half an hour, and remember that families who've had negative encounters with social services, immigration, or other authorities may feel uneasy with any kind of visit (York, 1991).

Opening the Culture Door

Creating a relationship with children and families who come from a different culture is particularly challenging and important. Research shows that they are less likely to consider teachers to be a source of information and support (Bowden, 1997; Kontos and Wells, 1986; Landy and Peters, 1991) and that families coping with poverty or minority status—those most in need—are the least likely to receive backing (Galinsky and Weissbourd, 1992).

A study in Canadian child-care centers found that minority families had less contact with their child's teacher than families from the mainstream culture (Bernhard, Lefebvre, Chud, and Lange, 1995). Contrary to what teachers believed, parents had a great deal of respect for them and were very interested in what they had to say. Parents were especially eager to learn more about their children's progress, but they often didn't ask questions or come to meetings because their English was inadequate, because the teachers seemed too busy or unwilling to talk with them, or because in their culture keeping a respectful and unquestioning distance is the most appropriate behavior toward a teacher, whom parents regard as an authority. Both families and teachers wanted more communication, but each believed the other wasn't interested.

Perhaps it is human nature to relate more easily to people when we think we have something in common with them, or perhaps the blame lies with the system, where communication is traditionally one way (Bernhard, Lefebvre, Kilbride, Chud, and Lange, 1999). Whatever the problem, it clearly affects our relationship with the child and cuts us off from the family—a vital resource in dealing with challenging behavior. A giant step in remedying this situation is to get to know more about the family's culture.

What is culture?

Everyone has a culture, but most of the time we can't see it. As Eleanor Lynch points out in *Developing Cross-Cultural Competence* (1998), the book she edited with Marci Hanson, culture is like a "second skin" (p. 24), and it becomes visible only when we brush up against one that's different. This can be an important factor in your relationship with a child and her family when challenging behavior emerges.

"There is not one aspect of human life that is not touched and altered by culture," says anthropologist Edward T. Hall, one of the foremost authorities on culture. "This means personality, how people express themselves (including shows of emotion), the

Culture includes our food, clothing, furniture, art, games, and habits as well as our deep beliefs and values.

way they think, how they move, how problems are solved, how their cities are planned and laid out, how transportation systems function and are organized, as well as how economic and government systems are put together and function" (1977, pp. 16–17).

Our culture is the framework for our lives. It includes our food, clothing, furniture, art, games, and habits as well as our deep beliefs and values—the way we look at the world, the way we relate to one another, and the way we bring up our children (Ayers, 1993).

Within each culture there are many variations. Educational level, socioeconomic status, occupation, temperament, and personal experience all influence our values and beliefs. So do race, language, ethnicity, religion, gender, family, workplace, age, sexual orientation, lifestyle, political orientation, geography (Lynch, 1998).

What does culture have to do with identity?

Our culture is an integral part of our identity, whether we know it or not. We learn it from our families (who learned it from their families) effortlessly and unconsciously, and it is reasonably well established by the time we are five or six (Chud and Fahlman, 1985; Lynch, 1998). "There is nothing in a young child's day that comes separate from the cultural context," point out Janet Gonzalez-Mena and Judith Bernhard, experts in multicultural child care. "Culture is not directly taught but grows out of the interaction between caregiver and children" (1998, p. 15).

There are no "best" child-rearing methods, no universal norms or expectations (Chud and Fahlman, 1985). Children naturally develop the characteristics that their own culture values (Lubeck, 1994; New, 1994). Emotional display and affect, moral development, gender roles, even cognitive abilities depend on what competencies the culture requires of its citizens (New, 1994).

People who work with children have long understood how important it is for children to develop a positive self-concept. We believe that they have the need and the right to feel good about themselves. What is less well known is that their culture is a vital part of that self-concept and that children also have the need and the right to be proud of their cultural heritage (York, 1991).

Children begin to construct their identity—to understand who they are—from understanding their own culture and by responding to how others see and relate to them. To form a positive self-concept, children need to honor and respect their own culture and to have others honor and respect it, too. This is a vital human need. When we don't recognize a child's identity—or when we misrecognize it—we can actually harm her by putting her self-concept at risk (LaGrange, Clark, and Munroe, 1994).

Culture is a vital part of self-concept, and children have the need and the right to be proud of their cultural heritage.

Are cultures really so different?

In a word, yes. Mainstream American culture—that is, European American, middle-class culture, which is based on Western European culture—is different from many other cultures in the world.

Hall (1977) distinguishes between what he calls low-context cultures (such as Western Europe and the United States) and high-context cultures (such as Asia, South Asia, Southern Europe, Latino, African American, and Native American).

The low-context culture that European Americans live in values the individual person over the group and considers the individual's independence the greatest possible virtue. It sees each person as a unique and separate being who is born with needs, rights, and an identity all his or her own, and it teaches its citizens to assert themselves, take the initiative, explore, and achieve.

Children in low-context cultures begin to practice independence when they're very small. Their parents put them to bed alone in cribs in their own rooms; supply them with objects so they can comfort themselves; transport them in their own carriages, strollers, and infant seats; deposit them in playpens or on the floor to play alone; give them finger foods and cups so that they can feed themselves; and leave them with babysitters when they go out for the evening because they, too, are individuals with separate lives.

But in the context of the world's cultures, this notion of the separate, individual self is "a rather peculiar idea," writes anthropologist Clifford Geertz (as cited in Kağıtçıbaşı, 1996, p. 53). Outside of the European American culture, people value interdependence—being closely connected—and they are first and foremost members of a group. They teach their children that they are part of an extended family and a community and that they are responsible for looking after one another. They value harmony, and their self-esteem is based on their contributions to the good of the whole, not on their individual achievement—which high-context cultures view as selfish and as a rejection of the family (Lynch, 1998).

As Lynch puts it, "The majority of people throughout the world have nurtured children for centuries by having them sleep in the parents' bed; following them around in order to feed them; keeping them in close physical proximity through holding, touching, and carrying long after they can walk alone; or taking them wherever the adults go" (1998, p. 59). Parents know that their children will eventually grow up to

Apron Strings

Cross-cultural researchers studied child-rearing values in nine countries (Kağıtçıbaşı, 1996). When asked to name the most desirable quality in children, 60 percent of Turkish parents chose "obeying their parents" first or second. A mere 18 percent selected "being independent and self-reliant." Thai, Filipino, and Indonesian parents made similar choices.

But parents in the fast-industrializing countries of Korea and Singapore valued their children's independence even more than U.S. parents.

become self-sufficient. While their children are young, the parents' idea is to forge a bond so strong that it will never break (Gonzalez-Mena and Bernhard, 1998).

Of course, in the end, every culture needs both group and individual loyalties. The question is, Which takes priority (Gonzalez-Mena, 1997)?

Communication is another area where there are distinct cultural differences. In low-context cultures, words are primary, and communication is direct, precise, and logical. Because babies are often in another room or a short distance away from their parents, they quickly learn to attract attention by crying or babbling, and their parents usually answer them by speaking (Gonzalez-Mena, 1997).

In high-context cultures, words take a back seat. Nonverbal cues (such as facial expression and movement) and contextual cues (such as shared experience, history, tradition, and social status) play a far greater role in communication. Pauses, silences, and indirect ways of communicating—such as empathy, storytelling, analogies, or talking around a subject—are also critical (Chud and Fahlman, 1995; Gonzalez-Mena, 1997; Lynch, 1998). Always ensconced on a lap or in someone's arms, babies in high-context cultures learn to communicate with their bodies. They find that tensed muscles or a change in position sends clear messages to their caregivers, who quickly calm them, feed them, put them on the toilet (Gonzalez-Mena, 1977).

Breaking the Code

Each culture has its own communication style. Perhaps you've encountered some of these varieties:

• In face-to-face conversation, the European American culture expects eye contact, which conveys honesty, attention, and trustworthiness. But African American, Asian Pacific, Latino, and Native American cultures consider direct eye contact aggressive, disrespectful, or impolite.

• Some cultures, such as the Mediterranean, display emotion openly and spontaneously; others, such as Chinese and Japanese, consider emotional restraint polite.

• European Americans laugh or smile when they're happy or amused. But in many Asian cultures, people smile when they're embarrassed, confused, or even sad.

• In Latino, Arabic, and African American cultures, people stand close together to converse; European Americans like to stay an arm's length away. Asian Pacific Islanders also prefer more space.

• Whereas frequent touching is an important part of communication in Mediterranean cultures, the Japanese, Chinese, and Korean cultures avoid physical contact (Chud and Fahlman, 1985; Lynch, 1998). And the Vietnamese believe that touching a person on the head robs her of her soul (Gonzalez-Mena, 1997).

How can you see your culture?

To care for any child—and a child with challenging behavior in particular—you have to understand where she is coming from. That means you have to understand her culture. But just as your feelings and perceptions create barriers, so does your own culture. Paradoxically, the first step in understanding someone else's culture is to become aware of your own. Then you can see how it influences your behavior and interactions with others—and that it isn't the only valid way to do things.

People who belong to the European American culture often have the mistaken idea that they don't have a culture. That's because they're surrounded by people who think the same way they do and because their way of thinking shapes their society. For the same reason, they know less about other people's cultures. People who are part of a less powerful culture have to learn more about the dominant culture—it's a matter of survival for them (Tatum, 1997). "Just as I know a lot more about male systems than [men] may know about female systems, so do . . . African Americans know more about my system than I know about theirs," says Gonzalez-Mena (1997, p. 97).

When you look at your family history, as you do when you're reflecting, you will get some insight into your culture. Another way to become more aware of your culture is to pay close attention when you come into contact with different ways of approaching the world—that is, whenever you interact with someone from a different gender, race, ethnic group, religion, nationality, age, or even family. If you put up your antennae in these encounters, you can begin to get a glimpse of your own assumptions.

Digging In

Louise Derman-Sparks, author of the *Anti-Bias Curriculum* (1989), and Gita Chud and Ruth Fahlman, who wrote *Early Childhood Education for a Multicultural Society* (1985), offer some suggestions for thinking about your own cultural beliefs and experiences:

- Do you remember the first time you met someone from another culture or ethnic group (Chud and Fahlman, 1985)?

- Do you remember how you first learned about your own ethnic identity (Derman-Sparks, 1989)?

- What is important to you about this aspect of yourself? What makes you proud and what gives you pain (Derman-Sparks)?

- Have you ever experienced prejudice or discrimination for any reason? How did it make you feel? What did you do? Thinking about it now, would you change your response (Derman-Sparks)?

- Do you and your parents agree about ethnic, cultural, and religious issues? If your beliefs are different, how did they evolve? What will you teach your children (Derman-Sparks)?

- If you've traveled to another country, or even to a different area, how did you feel in those strange surroundings?

The culture of child care and school

The field of early care and education has a culture, too. It's called *developmentally appropriate practice.*

Based mostly on the child development theory of Jean Piaget, who formulated it by observing his own white, Western European, middle-class children, developmentally appropriate practice became gospel in 1986, when the National Association for the Education of Young Children in Washington, DC, first published its guidelines for early childhood programs (Bredekamp, 1986, 1987). In the United States, teachers usually equate developmentally appropriate practice with high quality. Each day many thousands of them use its wisdom to make decisions and interact with children. Feeding, napping, guiding and disciplining, playing, communicating, socializing, and programming—developmentally appropriate practice pervades them all.

Because it is embedded in European American culture, developmentally appropriate practice naturally teaches the European American values of individualism and independence (among others), using European American methods of communication and learning. But these values and methods are not universal. As we have seen, other cultures in the world—including several with deep roots in the United States—bring up their children according to different beliefs and values. And when the children of

School Culture

In *Creating Culturally Responsive Classrooms*, Barbara J. Shade, Cynthia Kelly, and Mary Oberg (1997) point out some aspects of European American culture entrenched in schools in the United States:

- *Social distance.* [A] space bubble for interaction allows distance. [European Americans feel more comfortable when they're an arm's distance away.]

- *Authority.* The classroom is teacher centered and teacher directed.

- *Time.* Students are expected to adhere to exact time. Students think about the future rather than [the] past or present.

- *Regulation.* The teacher defines and monitors rules and procedures.

- *Language.* Standard English is required.

- *Sense of community.* Individuals compete against each other for rewards.

- *Competence demonstration.* Students demonstrate [competence] through paper and pencil tests. (p. 35)

As soon as they're born, children start to acquire the skills they need to become competent adults in their culture.

these cultures enter European American child-care and education systems, children, families, and teachers all face new challenges.

The worst part is that we don't really know how confused we are. Locked in our own cultures, families and teachers can see only the most obvious differences, such as differences in food. A mother doesn't think to tell you that she never puts her baby on the floor to play because in her culture historically the floor wasn't a safe place—and it doesn't occur to you to tell her that you're putting her daughter there or why you think it's good for her. Likewise, when a child is having trouble at nap, you don't think to tell her mother that in your center children sleep by themselves on cots—and the mother doesn't think to tell you that her child has always slept with her, never alone, on a mat on the floor. Nor do you say to parents that you encourage children to articulate their personal rights to resolve conflicts, and they don't mention that they want their child to learn to preserve peace and harmony in the group, not to express her own personal feelings. And the child, who may not speak much English—or who may not speak at all—certainly cannot tell you.

Schools also have a culture. Because they are usually funded and run according to the state's rules and goals, the school culture is much more ingrained and institutionalized than the culture of child care. And of course the values schools stress—self-direction, initiative, independence, and competitiveness—are thoroughly European American. Gonzalez-Mena points out, "Expected school behavior may be quite alien to what's needed by some children at home and in the neighborhood where they live" (2002, p. 293).

What happens when children move from one culture to another?

When the child care or school situation resembles home, a child experiences less stress, and home values are apt to be reinforced (Kuhn, 2001). When home is different from child care or school, there is discontinuity—hence there are more risks.

As soon as they're born, children start to acquire the skills they need to become competent adults in their culture, and by the time they enter child care or school, they're already well on their way. In the new environment, a lot of what they've learned so far simply doesn't apply. They must start again from scratch, feeling much less competent.

Children who find themselves in a strange environment are likely to be confused and may experience feelings of isolation, alienation, and conflict (Chud and Fahlman, 1995). Their talents, competencies, and abilities may not be recognized or appreciated, and behavior that was perfectly acceptable at home may be suddenly and inexplicably inappropriate at child care or school. Teachers from a different culture may even regard it as a problem requiring intervention (García Coll and Magnuson, 2000; Kağıtçıbaşı,

Two Cultures Are Better Than One

Discontinuity can have advantages, too. Research shows that learning more than one language and culture has decided benefits for children—if it's done right (Freire and Bernhard, 1997; Gonzalez-Mena, 1997).

- They perform better on school tests and are clear thinkers.
- They are less likely to drop out of school.
- Their risk of emotional or psychiatric illness is lower.
- They can move easily and comfortably from one culture to the other, and they're more likely to adapt well to a new situation.

1996). When teachers don't recognize and support their culture, children do not feel accepted, respected, or valued, and their self-concept suffers (LaGrange et al., 1994). Experts often blame discontinuity for the high rate of school failure among children from poor and minority families (Powell, 1989).

The dangers of discontinuity are greater when the discrepancy is large and long-lasting, especially if the child is very young or doesn't adapt easily to change (Powell, 1989). Carol Brunson Phillips, a specialist in cultural influences on human development, writes, "Remember what happened to E.T. when he got too far from home? He lost his power over the world. And so it is with our children when their school settings are so different from home that they represent an alien culture to them. They too lose their power" (p. 47). The way teachers handle these risks can make a big difference in children's lives.

How does culture influence behavior?

Sometimes a cultural conflict, visible or invisible, causes or contributes to challenging behavior. Maybe behavior that is inappropriate in the child-care setting or school is acceptable—or even desirable—at home. If a child doesn't answer when you ask her how she feels, her behavior may be culturally appropriate, not defiant, stupid, or devel-

Sometimes a cultural conflict causes or contributes to challenging behavior. It is extremely important to understand both the child's cultural assumptions and your own.

opmentally delayed. She may not know how, or wish, to answer because in her culture it is considered rude for people to express their personal feelings. A 3-year-old who spills her apple juice may not be clumsy or immature; she may not know how to drink from a cup because in her culture many generations ago liquid was too precious to present to a child in a spillable form and she still drinks from a bottle.

It is extremely important to understand the cultural assumptions on both sides—why you expect a child to express her feelings (and to drink from a cup) as well as why for some children that is an unreasonable (or unfamiliar) demand. If you are not from the European American culture, you will have cultural expectations of your own—and you'll also encounter behavior that perplexes you. For a teacher from a Latino culture, for example, a child who requires an explanation of why she should do things the way you ask may seem rude and lacking in respect rather than assertive or logical.

When a child from a different culture behaves unexpectedly, it's a good idea to try to figure out if culture is the culprit. One way to do this is to learn as much as you can about the child's culture. Study its history, read its literature, eat its food, visit its churches, attend its festivals, learn to speak a few words of its language. Of course, if the children in your class come from 16 different cultures (or even 6) it will be impossible to do this. But at least make a start, and try to stay as open as you can to the opportunities

Ogbu's Theory

Anthropologist John U. Ogbu of the University of California has developed an influential theory about why different cultural groups have different status in the United States (1994).

Some are what he calls *voluntary* or *immigrant minorities*, who move to the United States by choice. They believe they will have more freedom, more opportunity, and a better standard of living in this country. Although they would like to retain their own culture, they realize that they will have to learn some aspects of the European American culture in order to succeed in it, and they don't feel that their cultural identity will be threatened if they do. Their children do relatively well in school.

Other cultural groups are *involuntary minorities*, Ogbu says—"those groups (and their descendants) who were initially incorporated into U.S. society against their will by Euro-Americans through slavery, conquest, or colonization. Thereafter, these minorities were relegated to menial positions and denied true assimilation into the mainstream U.S. society" (p. 373). Native Americans, African Americans, and Mexican Americans (because the United States conquered and annexed their territory) make up this group. Because the United States tried to wipe out the cultures of the involuntary minorities and because they are aware of the racism in U.S. society, the involuntary minorities have defined themselves in opposition to the attitudes, beliefs, and preferences of the dominant culture. As a result, they feel they cannot adopt the majority's ways without losing their own culture. Children who grow up with these beliefs and attitudes may find it very difficult to succeed in European American schools. Those who do well are likely to be accused of "acting white" and be rejected by their peers (Ogbu, 1994; Tatum, 1997).

Refugees—who haven't been able to plan either their departure from their former home or their entry into the United States—do not fall comfortably into either category.

that come your way. You'll be amazed at how often you find yourself reading newspaper articles, watching television programs, and talking to people about the cultures of the families in your classroom.

What's most important—and most informative—is to get to know the families themselves. As you confer and collaborate, they will help you to better understand their culture and their child, and they will shed considerable light on the challenging behavior.

Researchers have identified some cultural traits that can help to explain different behavioral expectations and outcomes. The brief cultural profiles that follow are intended to illuminate areas where cultural confusion about challenging behavior may arise. Please note, however, that they are simply characteristics that are often found, and we present them as a way to help you to think about and understand the behavior that you're observing. Remember, too, that people from different places with similar educational and socioeconomic backgrounds may have more in common with each other than with some members of their own culture. Ultimately, the culture of each child and each family is unique.

African American culture

Most African American children, often using Ebonics, learn to express themselves openly, frankly, and freely, playing with words and trading insults from an early age. They quickly learn to handle intense feelings without being overwhelmed. Although this behavior might lead some people to label them as aggressive or confrontational, it has a clear survival value for children growing up in an inhospitable environment (Kochman, 1987; Shade et al., 1997). This verbal expressiveness (along with expressive clothing and hairstyles) also helps them to establish unique identities, which are an important part of African American culture (Peters, 1988; Shade et al., 1997).

Tough Love

Many African American parents feel that stern discipline is appropriate for teaching their children to function in a society that is full of stereotypes, misconceptions, and overt biases. One mother explained her views to researchers Ramona Denby and Keith Alford this way:

> I'm real conscious of making sure my cute little black son here doesn't become one of the people [European Americans] are afraid of [when they're] walking down the street [in] five more years. He's still the same child. He'll be bigger, but he'll become an automatic society threat at age 14.... I'm fighting against that already. No matter what... he'll be noticed and [people will] be suspicious of him.... [I teach him] you go look [at something in a store] but don't pick it up ... because a person will say that the little black child picked something up. If he were white, they wouldn't even think about watching. (1996, p. 89)

Source: From "Understanding African American Discipline Styles: Suggestions for Effective Social Work Intervention" by R. Denby and K. Alford, 1996, *Journal of Multicultural Social Work, 4*, p. 89. Copyright 1996 by Haworth Press. Reprinted by permission.

African American parents are often strict. They use directives and commands, and they expect obedience and respect (Greenfield and Suzuki, 1998). Discipline may be direct and physical, and it is administered as a way to teach, with love and warmth rather than anger. A recent study found that higher levels of physical punishment led to higher rates of aggressive behavior in European American children—but not in African American children (Deater-Deckard, Bates, Dodge, and Pettit, 1996).

In the inner city, strict discipline may be an adaptive response to reality, intended to prevent children from becoming either victims or perpetrators of violence. To keep them safe, parents may restrict their play (which in turn may limit their opportunities to have friends and practice social skills) (Kupersmidt, Griesler, DeRosier, Patterson, and Davis, 1995), teach them to view the environment as hostile, and encourage them to use aggressive tactics when necessary.

Although perhaps less now than in the not-so-distant past, every responsible adult in the African American community takes part in raising children (Gonzalez-Mena, 2002; Hale, 1986). This provides children with the assurance that an adult will correct their unacceptable behavior, and they feel free to move, explore, and assert themselves as their culture demands. Having this external locus of control can become a problem

Code of the Street

Sociologist Elijah Anderson of the University of Pennsylvania carried out an ethnographic study of a poor inner-city African American community (1997, 1998). He found two value orientations among the residents.

Most people identify themselves as "decent." They are strong, loving, church-going, and committed to the middle-class values of hard work, self-reliance, and education for their children. Keenly aware of the dangerous environment they live in, they are strict disciplinarians who supervise their children closely and use physical punishment to teach them to respect authority and stay out of trouble. They are careful to explain the reasons for it.

Other residents belong to what they call the "street" culture. A response to the failure of the police and justice systems to protect people in the inner city, it deliberately opposes the mainstream way of life. "Street" families are usually not as well off as their "decent" neighbors, and they tend to lead disorganized, isolated lives. Anderson writes, "Frustrations mount over bills, food, and, at times, drink, cigarettes, and drugs. Some tend toward self-destructive behavior; many street-oriented women are crack-addicted...alcoholic, or repeatedly involved...with men who abuse them" (1997, p. 10). Without resources or support, they often lash out at their children without explanation. As a result, the children learn to use violence to solve their problems, a lesson that is reinforced on the street, where the winner prevails and earns the respect of the others. The rules that govern respect and the use of violence are called the "code of the street."

As the "decent" children start to venture out on their own, they must learn the code of the street in order to survive, and many learn to "code-switch," or shift back and forth between the two styles of behavior. Because they may look and behave like "street" children, teachers may have difficulty distinguishing these "decent" children from the real "street" children.

when teachers expect them to control their behavior from within. Writes Gonzalez-Mena, "It's not too hard to see what kind of problems might arise for children who are disciplined one way at home and another in child care. When no one gives 'directives' . . . do they wonder if no one cares what they do? That would be a strange feeling indeed" (1997, p. 84).

Latino culture

With the 2000 census, it became clear that the number of Latinos in the United States was surpassing the number of African Americans to become the largest minority group in the country (U.S. Census Bureau, 2001). Latinos come from several different Spanish-speaking areas—most notably Mexico, Cuba, Puerto Rico, and South and Central America. These groups have a lot in common and—depending on the country of origin, education, and socioeconomic status of the family—a lot of differences.

Respect for authority and group harmony are important values in the Latino culture (Shade et al., 1997). Children receive directives to follow, and they are expected to respect and obey their elders (including their teachers). It is not considered polite to question adults, to argue, or to express negative feelings. There may be real cultural conflict for children with Latino values in a European American child-care center or school where children are supposed to ask questions and speak up for their rights. Latino children may be more inclined to participate and function better when they're working in a group of their peers (Greenfield and Suzuki, 1998; Rotheram and Phinney, 1987). Humor is also important—a good way to relieve tension and avoid disagreement (Shade et al., 1997).

Courtesy indicates caring, and discipline in the Latino home is polite, indirect, and affectionate (Delgado-Gaitan, 1994; Shade et al., 1997). Children are sensitive to social cues and the nonverbal expression of emotion (Rotheram and Phinney, 1987; Zuniga, 1998). Because direct criticism is a sign of disrespect, it's important for discipline in child care and school to be indirect and polite, too (Shade et al., 1997). A younger Latino child may cry when she is being reprimanded or corrected, and an older one may be upset. Though neither will respond, both are listening all the same. Eye contact may indicate disrespect, so they may also lower their eyes. Because being part of the group is extremely important to Latino children time-out is especially humiliating.

Indirect methods may also be more effective in persuading a Latino child to do something. For example, a child who hears that she's going sledding will be more likely to put on her hat than a child who hears that it's cold outside. Seeing the matter from the child's perspective is very important!

In the interdependent Latino culture, where parents prefer their children to remain dependent as long as possible, it's common for 3- and 4-year-olds to drink from bottles and be spoon-fed. A child who's expected to fend for herself in child care may cry and be unable to comfort herself. An older child whose mother always makes sure she has everything she needs may feel unsure of herself when she's asked to do something she's never done before. In both cases, adult soothing and close physical contact will help to calm her (B. Burton, personal communication, July 2001).

Because Latino children are used to being part of a large group, they are accustomed to noise and may speak loudly without realizing it (B. Burton, personal communication, July 2001). They may also prefer to make clean-up an activity they do together at the end of playtime instead of putting away toys individually (Greenfield and Suzuki, 1998).

Depending on where they come from, some Latinos tend to sit and stand close together and often touch each other, so children of other cultures may feel uncomfortable and push away a Latino child who comes too close. On the other hand, a teacher who keeps her distance may lead a child to think she isn't sincere, and the child may withdraw or refuse to cooperate (B. Burton, personal communication, July 2001).

Native American culture

There are over 550 Native American tribes, each with its own history, culture, and/or language, but some beliefs are widely shared (Beach Center on Disability, 2002).

In this interdependent culture, individuals cooperate, share, achieve, and excel for the good of the group (Suina and Smolkin, 1994). Being singled out for either praise or criticism will make a child feel uneasy and may lead to misbehavior or noncompliance, especially at the beginning of the year, before she has established a comfortable relationship with the teacher. Group recognition and group activities—for example, murals instead of individual easels—are far more appropriate. Because group harmony is so important, children are usually left on their own to work out conflicts.

Traditionally, Native American children learn by careful observation, by listening to respected adults (who are regarded as keepers of knowledge) (Williams, 1994), and by practicing in private (Tharp, 1994). Although someone unskilled in their culture may be unable to read their body language and feel that they aren't listening or interested, they are actually taking everything in.

Native American children are not brought up to "comply." They don't do things simply because you ask; they need a reason that stems from respecting the rules or from respecting others. For example, they will put things away in their proper place if told, "We need to take care of the puzzles," or "If we want to go outside, we should put away the blocks so that we can play with them again" (D. Van Raalte, personal communication, April 2001; P. Clements, personal communication, April 2001).

Direct eye contact, interrupting, and following another's words too closely are considered rude and disrespectful, which means that conversations may contain long pauses. Native Americans are very comfortable with silences (Shade et al., 1997; Williams, 1994).

Children of this culture care for themselves at an early age and exercise a great deal of autonomy, usually deciding what they want to do without asking for adult permission. As Chud and Fahlman point out (1985), a child who's used to this much freedom of choice and action may find the activities and routines of a school or child-care environment very limiting.

Asian Pacific culture

Asian Pacific Americans come from a number of different countries and cultures—among them Pacific Island, Chinese, Japanese, Korean, Vietnamese, and Hmong. Again, they share certain values, which often stem from their common Confucian heritage (Chao, 1994; Ho, 1994).

A Mother Speaks

In *To Teach* (1993), Ayers published the following letter from a Native American mother. The author is unknown, but the letter has been widely circulated among teachers.

Before you take charge of the classroom that contains my child, please ask yourself why you are going to teach Indian children. What are your expectations? What are the stereotypes and untested assumptions that you bring with you into the classroom?

...My child has a culture, probably older than yours; he has meaningful values and a rich and varied experiential background. However strange or incomprehensible it may seem to you, you have no right to do or say anything that implies to him that it is less than satisfactory....

Like most Indian children his age, he is competent. He can dress himself, prepare a meal for himself, clean up afterwards, care for a younger child. He knows his Reserve, all of which is his home, like the back of his hand.

He is not accustomed to having to ask permission to do the ordinary things that are part of normal living. He is seldom forbidden to do anything; more usually the consequences of an action are explained to him, and he is allowed to decide for himself whether or not to act. His entire existence ... has been an experiential learning situation, arranged to provide him with the opportunity to develop his skills and confidence in his own capacities. Didactic teaching will be an alien experience for him....

He has been taught, by precept, that courtesy is an essential part of human conduct and rudeness is any action that makes another person feel stupid or foolish. Do not mistake his patient courtesy for indifference or passivity.

...You will be well advised to remember that our children are skilful interpreters of the silent language. They will know your feelings and attitudes with unerring precision, no matter how carefully you arrange your smile or modulate your voice....

Will [my child] learn that his sense of his own value and dignity is valid, or will he learn that he must forever be apologetic and "trying harder" because he isn't white? Can you help him to acquire the intellectual skills he needs without ... imposing your values on top of those he already has?

Respect my child. He is a person. He has a right to be himself. (pp. 40–41)

The Asian Pacific cultures are highly interdependent. Family is central, and individuals garner self-esteem by contributing to the success and happiness of the group (Kim and Choi, 1994). Parents are prepared to make great personal sacrifices for their children, whom they see as extensions of themselves, and they expect loyalty, respect, and obedience in return (Chan, 1998).

Because an individual's behavior and achievement reflect on the honor of the family and its ancestors, parents of Asian Pacific descent emphasize good conduct, even in play. They are careful to model appropriate behavior, instill an ethic of hard work, help children to succeed in school, and teach empathy and concern for others—qualities that ultimately control social behavior (Chao, 1994). Such parenting may be strict, but it clearly indicates warmth and caring (Chao; Lebra, 1994).

It also promotes social harmony, another key value. In the Asian Pacific culture, communication is indirect—it is essential to attend to the needs of others, to pay them proper respect, and to avoid direct confrontation and criticism (Chan, 1998; Greenfield and Suzuki, 1998). A person does not express his or her own needs; others are expected to use empathy and read body language and other signs to anticipate them (Greenfield and Suzuki, 1998). (A child who uses her body, not her words, to let you know that she needs to go to the bathroom may be extremely frustrated, and wet, if you don't read her signals correctly.) It is also important to be modest, polite, and self-restrained rather than assertive—qualities that people from an individualistic culture may mistake for lack of interest or drive (Greenfield and Suzuki, 1998).

The Asian Pacific culture has great respect for teachers, who are considered authorities. A child who asks questions is challenging their competence or admitting her own failure to understand, so she may remain silent. This behavior is also easily misunderstood.

Middle Eastern American culture

The Middle Eastern American community has its roots not only in the areas in Asia and Africa (that Americans usually consider the Middle East) but also in neighboring countries such as Afghanistan and Pakistan that share their religions, languages, and values (Sharifzadeh, 1998). Like the places they or their ancestors come from, Middle Eastern Americans are an enormously diverse group. They can be Christian, Muslim, or Druze, rural or urban, affluent or poor, nineteenth-century settlers or brand-new immigrants. Most are born in the United States and are well educated (Adeed and Smith, 1997) and even newcomers speak English, but they may also speak Arabic, Farsi, Turkish, or other languages (Sharifzadeh, 1998).

Middle Eastern Americans have an interdependent culture, where the group takes precedence over the individual and the family is paramount. An individual's identity comes from her family's name, honor, reputation, and achievements more than from her own, but at the same time she represents the family in everything she does (Ajrouch, 1999). Family members take responsibility for one another and provide each other with guidance, support, and a social life (Sharifzadeh, 1998).

Children are extremely important in the Middle Eastern culture, and everyone fusses over them. Although child rearing is changing among the new generation of parents, children still may not have quite the self-help skills of European American children because in their culture there is less rush for them to learn to eat, dress, sleep, bathe, or use the toilet by themselves. On the contrary, in some Middle Eastern parents' eyes, such independence may indicate a failure of parental love and duty (Sharifzadeh, 1998). To spend as much time as possible with their parents, children may stay up late and as a result may arrive tired at child care or school. Until the age of 3, they follow few rules or routines. Then they learn to respect and obey their parents more by observing others than by asking questions or listening to explanations (Sharifzadeh, 1998)—although this, too, is changing (A. Al Futaisi, personal communication, January 19, 2002). All members of the extended family help with discipline, but if they aren't around, the children may easily get out of control (Sharifzadeh, 1998). Fathers may take more direct responsibility for discipline after the children are 4 or 5 years old (Sharifzadeh, 1998), and boys in particular may have trouble listening to women—such as their teachers—in positions of authority (Adeed and Smith, 1997). Education is highly valued and children of both genders are expected to do well at school (Sharifzadeh, 1998).

In this high-context Middle Eastern culture, harmony is important, communication is indirect, and it's essential to pay attention to nonverbal cues. When there's a problem with a child's behavior, be careful to share concerns so that no one loses face (Adeed and Smith, 1997; Schwartz, 1999). In *Developing Cross-Cultural Competence* (1998), Virginia-Shirin Sharifzadeh points out that it's impolite to say "no" and hurt another's feelings, so a person may say "maybe" or "yes" weakly instead. It is up to the listener to infer that the speaker means "no." Likewise, the listener must understand that "thank you" or "don't trouble yourself" means "yes."

People of the Middle Eastern American culture are comfortable standing and sitting close to one another, and it's useful to remember that this close personal space isn't meant to intimidate. Talk about it with the children so that everyone is aware of it and can respond appropriately. There is also lots of holding hands and hugging among close friends of the same sex (Adeed and Smith, 1997). A child or adult sitting silently in the midst of a crowd probably isn't daydreaming or being rude; instead, she's taking a moment of privacy (Sharifzadeh, 1998). According to Patty Adeed and G. Pritchy Smith (1997), the spoken English of native Arabic speakers may sometimes seem loud, rude, or hostile to ears raised on European American English, but this is nothing personal. Rather, it has to do with the intonations inherent in the Arabic language itself.

The Middle Eastern cultures and religions are patriarchal and patrilineal, and gender roles are sharply defined. Men have power and status. They earn and control the money, deal with the outside world, make decisions, and act as the moral and disciplinary authority within the family (Abu-Laban and Abu-Laban, 1999; Sharifzadeh, 1998). Women, the guardians of the culture (Seikaly, 1999), are in charge of child bearing, child rearing, and homemaking, and girls start to learn these roles very early. To preserve their modesty, Muslim girls and women wear clothing that covers their heads and/or faces, though different mosques have different rules ("Arab Americans: Overview," 2001; Cohn and Cohen, 2001). Because modesty is so crucial, girls are protected and well supervised at home, especially in extremely religious families. Even in less devout families, parents may start warning girls not to have physical contact with boys starting at about the age of 7 or 8 (A. Al Futaisi, personal communication, January 19,

A Muslim Way

> In a focus group of immigrant Muslim Lebanese parents in Michigan, one father said of his daughter, "She knows she's a Muslim. . . . If anybody wants to meet her, and this when she was five or six years old, it was whispered in her ears, you do not ever talk to boys . . . never [let] a boy put his hand on your shoulder, never, except me—I'm the only one. Your uncle wouldn't kiss you. I'm the only one who can kiss you on . . . the forehead, and this was brought up with her as a Muslim way" (Ajrouch, 1999, p. 136).

2002). It's important to make every effort to be sensitive to their needs and to keep them with other girls as much as possible. It's especially important, even with younger children, to permit them to go to the bathroom in single-sex groups. At home they may learn to remove their shoes, socks, and pants before using the toilet (A. Al Futaisi, personal communication, January 19, 2002), and you need to allow for the extra time this may take.

As women join the workforce, these cultural divisions and attitudes begin to break down, and even though parents may not want to discuss their personal lives with a teacher (Schwartz, 1999), both will probably want to take part in any discussion of a problem with their child. However, it is possible that men in very traditional Muslim families, who consider it their responsibility to represent and protect their families outside the home, may not allow their wives to talk to strangers, and if they're acting as interpreters, they may say or report only what they deem appropriate (Sharifzadeh, 1998). In this case, Sharifzadeh suggests communicating via a trusted friend or relative instead of talking directly with the mother, who is a child's primary caregiver. But, she warns, "never discount the father or his role" (1998, p. 467). If you're using an interpreter, be sure to choose a man to talk with a man and a woman to talk with a woman.

Muslims do not eat pork in any form, and during Ramadan—the most important Muslim holiday—those who are fasting from sunrise to sunset may be tired and irritable. Children don't usually fast for the whole month until they're 13 or 14 years old, but they may fast at home for short periods during the day from about the age of 7.

Why all this matters

Good teachers do not succeed by accident. Good teaching is intentional—deliberately choosing what you want to do, based on your understanding of yourself, the child, the family, the culture, and your ability to design and implement a program that reflects and respects the values of all the learners in your group.

Whether you're teaching in child care or grade 2, what's important is trying to ensure that what you're doing in the classroom meshes well with the lives of the children you're teaching. To create meaningful learning experiences, you must know about both yourself and the children. When you have a basic understanding of who you are and how others perceive you as an individual and as a teacher, you're able to make better decisions when a problem arises. A knowledgeable and thoughtful choice is bound to be much more effective than an impulsive or automatic one.

All too often, unexamined attitudes and assumptions influence the way teachers interact with children. When we understand ourselves and our students, we have a far better chance of seeing children clearly, establishing warm and trusting relationships with them, maintaining self-control, and identifying alternate solutions to problems. Then it becomes possible to see that a child's challenging behavior is her attempt to communicate—and an opportunity for us to teach her a new skill.

A teacher's ability to put an effective strategy into place also depends on having those strategies within reach. The following chapters will introduce you to some of those strategies.

What Do You Think?

1. What traditional rituals and ceremonies does your family celebrate? What is their meaning? Think about the sayings and aphorisms that family members use. They sometimes reveal cultural values with very little disguise.

2. The box called "Digging In" on page 87 contains some questions that you might like to discuss.

3. People who belong to the same culture or ethnic group often like to be together. Why do you think this might be? Have you ever tried explaining your family's culture to someone else? How did it feel to you?

4. Were you brought up in a low-context or high-context culture? How has this affected your attitudes and your interactions with family, teachers, and peers?

Selected Reading

Fadiman, A. (1998). *The spirit catches you and you fall down*. New York: Farrar Straus & Giroux.

Gonzalez-Mena, J. (2000). *Multicultural issues in child care* (3rd ed.). Mountain View, CA: Mayfield.

Lynch, E., & Hanson, M. J. (Eds.). (1998). *Developing cross-cultural competence: A guide for working with children and their families* (2nd ed.). Baltimore, MD: Paul H. Brookes.

Tatum, B. D. (1999). *"Why are all the black kids sitting together in the cafeteria?" and other conversations about race*. New York: Basic Books.

York, S. (1991). *Roots and wings: Affirming culture in early childhood programs*. St. Paul, MN: Redleaf Press.

References

Abu-Laban, S. M., & Abu-Laban, B. (1999). Teens between: The public and private spheres of Arab-Canadian adolescents. In M. W. Suleiman (Ed.), *Arabs in America: Building a new future* (pp. 113–128). Philadelphia: Temple University Press.

Adeed, P., & Smith, G. P. (1997). Arab Americans: Concepts and materials. In J. A. Banks (Ed.), *Teaching strategies for ethnic studies* (6th ed., pp. 489–510). Boston: Allyn and Bacon.

Ajrouch, K. (1999). Family and ethnic identity in an Arab-American community. In M. W. Suleiman (Ed.), *Arabs in America: Building a new future* (pp. 129–139). Philadelphia: Temple University Press.

Anderson, E. (1997). Violence and the inner-city street code. In J. McCord (Ed.), *Violence and childhood in the inner city*. New York: Cambridge University Press.

Anderson, E. (1998). *Code of the street: Decency, violence, and the moral life of the inner city*. New York: W. W. Norton.

Arab Americans: Overview: 100 questions and answers about Arab Americans. (2001). Detroit: Detroit Free Press. Retrieved December 28, 2001, from http://www.freep.com/jobspage/arabs/arab1.html.

Ayers, W. (1993). *To teach: The journey of a teacher*. New York: Teachers College Press.

Beach Center on Disability. (2002). *How to deliver services to Native American families who have children with disabilities* (fact sheet). Retrieved January 22, 2002, from http://www.beachcenter.org.

Bernhard, J. K., Lefebvre, M. L., Chud, G., & Lange, R. (1995). *Paths to equity: Cultural, linguistic and racial diversity in Canadian early childhood education*. North York, Ontario: York Lanes Press.

Bernhard, J. K., Lefebvre, M. L., Kilbride, K. M., Chud, G., & Lange, R. (1999). Troubled relationships in early childhood education: Parent-teacher interactions in ethnoculturally diverse child care settings. In *Research connections Canada 1: Supporting children and families* (pp. 129–157). Ottawa, Ontario: Canadian Child Care Federation.

Bowden, F. (1997). *Supported child care: Enhancing accessibility*. Victoria: British Columbia Ministry for Children and Families and Human Resources Development Canada.

Bredekamp, S. (1986, 1987). *Developmentally appropriate practice in early childhood programs serving children from birth through age 8*. Washington, DC: National Association for the Education of Young Children.

Bronfenbrenner, U. (1979). *The ecology of human development: Experiments by nature and design*. Cambridge, MA: Harvard University Press.

Chan, S. (1998). Families with Asian roots. In E. W. Lynch & M. J. Hanson (Eds.), *Developing cross-cultural competence: A guide for working with children and their families* (pp. 251–344). Baltimore: Paul H. Brookes.

Chao, R. K. (1994). Beyond parental control and authoritarian parenting style: Understanding Chinese parenting through the cultural notion of training. *Child Development, 65*, 1111–1119.

Chud, G., & Fahlman, R. (1985). *Early childhood education for a multicultural society*. Vancouver: Faculty of Education, University of British Columbia.

Chud, G., & Fahlman, R. (1995). *Honouring diversity within child care and early education: An instructors guide*. Victoria: British Columbia Ministry of Skills, Training, and Labour and the Centre for Curriculum and Professional Development.

Cohn, D'V., & Cohen, S. (2001, November 20). Statistics portray settled, affluent Mideast community. *The Washington Post*. Retrieved January 2, 2002, from http://www.aaiusa.org/ newsandviews/worthreading/ 112001washpost.html.

Deater-Deckard, K., Bates, J. E., Dodge, K. A., & Pettit, G. S. (1996). Physical discipline among African American and European American mothers: Links to children's externalizing behaviors. *Developmental Psychology, 32*, 1065–1072.

Delgado-Gaitan, C. (1994). Socializing young children in Mexican-American families: An intergenerational perspective. In P. M. Greenfield & R. R. Cocking (Eds.), *Cross-cultural roots of minority child development* (pp. 55–86). Hillsdale, NJ: Erlbaum.

Denby, R., & Alford, K. (1996). Understanding African American discipline styles: Suggestions for effective social work intervention. *Journal of Multicultural Social Work, 4*, 81–98.

Derman-Sparks, L., & the A.B.C. Task Force. (1989). *Anti-bias curriculum: Tools for empowering young children*. Washington, DC: National Association for the Education of Young Children.

Endsley, R. C., Minish, P. A., and Zhou, Q. (1993). Parent involvement and quality day care in proprietary centers. *Journal of Research in Childhood Education, 7*, 53–61.

Freire, M., & Bernhard, J. K. (1997). Caring for and teaching children who speak other languages. In K. M. Kilbride (Ed.), *Include me too! Human diversity in early childhood* (pp. 160–176). Toronto, Ontario: Harcourt Brace & Company Canada.

Galinsky, E., & Weissbourd, B. (1992). Family-centered child care. In B. Spodek & O. Saracho (Eds.), *Issues in child care: Yearbook in early childhood education, Vol. 3* (pp. 47–65). New York: Teachers College Press.

García Coll, C., & Magnuson, K. (2000). Cultural differences as sources of developmental vulnerabilities and resources. In J. P. Shonkoff & S. J. Meisels (Eds.), *Handbook of early childhood intervention* (2nd ed., pp. 94–114). New York: Cambridge University Press.

Gonzalez-Mena, J. (1997). *Multicultural issues in child care*. Mountain View, CA: Mayfield.

Gonzalez-Mena, J. (2002). *The child in the family and the community* (3rd ed.). Upper Saddle River, NJ: Merrill Prentice-Hall.

Gonzalez-Mena, J., & Bernhard, J. K. (1998). Out-of-home care of infants and toddlers: A call for cultural linguistic continuity. *Interaction, 12*, 14–15.

Gorter-Reu, M. S., & Anderson, J. M. (1998). Home kits, home visits, and more! *Young Children, 53*, 71–74.

Greenfield, P. M., & Suzuki, L. K. (1998). Culture and human development: Implications for parenting, education, pediatrics, and mental health. In I. E. Sigel & K. A. Renninger (Eds.), *Handbook of child psychology: Vol. 4, Child psychology in practice* (5th ed., pp. 1059–1109). New York: Wiley.

Hale, J. E. (1986). *Black children: Their roots, culture, and learning styles*. Baltimore: Johns Hopkins Press.

Hall, E. T. (1977). *Beyond culture*. Garden City, NY: Anchor Press/Doubleday.

Ho, D. Y. F. (1994). Cognitive socialization in Confucian heritage cultures. In P. M. Greenfield & R. R. Cocking (Eds.), *Cross-cultural roots of minority child development* (pp. 285–314). Hillsdale, NJ: Erlbaum.

Hogan, E. L. (1991). *The importance of the mother-provider relationship in family child care homes*. Paper presented at the Midwest Regional Conference of the Association for the Education of Young Children, Des Moines, IA. (ERIC Document Reproduction Service No. ED340470).

Hoover-Dempsey, K. V., & Sandler, H. M. (1997). Why do parents become involved in their children's education? *Review of Educational Research, 67*, 3–42.

Kağıtçıbaşı, C. (1996). *Family and human development across cultures: A view from the other side.* Mahwah, NJ: Erlbaum.

Kim, U., & Choi, S.-H. (1994). Individualism, collectivism, and child development: A Korean perspective. In P. M. Greenfield & R. R. Cocking (Eds.), *Cross-cultural roots of minority child development* (pp. 227–258). Hillsdale, NJ: Erlbaum.

Kochman, T. (1987). The ethnic component in Black language and culture. In J. S. Phinney & M. J. Rotheram (Eds.), *Children's ethnic socialization: Pluralism and development* (pp. 219–238). Newbury Park, CA: Sage.

Kontos, S., & Wells, W. (1986). Attitudes of caregivers and the day care experiences of families. *Early Childhood Research Quarterly, 1*, 47–67.

Kuhn, M. (2001). Quality child care and partnerships with parents. *Research Connections Canada 6.* Ottawa, Ontario: Canadian Child Care Federation.

Kupersmidt, J. B., Griesler, P. C., DeRosier, M. E., Patterson, C. J., & Davis, P. W. (1995). Childhood aggression and peer relations in the context of family and neighborhood factors. *Child Development, 66*, 360–375.

LaGrange, A., Clark, D., & Munroe, E. (1994). *Culturally sensitive child care: The Alberta study.* Edmonton: Alberta Association for Young Children and Government of Alberta Citizenship and Heritage Secretariat.

Landy, S., & Peters, R. DeV. (1991). Understanding and treating the hyperaggressive toddler. *Zero to Three, 11*, 22–31.

Larner, M. (1994). *Parent perspectives on child care quality.* New Haven, CT: Quality 2000.

Lebra, T. S. (1994). Mother and child in Japanese socialization: A Japan-U.S. comparison. In P. M. Greenfield & R. R. Cocking (Eds.), *Cross-cultural roots of minority child development* (pp. 259–274). Hillsdale, NJ: Erlbaum.

Lubeck, S. (1994). The politics of developmentally appropriate practice: Exploring issues of culture, class, and curriculum. In B. L. Mallory & R. S. New (Eds.), *Diversity and developmentally appropriate practice: Challenges for early childhood education* (pp. 17–43). New York: Teachers College Press.

Lynch, E. W. (1998). Conceptual framework: From culture shock to cultural learning. In E. W. Lynch & M. J. Hanson (Eds.), *Developing cross-cultural competence: A guide for working with children and their families* (pp. 23–45). Baltimore: Paul H. Brookes.

Lynch, E. W. (1998). Developing cross-cultural competence. In E. W. Lynch & M. J. Hanson (Eds.), *Developing cross-cultural competence: A guide for working with children and their families* (pp. 47–86). Baltimore: Paul H. Brookes.

New, R. S. (1994). Culture, child development, and developmentally appropriate practice: Teachers as collaborative researchers. In B. L. Mallory & R. S. New (Eds.), *Diversity and developmentally appropriate practice: Challenges for early childhood education* (pp. 65–83). New York: Teachers College Press.

Ogbu, J. U. (1994). From cultural differences to differences in cultural frame of reference. In P. M. Greenfield & R. R. Cocking (Eds.), *Cross-cultural roots of minority child development* (pp. 365–395). Hillsdale, NJ: Erlbaum.

Peters, M. F. (1988). Parenting in Black families with young children: A historical perspective. In H. Pipes McAdoo (Ed.), *Black families* (2nd ed., pp. 228–241). Newbury Park, CA: Sage.

Phillips, C. B. (1988). Nurturing diversity for today's children and tomorrow's leaders. *Young Children, 43*, 42–47.

Powell, D. R. (1989). *Families and early childhood programs.* Washington, DC: National Association for the Education of Young Children.

Powell, D. R. (1998). Reweaving parents into the fabric of early childhood programs. *Young Children, 53*, 60–66.

Rotheram, M. J., & Phinney, J. S. (1987). Ethnic behavior patterns as an aspect of identity. In J. S. Phinney & M. J. Rotheram (Eds.). *Children's ethnic socialization: Pluralism and development* (pp. 201–218). Newbury Park, CA: Sage.

Schwartz, W. (1999, March). *Arab American students in public schools.* New York: ERIC Clearinghouse on Urban Education Digest, No. 142. (EDO-UD-99-2)

Seikaly, M. (1999). Attachment and identity: The Palestinian community of Detroit. In M. W. Suleiman (Ed.), *Arabs in America: Building a new future* (pp. 25–38). Philadelphia: Temple University Press.

Shade, B. J., Kelly, C., & Oberg, M. (1997). *Creating culturally responsive classrooms.* Washington, DC: American Psychological Association.

Sharifzadeh, V.-S. (1998). Families with Middle Eastern roots. In E. W. Lynch & M. J. Hanson (Eds.), *Developing cross-cultural competence: A guide for working with children and their families* (pp. 441–482). Baltimore: Paul H. Brookes.

Smith, A. B., & Hubbard, P. M. (1988). The relationship between parent/staff communication and children's behavior in early childhood settings. *Early Child Development and Care, 35,* 13–28.

Suina, J. H., & Smolkin, L. B. (1994). From natal culture to school culture to dominant society culture: Supporting transitions for Pueblo Indians. In P. M. Greenfield & R. R. Cocking (Eds.), *Cross-cultural roots of minority child development* (pp. 115–131). Hillsdale, NJ: Erlbaum.

Tatum, B. D. (1997). *"Why are all the Black kids sitting together in the cafeteria?" and other conversations about race.* New York: Basic Books.

Tharp, R. G. (1994). Intergroup differences among Native Americans in socialization and child cognition: An ethnogenetic analysis. In P. M. Greenfield & R. R. Cocking (Eds.), *Cross-cultural roots of minority child development* (pp. 87–106). Hillsdale, NJ: Erlbaum.

U.S. Census Bureau. (2001, August). *United States Census 2000—Rankings, comparisons, summaries.* Retrieved January 22, 2002, from http://www.census.gov/main/www/cen2000.html.

Williams, L. R. (1994). Developmentally appropriate practice and cultural values: A case in point. In B. L. Mallory & R. S. New (Eds.), *Diversity and developmentally appropriate practice: Challenges for early childhood education* (pp. 155–165). New York: Teachers College Press.

York, S. (1991). *Roots & wings: Affirming culture in early childhood programs.* St. Paul, MN: Redleaf.

Zuniga, M. E. (1998). Families with Latino roots. In E. W. Lynch & M. J. Hanson (Eds.), *Developing cross-cultural competence: A guide for working with children and their families* (pp. 209–250). Baltimore: Paul H. Brookes.

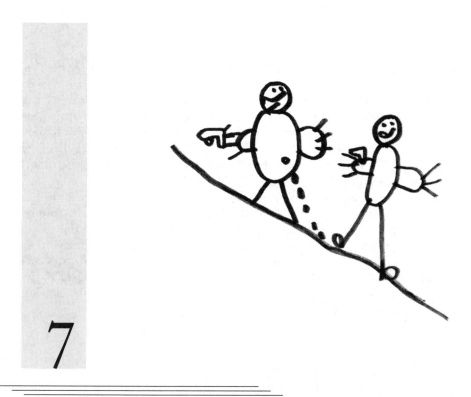

7

Preventing Challenging Behavior with the Right Physical Space and Program

Challenging behavior is troubling and puzzling, and people who work with young children naturally want to know how to respond to it. What do you do when Andrew throws a bucket of Legos across the room? What do you do when Jessica kicks you in the stomach? We will deal with these difficult questions in later chapters. But first consider this: Wouldn't it be wonderful if you never needed that information? Wouldn't you prefer it if challenging behavior never entered your classroom door?

This is a fantasy, of course. It is probably impossible to eliminate challenging behavior entirely. But it isn't a fantasy that a lot of challenging behavior can be prevented. Prevention isn't a particularly exciting topic, because it often involves small things, such as making transitions fun or controlling the number of children in a play space, and it works quietly, without flash or drama. But it can be enormously effective, and for that reason it's very important.

Prevention is also important because it can stop a child from accumulating risk factors. If he continues to behave aggressively, he can all too easily start on a downward spiral that makes him more likely to be rejected by his peers and teachers, fail at school, join a gang, abuse alcohol or drugs, or become delinquent. Preventing challenging behavior when a child is young can head off the development of more serious behaviors later (Guerra, 1997a; Kazdin, 1994; Pepler and Slaby, 1994).

The more teachers help children refrain from their challenging behavior, the less they're learning to use it—and the less likely it is to embed itself in their brains (Shore, 1997). Many children use the same challenging behavior for years because they don't know any other way to behave, and that behavior becomes firmly entrenched. If you can anticipate when and where the child will have trouble, prevent the situation from occurring, and remind him of what to do instead of waiting for him to make a mistake, you can build a new pattern: The child begins to reap the rewards of appropriate behavior, feels good about himself, and yearns to have that feeling again.

How does prevention work?

Prevention is a way to guide and control behavior. Because it increases a child's chances of success and doesn't tear him down, it helps to build self-esteem, competence, and resilience (Kazdin, 1995). Research shows that prevention is more likely to be effective when

- It starts early (Becker, Barham, Eron, and Chen, 1994; Reiss and Roth, 1993).

- It continues over a long period of time (Kazdin, 1987, 1994; Reiss and Roth, 1993).

- It is developmentally appropriate (Gagnon, 1991).

- It works on several fronts at the same time—for example, with parents as well as at school (Reiss and Roth, 1993).

- It takes place in a real-life setting instead of a psychologist's office or a special program (Guerra, 1997b). This last point is critical because it's hard for young children to use a new skill outside of the context where they learn it (Mize and Ladd, 1990).

Weighing In

In 1999, the Division for Early Childhood of the Council for Exceptional Children released a concept paper on challenging behavior. Among other things, it said, "Prevention is the best form of intervention. It is time- and cost-effective, and appears to be a major avenue by which to eliminate, not merely reduce, the incidence of challenging behavior" (p. 64).

As the old saying goes, an ounce of prevention is worth a pound of cure.

Prevention Places

Child care and the primary grades are excellent settings for preventing challenging behavior because

- The child is very young when he arrives.

- The teachers spend many hours a day with the child over months or even years.

- The teachers know the child well and have a warm and trusting relationship with him.

- The teachers can intervene consistently and systematically.

- The environment is safe and stable.

- The environment is a real-life setting.

- There are plenty of opportunities to work with and support the child's family.

Meeting children's needs

Children feel competent and are able to succeed when the environment meets their physical, cognitive, emotional, and social needs. Then they are less likely to resort to challenging behavior. If you can meet a child's needs before challenging behavior becomes necessary, you will enhance his self-esteem and allow him to begin to think of himself as a person who is capable of success. This is one of the basic ideas behind prevention, and it means that every aspect of the environment—the physical space, the program, the social context, and the teacher's teaching style—must take each child's needs into account.

Of course, you can't really figure out what an individual child requires until you get to know him. But you don't have to wait until then—research can help out in the meantime. It identifies many of the factors in the environment that encourage and discourage challenging behavior. The strategies that we will present here are based on that research, and they can help all children, not just those with challenging behavior.

We're all the same, yet we're all different

When you come to know the children better, you may find that some of the things you've planned don't work very well. If that happens, it's important to change them. You may even need to change things for just one child. When you enable that child to play successfully, it becomes possible for all the children to play successfully.

This idea of flexibility—rearranging the room, canceling or altering activities, changing your own management style to suit the needs of one child—shocks many teachers. They tend to think it's unfair. Some say that the child needs to learn to get along in the real world. Others think that they're giving one child more than they're

Glory in the Flower

Sixteen 4-year-olds were running to the oak tree at the far end of the field with one teacher at the front and the other at the rear. Everyone but Michael, that is. He ran off to the right. Instead of yelling at him to join the others, the second teacher followed him. When she reached him, he was smelling some small purple flowers. The snow had finally melted, and spring was just beginning. He had caught a glimpse of purple and wanted to investigate.

The teacher called the other children to see what Michael had found. Everyone started to talk about the flowers, their color, and spring. They decided to continue their outing looking for signs of spring. The other children asked for Michael's help, and he had a great time playing outside.

Had the teacher insisted he join the others without showing any interest in his find, his self-esteem would have been bruised, and he would have been frustrated. To get the acknowledgment he needed, he probably would have behaved inappropriately. Instead, seeing things from his perspective turned events around. Not only had this become a wonderful spontaneous science lesson, but the other children all thought that Michael was pretty smart, and he ended up feeling very proud of himself.

giving the others if they always become his partner during transitions or let him wash the tables while everyone else is listening to a story.

Lilian G. Katz, a guru of American child care, responds to this argument by turning it on its head. "Because children's needs, feelings, dispositions, and behavior vary, it would be unfair to treat them all alike," she and Diane E. McClellan write in *Fostering Children's Social Competence* (1997, p. 73). Some children need more individualized support than others in order to learn, and it's only fair to give them the chance. Fair is when every child has the opportunity to participate, learn, and flourish.

It's easy to confuse being fair with being consistent. The same rules apply to all the children, so any child who hurts another will learn that he is breaking a rule. But every child has different needs, and every child deserves the treatment that is appropriate for him, which means that you may respond one way to Andrew and another to Jessica. It's a good idea to give Jessica a head start when the class is getting ready to go outside, because she likes to do everything herself, and it takes her a bit longer. But it's better for Andrew to sit beside you in his cubby space so you can remind him about what comes next. Neither child is getting anything extra; they're just getting what they need. That is fair—both for them and for the other children.

If a child with challenging behavior can't function, he will keep other children from functioning by frightening them, destroying their work, grabbing their toys, or hitting or kicking them. In addition, he will take you away from them, monopolizing your time and depleting your resources, and prevent you from teaching anyone. If you can meet his needs before this happens, you will have more time and energy to give to all of the children, and the classroom can become a place that's pleasant, relaxed, and conducive to learning.

The children usually understand all of this very well. They know that Jessica takes longer to dress, so they don't mind if she starts before they do. They know that Andrew loses control when he's frustrated, so they don't mind if you sit beside him. If they don't understand, it's easy to explain. Ross W. Greene, author of *The Explosive Child* (1998), puts it this way: "Everyone in our classroom gets what he or she needs. If someone needs help with something, we all try to help him or her. And everyone in our class needs help with something" (p. 283).

Greene goes further. He suggests that when everyone gets what he or she needs, no one is stigmatized, and the children learn to help one another. They recognize each other's strengths and weaknesses, and they are quick to encourage and reinforce their classmates' positive efforts. Their support can make a real difference. They become part of the solution instead of part of the problem.

The Physical Space

"Space speaks to each of us," Jim Greenman writes in *Caring Spaces, Learning Places* (1988, p. 16). Every environment has a message. Think of a library or a hockey rink—each lets you know exactly what behavior is expected. So does a classroom. Creating an environment that fosters appropriate, prosocial behavior—cooperation, helping, sharing, negotiation, friendly interaction, consideration of others—requires just as much careful and conscious planning as any other part of a teacher's job. Such forethought goes a long way toward preventing challenging behavior (Katz and McClellan, 1997).

Depending on how it's arranged, the physical environment can elicit either aggressive or prosocial behavior. It is certainly much easier to change a space than it is to change behavior—but paradoxically, changing the environment frequently *can* change behavior (Katz and McClellan, 1997). Children with challenging behaviors often feel fenced in and restricted, and they will probably have trouble functioning in a physical space that's filled with rules, restrictions, and directions. Of course, all children need some limits, and we will talk more about that later. But too many imposed limits may actually make matters worse (Kritchevsky and Prescott, 1977). At a certain point,

Parental Guidance

Families sometimes have trouble understanding why teachers are treating children differently.

One center explained its philosophy of accommodating individual needs in its literature for parents. Some children have special needs, such as a disability, the literature said, but all children have unique needs, and the center believes in accommodating them. At times, parents may see a child receiving some special attention that their child doesn't get. But they can rest assured that their child's unique needs will also be addressed. This policy, says one teacher, "has made a huge difference with several children we used to describe as challenging" (Andersen, 2001a).

most children will stop listening, which is dangerous in an emergency. It is therefore a good idea to set up your room so that all the children can move about in it without reminders. Put toys, games, and puzzles within reach so that children don't have to climb on chairs or shelves to get them. Place art activities near the sink so that children don't have to walk across the room carrying containers of water or paint-laden brushes. If you can eliminate potential hazards, the children will feel safe and secure, and you won't have to clutter their world with warnings and admonitions.

Wide open spaces

As you make decisions about how to arrange your classroom, think about the empty space as well as what's in it. One study found that large numbers of children need lots of empty space. "No less than one-third to no more than one-half uncovered surface is appropriate to good organization," according to researchers Sybil Kritchevsky and Elizabeth Prescott, who examined the relationship between space and behavior (1977, p. 19).

But too much open space inspires running, chasing, and chaos. Use low bookcases to divide large spaces into uncluttered, well-organized areas with different functions, such as dramatic play, quiet reading and listening, or messy play. If you mark the boundaries clearly and lay out well-defined pathways from one area to another by putting masking tape on the floor, the children will feel more comfortable and their behavior will be more cooperative and less disruptive. Include at least two entrances to each area so that the children inside will welcome newcomers more readily (Ramsey, 1980).

Think carefully about where to locate each activity and learning center. For example, if the blocks are next to a high-traffic area, sooner or later someone will knock over a construction masterpiece, causing anger and frustration. Although it's hard to create a quiet corner in a noisy room, it's important to have one. Soft pillows and a couch nestled far away from noisy areas can help some children shut out the rest of the world. But this won't work for everyone. The most distractible and easily stimulated children, who really need a quiet escape from time to time, may unconsciously use challenging behavior just to enjoy some peace in the director's office.

One solution is to think about quiet times as well as quiet places. All the children can benefit from listening to the sound of silence. You don't have to schedule these moments; if you watch the children carefully, you'll know when they're in order. When Andrew is getting too excited, that's a good time to say, "Okay, everyone, stop everything, lie down on your back, and look at the ceiling. Think about how you're breathing." Ask them to think about their toes and each individual body part in turn. By the time you've reached the tops of their heads, the atmosphere will be completely altered.

What will go inside each area?

As the great American architect Louis Sullivan once said, "Form follows function." Again, set up your furniture, equipment, and materials to facilitate the behavior you're trying to nurture. The dramatic play area tops the list for spurring complex social interaction, followed by games, woodworking, sand, and manipulatives (Quay, Weaver, and Neel, 1986). Because there is more interaction in these areas, there is also more opportunity for aggression, so it's important to supervise closely. The likely result is more friendships and better social and negotiating skills. Create spaces that can accommodate these small group activities comfortably, and arrange the furniture and materials to encourage children to play together. For example, if the sand table is accessible on all four sides, two, even four, children can have their own space yet share the sand toys. As they get better at sharing, they can work on the same side of the table and eventually collaborate on a project (Smith and Gay, 1997).

If you want to cultivate independence and autonomy, make sure your shelves are well organized, inviting, and easily accessible to the children. An arrangement that clearly indicates where each item belongs will make clean-up time much easier. Be sure to close or cover the shelves during circle and story time if they're surrounding or dividing the large open space you use for group activities. Otherwise they're just too tempting.

What about the people?

One of the things that makes child care or school hard for children is that they are in groups all day and have to share their space, toys, and teachers' attention with other people. The National Association for the Education of Young Children (NAEYC) periodically makes recommendations about space per child, group size, and teacher-child ratio (Bredekamp, 1998), but state regulations often don't follow them, and many children end up in smaller spaces or larger groups with less satisfactory ratios. This makes it more difficult for children who require more space or adult attention to have their needs met.

Each child needs a different amount of space, depending on his culture and temperament. Children with challenging behaviors often have a definite idea of how much personal space they should have, but at the same time, they can be totally unaware of invading someone else's territory. No matter who's invading whose space, such incursions can easily set off escalating rounds of pushing and shoving. Help Andrew to understand that Eva didn't mean to come so near and he can use his words to tell her to move back—for example, "Tell Eva, 'I don't like it when you come so close.'" Such discussions enable Andrew to become aware of his own—and others'—space requirements and will help him extend his tolerance of another person's proximity.

When they're crowded together, children accidentally bump into each other, ruin one another's work, and have lots of misunderstandings, all of which can easily lead to

Close for Comfort

Culture has an impact on the way people use space. An environment that seems comfortable, exciting, and warm to one child may appear cold and uninteresting to another.

Kritchevsky and Prescott (1977) found that Mexican American preschoolers played and socialized comfortably in a space in their center that was cramped by middle-class European American norms. Though the researchers believed the conditions were conducive to aggressive behavior, there was no hint of conflict.

frustration and aggression. It therefore makes sense to limit and control the number who can play in each area. The size of the space, the activity, the availability of materials, and the chemistry of the participating children are all part of the equation. With the children's collaboration, figure out how many can fit comfortably into an area and set up a method to regulate it. Judy Lawry and her colleagues at the University of Colorado at Denver suggest that children hang name cards on hooks placed at the entrance to each learning center. When all the hooks at a center are filled, the children know they must look for a play space with an empty hook (Lawry, Danko, and Strain, 1999).

The numbers in an area may change as you come to know the children. Initially you might have set up a space for five in the block area. After a few days, you may discover that Andrew can't function with so many children around him. When this happens, change the number of children permitted in the area so that it works for everyone—if Andrew is fine when there are four children, reduce the number permitted to four. Explain the change to the children without pointing to a particular child: "I notice that people are having more fun when there are four instead of five children in the block area. What do you say if we change the number to four and see how it goes?"

Because there are rarely enough sinks for everyone to have one of his own, the sink area always attracts a mob during hand-washing and tooth-brushing times. Merely limiting the numbers won't fix the problem; you need a system. Figure out how many

When they're crowded together, children bump into each other, ruin one another's work, and have misunderstandings, all of which can lead to aggression. It makes sense to limit and control the number who can play in each area.

Crowd Control

After lunch all eight 4-year-olds went into the bathroom at once. It was small, with two toilet cubicles and two sinks. The children who were waiting to use the toilet congregated in the narrow space between the cubicles and the sink, pushing each other, banging the cubicle doors, and sliding under them.

The children who had finished using the toilet were everywhere. Several stood on a chair at the sink brushing their teeth; others brushed in the middle of the bathroom and pushed their way to the sink to spit. Those who were done with the whole hand-washing and tooth-brushing routine hung around, pushing each other, climbing onto the sinks, and crawling under the cubicle doors.

The two teachers were fully occupied with finding each child's toothbrush, putting on the toothpaste, washing and putting away the toothbrush, and handing the child a damp washcloth to wash his face. Amid tears and warnings, the children finished and lined up to go back to their room.

A consultant suggested some simple changes to both the space and the routine.

• First the consultant proposed putting hooks on the cubicle doors to keep them open and prevent slamming.

• Since all the children could reach the sink, she suggested removing the chair.

• She recommended the group move to the bathroom in a more orderly fashion with an adult in the lead. To accomplish this, they could pretend to be a train, with one teacher the locomotive and the other the caboose.

• To keep peace inside the bathroom, she advised the teachers to place a box of books for the children to read in a predesignated station area right outside the bathroom. As each child finished his bathroom routine, he would select a book and sit down in the station's waiting room. After everyone had finished, they could all spend a few minutes reading before getting back on the train and returning to their room.

• Once the teacher had eliminated the danger of the doors and chair, one teacher could manage the bathroom alone. The other controlled the children's entrance and exit.

children can use the sink comfortably at once, then devise a way to stagger the washers while you keep the others engaged elsewhere.

Does the level of stimulation make a difference?

An active classroom is a busy, noisy place. Although most children and teachers seem immune to the hubbub, others find it hard to deal with the movement, smells, bright lights, colors, and, above all, the noise. When it's hard to hear, it's harder to focus, harder to talk quietly, and harder to settle disputes peacefully (Slaby, Roedell, Arezzo, and Hendrix, 1995). Children with attention deficit hyperactivity disorder (ADHD), fetal alcohol syndrome (FAS), alcohol-related neurodevelopmental disorder (ARND, formerly fetal alcohol effects), hearing loss, or sensitive temperaments—the ones who feel the seams in their socks—may be particularly affected, and challenging behavior is more likely. It takes a special effort to reduce the level of stimulation. Consider leaving some of the wall space blank, organizing children's artwork by color, putting away some of the toys, reducing clutter, installing a dimmer switch for the lights, turning off the music. And strive to become aware of the volume of the buzz as you move through the day.

Consider the results

The best way to evaluate the use of space in your classroom is to look at it from the child's perspective. When you're alone in the room, try getting down on your knees—you'll quickly see if it's inviting and the equipment is accessible. Is there too much visual clutter? Or does it look cold and empty? Are there obvious corridors that invite running? Are the learning centers visible, clearly defined, large enough, and welcoming? Is the artwork on the walls at the children's eye level? Is it confusing? From this angle, the world shouldn't look like a maze.

The Program

A child with challenging behavior dares you to examine your schedule and program. Once again, it's important to think not only of the skill you want to teach but also of the behavior you are trying to encourage. In general, children enjoy a varied and balanced day with quiet and active, indoor and outdoor time, small- and large-group, teacher- and child-directed activities. But the ultimate success of the program will depend on how well it reflects the interests, abilities, cultures, temperaments, and developmental levels of the children in your group.

If a task is too difficult, a child will do whatever he needs to do to avoid participating and failing. Whether it's a puzzle with 40 pieces for a child who can do only puzzles with 25 pieces, a circle activity that requires a Native American child to respond individually, or an art project that demands a lot of sitting from a very active child, the result will be frustration, and he will probably find a challenging way to escape. Instead of forcing children to fit into the program, help them to learn by designing and bending the program to meet their needs. If you provide a puzzle with the appropriate number of pieces, design a circle activity with lots of group responses and choral singing, and create an art activity that doesn't require him to sit down, the child will succeed—and challenging behavior won't be necessary.

Offering choices

Every teacher needs some structured time to introduce new skills and concepts. But research shows that programs with less structure—where children have a lot of freedom to choose and use open-ended materials and activities in their own way—engender more social interaction and prosocial behavior (Field, 1991; Huston-Stein, Friedrich-Cofer, and Susman, 1977; Slaby et al., 1995).

Since Friedrich Froebel founded the first kindergarten, European American theorists have maintained that children are empowered when they are able to make meaningful choices about the way they spend their time (Hewes, 2001). If you allow the children to decide for themselves—rather than controlling them—they don't have to look for inappropriate ways to seek power and assert their independence. You can give them the opportunity to make their own decisions by building choice into your program. One way to do this is to create a variety of learning centers where they can choose among several related activities; another is to designate times of the day when they can decide what to do. Be sure these periods are long enough—children need a lot of uninterrupted play to nourish their creativity and imagination. Having enough time also helps them to feel more satisfied and more willing to share and cooperate.

But a lack of structure allows more aggressive behavior, too (Slaby et al., 1995), so be careful not to overdo it. Carefully observe how long the children can play constructively without structure, and gradually extend the time as they learn how to cope. They'll let you know if they're bored and need more stimulation: The dramatic play area will suddenly become too small for cooperative play; the room will get noisier and

Some children need extra structure and guidance during free-play. Close monitoring will help you figure out how much help to give each child.

messier; and the children will start wandering around looking for something to do. Keep your eyes open, and be sure to end the activity and offer new options before they reach this point.

Some children need extra structure and guidance during free-play. Close monitoring will help you figure out how much help to give each child. Knowing the child is the key. Some children may have limited play skills and easily become frustrated or bored. They need help finding something suitable to do or support from you while they're learning something new. Other children feel anxious because no one is telling them what to do. It's a good idea to reduce their choices and let them know that they can ask you for help.

Still others arrive knowing exactly what and who they want to play with, and if their plans are thwarted they respond with frustration, anxiety, or even anger. Jessica expected to draw with Jenny when she came to school, but Jenny was in the dramatic play area. Jessica was lost, unable to connect with any child or activity, perhaps afraid that no one else would want to play with her. In this situation you can support Jessica by helping her to choose an activity you know she enjoys or a playmate you know she can play with successfully, going with her as she approaches, helping her to engage, and staying as long as you have to. When Jessica has your guidance, she won't need to get your attention (or Jenny's) by throwing a block across the room.

Close supervision will also help you decide how many choices to offer and what they should be. Too many choices and/or too many toys create confusion both during playtime and at clean-up—but too few create conflict. Resolving this dilemma requires careful judgment. Very young children will do better if you provide duplicates of popular toys and materials. Older children can share—within reason. You might try doubles at the beginning of the year and gradually replace them with materials that extend the use of your other toys. In the block corner, for example, you could add animals, trees, cars, trucks, and people so that the children can make a total environment.

When you're planning, don't forget that children have different needs on different days. It's a good idea to offer fewer and less challenging options on Mondays. Many children have trouble returning to school, group activities, and a completely different set of expectations after spending an unstructured weekend at home or with a father they see twice a month. They are usually back in the groove by midweek, but by the time Friday rolls around they're tired and wondering who will pick them up and what the weekend will bring. This means that you must reconsider your expectations and rearrange the program to coincide with their ability to succeed. Certain times of the year—Christmas, Halloween, flu season, to name a few—also unsettle them and require a rethinking of the program.

Choosing materials

The materials, toys, games, and books that you select also have an impact on children's behavior. As we've said, to be engaging and satisfying they must match the children's interests, abilities, cultures, temperaments, and developmental levels. If a construction toy is too difficult, for example, you may find the children making simple shapes with it—such as guns. Materials and activities that require cooperation—parachutes, tire swings, murals—are more likely to reduce aggressive behavior, whereas competitive games inspire it (Slaby et al., 1995; Sobel, 1983), as do superheroes, soldiers, games that require a lot of waiting (Slaby et al., 1995), and toys based on violent television shows (National Association for the Education of Young Children, 1990, 1994). Tactile experiences—such as play dough, sand, or water play—help the children to relax and ride over difficult patches. To increase the variety and range of toys that you can offer, trade with other teachers and visit your local garage sales, flea markets, and thrift shops (Lawry et al., 1999).

Although toys and objects from home may supplement the toy supply and ease the transition to child care or school for some children, they create a whole new set of problems. Some children appear with totally inappropriate toys (such as toy guns or swords), and others can't concentrate on activities because they're worrying about sharing or protecting their property. Conflict is all too common.

Parents also become embroiled. When they're running late in the morning, they may decline to argue with their child over an action-hero toy, and it ends up at child care or school despite the rules. It's important to negotiate the solution to this problem with the parents. One center reached this compromise: Unsuitable toys such as weapons went straight into the director's office for the day; other toys were allowed until 9:30 A.M., when they had to be placed in the children's cubbies.

On the other hand, you might want to encourage the children to bring things from home that they can share—perhaps a book that you can read to everyone or a tape of music from their own culture that the class can listen or dance to (Slaby et al., 1995).

War on Violence

In her book, *Remote Control Childhood? Combating the Hazards of Media Culture* (1998), Diane E. Levin of Wheelock College in Boston, writes:

> Many teachers . . . would like to ban media-linked war play and toys from their children's lives. This is totally understandable. But . . . banning such play often just pushes the issues underground. It does not give children a chance to work through their feelings about and experiences with media violence. It also cuts off adults from influencing how children process the violent content they see and what they learn from it. For these reasons, it is important to find safe ways to help children work through the violent content they see in the media. For young children, this usually means in their play. (p. 83)

Levin makes these suggestions:

- Encourage children to play with toys that they can use in many ways rather than play with highly realistic, media-linked toys that dictate what and how to play.

- Observe and talk to children as they engage in play with violence. This will help you to learn more about what they know and think so you are in a better position to determine if and how their play is imitative or creative. You also can gather the information you need to decide if, when, and how to intervene.

- Make give-and-take discussions about issues of play, toys, and violence a regular part of any approach you take with children. (p. 87)

Are some activities harder for children with challenging behavior?

For some children with challenging behavior, the hardest time of day is arrival. They are bringing emotional baggage from home, and there is no way to know what's inside it—whether they're angry because they had to wear their rain boots or exhausted because they stayed up too late. On top of that, you may not be available or tuned into their needs because everyone is arriving, parents want to talk to you, and someone left his lunch box on the bus. Your relationship with the parents plays an important role here. They should know that it's appropriate to inform you if their child needs some special moments with you, and you should have a way to let them know if you need their assistance in getting him settled. Probably the best solution is to talk to the parents and ask them to bring the child directly to you.

Naptime is another potential minefield. There are many children who don't need to sleep or even rest for the designated period of time. For some with specific behavioral disorders, a nap just isn't a possibility. Others who sail through the rest of the day without difficulty glow with the effort of staying awake and entertaining their classmates during nap. All of this can transform you into a dictator or turn nap into a time to dread. How you respond to these different needs depends on the group, the physical facilities, and your philosophy. The ideal solution is to arrange separate areas for sleepers, resters, and those who can play quietly. Everyone benefits if you send the most tired children to nap first.

As we've said, dramatic play, woodworking, and blocks present lots of opportunities for social interaction. But they also present more opportunities for aggression (Quay et al., 1986), so children in those areas require close supervision. This is especially true when a child with challenging behavior is part of the group because there are so many potential weapons close at hand—saws, hammers, heavy blocks, even scarves. Although you don't want to stifle the children's interactions and imagination by coming too close, it's essential to stay near enough to act quickly in case you're needed. Trust your instincts and your knowledge of the children, even if that means removing the woodworking tools and replacing them with their plastic counterparts and styrofoam or plastic "wood."

Because art is an opportunity for children to express themselves, it isn't usually considered a matter of concern for children with challenging behavior. But the fact is that children with challenging behavior often have poor fine-motor control, so they don't enjoy art activities—a situation that breeds challenging behavior. If you can create activities that they can do successfully, they will have a much better time and become more interested. Try taking away the chairs, allowing everyone to work standing up, and arranging the table so that each child has enough space and ready access to the materials. Cover the table with a large piece of paper, and select tools and materials that are easy to handle—large brushes, toothbrushes, and popsicle sticks; fabric, cotton balls, and wallpaper scraps; feathers, cellophane, magazine photos, and pieces of colored paper. If you make the project open ended rather than creating a model for the children to follow, those who have trouble won't feel they've failed. After they've worked for as long as they like, allow them to choose another activity. Books and play dough may help them to feel calm.

A day in child care or primary school doesn't feel complete without a circle and story time. The children love to sing, clap, jump, and learn new songs, and they usually hang on every word of a story. But when a child with challenging behavior enters the picture, everything begins to unravel, and it is time to reevaluate. Begin by thinking about the circle activity or the book itself. Does it go on for too long? Is it interesting and varied enough? Do the children get enough opportunities to participate actively? Does the book have too many words and not enough pictures? Are there too many unfamiliar songs in the circle? You can introduce only one new song at a time effectively, and it takes several more circle times for the children to become comfortable singing it.

If you have a child who is easily distracted, seat him facing you with his back to the door and windows. If there's a child in the group who's very restless or fidgety, consider letting everyone sit on balls or sit-and-move cushions used by occupational therapists. Kate Andersen, an educator with a special interest in temperament, suggests allowing children to select a "squishy" (a soft foam ball) to hold (Andersen, 2001b). She also advises stopping often to link what's happening in the story to the children's lives—but be careful not to disturb the flow of the story. To extend a child's ability to stay in the circle, change the content to suit his needs, reinforce his efforts to stay and take part, and allow him to leave if he asks appropriately.

When you know a child isn't ready to participate successfully in story or circle time, even with help, you can avoid disrupting the group and singling him out by allowing him to play quietly in a designated area. If your circle is fun and interesting, the

Dramatic play, woodworking, and blocks present more opportunities for social interaction—and also for aggression.

other children won't look for excuses to join him but will appreciate having an uninterrupted circle that also accommodates individual needs. You'll be surprised at how well a child can listen and learn without participating directly. This preventive approach means you probably won't have to stop reading or end the circle abruptly, punishing all the children and bestowing extra attention on the child with challenging behavior.

If you find that circle time isn't working at all—for example, if half your group can't handle it—it might be wise to eliminate it for a while. Or hold it on Wednesdays and Thursdays only, when the children are functioning at their best. What is the value of circle time if the children aren't learning or having a good time?

Show and tell has long been a staple of preschool programs, but it, too, is fraught with problems. Parents often forget the day, so some children have nothing to "show." It emphasizes material possessions, and as a result children become competitive, envious of others' things, and feel themselves wanting if they don't own a particular item. Show and tell itself tends to go on for much too long because each child must have a turn, which means children have to wait—and wait—with potentially dangerous objects in their hands. Many teachers have dropped this activity from their program.

How do you get from A to B?

Transitions are a special challenge for children with challenging behaviors. If Andrew, who has a very persistent and negative temperament, has finally settled down to listen at story time, he is going to find it hard to get into the right frame of mind to go outside. Children with ADHD, FAS, or ARND may be particularly susceptible to this problem. A few minutes' warning can make a big difference. Telling the group as a whole will facilitate the transition for everyone: "When I finish this story, we will be going outside." Or go around to the various play centers and deliver the message to each small group. You can also flash the lights or sing a clean-up song, but giving an explanation will be more helpful for a child who needs a proper reason to finish what he's doing.

If a child such as Andrew has particular difficulty adapting, give him some extra help; don't wait for him to demand it with his behavior. To ensure that he'll get to the park without incident, ask him to be your partner, labeling his feelings: "I know change is hard for you, but let's be partners and we can talk some more about the story on the way to the park." This is not a punishment but a way to help him to succeed, and he should be your partner as often as he needs to be. If you think ahead of time about providing the support the children require to act appropriately, their self-esteem remains intact and the whole group moves more smoothly from one activity to another.

Because transitions are so problematic, there should be as few as possible. But even after you've examined your program with a magnifying glass there will be some that you just can't change or eliminate, such as putting on snowsuits, hats, scarves, and boots when it's time to go outside in the winter. So transitions should be fun. Float down the hall like astronauts; sing the song about the five little ducks following their mother; take a theme from the story you just read and ask the children to fly to the gym like Stella Luna the bat. There are many songs and games that adapt well to these unavoidable moments.

Transitions should be fun.

Clean-up is always difficult. When you assign tasks to everyone ("You are responsible for putting away the costumes") it helps those children who need extra direction to have a goal and a limited responsibility. It also enables you to provide a rationale for the children who need one ("You are responsible for putting the trucks in the garage so we'll know where they are when you want to play with them again"). Be sure to relate the task to what the child has been doing, and make it achievable ("You are responsible for putting away all the scissors"—not "You are responsible for cleaning up the art table"). Another strategy for making the clean-up process more fun is to put on music with a driving beat that makes everyone want to dance—big band music, for example. Give the children some dancing time when everything is back in place. Another way to smooth clean-up is to ensure that it isn't overwhelming. That means thinking ahead about the number of objects you make available and making it very obvious where each belongs.

Sometimes the transition itself causes the problem. Is an orderly line really necessary? You'll need one when the children are crossing the street, but do you need it when they're going to the bathroom? Waiting is hard, and children tend to find interesting—and not always appropriate—ways to entertain themselves. If you can avoid waiting, you can avoid its consequences.

Instead of moving all the children at once, it sometimes makes more sense to divide the group into smaller units. This can even become a teaching opportunity if you ask the children, "Who's wearing running shoes?" or "Who's wearing green socks?"

One very good way to ease the pain of transition is to have all the materials ready before an activity begins. If you are team-teaching, one person can do the preparation while the other reads a story or guides another activity.

All children function better when there is a consistent routine: They feel more secure knowing what to do, when to do it, and what is coming next. Post a picture schedule to help them remember and understand. If you're going on a field trip or the season changes and you're going swimming instead of to the gym, tell the children in advance, and move the pictures accordingly.

Here are some other techniques to ease transitions:

- Allow children who are slow to adapt to have more time to make a change.

- Some children may want to hear all the concrete details about what's coming up next: the time (after story), the place, who's going, when you'll be coming back.

- Some children do better if they have a job to perform during a transition: be a leader, carry the backpack with the food, carry the diaper bag.

- Some children can use a peer buddy to guide and reinforce them.

Picture This

Children feel better when they know what's next on the agenda. You can make an engaging picture schedule with their help.

- Take photographs of them participating in every facet of the daily routine. Include snack, bathroom, dressing for outdoors, recess, nap, and so on.

- Have the photos printed in 4" x 6" size and laminated.

- Brainstorm with the children: How do they see the day? Begin with drop-off time or school bus arrival.

- Put the photos in an album or on a ring, or post them on the wall at eye level with velcro strips.

- Take new pictures throughout the year so that you can update the schedule and give every child a chance to appear in it.

- Don't throw away the old photos. You can use them for events that haven't occurred yet, such as field trips.

When circumstances change

When there are extraordinary events such as those of September 11, 2001, everyone is affected. With confused and frightened adults all around them, children feel unsafe and insecure, and providing a safe haven for them and their families must become your top priority. Anything else you'd planned goes straight out the window.

Reassuring the children

Because there is fear in the air, even very young children are probably aware that something terrible has happened. In *What Happened to the World? Helping Children Cope in Turbulent Times* (2001), Jim Greenman says that children want to know three things:

- Will I be okay?
- Will you be okay?
- Will everyone I care about be okay? (p. 12)

Your first job is to reassure them that you will take care of them and keep them safe. Even if a child is in danger, you can point out that adults are responsible for taking care of the danger and the children and will do their very best, says Sydney Gurewitz Clemens (2001). You are a bit like the flight attendants on a turbulent flight. If they continue to walk calmly down the aisles, politely serving lunch, everyone feels safe. Their relaxed demeanor tells the passengers the turbulence may be uncomfortable but it isn't dangerous. When you are calm and demonstrate coping skills in the classroom, the children feel more secure and even imitate you (Farish, 2001), and the risk of challenging behavior diminishes.

How do you accomplish this feat when you are feeling confused and fearful yourself? If you can, take some time to sort through your own feelings and get the support you need before you meet the children again. Greenman (2001) suggests:

- Talk about your feelings with adults with whom you feel secure.
- Try to create a daily routine and rituals that support your current needs. . . .
- Try to create a daily routine and rituals that support your family's current needs.
- Live well: eat right, get exercise, sleep.
- Cry when you need to, and seek solitude when you have to.
- Take breaks from the news and headlines.
- Take breaks from others who bring you down.
- Give yourself and those around you some slack for poor behavior under stress.
- Seek help if you feel that life is not becoming more manageable.
- Replenish your spirit with friends, faith, family, music, or nature. (p. 17)

Talking about feelings

After you have reassured the children, your second job is to offer children opportunities to ask questions and express their feelings and thoughts. No matter what they've

Stressed Out

Traumatic events take a toll on teachers, just as they do on children. One study of Head Start teachers who lived through the 1992 riots in Los Angeles showed that 7 percent had severe symptoms of posttraumatic stress disorder, and 29 percent had moderate symptoms (National Institute of Mental Health [NIMH], 2001).

heard, they're likely to be confused. It's important for them to have a chance to talk to adults they trust. If you don't allow them to do this, they get the message that you're too scared and upset to deal with the situation and they become even more frightened.

You can talk with them as a group during circle time; the children may find it helpful to hear that others share their feelings. But be prepared for the possibility that what they hear will also scare them. As you respond to each child and help him put events into perspective, you'll be helping the whole group.

Because not all children share the same concerns, and because they process information in different ways, it makes sense to talk to each child individually as well. A child who's been directly affected should be at the top of your list. Look for a moment when he feels ready to talk, find out what he knows and is trying to understand by asking open-ended questions ("What have you heard about what happened in New York City?"), and base your response on what he says. Diane E. Levin suggests, "Answer questions and clear up misconceptions, but don't try to give children all the information available. . . . The best guide is to follow the child's lead, giving small pieces of information at a time and seeing how the child responds before deciding what to say next" (National Association for the Education of Young Children, 2001). Listen calmly and without judging, and validate the child's feelings. Let him know that it's normal to feel upset or angry. Emphasize his strengths and remind him of how he's coped with problems in the past. Children don't have to think you have all the answers, but they do need to feel as though you understand and value their concerns and will keep them safe.

Let the children know what you're feeling, too. It frightens them if you hide it. It's most reassuring when you show them that you're still all right even though you feel sad or worried or angry. When they see that you can cope, it makes it more possible for them to do the same. You can say, "I'm very sad, but I know I'll get through it, and you will, too."

Encouraging play

More than ever, children will need opportunities to express themselves through play, which is one of the important ways that they can overcome their feelings of helplessness (Farish, 2001). They may recreate the same scenes over and over. Normal and therapeutic, this activity helps them to gain control of the trauma (American Academy of Pediatrics, Work Group on Disasters, n.d.). Children want to be big and strong; they want to be heroes who save the world; and sometimes they even want to be villains. Play is how they acquire this power. Look and listen carefully so that you can support their efforts. You can help them find new heroes by placing props in the dramatic play and block areas so that they can pretend to be firefighters, police, doctors, nurses, and other helpers.

Drawing and writing are also extremely useful in helping children to deal with their feelings, and both physical activity and tactile play with sand, water, or play dough help them to release tension.

Maintaining routines and activities

When their lives feel insecure and unpredictable, children need routine more than ever. Consistency brings a sense of comfort and a feeling that everyday things are unchanged. After children have had time to talk about what's on their minds, return to your normal activities (NIMH, 2001). In order to minimize frustration do not introduce new or difficult concepts. If you were planning a field trip or a change in schedule, it would be best to wait for a while.

Some children will find it hard to make choices, but others will need choices in order to have more control. Some children will need more physical contact and structure and others less. Some will regress into patterns of behavior that are appropriate for younger children and be able to meet fewer demands. Be sensitive to what each child needs and adjust the program accordingly.

When there is so much anger and pain, children need positive ways to express their feelings. They feel better if they can do something to help. Making cookies, writing letters, or drawing pictures for the rescue workers—or the president or the mayor—can direct some of that potentially negative energy in a constructive way and give them a sense that one person can make a difference.

Natural Play

Anna's school in downtown New York City reopened almost a week after the terrorist attacks on the World Trade Center. Even before school closed on September 11, some children in her kindergarten class were still struggling with separation anxiety, and Anna's own normal anxiety about the beginning of the school year just 10 days earlier was now exacerbated by what had happened. The drive to school didn't help. National Guardsmen were stopping cars on the highway, and half the tunnels and bridges were still closed.

Anna was relieved to see that all of the children were there and none had lost a parent. There was an eerie calm in the classroom until Max and Alex arrived. "Max, you get the planes and let's build the towers," Alex shouted. Max selected two toy planes while Alex began working in the block corner. When Anna asked what they were planning to do, Alex replied, "Build the two towers and crash the planes into them."

Anna's first thought was to say, "Not in my classroom!" She wasn't prepared for this. But she took a deep breath and remembered that this is how children come to terms with things that frighten them. Such games help them feel safe and gain control. In a warm, firm voice she said, "Why don't you get some ambulances and fire engines and plan the rescue? There are a lot of people who want to help."

You may also find that the previously engaging hustle and bustle of the classroom has become overstimulating. Slow things down and calm everyone's nerves, including your own, by playing quiet music, speaking in a calm voice, and moving more slowly (Farish, 2001).

Connecting with parents

In a crisis that affects everyone, it's also essential to communicate with families. Children need to know that all the adults in their lives are working together to keep them safe. But you can't rely on the parents to come to you. Their world has collapsed, and like everyone else, they are trying hard to redefine their reality. Different families have different resources for meeting this challenge. Those who cope well will probably have children who cope well, whereas those who are struggling may have difficulty reassuring their children.

If you reach out to them both in writing and in person, you'll have a better chance to connect. A parent evening, complete with food and child care, will provide an opportunity for parents to talk with each other and share what they are going through. It will also allow you to hear what's on their minds. Some parents will look to you for guidance; others will want to handle things their own way. They will probably also have diverse views about what you're doing in the classroom. Although some parents will be eager for you to discuss the events with their children, there will be others who consider the subject taboo. Explain to them why you feel it's important for the children to express themselves, ask questions, and have the opportunity to come to terms with what has happened on their own level. Reassure the parents that you're dealing with the events in a caring, sensitive way.

You can also provide information parents need to help their children get through these hard times. Most parents probably won't be aware of what is developmentally appropriate for their child to know or how much he can understand. Although watching television may alleviate their own anxiety, they probably don't realize what impact the news has on their children. They may not have grasped that each time their children saw the World Trade Center crumble, they thought a different building was collapsing, and that their own homes and their parents' workplaces might be next. Gently help parents understand the need to limit what they watch when their child is present. When you work together, children, families, and teachers all benefit, and a deep sense of community is likely to emerge.

What Do You Think? _____

1. How does preventing challenging behavior help a child at risk to become more resilient?

2. You often hear children say, "That's not fair!" What does being *fair* mean to you? How would you explain to parents that you do not teach all the children the same way?

3. If the physical space in your classroom sends a message, what message would you want your classroom to send? How would you convey the message?

4. When you plan an art activity, what important things do you need to do so that everyone, including the child with challenging

behavior, will participate and benefit from it? What will you ask the children to do? How will you set up the physical space? What materials will you set out? How will you introduce it and bring it to a close?

5. Transitions are an inevitable part of the day. Develop five ways to make transitions fun. Describe where the children are coming from, where they're going, and how you'll get them there.

Suggested Reading

Feldman, J., & Jones, R. (1995). *Transition time: Let's do something different!* Beltsville, MD: Gryphon House.

Greenman, J. (1988). *Caring spaces, learning places: Children's environments that work.* Redmond, WA: Exchange Press.

Kritchevsky, S., & Prescott, E. (1977). *Planning environments for young children: Physical space.* Washington, DC: National Association for the Education of Young Children.

References

American Academy of Pediatrics, Work Group on Disasters. (n.d.). *Psychosocial issues for children and families in disasters: A guide for the primary care physician.* Elk Grove, IL: American Academy of Pediatrics. Retrieved September 24, 2001, from http://www.mentalhealth.org/publications/allpubs/SMA95-3022/SMA3022.htm.

Andersen, K. (2001a, February). More than one challenging child in a group setting. *BDINews—A Newsletter about Caring for the High Maintenance Child*, 3(7). Retrieved from http://www.b-di.com.

Andersen, K. (2001b, May). Teaching functionally equivalent replacement behaviors. *BDINews—A Newsletter about Caring for the High Maintenance Child*, 3(10). Retrieved from http://www.b-di.com.

Becker, J. V., Barham, J., Eron, L. D., & Chen, S. A. (1994). In L. D. Eron, J. H. Gentry, & P. Schlegel (Eds.), *Reason to hope: A psychosocial perspective on violence & youth* (pp. 435–446). Washington, DC: American Psychological Association.

Bredekamp, S. (Ed.). (1998). *Accreditation criteria and procedures.* Washington, DC: National Association for the Education of Young Children.

Clemens, S. G. (2001). Discussing the news with 3- to 7-year-olds: What to do? Washington, DC: National Association for the Education of Young Children. Retrieved September 24, 2001, from http://www.naeyc.org/resources/eyly/1998/22.htm.

Division for Early Childhood of the Council for Exceptional Children. (1999). Concept paper on the identification of and intervention with challeng-ing behavior. In S. Sandall & M. Ostrosky (Eds.), *Practical ideas for addressing challenging behaviors* (pp. 63–70). Longmont, CO: Sopris West.

Farish, J. M. (2001). Helping children cope with disaster. Adapted from *When disaster strikes: Helping young children cope.* Washington, DC: National Association for the Education of Young Children. Retrieved September 24, 2001, from http://www.naeyc.org/coping_with_disaster.htm.

Field, T. (1991). Quality infant day-care and grade school behavior and performance. *Child Development*, 62, 863–870.

Gagnon, C. (1991). Commentary: School-based interventions for aggressive children: Possibilities, limitations, and future directions. In D. J. Pepler & K. H. Rubin (Eds.), *The development and treatment of childhood aggression* (pp. 449–455). Hillsdale, NJ: Erlbaum.

Greene, R. W. (1998). *The explosive child: A new approach for understanding and parenting easily frustrated, "chronically inflexible" children.* New York: HarperCollins.

Greenman, J. (1988). *Caring spaces, learning places: Children's environments that work.* Redmond, WA: Exchange Press.

Greenman, J. (2001). *What happened to the world? Helping children cope in turbulent times.* Retrieved February 1, 2002, from www.brighthorizons.com/talktochildren/whathapp.pdf.

Guerra, N. G. (1997a). Intervening to prevent childhood aggression in the inner city. In J. McCord (Ed.), *Violence and childhood in the inner city* (pp. 256–312). New York: Cambridge University Press.

Guerra, N. G. (1997b, May). *Violence in schools: Interventions to reduce school-based violence.* Paper presented at the meeting of the Centre for Studies of Children at Risk, Hamilton, Ontario.

Hewes, D. W. (2001). *W. N. Hailmann: Defender of Froebel.* Grand Rapids, MI: Froebel Foundation.

Huston-Stein, A. C., Friedrich-Cofer, L., & Susman, E. J. (1977). The relationship of classroom structure to social behavior, imaginative play, and self-regulation of economically disadvantaged children. *Child Development, 48,* 908–916.

Katz, L. G., & McClellan, D. E. (1997). *Fostering children's social competence: The teacher's role.* Washington, DC: National Association for the Education of Young Children.

Kazdin, A. E. (1987). Treatment of antisocial behavior in children: Current status and future directions. *Psychological Bulletin, 102,* 187–203.

Kazdin, A. E. (1994). Interventions for aggressive and antisocial children. In L. D. Eron, J. H. Gentry, & P. Schlegel (Eds.), *Reason to hope: A psychosocial perspective on violence & youth* (pp. 341–382). Washington, DC: American Psychological Association.

Kazdin, A. E. (1995). *Conduct disorders in childhood and adolescence* (2nd ed.). Thousand Oaks, CA: Sage.

Kritchevsky, S., & Prescott, E., with Walling, L. (1977). *Planning environments for young children: Physical space.* Washington, DC: National Association for the Education of Young Children.

Lawry, J., Danko, C. D., & Strain, P. (1999). Examining the role of the classroom environment in the prevention of problem behaviors. In S. Sandall & M. Ostrosky (Eds.), *Practical ideas for addressing challenging behaviors* (pp. 49–61). Longmont, CO: Sopris West.

Levin, D. E. (1998). *Remote control childhood? Combating the hazards of media culture.* Washington, DC: National Association for the Education of Young Children.

Mize, J., & Ladd, G. W. (1990). Toward the development of successful social skills training for preschool children. In S. R. Asher & J. D. Coie (Eds.), *Peer rejection in childhood* (pp. 338–364). New York: Cambridge University Press.

National Association for the Education of Young Children. (1990, 1994). *Media violence in children's lives.* Washington, DC: Author. Retrieved February 11, 2002, from http://www.naeyc.org/resources/position_statements/psmevi98.htm.

National Association for the Education of Young Children. (2001). Helping children cope with violence. Washington, DC: Author. Retrieved September 24, 2001, from http://www.naeyc.org/resources/eyly/1998/01.htm.

National Institute of Mental Health. (2001). *Helping children and adolescents cope with violence and disasters* (NIH publication No. 01-3518). Bethesda, MD: Author. Retrieved November 28, 2001, from http://www.nimh.nih.gov/publicat/violence.cfm.

Pepler, D. J., & Slaby, R. G. (1994). Theoretical and developmental perspectives on youth and violence. In L. D. Eron, J. H. Gentry, & P. Schlegel (Eds.), *Reason to hope: A psychosocial perspective on violence & youth* (pp. 27–58). Washington, DC: American Psychological Association.

Quay, L. C., Weaver, J. H., & Neel, J. H. (1986). The effects of play materials on positive and negative social behaviors in preschool boys and girls. *Child Study Journal, 16*(1), 67–76.

Ramsey, P. G. (1980). Solving the dilemma of sharing. *Day Care and Early Education, 8*(4), 6–10.

Reiss, A. J., Jr., & Roth, J. A. (Eds.). (1993). *Understanding and preventing violence.* Washington, DC: National Academy Press.

Shore, R. (1997). *Rethinking the brain: New insights into early development.* New York: Families and Work Institute.

Slaby, R. G., Roedell, W. C., Arezzo, D., & Hendrix, K. (1995). *Early violence prevention: Tools for teachers of young children.* Washington, DC: National Association for the Education of Young Children.

Smith, C., & Gay, C. (1997, April). *Early childhood social integration: Making friends.* Workshop presented at SpeciaLink Institute on Children's Challenging Behaviours, Sydney, Nova Scotia.

Sobel, J. (1983). *Everybody wins: Noncompetitive games for young children.* New York: Walker.

8

Preventing Challenging Behavior with the Right Social Context

Creating the Social Context

In Chapter 7 we saw that you can prevent challenging behavior by altering the physical space and the program in your classroom. In this chapter you'll see that you can also prevent challenging behavior by the way you manage the social context. The physical space, the program, and the social context all influence one another.

What is the social context? Although you can't see or touch it, the social context is everywhere, affecting everything you do, whether you're in a supermarket, an elevator, or a classroom. In the classroom, the program and physical space play a role in creating and reinforcing the social context, but in the end, it depends much more on the people. The social context is a framework that tells us what kinds of attitudes and behaviors are expected, accepted, and valued in a setting or group, and it has amazing power to influence what happens there. The social context creates the social climate—the spirit of the group and the ambience of the classroom.

What kind of social context fosters prosocial behavior and discourages aggressive behavior?

Not surprisingly, the social context influences the appearance of aggressive behavior. Rough-and-tumble play on the playground, for example, is more conducive to aggressive behavior than cooperative play in the classroom (DeRosier, Cillessen, Coie, and Dodge, 1994). In an experimental play group study, researchers found that first- and third-grade boys were less likely to act aggressively when the social climate was cohesive and friendly (DeRosier et al., 1994). Such a climate doesn't happen automatically. On the contrary, researchers have found very little naturally occurring prosocial behavior in the preschool classroom (Eisenberg and Fabes, 1998).

Cohesiveness and friendliness seem more ready to appear when a group has a strong sense of community. A community, Lilian G. Katz and Diane E. McClellan state, is "a group of individuals who have a serious stake in each other's well-being and who can accomplish together that which they could not do alone" (1997, p. 17). A community is like a family: People have a sense of belonging, nurture and support one another, and work together toward common goals. Katz and McClellan believe that feeling part of a community is crucial to a child's social and emotional development.

Cooperation, which emphasizes the group more than the individuals in it, also seems to promote cohesiveness and friendliness. When children participate in structured cooperative activities, they behave less aggressively and are more likely to cooperate during unstructured times—even when they're frustrated. They learn to see things from another's point of view, work together, negotiate, problem solve, share, accept, and support one another (Slaby, Roedell, Arezzo, and Hendrix, 1995). "Increasing children's cooperative interaction skills is an important part of any approach to reducing violence," Ronald G. Slaby, Wendy Roedell, Diana Arezzo, and Kate Hendrix write in *Early Violence Prevention* (1995, pp. 45–46).

What is the teacher's role in the social context?

When it comes to establishing the social context, teachers set the stage and play the lead. They are the primary role models, teaching by everything they say and do, whether they intend to or not. As Daniel Goleman writes in *Emotional Intelligence*, "Whenever a teacher responds to one student, 20 or 30 others learn a lesson" (1997, p. 279). Because children pay more attention to people they trust and care about, teachers are most effective when their relationships with children are warm and nurturing. Their consistent awareness of children's needs and feelings and their caring, helpful behavior set a powerful example.

The children are also quick to notice how their teachers behave with other members of the staff. When they work together as a team, share resources, and help each other, the children catch the adults' cooperative spirit; when there's tension and acri-

"Whenever a teacher responds to one student, 20 or 30 others learn a lesson," says Daniel Goleman in Emotional Intelligence.

mony, that's contagious, too. The same holds true for interactions with parents, administrators, and even visitors to the classroom. Research-based bullying- and violence-prevention programs advocate a whole-school (or whole child-care-center) approach for exactly this reason. The impact of the intervention increases because the children see that the entire community values prosocial, nonviolent, cooperative interaction and problem solving (Olweus, Limber, and Mihalic, 1999; Thornton, Craft, Dahlberg, Lynch, and Baer, 2000).

In addition to being a role model, the teacher is the group's leader. In *The Nurture Assumption* (1999), Judith Rich Harris describes a leader's power this way:

> First, a leader can influence the group's norms—the attitudes its members adopt and the behaviors they consider appropriate. To do this it is not necessary to influence every member of the group directly: influencing a majority of them is enough, or even just a few if they are dominant members....
>
> Second, a leader can define the boundaries of the group: who is *us* and who is *them*....
>
> Third, a leader can define the image—the stereotype—a group has of itself.
>
> A truly gifted teacher can exert leadership in all three of these ways. A truly gifted teacher can prevent a classroom of diverse students from falling apart into separate groups and can turn the entire class into an *us*—an *us* that sees itself as scholars. An *us* that sees itself as capable and hard-working. (p. 245)

Us is a community, of course. In a class like this, Harris points out, the children cheer on the slow learners. And just as they can offer a round of applause to an emerging reader, so they can enthusiastically support a child who's beginning to ask instead of push. Once again, the children can become part of the solution instead of part of the problem.

The teacher's attitude toward the children also helps form the social context. Having high expectations—believing that the children have, or can develop, the skills to make friends, complete the puzzle, enjoy circle time, or read the assigned text—increases their potential for success, develops resiliency, and helps build a positive social climate. When children have the support they need to succeed, they are much less likely to resort to challenging behavior.

How can you create a cooperative and inclusive community?

The following strategies can enhance the spirit of community and cooperation in the classroom.

Language

One of the key elements of a classroom's social context is language—what you say and how you say it. Your tone of voice, speed, intensity, and vocabulary all set an example. Addressing individuals by name, saying "please" and "thank you," expressing your feelings, being sensitive to others' feelings, offering your help, and accepting the help of others all show the children that you value them—and demonstrate how they can show that they value each other.

Without realizing it, the teacher may establish an unfriendly social context by shouting or filling the air with negative imperatives like "don't" and "stop." It is important to speak, not shout. If you're constantly raising your voice, the children tune you out; and because you're a role model, they shout more often, too. No one can hear or concentrate, and the atmosphere becomes unpleasant and unfriendly. When you want to talk with a child, take the time to walk over to her so that you can communicate in a normal tone of voice.

Be positive and tell the children what to do, not what *not* to do. When you say, "Stop running!" the child doesn't actually know what to do. Should she hop, skip, jump? "Please walk in the hallway," stated clearly, calmly, and respectfully, informs the child of the expected and desired behavior. It also deemphasizes the messages hidden in "don't," "stop," and "no" sentences, such as "Don't spill the milk" and "No throwing sand."

No is another word to expunge from your vocabulary. It, too, creates negative vibes and fails to tell a child what to do. And using it frequently also devalues it. Because you want the children to pay close attention when you say *no*, it is important to save it for an emergency—such as when a child is about to step into the street or push over a bookcase.

When challenging behavior is involved, the question *why* doesn't help much either. Jessica doesn't actually know why she kicked Sonia, and when you ask, she's likely to make up a reason. She may even come to believe that a good explanation will make the behavior acceptable. But the bottom line is that unacceptable behavior is always unacceptable, whatever the reason for it. *Why* also puts some children on the defensive, making it harder for them to calm down.

Although it's difficult, eliminating these little words is worth the effort. Without them, both the learning environment and the social climate are much more positive.

Rules and policies

By setting boundaries for acceptable behavior and teaching children about limits and expectations, rules and policies also contribute substantially to the social context. It is easier for the children to remember rules when there aren't too many of them. You can base them on whatever is most important to you and the children, but it's common to begin with the primary need of everyone in the room—to be safe. Child Care plus+ at the University of Montana (Mulligan, Morris, Miller-Green, and Harper-Whalen, 1998) has suggested three basic rules:

- Respect the rights of others.

- Avoid danger.

- Take care of the environment (toys, materials, rooms, etc.).

Children understand and respect the rules more readily if they participate in creating them. This gives the children a sense of ownership and makes the rules seem more important and fair, which probably means they'll be followed (Brooks, 1994). Involving the children shows that you consider them capable and responsible and allows them to practice using their reason and judgment (Katz and McClellan, 1997).

Use language that the children understand, and make the final wording of the rules clear, explicit, and positive. Once again, they should tell the children what to do, not what not to do.

To increase the children's understanding, encourage them to draw pictures and talk about what the rules mean. Post the pictures along with the rules in a prominent place in the classroom. Use natural opportunities and activities such as story-telling, puppets, and role-playing to reinforce them throughout the year, and remind the children about the rules whenever they seem to need an extra nudge. They're young, they forget, and practice helps them to remember.

Parents and other adults who come into your classroom should also know and understand the rules. Evaluate them periodically to ensure that they're still relevant.

Group projects and activities

Cooperative activities and routines reduce aggression and strengthen prosocial behavior and acceptance of others (Eisenberg and Fabes, 1998). When children work together toward a common goal, they come to know and like each other and have more of a chance to become friends. Planting a class garden, for example—planning what to plant and where to plant it, preparing the ground, buying the seeds and plants, putting them into the earth, watering, weeding, and harvesting the bounty—requires children to listen to one another's ideas, negotiate, share, and help. Murals and large construc-

You Can't Say You Can't Play

Vivian Paley, a kindergarten teacher at the University of Chicago Laboratory Schools and the recipient of a prestigious MacArthur Foundation award, was more and more disturbed by exclusion in her classroom. She couldn't accept that some children had the right to limit the social experiences of their classmates, and after extensive consultation with the children from kindergarten through grade 5, she brought in a new rule: You can't say you can't play.

"In general," Paley writes, "the approach has been to help the outsiders develop the characteristics that will make them more acceptable to the insiders. I am suggesting something different: the *group* must change its attitudes and expectations toward those who, for whatever reason, are not yet part of the system" (1992, p. 33).

Though it took time to institute, this straightforward assault on the social climate was a resounding success. The most popular girl in the class invited two girls who'd been on her worst-friend list to play, no one was left out, everyone had more turns, the children were nicer to one another, and they were far more willing to try out new roles and new ideas.

tion projects lend themselves particularly well to cooperative social interaction, as do cooking projects such as soups and stews. Music and singing also create a strong group feeling (Katz and McClellan, 1997).

A child with challenging behavior can enjoy participating in these activities if you assign her a specific role, encourage her attempts to cooperate, and remind her that she has the ability to succeed. It's also wise to place her beside a supportive peer and to ensure that she has enough personal space so that another child won't accidentally bump or push her.

Peer partners

When children choose peers to play or sit with during free-play and lunch, the same child often finds herself alone. Children need to feel welcome and accepted by their peers, and when they are confronted with regular rejection, they will turn to other, usually inappropriate, means of getting their attention. Although your goal is for children to form friendships and solve problems on their own, it's important to anticipate that some children will have a tough time socially. Try to figure out potential play partners for them—those with similar interests who might be compatible—and bring them together in nonthreatening situations in class. You might even suggest play dates to the family (Andrews and Trawick-Smith, 1996). The sooner you act, the better; after a child acquires a negative reputation with her peers, it will be much harder to find a playmate for her (Ladd, Price, and Hart, 1990).

At times it may be necessary to give the children permanent compatible partners for transitions or to assign seats at lunchtime and snack so that Andrew isn't always left looking for a partner and Thomas and Chloe, who fight when they're together, sit at different tables. If you have more than one teacher for the group, divide the children into smaller groups to keep those flammable elements apart and give them the chance to learn from their more socially adept peers.

Pairing a more socially skilled child with one who's less skillful can be very effective (Hymel, Wagner, and Butler, 1990; Katz and McClellan, 1997; Wittmer and Honig, 1994). Whether you ask them to sit together, clear the tables together, or carry the library books together, the more expert child is always modeling social skills, and this one-on-one situation presents a chance for her to discover a more likeable side to her awkward peer.

Open-ended activities and cooperative games

The dramatic play area, the block corner, and the sand and water tables all provide myriad opportunities for social interaction and cooperation (Quay, Weaver, and Neel, 1986). But remember that they also require your close supervision to prevent the inappropriate behavior that often pops up when there's lots of interaction. Noncompetitive games also foster cooperation and prosocial behavior (Slaby et al., 1995; Sobel, 1983). See Chapter 7 for more on this topic.

Testing the Social Context

As much as you'd like to protect children from all the awful things that happen in the world, you can't shield them from reality. A crisis such as September 11, 2001, will have an enormous impact on the social context of your classroom.

When the media and the politicians talk about nothing but revenge and violence, the president says he will get Osama Bin Laden dead or alive, and people rush out to buy guns (Baker, 2001), the social context that you had previously established is put to the test. Children see adults using violence and power to solve problems, and they hear intolerance and hatred everywhere.

In this situation it's important to continue to model and teach peaceful problem solving. Tell the children that it's normal to feel angry, but it's not all right to hurt others. Instead of solving problems, striking back leads to more anger and violence. Diane E. Levin suggests saying something like, "I really get upset when people solve their problems by hurting each other," and reminding children of times when they solved their own problems in a peaceful way (National Association for the Education of Young Children, 2001). This is also an opportunity to encourage empathy.

To explain terrorism and adults' violent behavior, Fred Rogers says, "There are some people in this world who are very angry and haven't learned how to live with people they don't agree with" (Greenman, 2001, p. 44).

"There are many more people who know how to get along, and they are all over the world working hard to stop these people who do terrible things," adds Jim Greenman (2001, p. 44).

It is also critical to watch out for racism and stereotyping and to teach children to respect differences (Greenman, 2001). Provide them with information about other cultures and explain that most people don't believe in hurting others and find the terrorist attacks just as upsetting and shocking as we do.

Teaching Social Skills

You can also tackle the social context head on by teaching the children social skills. Social skills (and their cousin, social competence) are the behaviors, attitudes, gestures, and words that enable children to initiate and maintain positive social relationships (Rubin, Bukowski, and Parker, 1998). Historically, social skills have been the bread and butter of early care and education, one of the main reasons parents sent their children to preschool (Clarke-Stewart, 1982).

People have often assumed that it was enough for children to be together, that the group itself offered whatever they needed to learn social skills, and the role of the teacher was simply to create opportunities for this learning to take place (Beaty, 1992). There is no doubt that children need and learn from the opportunities a teacher and group provide, but they learn even more when social skills are taught proactively. Giving social skills formal status in the program highlights their value and changes the entire ambience of the classroom. In addition, it offers children with challenging behavior a chance to learn that they might not otherwise have had.

Why are social skills important?

Social skills are important for one very fundamental reason: They enable people to get along with others. But social skills have other virtues as well, some with lifelong implications. They enable children to:

- Make friends.

- Gain self-confidence and self-esteem, which increase their resilience (Michelson and Mannarino, 1986).

- Resolve conflicts more readily and less aggressively (Fabes and Eisenberg, 1992).

- Avoid peer rejection and victimization (Perry, Kusel, and Perry, 1988).

- Perform better at school (Cartledge and Milburn, 1995).

- Lower their risk for later delinquency and violence (Nagin and Tremblay, 2001; Tremblay, 1997).

- Become better adjusted adults (Michelson and Mannarino, 1986).

Because children with aggressive behavior are often rejected by their peers and have no friends, they have little opportunity to learn or practice social skills. As a result, they may become more aggressive and disruptive, making matters worse (Coie and Koeppl, 1990).

Children who behave aggressively also have difficulty processing social information. They don't understand social cues very well, or they tend to assume that others have hostile intentions, whether they do or not. It may not occur to them to look around for additional information or think of alternative solutions to problems, and they may not consider what will happen if they respond aggressively (see Chapter 1).

Nice Is Powerful

Daniel S. Nagin of Carnegie Mellon University and Richard E. Tremblay of the University of Montreal followed more than 1,000 boys from ages 6 to 15 at high risk for aggression.

The researchers found that boys with high scores on a scale of prosocial behavior—those who tried to stop quarrels, help someone who was hurt, comforted a child who was crying or having trouble with a task, for example—were half as likely as the boys in the control group to behave aggressively at age 15 (Nagin and Tremblay, 2001). Their prosocial skills protected them.

Other children (and teachers) are afraid of children who behave aggressively and are more inclined to put a negative spin on their behavior. Even when children who behave aggressively begin to learn social skills, their reputation makes it hard for them to be accepted (Coie and Koeppl, 1990). These are the children who need social skills the most.

How do children learn social skills?

Children learn social skills—a major developmental task of early childhood—through lots of observation, repetition, and practice with their peers. With their social equals, children play roles and face dilemmas they don't encounter with adults, so they learn to lead, follow, contribute ideas, respond assertively to threats and demands, negotiate, compromise, defer, problem solve, see multiple perspectives, work through issues of power, persuade, take turns, reason, cooperate, share, and learn the rules and niceties that make interactions run smoothly. The more time they spend interacting with their peers, the better they become at it. Even conflict is useful: It helps them hone all of these skills and understand other people's feelings as well. Adults are important because they model, teach, and reinforce the appropriate behavior that children need to practice.

Obstacle Course

Children with challenging behavior often have trouble with social skills, says Kathleen R. Beland (1996) of the Committee for Children in Seattle:

• They do not know what appropriate behavior is, because of a lack of modeling of alternative ways of resolving conflict.

• They have the knowledge but lack the practice because of inadequate reinforcement.

• They have emotional responses, such as anger, fear, or anxiety, that inhibit the performance of desirable behavior. . . .

• They have inappropriate beliefs and attributions regarding aggression. (p. 212)

Monkey Love

After a fight, most primates go out of their way to make peace with their opponents. Depending on the species, this reconciliation may take the form of mouth-to-mouth kissing, embracing, clasping the other's hips, grooming, grunting, and holding hands. These reunions reduce the possibility of more aggression, enabling the animals to maintain social relationships that are vital to them as individuals and to the group as a whole. Grooming is particularly important. It fosters valuable partnerships and alliances.

Similarly, children make up after a fight by inviting their friends to play, offering toys, gently touching one another, apologizing, and similar gestures (deWaal, 2000).

Friendship is extremely important for gaining social competence (Katz, Kramer, and Gottman, 1992; Shonkoff and Phillips, 2000). Children as young as 14 months prefer one child to another, and toddlers are quite capable of forming stable friendships (Andrews and Trawick-Smith, 1996). It requires considerable skill to maintain a relationship with a friend. Friends have more disputes because they're together more often. But their conflicts are less intense and they resolve them more equitably, with more negotiation and compromise, because the friendship matters to them. An altercation will bring interaction between nonfriends to a halt, but friends will continue to play (Rubin et al., 1998). A child can have a friend even after the group has rejected her (Katz and McClellan, 1997), and that friendship will insulate her from some of the pernicious effects of rejection (Andrews and Trawick-Smith, 1996).

Why should we include children with challenging behaviors?

Sometimes people think it is pointless to try to help children with challenging behaviors become accepted members of the group—that they are better off in special settings with more expert staff and better ratios. Of course it depends on the child's needs, but in general if children are going to learn to function in society, they must be *in* society. Peers are extremely important role models: Children tend to imitate those most like themselves (Michelson and Mannarino, 1986). Research shows that when socially skilled peers are involved in an intervention, children with challenging behavior are more likely to become both more accepted and less aggressive (Bierman, 1986; Bierman and Furman, 1984). In one study, abused and neglected children usually interrupted their desirable behavior when their teachers remarked on it—in fact, teachers' reinforcement worked only 12 percent of the time. But when peers paid attention, the children responded positively 53 percent of the time (Strayhorn and Strain, 1986). Socially competent peers who can model and reinforce appropriate behavior every day are the best possible teachers for children with challenging behavior (Slaby et al., 1995; Vitaro and Tremblay, 1994). Being part of the ordinary community also enables children to develop a bond to conventional social life—another factor that protects them from behaving aggressively (Guerra, 1997a).

How do you teach social skills?

Because children with challenging behavior learn best when they're with their socially skilled peers, it's a good idea to teach social skills to the whole class—or the whole school. No one is singled out or stigmatized, and children and teachers all learn the same concepts and vocabulary, making it much easier for both teachers and children to model, use, and reinforce the skills during the school day.

Some experts consider the preschool years the optimal time to start (Mize and Ladd, 1990). Children are likely to suffer from peer rejection and its consequences if they don't learn social skills before they start school, and it's easier to change a child's social status when she's young. Even young children can learn social concepts if they can see why they're important to their lives (playing with other children makes you feel happy), if you define them in terms they can understand (asking someone to play), and if you give them plenty of concrete examples and chances to generalize the information (Mize and Ladd, 1990). But training in social skills is beneficial later, too, and should probably continue over several years (Mize and Ladd, 1990; Thornton, Craft, Dahlberg, Lynch, and Baer, 2000). Learning social skills is a lifelong process.

Successful social skills training programs are often based on Bandura's social cognitive learning theory, and they use a variety of methods, including didactic teaching, modeling, group discussion, and role-playing. Regular, plentiful rehearsal and practice—with peers, puppets, and/or teachers—are essential, as are follow-up and reinforcement in real-life interactions in the classroom, because it's hard for children to transfer these skills into their real lives (Guerra, 1997b; Mize and Ladd, 1990).

When you're presenting a social skills activity, remember that you're a role model, and concentrate on being your prosocial best. It is also extremely important to be aware of the needs of individual children. Often, the child who stands to benefit the most may be the least interested in taking part. Perhaps the ideas threaten a pattern of behavior she relies on, or she lacks the self-esteem to believe that anything can change her status in the group. If she doesn't want to participate, use her own stuffed animals to try to engage her interest, or let her listen from elsewhere in the room. Disguise and recycle real incidents using puppets, photographs, drawings, books, role-playing, and discussion. With this impersonal, externalized approach, no one feels picked on and everyone develops skills for the next time.

Of course, like anything else you teach, social skills training should be fun, developmentally appropriate, and culturally sensitive. Here are some ideas to keep things lively:

- Include games.
- Videotape what you're doing.
- Ask children to share stories about prosocial behavior they see.
- Publicly celebrate accomplishments.
- Connect activities to the children's goals—more friends, better academic performance, a safer school (Thornton et al., 2000).

When children are applying what they've learned in real situations at recess or in the classroom, your job is to stay closely attuned and to coach, prompt, cue, and reinforce them to ensure that they get the desired results. Reinforcing approximations of their intended behavior tells children that they're on the right track and encourages them to keep trying. Once a child's skills are firmly established, you can gradually and systematically decrease your reinforcement because the natural rewards—better peer relationships—will be enough.

Researchers have found that a teacher's enthusiasm is key in teaching social skills successfully (Thornton, et al., 2000). To be effective, you have to believe that violence can be prevented and that you can make a difference!

What skills do children need to learn?

The first step in planning a social skills program is to identify the skills that are likely to promote peer acceptance and the social context you want to create in your classroom.

Practice Makes Perfect

In *Teaching and Working with Children Who Have Emotional and Behavioral Challenges* (2000), Mary M. Quinn and her colleagues outline the following steps for teaching children new behaviors:

- *Modeling.* Show the student the appropriate behavior.

- *Rehearsing appropriate behavior.* Provide opportunities for the student to practice the behavior.

- *Role-playing.* Provide students the opportunity to practice the behavior in the context of a situation in which the behavior might be needed.

- *Continuous reinforcement.* Provide reinforcement to the student as he or she practices the new behaviors.

- *Prompting.* Give students cues to help them remember how and when to use the new behaviors. (p. 35)

Research-based social skills programs usually focus on emotional regulation and empathy, impulse control, entering groups, social problem solving, anger management, and responding assertively.

Emotional regulation and empathy

Children who manage emotion well have an easier time getting along with their peers (Shonkoff and Phillips, 2000). The process of understanding and regulating feelings is a complicated one that starts as soon as a baby looks into her parents' eyes and begins to establish a relationship. Infants can't regulate their own internal states and emotions; they depend on their caregivers to sensitively decipher the clues they provide and promptly respond with the help they need (Cicchetti, Ganiban, and Barnett, 1991). That is, caregivers act as a kind of external arm of the baby's own internal regulatory system.

As babies grow, they get better at communicating their distress, pain, fear, surprise, and happiness, and caregivers get better at reading their signals. This relationship, which develops at about 9 to 12 months, is called *attachment*, and it is crucial to the baby's ability to regulate her affect and deal with stress and frustration (Landy and Peters, 1991). It also becomes a model for her future relationships.

Little by little, with the picture of her principal warm, consistent caregivers in her mind, the baby can take over managing her emotions herself, internalizing what they've taught her. Temperament definitely plays a role here—a child who feels everything intensely may find this process much more difficult.

Language, observation, pretend play, and asking questions all help children learn how to regulate their emotions (Dunn and Brown, 1991). Learning to control impulses, tolerate frustration, delay gratification, inhibit action, and accept rules are all part and parcel of the emotional regulation a child is developing in the first five years.

Empathy, which is the ability to understand what others are feeling and to put one-self in their shoes, begins to develop by the age of 2 (and sometimes earlier), when a child is likely to try to console her crying brother by patting him or bringing him blan-kets, drinks, toys—anything that she associates with relieving her own pain (Dunn and Brown, 1991). In *The Scientist in the Crib*, Alison Gopnik, a developmental psychologist at the University of California at Berkeley, describes how her son, then almost 2 years old, found her in tears after a particularly discouraging day at work. In a valiant attempt to fix whatever ailed her, he rushed to the bathroom and returned with a large box of Band-Aids, which he plastered all over her (Gopnik, Meltzoff, and Kuhl, 2001).

As children realize that not everyone feels what they feel and that different people can have different feelings, they can learn to anticipate how others might feel and to respond appropriately to someone in distress.

Before we can tune into other people's feelings, we have to be able to understand our own. Daniel Goleman calls this understanding the "fundamental emotional com-petence" (1997, p. 47). It helps us to run our lives, organize our experience, and make appropriate decisions. It is also the basis for emotional self-control and empathy. Being able to say what they feel helps children to feel listened to, respected, and valued—feel-ings that help them value and care for others as well. In a classroom where feelings are acknowledged and spoken about, it may not be so necessary to act them out (Aderem, 1995).

The ability to see things from another's perspective makes a considerable differ-ence in the way children perceive the world, and it's crucial when it comes to control-ling aggressive behavior (Beland, 1996; Cartledge and Milburn, 1995). Bullies and other children with challenging behavior find it hard to see things from someone else's point of view (Webster-Stratton and Herbert, 1994), and children who've been abused or who've witnessed abuse often close down their empathic responses in an attempt to cope (Beland, 1996).

Conversely, children who can imagine another's feelings are less likely to act aggressively. When they can identify and sympathize with a peer, they're more likely to help her and less likely to become angry or misinterpret events and intentions (Beland, 1996; Eisenberg and Fabes, 1998). They can anticipate the effect of their actions and

Emotional Acrobatics

When it comes to regulating and displaying emotion, different cultures have different beliefs and values. In the individualistic European American culture, children are encour-aged to express their feelings. But in collective cultures, such as those of Japan and China, where the harmony of the group takes precedence, people keep their feelings to themselves so that they won't hurt others (Chan, 1998).

When children cross from one culture to another to go to child care or school, they may find it hard to switch their emotional mode (Shonkoff and Phillips, 2000).

words and understand that if they push or tease, someone will get hurt. They make better decisions (Greenberg and Kusche, 1998), and they're more likely to take others' feelings into account when they're trying to solve problems, increasing the chances that the solutions they reach will satisfy everyone (Ianotti, 1985).

To help children understand others' feelings, focus on their own feelings first (Slaby et al., 1995). You can help them learn to differentiate and label their feelings both in calm times and when they occur ("You feel sad because your friends are leaving you out"). You can also help them figure out which situations may provoke which feelings ("I feel angry when you take away the bike"). Children also need to understand that different people may have different feelings about the same situation (Juan may be happy at the top of the big slide, but Ines might be scared). When you talk about feelings—and encourage children to talk about them—it helps children regulate their emotions (Dunn and Brown 1991; Shonkoff and Phillips, 2000).

Impulse control

Impulse control has nothing to do with knowing the rules or the consequences of breaking them. Many children with challenging behavior—especially those who interrupt and talk over others, blurt out answers without raising their hands, and have difficulty taking turns—can tell you all about the rules and why their behavior was inappropriate, but this knowledge doesn't help them. Children with FAS or ARND also have a problem with impulse control because prenatal exposure to alcohol damages the frontal lobe, which controls inhibitions and judgment.

Daniel Goleman writes, "There is perhaps no psychological skill more fundamental than resisting impulse. It is the root of all emotional self-control, since all emotions, by their very nature, lead to one or another impulse to act" (1997, p. 81).

The Marshmallow Test

Daniel Goleman describes an extraordinary study begun by psychologist Walter Mischel in the 1960s. In this study, researchers told 4-year-olds that they could have two marshmallows if they could wait about 15 minutes for the researcher to do an errand. If they couldn't wait, they could have a marshmallow right away—but just one.

About two-thirds of the children earned both marshmallows. They covered their eyes, sang, talked to themselves, and played games with their hands and feet to fend off temptation.

The researchers sought out these children again when they were graduating from high school. They discovered that the double-marshmallow children were extremely socially competent—"personally effective, self-assertive, and better able to cope with the frustrations of life." In addition, they were superior students, with SAT scores 210 points higher, on average, than the single-marshmallow children.

The impulsive children's inability to delay gratification had them cost dearly. As adolescents, they were more likely to be seen as stubborn, indecisive, easily upset by frustration, mistrustful, jealous, and prone to fights and arguments (Goleman, 1997, pp. 80–82).

Children learn self-control skills between the ages of 2 and 5. Besides the ability to delay gratification (if you can wait, you can have two marshmallows), these include:

- Tolerating frustration (putting away the blocks without getting angry when it's time for lunch)

- Inhibiting action or effortful control (waiting at the starting line for the race to begin rather than starting to run immediately)

- Adapting behavior to the context (talking quietly in the library) (Giuliani, 1997)

In the hurly-burly of classroom give-and-take, children often go on automatic pilot and act impulsively. They do what they've always done, and if they've behaved aggressively in the past, then aggressive behavior just reappears. According to Ronald G. Slaby and his colleagues (1995), children act impulsively for several reasons:

- They have trouble regulating their emotions.

- They don't listen carefully.

- If they have verbal skills that could help them to stop and think, they may not use them.

- It doesn't occur to them to consider what else they could do or what will happen if they respond aggressively. To them, passive or aggressive solutions seem perfectly all right.

One of the secrets to impulse control is learning the difference between feelings and actions, Goleman says (1997). When a child learns to recognize that she's feeling angry or frustrated, she can also learn that having that feeling is a signal to stop and think—not a signal to act. Part of learning to identify the feeling is learning that it's all right to feel whatever she's feeling and that she can express those feelings without behaving aggressively.

Remaining calm is also central. The two-marshmallow 4-year-olds employed a strategy that works very well: "self-speak" or verbal mediation. The child thinks out loud to guide her own behavior. Several research-based social skills programs teach children to remind themselves aloud to "Stop, look, and listen" when they realize they're becoming angry or frustrated. Teachers can model this method, making the usually hidden process of reasoning more apparent to all the children. Children can also learn to take deep breaths, count to five, or do relaxation exercises.

Practice these techniques with the children when they're composed, and rehearse them in role-plays of potentially provocative situations with puppets, teachers, and peers before trying them in real life. Provide lots of cues, prompts, and reinforcement when children are using them with their peers in the classroom.

Prevention is extremely important when you're teaching impulse control. As always, knowing the child is key: It enables you to predict when and where she's likely to explode. If you monitor closely, remind her of the rules and expected behavior, help her identify her feelings, and give her a script of what to say before she loses control, you are providing useful information and cues that will eventually enable her to control herself. Give the child plenty of encouragement and as much help—both physical and verbal—as she needs to ensure that she'll succeed (Schmidt, 1996).

Entering groups

Group entry is a vital skill. In order for children to interact, they must enter groups over and over again each day. But entering a group is very difficult. In studies, 3- and 4-year-olds who knew each other rejected 54 percent of all initial entry attempts by their peers, and even popular second- and third-graders were rejected or ignored 26 percent of the time (Putallaz and Wasserman, 1990).

Impulse control is essential to success. Children who can wait have more opportunity to figure out what the group is doing, and when they try again, their peers are more receptive to them. Children who try at least three times generally make it, so persistence pays off, too (Putallaz and Wasserman, 1990).

The sequence of tactics also matters. The most successful route seems to be:

- *Waiting and hovering* on the outskirts of the group without speaking. Again, this strategy enables the child to observe and gain some understanding of the group's frame of reference.

- *Mimicking* what the children in the group are doing. (Parallel play is a useful bridge.)

- *Saying something positive that relates to the group's activity* (Putallaz and Wasserman, 1990).

Asking to join usually works, but children hesitate to try this direct approach, probably because it's harder for them to try again if they're rejected (Putallaz and Wasserman, 1990). It's useful to have the other child's attention before speaking, to

Rewarding Control

Kate Andersen, an educator with a special interest in temperament, sometimes uses behavior modification techniques to train a child in frustration tolerance and self-control. She begins by observing closely to figure out exactly what triggers the child's impulsive aggressive behavior. Andersen then shares this information and her strategy with the child: "Whenever you don't get what you want, you get a feeling called 'frustration,' and then you push someone. I'm going to watch you from now on, and every time I see you stopping yourself from pushing when you're frustrated I'm going to give you a hug and say, 'Good self-control, Elena.'"

As she watches, she can see the little beginnings of self-control: Elena actually puts out her hand and pulls it back—and Andersen reinforces and reinforces. The goal, she emphasizes, is improvement, not perfection (Andersen, 1996).

speak clearly, and to ask friendly questions (Guralnick, 1986). What's most important is for the child to focus on the social interaction and the other children's needs and interests and to show that she understands the group's frame of reference (Putallaz and Sheppard, 1992).

Disrupting play by introducing new topics, directing the conversation to oneself, or disagreeing with others will almost certainly lead to failure. Boys are more likely to adopt these strategies, which enable them to save face after they've been rejected (Putallaz and Wasserman, 1990). Researchers believe that status is more important to boys than actually entering the group.

Teachers can facilitate the process by designing an activity for the entire group that's geared to the needs and interests of a specific child. If you know that Luke, who's often left out because of his aggressive behavior, loves trains and knows all about them, create a train activity in the classroom. Because of his expertise, Luke will become an attractive member of the group and enter the play with relative ease (Carr, Kikais, Smith, and Littmann, n.d.). Once again, teach these skills with discussion, role-playing, rehearsal, prompting, and reinforcement.

Problem solving or conflict resolution

Once they have successfully inhibited their impulse to strike out or yell, children can begin to solve their problems nonviolently. Good problem-solving skills enable children to avoid aggression (Richard and Dodge, 1982; Spivack and Shure, 1974), stand up for themselves, and build competence and self-esteem (Dinwiddle, 1994; Gonzalez-Mena, 2002).

The process requires them to be calm and able to listen. They will need your help as a facilitator, and you will need enough time and energy to carry through from beginning to end. There's no point in starting the process if everyone is exhausted or if you know you'll have to stop for a snack in the middle (Dinwiddle, 1994). It's useful to remember that conflicts are normal events that provide excellent teaching and learning opportunities and that children are more likely to honor solutions they've thought up themselves.

Most experts agree about how to proceed. There are five basic steps (Committee for Children, 2002; Gonzalez-Mena, 2002; Slaby et al., 1995):

• *Identify the problem.*   All participants in the dispute must have a chance to define the problem. They have to frame it so that it has a solution, which isn't always easy for young children. "Johnny took my bike" is a fact, not a problem that can be easily solved. If Laura says, "Johnny wants my bike," Johnny can reply that Laura has had the bike for a very long time, and they can agree that the problem is "both children want the bike." Then they can begin to find solutions.

• *Brainstorm solutions.*   It's good to have a selection to choose from, and it's important to accept them all, no matter how silly or unworkable they seem. To elicit them nonjudgmentally, use a phrase like, "That's one idea. What's another?" In *The Explosive Child* (1998), Ross W. Greene suggests reminding children of satisfactory ways they've handled similar problems in the past.

- *Evaluate solutions.* This is the time to examine what might work and why. The Second Step program (Committee for Children, 2002) asks the question, "What might happen if . . . ?" to help children learn to think about the possible consequences of a proposed action.

- *Choose a solution and try it.*

- *Evaluate the outcome.* If the first solution doesn't work, tackle the process again.

Although young children can't learn all of this at once, they can begin to learn and use one skill at a time.

It's especially important for children who have difficulty processing social information to learn and practice these skills. If they believe that their failures are their own fault while their successes are due to luck—and many children with problems processing social information do—they may give up far too easily (Rubin et al., 1998). Learning to problem-solve may empower them at the same time that it boosts their skills. Because they often think that the other person in the conflict has hostile intentions, they may also have trouble coming up with nonaggressive alternative solutions, and they may believe that aggressive solutions will get them what they want (Price and Dodge, 1989). Social skills programs often help children learn to distinguish accidents from intentional acts. However, it's important to remember that in some environments attributing hostile intent to others is adaptive—and can be a matter of life and death (Guerra, 1997b).

Anger management

When Case Western Reserve University psychologist Diane Tice asked 400 people about how they manage their moods, she discovered that they had the most trouble with anger (Goleman, 1997).

Anger both in children and adults comes from a feeling of being in danger—either physical or emotional. When you're insulted, treated unfairly, or thwarted in reaching an important goal, you're self-esteem or dignity feels threatened (Goleman, 1997), and the body's first response is to gear up for fight or flight. Then, thanks to the adrenocortical system, the body remains in a state of arousal, ready to convert any new offense into more anger. Even mulling over the original provocative incident—for instance, thinking "That makes me so mad!"—has the effect of escalating anger (Goleman, 1997; Novaco, 1975). This is why venting anger or hitting a pillow doesn't calm a child down or teach her to regulate her feelings. On the contrary, it can actually increase aggression (Bandura, 1973; Berkowitz, 1993; Mallick and McCandless, 1966).

The world of a child with challenging behavior seems to be filled with threats and potential sources of anger. Because she can't process social information correctly, she misunderstands others' actions, and she is frequently rejected by her peers, excluded from activities, or frustrated by the task at hand. When she has a math problem that's too difficult, she will probably get angry—angry at her parents for making her go to school, angry at the teacher for giving her such a hard problem, angry at her classmates for being able to solve it. To keep this anger from blowing up, it's important to intervene early in the anger cycle, while it's still possible to interrupt it. That is precisely what anger management programs teach children to do.

Good problem-solving skills enable children to avoid aggression, stand up for themselves, and build competence and self-esteem.

The best time for children to learn is when they're calm. They aren't listening when they're in the middle of an angry outburst; and talking may actually add to their frustration and anger. Instead, map out a strategy ahead of time for situations where tempers flare, such as when a child doesn't get what she wants; a child is frustrated, hurt, or called a name; or another child takes away a toy.

The first step is to learn to recognize and label anger, usually by becoming sensitive to body cues: a hot face, clenched fists, a frowning mouth, a wrinkled forehead. Children also need to learn that it's all right to feel angry, that feelings—even feelings that make them uncomfortable, such as anger and frustration—are natural responses to events or actions, and that learning to understand, accept, and label feelings is crucial to managing them and solving problems.

They must also learn that feelings are signals, and feeling angry is a signal to stop and consider what to do next. Anger management programs teach direct techniques, such as those used for impulse control—self-speak ("Stop," "Calm down," "I'm getting angry; I'm not going to lose my temper"), slow breathing, relaxation, and counting slowly to five (Coie and Koepll, 1990; Kreidler and Whittall, 1999; Moore and Blaxall, 1995; Wittmer and Honig, 1994). One preschool teacher asks children to put their hands over their hearts to check out how they feel. "I point out that a wildly beating heart is a sign of being out of control," he says (Bauer and Sheerer, 1997). The Turtle Technique, created by A. L. Robin, M. Schneider, and M. Dolnick (1976; see also Greenberg and Kusche, 1998), teaches children to go inside their "shell" when they feel angry or upset. It, too, emphasizes bringing arms and hands toward the body—behavior that helps to inhibit physical action.

A teacher can also help children reframe their anger by using empathy to look at the situation from a different point of view (perhaps realizing that Emma spilled the juice because she hurt her hand yesterday) or by suggesting possible explanations for the event (Maria bumped into Emma and she wasn't actually trying to spoil Jessica's lunch). Another way to reframe anger is to externalize it. One teacher talks about a temper monster who makes children lose their tempers and helps them figure out how to stop the temper monster from controlling them (Milne-Smith, 1995). A different frame for older children (who reacted angrily because they felt their honor was at stake) convinced them that when they were provoked into losing their tempers, the other party in the dispute came out on top (Coie and Koeppl, 1990; Coie, Underwood, and Lochman, 1991).

Once the child's anger is under control, it's time to apply problem solving to the original problem. At that point the child can say, "I'm angry because the math problem is too hard and I don't know what to do," and with the teacher's help, she can begin to brainstorm ideas to solve the problem—asking for help, teaming up with a classmate, breaking it down into smaller, more achievable steps. Throughout this process it is necessary to ensure that the child understands that feeling angry is all right but that pushing Joshua or throwing her math book across the room is not.

Assertiveness

Whenever a child behaves aggressively, there is also a child on the receiving end of that aggression. She is at risk for more than just physical injury.

A child who's harassed isn't usually chosen at random—she has a kind of "anxious vulnerability" that tells a child who behaves aggressively that she's an easy target, according to Michael Troy and L. Alan Sroufe (1987; Crick, Casas, and Ku, 1999). She tends to cry easily; be anxious and withdrawn; lack humor, self-confidence, and self-esteem; and have a hard time finding friends and persuading other children to do what she wants (Hodges et al., 1999; Olweus, 1991). Most of all, she doesn't defend herself, and by giving in, she reinforces the aggression and increases the odds that she'll be attacked again (Coie and Dodge, 1998; Hodges et al., 1999; Schwartz, Dodge, and Coie, 1993). Other children may even follow the example of the child with aggressive behavior (Patterson, Littman, and Bricker, 1967).

Some children who are victimized are not so passive—in fact, they're quick to anger, provocative, and aggressive. The double whammy of being both victimized and aggressive makes them even more likely to be rejected by their peers than children who don't fight back (Schwartz, Dodge, Pettit, and Bates, 1997).

It is during the preschool and early elementary years that children develop a stable tendency to be victimized (Crick et al., 1999; Schwartz et al., 1993). When they play this role over and over again, they come to believe that they deserve the attacks, and they may face serious adjustment problems both in school and in their adult lives (Crick et al., 1999).

If teachers solve the children's problems for them, children who are victimized may learn helplessness and dependency. One way to empower them and help prevent them from being targeted is to teach them assertiveness skills—how to express their feelings, needs, and opinions and to stick up for themselves without violating the rights of others. In European American culture, assertiveness is associated with social competence (Rotheram, 1987). Children who assert themselves are unlikely to be harassed and more likely to have friends who protect them from aggression (Hodges et al., 1999; Rose, 1983). For more on this subject, see Chapter 13.

The European American school day is constantly presenting situations that call for assertive behavior—a child wants to enter a group or have a turn on the swing; another child bosses, intrudes, calls her names, or attacks her (Buell and Snyder, 1981). Knowing how to approach or respond assertively offers children a means to achieve their goals without aggression. By using an assertive overture, a child who tends to behave aggressively can get what she wants without resorting to aggression. An assertive response can protect a child from being victimized and get a child who's potentially aggressive to back down. When all the children learn these skills, they help one another, assertive behavior is reinforced, and no one is blamed or stigmatized.

Assertive behavior lies on a continuum about halfway between passive behavior (when an individual disregards her own needs in favor of another's) and aggressive behavior (when a person denies other people's rights altogether) (Bedell and Lennox, 1997). Children need a wide range of responses along this continuum so that they can choose the one that best fits a particular situation (Rotheram-Borus, 1988).

European American Straight Talk

Assertiveness is culture bound. In cultures where humility and group harmony are important values, it may even be frowned upon (Bedell and Lennox, 1997; Hargie, Saunders, and Dickson, 1994). In European American culture, assertive responses usually involve the following verbal and nonverbal behaviors:

- Facing and looking at the other person without staring
- Speaking loudly, clearly, and directly to the other person in a firm, well-modulated voice
- Using "I" statements ("I don't like it when you push me")
- Having a facial expression and body language that match the verbal message
- Standing straight, 1½ to 3 feet from the other person
- Replying promptly (Bedell and Lennox, 1997; Rose, 1983; Slaby et al., 1995; Weist and Ollendick, 1991)

Researchers who looked at the assertive responses of popular children noticed that they had a high energy level and gave reasons for their requests and for not complying with unreasonable requests (Weist and Ollendick, 1991). In *Skill-Streaming in Early Childhood* (1990), Ellen McGinnis and Arnold P. Goldstein call this "brave talk" (p. 117).

Taking a Stand

Slaby and his colleagues (1995) suggest teaching children to use the following assertive responses—immediately, directly, and firmly—to avoid being victimized:

- To physical attack, "I don't like it when you hit," "Stop kicking me; that hurts."

- To a seizure of objects or territory, "I'm not done with that," "I'm staying here."

- To verbal abuse or discrimination, "I don't like it when you say that," "Everyone is allowed to play here."

- To unfair treatment, "It's my turn now."

In *Early Violence Prevention*, Ronald G. Slaby and his colleagues describe two kinds of assertive behaviors (1995). The more familiar kind, *reactive assertive behavior*, is what a person uses to respond to someone else: to express a different opinion, ask someone to change her behavior, refuse an unreasonable request. The other kind, *proactive assertive behaviors*, help a person to initiate and maintain interactions, express positive feelings, give and receive compliments, make requests and suggestions, and offer things in a polite open-ended manner (Hargie, Saunders, and Dickson, 1994). This version of assertiveness comes with a smile and is softer, friendlier, quieter, and more open than the reactive version.

Assertiveness requires several skills. Perhaps the most important is for a child to recognize her own feelings and thoughts, positive and negative. Without this awareness, she can't figure out what she wants to say and do. Being attuned to her own feelings also helps her have more empathy for others and make better decisions (Rotheram-Borus, 1988). Because self-esteem also helps a child to express disagreement or stand up for her rights, some programs try to bolster confidence by asking children to make positive statements about themselves (Rotheram, 1987). Assertiveness also requires impulse control—the ability to express oneself in an appropriate way and to problem-solve and compromise without losing one's temper.

Like other social skills, assertiveness should be introduced and taught away from the heat of the moment. Coaching and reinforcement are especially important, both in practice sessions and when children are putting their new skills to use in the classroom. When Irene says, "Jody hit me," that is your cue to teach: "No one is allowed to hurt you. Did you tell her you don't like that?" If Irene needs more assistance, accompany her to the scene and give her a script ("Say, 'I don't like it when you hit me. Hitting isn't allowed. It hurts.'"). In this way you teach Irene (and the other children) the value of an assertive response and remind Jody of the rules without giving her any direct attention.

Once again, we repeat our mantra: Whether you're teaching empathy, impulse control, group entry skills, problem solving, anger management, or assertiveness, it's essential to present, rehearse, and role-play these techniques when the children are calm and collected. When they actually put them into practice in the classroom, they'll need plenty of prompting, coaching, cuing, and reinforcement from you.

Although learning social and emotional skills won't solve all the problems that children face, it can go a long way toward creating a positive social climate and helping them to feel comfortable and safe.

What Do You Think?

1. Describe the social climate in your class. What role has the professor played in developing and supporting the social context that created this climate?

2. What does "You can't say you can't play" mean to you? Has anyone ever told you that you couldn't play? How did it make you feel? How did you respond?

3. Cut out a series of photographs from magazines and identify the subjects' emotions. What are the clues (e.g., body language, facial expression) that led you to your conclusions? Be specific.

4. Think about times when you were trying to enter a group. What did you feel? Do you remember what you did? Do you remember what worked and what didn't?

5. Do a role-play with a classmate where you are supposed to do a class project together but you disagree about what to do. Try to resolve the problem by using problem-solving techniques.

6. How do you know that you are angry? What are your personal cues? How does knowing that you feel angry help you to manage your anger?

Suggested Reading and Resources

Goleman, D. (1997). *Emotional intelligence*. New York: Bantam Books.

Katz, L. G., & McClellan, D. E. (1997). *Fostering children's social competence: The teacher's role*. Washington, DC: National Association for the Education of Young Children.

Paley, V. (1993). *You can't say you can't play*. Cambridge, MA: Harvard University Press.

Slaby, R. G., Roedell, W., Arezzo, D., & Hendrix, K. (1995). *Early violence prevention: Tools for teachers of young children*. Washington, DC: National Association for the Education of Young Children.

Webster-Stratton, C. (2000). *How to promote children's social and emotional competence*. London: Paul Chapman.

In the last few years, a virtual library of user-friendly social skills programs has appeared on the market.

Second Step: A Violence Prevention Curriculum (preschool to kindergarten level) aims to reduce aggression and increase prosocial behavior by teaching empathy, emotion management, and problem-solving skills using concrete tools such as photos, puppets, stories, and songs, along with role-playing and dramatizations. Committee for Children, 568 First Avenue South, Suite 600, Seattle, WA 98104-2804; phone 800-634-4449; http://www.cfchildren.org/violence.htm.

RCCP, Resolving Conflict Creatively Program, is a collaborative effort of the New York City Board of Education and Educators for Social Responsibility. In its comprehensive conflict resolution program for kindergarten through grade 12, regular classroom teachers teach the curricula with training and support from RCCP staff throughout the year. The program concentrates on active listening, assertiveness, expressing feelings, perspective taking, cooperation, negotiation, and ways of interrupting expressions of bias or prejudice. Resolving Conflict Creatively Program, National Center, 163 Third Avenue, Room 103, New York, NY 10003; phone 212-387-0225 (contact Linda Lantieri, director); http://www.esrnational.org/about-rccp.html.

Peace Builders is an elementary-school-based project to reduce physical and verbal aggression. Throughout the school year, school counselors or other trained instructors use modeling, role play, self-monitoring, and generalization strategies to teach students to interact socially in a positive way. The main messages are to praise others, avoid insults, seek the advice of wise people, and speak up about hurt feelings. Peace Builders, P.O. Box 12158, Tucson, AZ 85732; phone 877-473-2236; http://www.peacebuilders.com/.

PATHS, Promoting Alternative Thinking Strategies, a curriculum for kindergarten through grade 5, focuses on the developmental integration of affect, behavior, and cognitive understanding. It provides children with the knowledge and skills necessary for self-control, understanding, expressing and regulating their emotions, and effective social problem solving. It also works to improve classroom and school ecology. Blueprints for Violence Prevention, Center for the Study and Prevention of Violence, Institute of Behavioral Science, University of Colorado at Boulder, 900 28th Street, Suite 107, 439 UCB, Boulder, CO 80309-0439; phone 303-492-1032; http://www.colorado.edu/cspv/blueprints.

References

Aderem, M. (1995). Dealing with challenging behaviours: A viewpoint from the PACE Program. *Early Childhood Educator, 10,* 7.

Andersen, K. (1996, May). *Earlier help for children with spirited temperaments, please.* Workshop presented at the meeting of the Early Childhood Educators of British Columbia, Vancouver.

Andrews, L., & Trawick-Smith, J. (1996). An ecological model for early childhood violence prevention. In R. L. Hampton, P. Jenkins, & T. P. Gullotta (Eds.), *Preventing violence in America* (pp. 233–261). Thousand Oaks, CA: Sage.

Baker, A. (2001, December 16). Steep rise in gun sales reflects post-attack fears. *The New York Times,* pp. A1, B10.

Bandura, A. (1973). *Aggression: A social learning analysis.* Englewood Cliffs, NJ: Prentice-Hall.

Bauer, K. L., & Sheerer, M. A., with Dettore, E., Jr. (1997). Creative strategies in Ernie's early childhood classroom. *Young Children, 52,* 47–52.

Beaty, J. J. (1992). *Skills for preschool teachers* (4th ed.). New York: Merrill.

Bedell, J. R., & Lennox, S. S. (1997). *Handbook for communication and problem-solving skills training: A cognitive-behavioral approach.* New York: Wiley.

Beland, K. R. (1996). A schoolwide approach to violence prevention. In R. L. Hampton, P. Jenkins, & T. P. Gullotta (Eds.), *Preventing violence in America* (pp. 209–231). Thousand Oaks, CA: Sage.

Berkowitz, L. (1993). *Aggression: Its causes, consequences, and control.* New York: McGraw-Hill.

Bierman, K. L. (1986). Process of change during social skills training with preadolescents and its relation to treatment outcomes. *Child Development, 57,* 230–240.

Bierman, K. L., & Furman, W. (1984). The effects of social skills training and peer involvement on the social adjustment of preadolescents. *Child Development, 55,* 151–162.

Brooks, R. B. (1994). Children at risk: Fostering resilience and hope. *American Journal of Orthopsychiatry, 64,* 545–553.

Buell, G., & Snyder, J. (1981). Assertiveness training with children. *Psychological Reports, 49,* 71–80.

Carr, A., Kikais, T., Smith, C., & Littmann, E. (n.d.). *Making friends: A guide to using the assessment of peer relations and planning interventions.* Vancouver, British Columbia: Making Friends.

Cartledge, G., & Milburn, J. F. (1995). *Teaching social skills to children: Innovative approaches* (3rd ed.). Boston: Allyn and Bacon.

Chan, S. (1998) Families with Asian roots, In E. W. Lynch & M. J. Hanson (Eds), *Developing cross-cultural competence: A guide for working with children and their families* (pp 251–344). Baltimore: Paul H. Brookes.

Cicchetti, D., Ganiban, J., & Barnett, D. (1991). Contributions from the study of high risk populations to understanding the development of emotional regulation. In J. Garber & K. A. Dodge (Eds.), *The development of emotional regulation and dysregulation* (pp. 15–48). New York: Cambridge University Press.

Clarke-Stewart, A. (1982). *Daycare.* Cambridge, MA: Harvard University Press.

Coie, J. D., & Dodge, K. A. (1998). Aggression and antisocial behavior. In N. Eisenberg (Ed.), *Handbook of child psychology: Vol. 3, Social, emotional, and personality development* (5th ed., pp. 779–862). New York: Wiley.

Coie, J. D., & Koeppl, G. K. (1990). Adapting intervention to the problems of aggressive and disruptive rejected children. In S. R. Asher & J. D. Coie (Eds.), *Peer rejection in childhood* (pp. 309–337). New York: Cambridge University Press.

Coie, J. D., Underwood, M., & Lochman, J. E. (1991). Programmatic intervention with aggressive children in the school setting. In D. J. Pepler & K. H. Rubin (Eds.), *The development and treatment of childhood aggression* (pp. 389–410). Hillsdale, NJ: Erlbaum.

Committee for Children. (2002). *Second Step: A violence-prevention curriculum*. Seattle: Author.

Crick, N. R., Casas, J. F., & Ku, H.-C. (1999). Relational and physical forms of peer victimization in preschool. *Developmental Psychology, 35,* 376–385.

DeRosier, M. E., Cillessen, A. H. N., Coie, J. D., & Dodge, K. A. (1994). Group social context and children's aggressive behavior. *Child Development, 65,* 1068–1079.

deWaal, F. B. M. (2000). Primates—A natural heritage of conflict resolution. *Science, 289,* 586–590.

Dinwiddle, S. A. (1994). The saga of Sally, Sammy, and the red pen: Facilitating children's social problem solving. *Young Children, 49,* 13–19.

Dunn, J., & Brown, J. (1991). Relationships, talk about feelings, and the development of affect regulation in early childhood. In J. Garber & K. A. Dodge (Eds.), *The development of emotional regulation and dysregulation* (pp. 89–108). New York: Cambridge University Press.

Eisenberg, N., & Fabes, R. A. (1998). Prosocial development. In N. Eisenberg (Ed.), *Handbook of child psychology: Vol. 3, Social, emotional, and personality development* (5th ed., pp. 701–778). New York: Wiley.

Fabes, R. A., & Eisenberg, N. (1992). Young children's coping with interpersonal anger. *Child Development, 63,* 116–128.

Giuliani, L. (1997, April). *Anger and aggressivity in pre-schoolers.* Workshop presented at Centre de Psychoeducation, Montreal, Quebec.

Goleman, D. (1997) *Emotional intelligence.* New York: Bantam Books.

Gonzalez–Mena, J. (2002). *The child in the family and the community* (3rd ed.). Upper Saddle River, NJ: Merrill Prentice-Hall.

Gopnik, A., Meltzoff, A. N., & Kuhl, P. K. (2001). *The scientist in the crib: What early learning tells us about the mind.* New York: Perennial.

Greenberg, M. T., & Kusche, C. (1998). *Blueprints for violence prevention: Book 10, Promoting Alternative Thinking Strategies (PATHS).* Boulder: Institute of Behavioral Science, University of Colorado.

Greene, R. W. (1998). *The explosive child: A new approach for understanding and parenting easily frustrated, "chronically inflexible" children.* New York: HarperCollins.

Greenman, J. (2001). *What happened to the world? Helping children cope in turbulent times.* Retrieved February 1, 2002, from www.brighthorizons.com/talktochildren/whathapp.pdf.

Guerra, N. G. (1997a). Intervening to prevent childhood aggression in the inner city. In J. McCord (Ed.), *Violence and childhood in the inner city* (pp. 256–312). New York: Cambridge University Press.

Guerra, N. G. (1997b, May). *Violence in schools: Interventions to reduce school-based violence.* Paper presented at the meeting of the Centre for Studies of Children at Risk, Hamilton, Ontario.

Guralnick, M. J. (1986). The peer relationships of young handicapped and nonhandicapped children. In P. S. Strain, M. J. Guralnick, & H. M. Walker (Eds.), *Children's social behavior: Development, assessment, and modification* (pp. 93–140). Orlando: Academic Press.

Hargie, O., Saunders, C., & Dickson, D. (1994). *Social skills in interpersonal communication* (3rd ed.). New York: Routledge.

Harris, J. R. (1999). *The nurture assumption: Why children turn out the way they do.* New York: Touchstone.

Hodges, E. V. E., Boivin, M., Vitaro, F., & Bukowski, W. M. (1999). The power of friendship: Protection against an escalating cycle of peer victimization. *Developmental Psychology, 35,* 94–101.

Hymel, S., Wagner, E., & Butler, L. J. (1990). Reputational bias: View from the peer group. In S. R. Asher & J. D. Coie (Eds.), *Peer rejection in childhood* (pp. 156–186). New York: Cambridge University Press.

Ianotti, R. J. (1985). Naturalistic and structured assessments of prosocial behavior in preschool children: The influence of empathy and perspective taking. *Developmental Psychology, 21,* 46–55.

Katz, L. F., Kramer, L., & Gottman, J. M. (1992). Conflict and emotions in marital, sibling, and peer relationships. In C. U. Shantz & W. W. Hartup (Eds.), *Conflict in child and adolescent development* (pp. 122–149). New York: Cambridge University Press.

Katz, L. G., & McClellan, D. E. (1997). *Fostering children's social competence: The teacher's role.* Washington, DC: National Association for the Education of Young Children.

Kreidler, W. J., & Whittall, S. T., with Doty, N., Johns, R., Logan, C., Roerden, L. P., Raner, C. & Wintle, C. (1999). *Early childhood adventures in peacemaking.* Cambridge, MA: Educators for Social Responsibility.

Ladd, G. W., Price, J. M., & Hart, C. H. (1990). Preschoolers' behavioral orientations and patterns of peer contact: Predictive of peer status? In S. R. Asher & J. D. Coie (Eds.), *Peer rejection in childhood* (pp. 90–115). New York: Cambridge University Press.

Landy, S., & Peters, R. DeV. (1991). Understanding and treating the hyperaggressive toddler. *Zero to Three, 11,* 22–31.

Mallick, S. K., & McCandless, B. R. (1966). A study of catharsis aggression. *Journal of Personality and Social Psychology, 4,* 591–596.

McGinnis, E., & Goldstein, A. P. (1990). *Skill-streaming in early childhood: Teaching prosocial skills to the preschool and kindergarten child.* Champaign, IL: Research Press.

Michelson, L., & Mannarino, A. (1986). Social skills training with children: Research and clinical applications. In P. S. Strain, M. J. Guralnick, & H. M. Walker (Eds.), *Children's social behavior: Development, assessment, and modification* (pp. 373–406). Orlando: Academic Press.

Milne-Smith, J. (1995, November). *Working with high needs children.* Workshop sponsored by Quebec Association for Preschool Professional Development, Montreal, Quebec.

Mize, J., & Ladd, G. W. (1990). Toward the development of successful social skills training for preschool children. In S. R. Asher & J. D. Coie (Eds.), *Peer rejection in childhood* (pp. 338–361). New York: Cambridge University Press.

Moore, K., & Blaxall, J. (1995, October). Developing empathy and building social skills. *Ideas, 2*(2), 16–21.

Mulligan, S., Morris, S., Miller-Green, K., & Harper-Whalen, S. (1998). *The Child Care plus+ curriculum on inclusion: Practical strategies for early childhood programs.* Missoula, MT: Rural Institute on Disabilities/University of Montana.

Nagin, D. S., & Tremblay, R. E. (2001). Parental and early childhood predictors of persistent physical aggression in boys from kindergarten to high school. *Archives of General Psychiatry, 58,* 389–394.

National Association for the Education of Young Children. (2001). *Helping children cope with violence.* Washington, DC: Author. Retrieved September 24, 2001, from http://www.naeyc.org/resources/eyly/1998/01.htm.

Novaco, R. W. (1975). *Anger control: The development and evaluation of an experimental treatment.* Lexington, MA: Heath.

Olweus, D. (1991). Bully/victim problems among schoolchildren: Basic facts and effects of a school-based intervention program. In D. J. Pepler & K. H. Rubin (Eds.), *The development and treatment of childhood aggression* (pp. 411–448). Hillsdale, NJ: Erlbaum.

Olweus, D., Limber, S., & Mihalic, S. F. (1999). History and description of the Bullying Prevention Program. Excerpted from *Blueprints for violence prevention: Book 9, Bullying Prevention Program.* Boulder, CO: Center for the Study and Prevention of Violence. Retrieved November 3, 2001, from http://www.colorado.edu/cspv/blueprints/model/chapt/BullyExec.htm.

Paley, V. G. (1992). *You can't say you can't play.* Cambridge, MA: Harvard University Press.

Patterson, G. R., Littman, R. A., & Bricker, W. (1967). Assertive behavior in children: A step toward a theory of aggression. *Monographs of the Society for Research in Child Development, 32* (5, Serial No. 113).

Perry, D. G., Kusel, S. L., & Perry, L. C. (1988). Victims of peer aggression. *Developmental Psychology, 24,* 807–814.

Price, J. M., & Dodge, K. A. (1989). Peers' contributions to children's social maladjustment. In T. J. Berndt & G. W. Ladd (Eds.), *Peer relationships in child development* (pp. 341–370). New York: Wiley.

Putallaz, M., & Sheppard, B. H. (1992). Conflict management and social competence. In C. U. Shantz & W. W. Hartup (Eds.), *Conflict in child and adolescent development* (pp. 330–355). New York: Cambridge University Press.

Putallaz, M., & Wasserman, A. (1990). Children's entry behavior. In S. R. Asher & J. D. Coie (Eds.), *Peer rejection in childhood* (pp. 60–89). New York: Cambridge University Press.

Quay, L. C., Weaver, J. H., & Neel, J. H. (1986). The effects of play materials on positive and negative social behaviors in preschool boys and girls. *Child Study Journal, 16*(1), 67–76.

Quinn, M. M., Osher, D., Warger, C. L., Hanley, T. V., Bader, B. D., & Hoffman, C. C. (2000). *Teaching and working with children who have emotional and behavioral challenges.* Longmont, CO: Sopris West.

Richard, B. A., & Dodge, K. A. (1982). Social maladjustment and problem-solving in school aged children. *Journal of Consulting and Clinical Psychology, 50,* 226–233.

Robin, A. L., Schneider, M., & Dolnick, M. (1976). The turtle technique: An extended case study of self control in the classroom. *Psychology in the Schools, 13,* 449–453.

Rose, S. R. (1983). Promoting social competence in children: A classroom approach to social and cognitive skill training. In C. W. LeCroy (Ed.), *Social skills training for children and youth.* New York: Haworth.

Rotheram, M. J. (1987). Children's social and academic competence. *Journal of Educational Research, 80,* 206–211.

Rotheram-Borus, M. J. (1988). Assertiveness training with children. In R. H. Price, E. L. Cowen, R. P. Lorion, & J. Ramos-McKay (Eds.), *Fourteen ounces of prevention: A casebook for practitioners.* Washington, DC: American Psychological Association.

Rubin, K. H., Bukowski, W., & Parker, J. G. (1998). Peer interactions, relationships, and groups. In N. Eisenberg (Ed.), *Handbook of child psychology: Vol. 3, Social, emotional, and personality development* (5th ed., pp. 619–699). New York: Wiley.

Schmidt, R. (1996, May). *Difficult social behavior problems: A consideration of behaviour teaching strategies.* Workshop presented at the meeting of the Early Childhood Educators of British Columbia, Vancouver.

Schwartz, D., Dodge, K. A., & Coie, J. D. (1993). The emergence of chronic peer victimization in boys' play groups. *Child Development, 64,* 1755–1772.

Schwartz, D., Dodge, K. A., Pettit, G. S., & Bates, J. E. (1997). The early socialization of aggressive victims of bullying. *Child Development, 68,* 665–675.

Shonkoff, J. P., & Phillips, D. A. (Eds.) (2000). *From neurons to neighborhoods: The science of early childhood development.* National Research Council and Institute of Medicine, Committee on Integrating the Science of Early Childhood Development, Board on Children, Youth, and Families, Commission on Behavioral and Social Sciences and Education. Washington, DC: National Academy Press.

Slaby, R. G., Roedell, W. C., Arezzo, D., & Hendrix, K. (1995). *Early violence prevention: Tools for teachers of young children.* Washington, DC: National Association for the Education of Young Children.

Sobel, J. (1983). *Everybody wins: Noncompetitive games for young children.* New York: Walker.

Spivack, G., & Shure, M. B. (1974). *Social adjustment of young children. A cognitive approach to solving real-life problems.* San Francisco: Jossey-Bass.

Strayhorn, J. M., & Strain, P. S. (1986). Social and language skills for preventive mental health: What, how, who, and when. In P. S. Strain, M. J. Guralnick, & H. M. Walker (Eds.), *Children's social behavior: Development, assessment, and modification* (pp. 287–330). Orlando: Academic Press.

Thornton, T. N., Craft, C. A., Dahlberg, L. L., Lynch, B. S., & Baer, K. (2000). *Best practices of youth violence prevention: A sourcebook for community action.* Atlanta: Centers for Disease Control and Prevention, National Center for Injury Prevention and Control. Retrieved January 18, 2002, from http://www.cdc.gov/ncipc/dvp/bestpractices.htm.

Tremblay, R. E. (1997, May). *Early identification and intervention.* Paper presented at the meeting of the Centre for Studies of Children at Risk, Hamilton, Ontario.

Troy, M., & Sroufe, L. A. (1987). Victimization among preschoolers. *Journal of the American Academy of Child and Adolescent Psychiatry, 26,* 166–172.

Vitaro, F., & Tremblay, R. E. (1994). Impact of a prevention program on aggressive children's friendships and social adjustment. *Journal of Abnormal Child Psychology, 22,* 457–475.

Webster-Stratton, C. (1997). Early intervention for families of preschool children with conduct problems. In M. J. Guralnick (Ed.), *The effectiveness of early intervention: Second generation research* (pp. 429–454). Baltimore: Paul H. Brookes.

Webster-Stratton, C., & Herbert, M. (1994). *Troubled families—Problem children: Working with parents: A collaborative process.* Chichester, England: Wiley.

Weist, M. D., & Ollendick, T. H. (1991). Toward empirically valid target selection: The case of assertiveness in children. *Behavior Modification, 15,* 213–227.

Wittmer, D. S., & Honig, A. S. (1994). Encouraging positive social development in young children. *Young Children, 49,* 4–12.

9

Guidance and Punishment

Unlike the previous chapters, which deal with the child's surroundings and can make any classroom a safer, happier place for all children, this chapter and the two that follow describe several strategies for working directly with children with challenging behavior. These strategies come from various theoretical perspectives, notably social learning and behaviorist theory, the work of Alfred Adler, and the work of Carl Rogers. Because they aren't recipes or formulas, you can use one strategy at a time or mix and match them. Since no behavior exists in a vacuum, all of these strategies will be more effective when you have a warm and trusting relationship with the child and when the physical environment, the program, and the social context are also set up to prevent aggressive behavior and to enable children to find appropriate alternative behaviors.

   We offer you several strategies for two reasons. First, people have different styles, philosophies, and life experiences, and what suits the teachers in the child-care center or school around the corner might not suit you at all. It's important to believe in the strategy you're using; if you don't feel comfortable with it or understand the philosophy behind it, it probably won't work for you. Second, every child is unique, and each requires an approach that fits his state of mind, to say nothing of his unique temperament, stage of development, and culture. When you know how to use several strategies, possibilities open up, and you can choose the one that's most appropriate for the circumstances. As Abraham Maslow once said, "If the only tool you have is a hammer, you tend to see every problem as a nail."

There are two keys to using these strategies: you and the child. Your knowledge and understanding of both will determine how effective you'll be.

This chapter will look at some of the most familiar strategies teachers use to guide children's behavior: positive reinforcement (including praise and encouragement), natural and logical consequences, time-out, and punishment.

What information will you need?

No matter which approach you decide to use, your intervention will be more effective if you've collected some basic data about the child's challenging behavior. Set aside time to observe how frequently it actually occurs—how many times a day, how many times a week. It's also useful to know whether it happens at specific times—for example, only in the afternoon, when the child is tired; or only on Mondays, after the weekend.

Notice and record the duration, too. How long does the behavior go on? Is he screaming for 10 minutes or 10 seconds? (A watch with a second hand is useful.) And try to measure the intensity—how serious or destructive is it? You may discover that although it's driving you nuts, it isn't really bothering anyone else.

It helps to make a graph. Write down each challenging behavior, and put a checkmark next to it every time you see it. If you can, note the duration as well. At the end of the day, you'll know how many times the behavior occurred, and after a week or so you

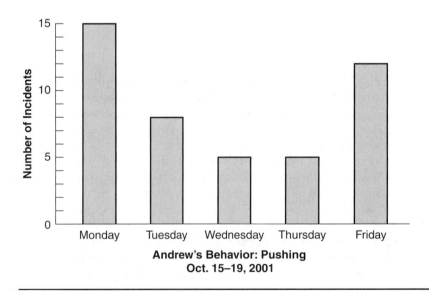

FIGURE 9.1   *Graph of Child's Behavior*

can make a simple line graph or bar graph that will enable you to visualize exactly what's happening. Put the dates or days of the week along the bottom axis, and the frequencies along the side (see Figure 9.1). If you keep track of the time of day that the challenging behavior takes place, you can make another graph that shows the times or activities (such as art or outside play) when the challenging behavior occurs. For future reference, don't forget to label the graph with the child's name, the behavior you've observed, and the dates. This information provides you with a reality check: It tells you that you're dealing with real events. It also gives you a much better sense of what provokes the child's challenging behavior and which strategies will work best with him. Chapter 11 presents more information about observing and recording behavior.

How useful is positive reinforcement?

Positive reinforcement is perhaps the most basic of all guidance strategies—so prevalent that we use it almost without noticing. As a formal technique, it draws its inspiration from social learning theory, the behaviorists, and operant conditioning. It is, of course, a reward, a pleasant response that follows a behavior and usually increases its frequency or intensity (Neilsen, Olive, Donovan, and McEvoy, 1999; Webster-Stratton and Herbert, 1994). Positive reinforcement is a very effective way to influence children's behavior. Janet Gonzalez-Mena says it succinctly in *The Child in the Family and the Community* (2002): "Behavior that's rewarded tends to continue. Behavior that's ignored tends to disappear" (p. 161).

Positive reinforcement comes in several flavors. It can be verbal or physical, social or tangible (such as an encouraging phrase, a pat on the back, a smile, a favorite activity,

Myriad Possibilities

There are endless opportunities to provide positive reinforcement to children throughout the day, and almost anything can turn out to be a reinforcer.

- *Verbal reinforcement.* Talk to a child about what he's doing; ask questions about his family, his pet, his culture, what he likes to do at school and at home, and listen attentively to the answers; share jokes; ask him to help you or another child with a task; ask him what he would like to do; let him know that you enjoy being with him and are glad that he is in your class; show appreciation for his contributions to the group, his sense of humor, or his sensitivity; tell him that he is a good friend and that the other children like him.

- *Nonverbal reinforcement.* Give a child a friendly smile, a high-five, a hug, or a cuddle; be his partner or let him sit on your lap; offer help; take the time to teach him a new skill; readily comply with a child's request. Some children are tickled pink when the teacher chooses to sit by them or join in their activity. Sometimes giving a child the time to finish his work or putting it on the wall is enough to let him know that you think what he is doing is important.

Children respond to different positive reinforcers, so it's very important to take the time to observe closely and discover which ones each child understands and values.

a sticker, or a jelly bean). Although tangible rewards are useful with children with developmental or emotional problems, by and large teachers eschew their use with children who are developing normally.

Each child responds to different positive reinforcers, so it's very important to take the time to observe closely and discover which kinds he understands and values. Some children prefer enthusiastic, intense reinforcement. Others, who are easily excited and stimulated, need their reinforcement in small, low-key doses. Many children with challenging behavior don't like to be touched, so give them a wink, a nod, or a thumbs up instead.

Whatever form positive reinforcement takes, the bottom line is always the same: You are giving the child your attention and support. For this reason any reinforcer works best when you and the child have a warm and open relationship. Positive reinforcement helps to build that relationship.

A child who receives a lot of positive messages will probably behave more positively (Webster-Stratton and Herbert, 1994). Because children need attention, a child who doesn't get enough positive attention will set out in search of negative attention (Webster-Stratton and Herbert), and he'll probably become a master at finding it. When a child with challenging behavior acts appropriately, teachers are so unsure of how to respond and so reluctant to rock the boat that they withdraw ever so quietly. On the other hand, they have eyes in the back of their heads when it comes to inappropriate behavior. The result? Most of a teacher's interactions with a child with challenging behavior are negative, and the child (and his classmates) learn that the best way to get the teacher's attention is to make her angry. The less acceptable the child's behavior, the more attention he receives.

One part of the solution to this problem is to figure out ways to give the child positive attention instead of negative attention. Every child—even one whose behavior is driving you crazy—does things right some of the time. It's extremely important to keep an eagle eye out for those moments—to catch him being good, as the expression goes—and reward him with positive reinforcement (Gonzalez-Mena, 2002). When you give proper recognition to the positive times, you are emphasizing the child's strengths and helping him to enlarge them, helping him to replace inappropriate behavior with appropriate behavior. If he can capture your attention this way and learn to accept your encouragement, he will probably feel less need for challenging behavior. And if you can manage to recognize the strengths in a child who's making your job difficult, chances are you'll find yourself feeling more positive, forgiving, and empathetic toward him— which may induce him to behave more appropriately.

Positive reinforcement is actually feedback. It gives children information about what behavior you accept and value in your classroom, and it gives them support while they're trying it out, making mistakes, and trying again. For this reason it's also important to reinforce *approximations* of desired behavior—and even pauses in challenging behavior—rather than demanding perfection (Barton, 1986). If Gabriella puts her coat under the hook in her cubby instead of the middle of the cloakroom floor where she usually drops it, that's progress and deserves commendation ("Well done, Gabriella; now no one will trip over your coat"). If you're inclined to be sarcastic or to add advice about what she should do the next time, bite your tongue. For this tactic to work, the reinforcement has to be positive and unequivocal, with no implied criticism of past performance or reminders about the future (Andersen, 2000; Webster-Stratton and Herbert, 1994).

Research gives us these hints about how to make positive reinforcement more effective:

- Deliver the reinforcement immediately (as soon as he starts putting away the blocks).

- Describe exactly what you're reinforcing ("You're getting good at remembering to walk indoors").

Different Strokes

In many cultures, positive reinforcement doesn't hold the prominent position it has in European American culture. In India, for example, once a person is part of a group, he is completely accepted, and he is expected to fulfill all his obligations without prompting, thanks, or recognition (Greenfield and Suzuki, 1998).

• Give it consistently, each time you see the behavior you're looking for. As the child learns, you can switch to intermittent reinforcement, which is very effective at maintaining behavior (Strayhorn and Strain, 1986; Webster-Stratton and Herbert, 1994).

• Be honest and sincere. Children can spot a phony a mile away.

Which is better: Praise or encouragement?

What exactly do you say when you're giving a child positive reinforcement? This question evokes remarkably strong reactions from teachers. Some believe that praise— the traditional positive reinforcer—is an enemy that's "dangerous," "coercive," "does more harm than good," and even damages relationships (Fields and Boesser, 1998; Kohn, 2001; Reynolds, 1990). These critics charge that praise motivates children to do things for extrinsic reasons (to please others) and not for intrinsic reasons (to please themselves or because the task is inherently worth doing). They say that because praise is an adult's judgment of a child's performance, children come to rely on the views of others and

Accentuate the Positive

To make your positive comments more effective, try the following:

• Name the behavior you want to reinforce. ("Thank you for putting your puzzle on the puzzle shelf so nicely.")

• Focus on specific attributes of the child's work rather than on generalities. ("Your collage has a lot of sparkles," "The ending of your story surprised me.")

• Emphasize the process, not the product, and let the child know that mistakes are part of learning. ("You worked on that dinosaur for a long time. Can you show me how you finally made it stand up?")

• Point out how a child's action affects his peers. ("Look at Caitlin's smile! You really made her happy when you let her be a firefighter!")

• Be sincere and direct.

• Deliver your encouragement privately.

• Use your natural voice, but be aware that some children may need quieter or more intense encouragement.

• Avoid comparisons between children.

• Help children appreciate their own behavior and achievements. ("You must feel proud of the way you shared the markers with Lan Ying," rather than "I like the way you. . . .") (Kohn, 2001; Mulligan, Morris, Miller-Green, and Harper-Whalen, 1998; Slaby, Roedell, Arezzo, and Hendrix, 1995).

don't develop their own judgment or learn to evaluate their own effort and satisfaction. Praise, the argument concludes, dampens children's autonomy, creativity, self-control, self-esteem, and pleasure. Opponents reserve special scorn for evaluative praise, which expresses the teacher's approval, compares children to one another, or is very general. Most teachers (and many children!) agree that phrases such as "Good girl" and "What a beautiful painting" are meaningless.

On the other hand, encouragement—another form of positive reinforcement—"is more important than any other aspect of child raising" (Dreikurs, 1964, p. 36). According to its supporters, encouragement is not judgmental and it expresses trust and confidence in the child (Coloroso, 1995). Encouragement, it is said, places the emphasis on the behavior and the process as opposed to the person and the product. By recognizing effort and improvement rather than achievement (Reynolds, 1990; Rodd, 1996), it nourishes autonomy and self-esteem.

Sometimes, however, it's hard to understand the difference between praise and encouragement. In fact, a meta-analysis (Cameron and Pierce, 1994) shows that praise *does* increase intrinsic motivation, so the sky won't fall if we use it occasionally. When you get right down to it, what's most important is to give positive attention to the child whenever he's acting appropriately.

What if positive reinforcement provokes challenging behavior?

With some children, positive reinforcement seems to have exactly the opposite effect from what you expect. At the first kind word, they throw games on the floor or kick the nearest person.

Why do children react this way? One reason is that your style or choice of reinforcement may not suit that particular child. Perhaps he's accustomed to living in a much more intense emotional environment, and everything at school or child care seems bland by comparison. Your gentle positive attention can't begin to compete with the excitement he generates by standing up and pushing over his table while you're quietly explaining the math to him. To deal with this problem, psychologists Carolyn Webster-Stratton and Martin Herbert (1994) suggest that you provide yourself with a metaphorical megaphone to make your reinforcement stronger. Sometimes, they write, children with challenging behavior seem deaf, "as if hidden in a suit of armor and a helmet" (p.136). Another possibility is that your positive attention is too intense and the child's neurological or sensory system can't handle it. In that case, you need to tone it down. If the child is old enough, you could ask him what kind of feedback he'd prefer (Andersen, 2000). If another teacher has more success with this child, watch her, talk to her about what she does, and try it. Ask yourself, "What would Louise do in this situation?"

But the most likely explanation is that the child rarely receives positive attention, and it scares and worries him. When he punches the child beside him, he knows exactly what to expect from the people around him and he's far more comfortable. Children like this eventually become used to criticism from adults and rejection from their peers, and they begin to believe that they deserve this treatment. Convinced that they're bad,

When children have trouble with positive reinforcement, they need more encouragement, not less.

they dedicate themselves to proving it. Their motto seems to be, "If you think that I'm bad, why should I be good?" If their negative self-image is too strong, they will try to get you to treat them the way everyone else does—negatively—because in their own eyes they couldn't possibly be worthy of your positive attention (Giuliani, 1997; Milne-Smith, 1995). This state of affairs severely damages their self-esteem and makes it difficult for them to succeed in the future.

When a child has so much trouble with positive reinforcement, it is tempting to conclude that it is the last thing he needs. But such children need *more* encouragement, not less. So what can you do? Combating the child's negative view of himself takes commitment, patience, and perseverance. It requires you to trust, respect, and care for the child so that he can learn to trust, respect, and care for himself. It's important to believe in the child's ability to succeed, to look for what he can do instead of what he can't do. If you expect him to hurt others, that's what he will do. But if you believe that he can learn to make friends, enjoy circle time, finish the assignment, wait his turn, his potential for success will increase. Your confidence in him can't guarantee it, but it will help.

Give the child lots of nonverbal positive reinforcement, showing your affection and your belief in him in your body language, tone of voice, and behavior. Watch carefully to see what he likes, what he's good at, what works as a reinforcer for him. Each day find opportunities to offer him activities you know he enjoys, books he can read successfully, games that entice him to cooperate. Notice and create positive moments with him, playing at something he chooses himself, letting him direct the play, and telling him that you like talking and playing with him. Include other children when you can. Gradually you will increase his comfort zone and accustom him to feeling better about himself and less anxious when he is behaving appropriately.

What about natural and logical consequences?

In addition to being a strategy in its own right, positive reinforcement is one half of another familiar guidance technique: natural and logical consequences. In fact, positive reinforcement *is* a consequence, and as you've just seen, it can be an effective motivating force that also helps children to know they're behaving appropriately ("When you've finished putting away the blocks, we're going to have watermelon for snack"). Most of the time, however, teachers focus on the other kind of consequence, one that's a response to negative behavior.

The idea comes from the work of the Adlerians, but Rudolf Dreikurs (1964) and Barbara Coloroso (1995) made it famous. Whether they're positive or negative, consequences flow from the natural or social order of the real world, not from the power or control of adults (Coloroso, 1995; Gonzalez-Mena, 2002; Marion, 1999). The child does something, and something happens as a result of his action.

Some consequences occur naturally. If the child goes outside without his mittens when it's below freezing, his hands will be cold. But in a situation where natural consequences are too remote or dangerous, teachers often create logical or reasonable con-

The teacher's respectful, calm, matter-of-fact demeanor will make it possible for the consequences to do their job.

sequences instead. On a sunny day either the child can put on a sun hat, or he has to play in the shade. Whether they're natural or logical, consequences are a teaching tool, because the child learns from experiencing the consequences of his own behavior (Dreikurs, 1964). The consequences tell him that he has control over his own life and responsibility for what he does (Coloroso, 1995; Dreikurs, 1964) and help him learn to make decisions and profit from his mistakes (Webster-Stratton and Herbert, 1994).

Although consequences are helpful for children, they can be very tricky for teachers in both design and application. When you're constructing consequences, you're offering the child a choice. First of all, both options must relate directly, reasonably, and logically to his behavior. A child who refuses to put on a sun hat can choose between wearing it or staying in the shade. Or, to put it another way, when he wears a hat, he can play wherever he likes. It makes sense for the child to stay in the shade if he isn't wearing a hat, and because this is a fair and reasonable consequence, he'll probably accept it and recognize that the next time he's outside he has to wear a hat if he wants to play on the climbing structure with his friends. On the other hand, restricting his access to the Legos for the rest of the day is not at all logical or reasonable. Such a consequence would provoke anger and resentment, and all it would teach is that his teacher is mean.

Consequences also have to be enforceable and enforced, because a consequence that isn't enforced doesn't teach what it's supposed to. (Instead the child learns that he can ignore the choices.) It's relatively easy to be sure the child stays in the shade, but keeping him inside for the day would present terrible logistical problems for the entire staff. This is what Barbara Coloroso (1995) means when she says consequences have to be simple and practical.

It's also extremely important to design consequences that aren't threatening or punitive. That's what happens when they're arbitrary (such as taking away the Legos), or when you're feeling angry or vengeful at the time that you're imposing them. In fact, your attitude is the major difference between negative consequences and punishment. A respectful, calm, matter-of-fact demeanor will make it possible for the consequences to do their job. Your tone of voice should be firm but friendly, and your words shouldn't be judgmental or critical.

State the choices clearly, and once the child has made his decision, allow the consequences to take their course immediately. If you're a very empathetic soul, you may

Use with Care

In *The Explosive Child* (1998), Ross W. Greene cautions that consequences don't work in every situation and with every child. "Motivational strategies don't make the impossible possible; they make the possible more possible," he writes (p. 92).

"Your child is drowning in a sea of frustration and inflexibility. You are the lifeguard. If you swim out to your drowning child, hold up a dollar bill, and yell "SWIM!" your child will continue to drown. If you ignore your child, he'll just as surely drown. Your days of trying to motivate your drowning child to swim are over. If your child could swim, he would. It's time for plan B" (p. 98).

be tempted to intervene before the natural consequences actually take effect. If so, restrain yourself. Such overprotectiveness deprives the child of the chance to learn and doesn't allow him to develop his own coping strategy. What you can do instead is offer him a chance to try again later (Webster-Stratton and Herbert, 1994).

When there are consequences for breaking class rules, it's a good idea for the children to help create them. If they've had a hand in designing them, they're more likely to understand and accept both the rule and the consequence.

Is it good practice to use time-out?

The early care and education community has been debating time-out for years. The practice has been misused and overused, and in some places it is now banned or restricted. Time-out comes from the same roots as positive reinforcement: social learning theory and behaviorism. An extreme way to ignore inappropriate behavior, it actually means a time-out from positive reinforcement (Quinn et al., 2000; Webster-Stratton and Herbert, 1994). Although there are many variations, time-out usually involves removing a child from the group to sit in a remote area of the room, perhaps on a specified chair, for one minute for each year of his age, to think about what he's done.

Adherents maintain that time-out tells the child that you care and want to help him keep himself in control. If it's used sensitively and correctly, they say, it assists in maintaining a respectful, trusting relationship. They also believe that time-out interrupts and prevents aggressive behavior, protects the rights and safety of the other children, and keeps them from turning into an admiring and encouraging audience (Milne-Smith, 1995; Rodd, 1996). It allows the child who behaves aggressively, the child who is victimized, and the adult enough time to compose themselves without giving undue attention to the aggressor. According to the yea-sayers, time-out works if it's used consistently and appropriately (American Academy of Pediatrics, 1998; Milne-Smith, 1995; Slaby et al., 1995).

Opponents argue that time-out is a form of punishment that teaches children it's all right to use power to control others. They point out that children don't understand the connection between their behavior and time-out, and time-out doesn't acknowledge their feelings (Katz and McClellan, 1997) or address the causes of their behavior (Marion, 1999). Because teachers tend to use time-out when they're angry, frustrated, or out of control themselves, their motives are suspect. Foes also say that rather than stopping challenging behavior, time-out actually increases it by making children more angry, hostile, and resentful. They suggest that when a teacher puts a child into time-out and tells him to think about what he's done, he's probably plotting his revenge (Katz and McClellan, 1997).

If the child refuses to move to the designated chair, you have created another problem, and no one remembers the reason for moving him in the first place. Why do teachers expect a child who's defiant and noncompliant to be agreeable about time-out? When he refuses, do you pick him up? Drag him? Wait until he changes his mind? Or just give up? If you make a fuss, you may be placing yourself and the rest of the class in danger, and you are once again demonstrating that the more challenging his behavior,

The Fearsome Chair

> Time-out frightens many children, as Kimberly Boulden (1998) relates in her reflection on the practice: "The time-out chair is forever retired in my classroom, and all the children feel more safe, even those children who were never in it. I know this because a parent told me that the thing her son likes best about his new school is that no one sits on the time-out chair. She said it used to terrify him when other children were left there at his previous school. Although he himself never experienced time-out, it caused him great anguish when others did" (p. 43).

the more attention you and his classmates will award him. The other children quickly learn this lesson, too. On the other hand, if you decide that you don't want to fight and don't follow through with your original request, the child learns that he may actually be in control. All of this scares the other children, who begin to doubt that you can keep them safe.

One of the most powerful arguments against time-out is that it damages self-esteem by punishing, embarrassing, and humiliating the child in front of his peers. In effect, it says, "You are bad, and I don't want you here." For children who belong to cultures where being part of the group is important, time-out is an especially dire punishment (Gonzalez-Mena, 2002). Techniques that preserve self-esteem are much more effective in the long run.

Last, but certainly not least, the adversaries of time-out note that it doesn't teach children how to behave appropriately (Katz and McClellan, 1997; Rodd, 1996). The proof is that the same children find themselves in time-out again and again. Indeed, time-out may unintentionally increase behaviors you're trying to eliminate. For example, if Andrew is throwing toys because he doesn't want to put them away and you respond by putting him in time-out, he doesn't have to clean up. If Jessica doesn't know how to string the beads, she might sweep them all to the floor and push over her chair in frustration. If you send her to time-out, she manages to avoid this dreaded activity entirely, and she is no better equipped to do it the next time. In both cases, time-out has reinforced the inappropriate behavior and raised the odds that it will happen again.

Outcast

> A mother who was searching for child care visited a center in her neighborhood, where a friendly 4-year-old helped the director to show her around. He saved his own group's room for last. "This is the science corner where we're weighing different stones," he said. Then he showed her the block corner, the dramatic play area, the art area, and the quiet space where children could curl up with music or a book.
>
> "And that," he said, pointing to a chair in a corner, "is Gary's chair. He's not my friend."

Likewise, a child who's sent to the principal's office doesn't have a chance to learn the material you're covering in class, and he will either fall behind or need your help to catch up—which may be what he wanted in the first place. This can have a domino effect. He won't be able to do tomorrow's work because he didn't learn today's, and he may spit on the floor rather than reveal his inability to solve the problem—and require another visit to the principal.

Interestingly enough, some of time-out's staunchest foes believe in "time away," "cool down," "take a break," "private time" or "sit and watch." This is because the two sides agree on the goals of time-out:

- To give everyone a chance to regain control in a safe place so that when the child reenters the group he is capable of success

- To teach children to recognize when their emotions are building to a dangerous level and to recognize when they are ready to function again

- To allow the rest of the group to continue its activities

Both sides also agree that to be effective, the adult must be calm and respectful, not angry or threatening (Chornoboy and Keffer, 1996; Kleinberg-Bassel, 1997; Slaby et al., 1995; Sussman, 1994).

Time away is really much more valuable—and not at all punitive—when you use it preventively. It is a kind of redirection, a way to teach impulse control and anger management. When the child feels himself becoming anxious or agitated, he can learn to move away, take a deep breath, close his eyes, do a puzzle, sort shapes, or play at the sand table. This self-directed change in locale, activity, or stimulation level allows him to settle his feelings, just as jogging or having a cup of tea often calms and restores an adult who's struggling with a problem. The child may return to the group whenever

Time Away

The other children in the block corner were coming too close to him, and Tyrone was feeling very nervous. He began to knock over all the structures, including his own.

His teacher realized that he needed some time away. In a matter-of-fact voice, she said, "Tyrone, being in the block area just isn't working for you this morning. You can try again later. In the meantime, would you like to draw at the art table or pick a book that we can read together?"

She selected the words and choices carefully. She wasn't punishing or threatening him; she was offering him an opportunity to regain control of himself. She knew that he enjoyed both activities and that they usually had a calming effect on him.

Tyrone chose to look at a book with the teacher. When she finished reading, she felt he was calm enough to go back to the blocks if he wanted to. "Tyrone," she said, "I need to help Megan now. Would you like to look at another book or try playing in the block corner again?"

he's ready, knowing you'll welcome him warmly. You can suggest that he take time away to begin with, but the ultimate goal is for him to figure out when to do this himself.

What's wrong with using punishment?

Punishment is a penalty for wrongdoing, imposed on purpose by someone in power who intends it to be unpleasant (Coloroso, 1995; Rodd, 1996). Like positive reinforcement, punishment originates with social learning and behavioral theory, and because it's aversive, it is supposed to decrease the inappropriate behavior that provoked it (Quinn et al., 2000).

Does punishment work? In the short term, yes. That's why teachers sometimes use it: It provides a quick fix. But its results are fleeting. To remain effective, it has to become stronger and stronger, and the child may behave the same way in other situations because it suppresses the undesirable behavior only in the punisher's presence.

In addition to those we mentioned when we were discussing time-out, there are several other powerful arguments against punishment:

- It makes children angry, resentful, and defiant and leads to more aggressive behavior.
- It teaches children that it's acceptable to use power to control other people.
- It frightens, embarrasses, and humiliates children.
- It damages their self-esteem and self-concept.
- It doesn't teach appropriate behavior.

Punishment also undermines the relationship between adult and child and creates a distrust of adults (Gartrell, 1997; Gonzalez-Mena, 2002; Hay, 1994–1995) because the child tends to focus on how awful the teacher is instead of on his own behavior. Rather than teaching self-discipline and impulse control, the punishment breeds confrontation—or its opposite, deviousness (Gonzalez-Mena, 2000; Hay, 1994–1995). As adults, children who've been punished are prone to depression and other internalizing disorders or to externalizing disorders such as aggressive behavior and delinquency (Hay, 1994–1995).

Skinner's View

In an interview with the *New York Times*, B. F. Skinner, the father of behaviorism, said, "What's wrong with punishments is that they work immediately but give no long-term results. The responses to punishment are either the urge to escape, to counterattack, or a stubborn apathy. These are the bad effects you get in prisons or schools, or wherever punishments are used" (Goleman, 1987, p. C1).

Words Hurt

Most people who work with children agree that physical punishment is never appropriate. But emotional punishment can cause even more developmental problems than minor physical punishment. Did you know that the following practices are also punitive and unacceptable (Hay, 1994–1995) ?

- Threatening
- Scaring
- Humiliating
- Yelling

- Embarrassing
- Insulting or putting someone down
- Teasing
- Intimidating

Punishment also hurts a child's sense of safety and interferes with learning and the development of initiative and autonomy (Gonzalez-Mena, 2002; Hay, 1994–1995). Janet Gonzalez-Mena describes the process this way: "When punishments hurt, the teachable moment is lost. Children are most open to learning right after they've done something wrong or made a mistake. That's the time for helping them see what went wrong. If they're wrapped up in pain (physical or psychological), they can't concentrate on the 'lesson' the adult has in mind" (p. 120).

Punishment is not so much an educational tool as an outlet for adult anger. But an effective teacher needs to regard challenging behavior as an opportunity to teach children skills that they'll need for the rest of their lives. Although empathy, emotional regulation, anger management, impulse control, and other social and problem-solving skills aren't usually part of the formal curriculum, they can be just as important as learning to read and write. When a child feels safe and respected, he is ready to learn and he can become an asset instead of a problem.

In the next two chapters, we'll describe some more positive strategies for addressing challenging behavior.

What Do You Think?

1. Some people believe that praise encourages children to do things for the reward, rather than for the joy of doing them. What do you believe? Do you think that encouragement is more effective? Why?

2. Why do some children have difficulty accepting positive reinforcement? What can you do about it?

3. What is the difference between natural and logical consequences? Give examples of both.

4. What is the difference between a consequence and a punishment? Do they work equally well? Why or why not?

5. Divide the class into two groups and debate the pros and cons of time-out.

Suggested Reading

Coloroso, B. (1995). *Kids are worth it! Giving your child the gift of inner discipline.* Toronto, Ontario: Somerville House.

Greene, R. W. (1998). *The explosive child: A new approach for understanding and parenting easily frustrated, "chronically inflexible" children.* New York: HarperCollins.

Sandall, S., & Ostrovsky, M. (Eds.). (1999). *Practical ideas for addressing challenging behaviors.* Longmont, CO: Sopris West.

References

American Academy of Pediatrics. (1998). Guidance for effective discipline (RE 9740). *Pediatrics, 101,* 723–728.

Andersen, C. J., with McDevitt, S. C. (2000). *The temperament guides: Resources for early intervention professionals.* Scottsdale, AZ: Behavioral-Development Initiatives.

Barton, E. J. (1986). Modification of children's prosocial behavior. In P. S. Strain, M. J. Guralnick, & H. M. Walker (Eds.), *Children's social behavior: Development, assessment, and modification* (pp. 331–372). Orlando: Academic Press.

Boulden, K. (1998). Guidance. In E. A. Tertell, S. M. Klein, & J. L. Jewett (Eds.), *When teachers reflect: Journeys toward effective, inclusive practice* (pp. 37–47). Washington, DC: National Association for the Education of Young Children.

Cameron, J., & Pierce, W. D. (1994). Reinforcement, reward, and intrinsic motivation: A meta-analysis. *Review of Educational Research, 64,* 363–423.

Chornoboy, E., & Keffer, L. (1996, October). *Working effectively with violent and aggressive students.* Workshop sponsored by Quebec Association for Preschool Professional Development, Montreal, Quebec.

Coloroso, B. (1995). *Kids are worth it! Giving your child the gift of inner discipline.* Toronto, Ontario: Somerville House.

Dreikurs, R., with Soltz, V. (1964). *Children: The challenge.* New York: Hawthorn.

Fields, M., & Boesser, C. (1998). *Constructive guidance and discipline: Preschool and primary education* (2nd ed.). Upper Saddle River, NJ: Prentice-Hall.

Gartrell, D. (1997). Beyond discipline to guidance. *Young Children, 52,* 34–42.

Giuliani, L. (1997, April). *Anger and aggressivity in preschoolers.* Workshop presented at Centre de Psychoeducation, Montreal, Quebec.

Goleman, D. (1987, August 25). Embattled giant of psychology speaks his mind. *The New York Times,* pp. B1, B3.

Gonzalez-Mena, J. (2002). *The child in the family and the community* (3rd ed.). Upper Saddle River, NJ: Merrill Prentice-Hall.

Greene, R. W. (1998). *The explosive child: A new approach for understanding and parenting easily frustrated, "chronically inflexible" children.* New York: HarperCollins.

Greenfield, P. M., & Suzuki, L. K. (1998). Culture and human development: Implications for parenting, education, pediatrics, and mental health. In I. E. Sigel & K. A. Renninger (Eds.), *Handbook of child psychology: Vol. 4, Child psychology in practice* (5th ed., pp. 1059–1109). New York: Wiley.

Hay, T. (1994–1995, Winter). The case against punishment. *IMPrint, 11,* 10–11.

Katz, L. G., & McClellan, D. E. (1997). *Fostering children's social competence: The teacher's role.* Washington, DC: National Association for the Education of Young Children.

Kleinberg-Bassel, A. (1997, April). *Tools for crisis management.* Workshop presented at the SpeciaLink Institute on Children's Challenging Behaviours, Sydney, Nova Scotia.

Kohn, A. (2001). Five reasons to stop saying "Good job!" *Young Children, 56,* 24–28.

Marion, M. (1999). *Guidance of young children* (5th ed.). Upper Saddle River, NJ: Merrill.

Milne-Smith, J. (1995, November). *Working with high needs children.* Workshop sponsored by Quebec Association for Preschool Professional Development, Montreal, Quebec.

Mulligan, S., Morris, S., Miller-Green, K., & Harper-Whalen, S. (1998). *The Child Care plus+ curriculum on inclusion: Practical strategies for early childhood programs.* Missoula, MT: Rural Institute on Disabilities/University of Montana.

Neilsen, S. L., Olive, M. L., Donovan, A., & McEvoy, M. (1999). Challenging behavior in your classroom? Don't react—Teach instead! In S. Sandall & M. Ostrosky (Eds.), *Practical ideas for addressing challenging behaviors* (pp. 5–15). Longmont, CO: Sopris West.

Quinn, M. M., Osher, D., Warger, C. L., Hanley, T. V., Bader, B. D., & Hoffman, C. C. (2000). *Teaching and working with children who have emotional and behavioral challenges.* Longmont, CO: Sopris West.

Reynolds, E. (1990). *Guiding young children: A child-centered approach.* Mountain View, CA: Mayfield.

Rodd, J. (1996). *Understanding young children's behavior: A guide for early childhood professionals.* New York: Teachers College Press.

Slaby, R. G., Roedell, W. C., Arezzo, D., & Hendrix, K. (1995). *Early violence prevention: Tools for teachers of young children.* Washington, DC: National Association for the Education of Young Children.

Strayhorn, J. M., & Strain, P. S. (1986). Social and language skills for preventive mental health: What, how, who, and when. In P. S. Strain, M. J. Guralnick, & H. M. Walker (Eds.), *Children's social behavior: Development, assessment, and modification* (pp. 287–330). Orlando: Academic Press.

Sussman, E. F. (1994, Summer). Alternatives to time out. *Show'N Tell Newsletter.*

Webster-Stratton, C., & Herbert, M. (1994). *Troubled families—Problem children: Working with parents: A collaborative process.* Chichester, England: Wiley.

10

The WEVAS Strategy

Even to the most experienced teacher, it sometimes seems as if challenging behavior comes out of nowhere. But according to Canadian psychologists Neil Butchard and Robert Spencler, children usually present warning signs. If you can recognize them and intervene early enough, you can prevent challenging behavior and help children return to a competent state, where their minds, bodies, and emotions are functioning well and geared up for learning. Butchard and Spencler have designed a research-based intervention program called WEVAS, Working Effectively with Violent and Aggressive States. Although it hasn't been formally evaluated, anecdotal evidence from the United States and Canada indicates that it is a very effective strategy.

One of the key ideas behind WEVAS is that any child, even a child who's prone to challenging behavior, can be in a competent state. And any child can drop out of this state at any time. Anxiety is a kind of early warning system that something is amiss, and

The WEVAS concepts and models are presented in this book with the written permission of WEVAS, Inc., 778 Ibister Street, Winnipeg, Manitoba R2Y 1R4, Canada. Email: neil@WEVAS.net or bob@WEVAS.net.

if it continues it can give way to agitation, aggressive behavior, or even assaultive behavior. The sooner teachers can stop this slide, the better.

No matter which state they're in, children need support and guidance to return to the competent state. The WEVAS strategy helps teachers provide this support and guidance by recognizing exactly where the child is, seeing things from her perspective, understanding how their own reactions contribute to the child's behavior, and matching their response to the child's needs. Psychologist Kevin Leman (1992) points out that there is no way to change anyone else's behavior. You can only change your own, and when you do, the strangest thing happens: Other people make the behavior changes you've been hoping for.

Calibration: Zeroing in on the child's state of mind

When you know a child well—her temperament, developmental level, play skills, family, and culture; what she enjoys, what frightens and frustrates her, what makes her sad or mad—you can tell whether she's in or out of a competent state. For example, you know that Amy is feeling "up" when she's talkative and bright eyed. If you see her looking at the floor, silently twirling her hair, you can tell that something's wrong—she's not feeling 100 percent. WEVAS calls this act of sizing up a child's mood and state of mind *calibration*. It is crucial to choosing a strategy that's effective for a particular situation—and crucial to letting you know whether that strategy is working. If you smile at Amy and she sits up straight and begins to talk to her neighbor, you can see that your intervention, subtle as it was, did the trick. Each child has her own characteristic physiological and behavioral signs that can help you to figure out her state of mind.

Tell-Tale Signs

You can prevent challenging behavior by catching it in its earliest phase, anxiety. The signs vary with the child. You can't know for sure what a child is thinking or feeling, but by knowing her well and watching her closely, you can identify these and other signs that indicate what she is feeling.

- *Physiology.* Tears, frequent urination, clenched teeth, blushing, pallor, rigidity, rapid breathing, sweating, fidgeting, vomiting, squeaky voice

- *Behavior.* Downcast eyes, withdrawing, hair twirling, thumb-sucking, sucking hair or clothes, hoarding, clinging, biting fingernails, whining, being noisy or quiet, screaming, masturbating, smirking, giggling, crying

- *Thoughts.* No one loves me; no one wants me; I'm no good; I don't like it here; I don't have any friends; no one will come to get me; I can't do it; I'm bad; I want my mommy

- *Feelings.* Concerned, distressed, troubled, afraid, nervous, excited, expectant, sad, irritable, grouchy, insecure, frustrated, worried, confused, panicky

Understanding the WEVAS Model

A child is centered in the competent state. When she moves out of the center into an anxious, agitated, aggressive, or assaultive state, the role of the teacher is to help the child return to her center. The child usually moves into the anxious state first, and each state is more intense than the one before it. In the diagram, arrows connect the states to one another because a child can move back and forth between them. The outermost circle shows that each state necessitates a different response. Anxiety requires open communication; agitation calls for a teaching or limiting response; aggression demands deescalation; and the assaultive state requires protection for both the teacher and the children. Each response is guided by and responds to a different level of consciousness: the heart, the mind, the body, or the community. The small circles between the competent state and each of the other states represent the open state or the way back. They differ in size because the way back is much more complex when a child is in the assaultive state than when she is in an anxious state.

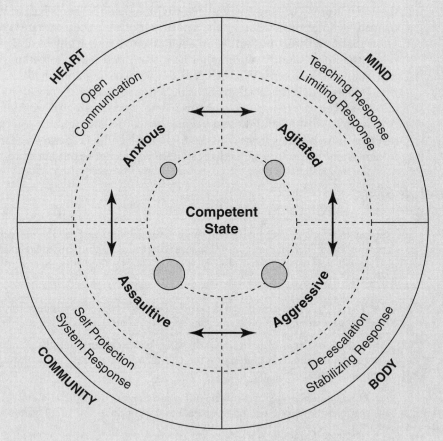

Source: © 2000, WEVAS, Inc. Reproduced with the written permission of WEVAS, Inc.

The anxious state: The early warning system

Anxiety is usually the first state a child reaches when her world is out of kilter. When you're in a child-care center where there are multiple demands or a school classroom with 26 students, it's easy not to notice that a child is anxious. Anxiety is internal; it doesn't show much and doesn't affect anyone but the child herself. But anxiety interferes with a child's ability to learn and interact with her peers, and it alerts you to trouble ahead. If it goes unnoticed, it may escalate. It is therefore extremely important to watch the child closely and learn to read whatever subtle physiological and behavioral clues she gives you as she tries to cope with her anxiety. The way she walks or the way she hangs up her coat may be enough to tip you off.

Recognizing the observable signs is only part of the solution. If you're going to help an anxious child return to her competent state, it's useful to have some insight into her thoughts and feelings, too. Every child has stresses in her life—everything from "Patrick is coming too close to me" to "Mommy and Daddy had a terrible fight last night." These stresses make the child anxious, and as they interact with her thoughts and feelings, her anxiety increases.

Here's how it works: The alarm didn't go off in 3-year-old Zaria's house this morning, so everything was rush, rush, rush. There was toast for breakfast, but Zaria didn't get a chance to eat it. Her mother dressed her because there wasn't time for her to dress herself, and when she dropped Zaria at the child-care center, she rushed off without kissing her goodbye. These were the external stressors.

Then there are internal stressors. Zaria is hungry, and she needs to go to the bathroom. (There wasn't time for that, either.) Her thoughts—irrational because she's anxious—filter the reality and contribute to the stress. "Mommy's mad at me," she thinks. "I didn't eat or dress fast enough. Does she still love me? Will she come back for me?" Her feelings add another layer of stress: Zaria feels sad, lonely, and worried.

Zaria may be hardly aware of all this, and she almost certainly isn't capable of articulating it, so the information isn't available to you. But when she appears at the classroom door, the characteristic behavioral and physiological signs of her anxiety are evident. She is whiny, and tears are starting to form in her eyes as she sits by herself at the art table.

How you respond to this child will make or break her day.

WEVAS advises us to put away our defenses and open ourselves to the child before us. (Your relationship with her is critical here.) Noticing the tears in her eyes and remembering that whining is a sign of anxiety in Zaria, try to understand what she's feeling and thinking so that you can respond to her honestly and completely. Your concern and empathy will tell her that you care about her, respect her feelings, and are there for her. WEVAS calls this strategy *open communication:* You are open emotionally and respond with your heart. Open communication can be as quick and simple as a hug, a smile, or sitting beside her. Two minutes of warm interaction now can spare you hours of trouble later.

The following techniques, drawn from the work of Jack R. Gibb (1961), Robert Carkhuff (1987), and Thomas Gordon (1970, 1974, 2000), facilitate open communication and help children return to a competent state:

- *Using door openers*. Gentle comments or questions ("Can I help?" "Can Miranda play with you?" "Do you want to sit with me for a while?") tell the child you care and are ready to listen. If she decides not to share her feelings or thoughts, respect her wishes.

- *Asking open-ended questions*. Genuine requests for information can reduce a child's anxiety by letting her tell her story and giving her a sense of control over events. They also facilitate problem solving because, as Gordon says in *Parent Effectiveness Training* (2000), "People do a better job of thinking a problem through when they can 'talk it out'" (p. 67). *Who, what, when, where*, and *how* questions (which aren't judgmental) help a child to think about what happened and what she feels. But stay away from *why* questions. Because they so often accompany disciplinary interventions, they make a child with challenging behavior clam right up (Quinn et al., 2000).

- *Validating and paraphrasing*. Enter the child's world and let her know that you understand the message and feelings behind her words by restating them in words of

Hard-Core Anxiety

Responding to anxiety is critical, especially when you're working with children who have extreme emotional and behavioral problems. Although children experience many different anxieties, psychologist Mary Wood (1986) has identified five that are central and often drive the anxieties that we see on the surface:

- *Feeling alone, abandoned, or rejected.* "I'm the only one who can't do this," "The other kids don't like me."

- *Feeling inadequacy or failure.* "I can't tie my shoelaces the way Christina can," "I can't figure out the answer to this math problem. I hope the teacher doesn't call on me."

- *Feeling guilt or shame.* "It's my fault that Mommy will be late to work," "It's my fault they're always arguing."

- *Feeling confused about identity.* "Daddy says I'm just a baby, but here they tell me I'm a big girl," "Why does Eddy say I'm black when my skin is brown?" (Tatum, 1997). Identity becomes more of an issue as children get older and grapple with who they are, how they perceive themselves, and how others see them. They worry about their color, ethnicity, sexuality, and dozens of other questions.

- *Feeling conflicted.* "My friends are all playing soccer, but I'd rather read," "I know I should stay, but I hate it here. I'm going to Grandma's." Like identity, conflict is an anxiety for older children as they struggle to find a balance between doing what they know is right and bending to peer pressure.

your own. It is her perceptions that matter here, not the reality (Gordon, 2000). To a child who says, "No one wants to play with me," you might answer, "You're feeling left out."

• *Reframing the child's statements.* Help the child see the event in a more positive light if you can do this honestly and without judging. ("You're learning something brand new," "Making mistakes isn't stupid; it's how we learn.")

• *Responding to the need within the child's message.* Try to hear what the child is really saying. Though the words are "This is stupid!" she may actually be asking for help. When you offer your assistance, she feels that her needs can be met, and her anxiety will abate.

• *Paying attention to your tone of voice.* Those who study interpersonal communication usually agree that words convey just a small fraction of a message, somewhere between 7 and 15 percent (Mehrabian, 1972). The bulk of what people communicate comes from their tone of voice, facial expressions, and body language. Your tone, cadence, speed, volume, and pattern of speech should match your message. It's helpful to notice the quality of the child's voice as well. When a child is anxious, her speech may go to extremes and become fast or slow, high or low, loud or soft. If you match her voice pattern, then slowly make your own more normal, you can lead the child into speaking more normally and feeling less anxious.

• *Paying attention to your body language.* In situations where a child is highly anxious and distant and doesn't respond to your efforts to help, it's a good idea to match your facial expression and body language to your message—and to the expression and body language of the child. This technique, called *mirroring*, often occurs when two people are communicating well. To use it effectively, take your cues from the child. If she's sitting back with her legs crossed, she's letting you know that she's listening but withdrawn. To encourage her to become engaged, try mirroring her stance—her facial expressions, her posture, even her mannerisms—to begin with, and then take the lead by moving closer, leaning forward, or placing your arms at your sides. If she mirrors your actions, you'll know she's ready for more personal contact. If she doesn't, or if she withdraws, step back and wait until she's ready.

The agitated state: Reactions intensify

When a teacher doesn't respond to a child's signs of anxiety or when open communication doesn't work, a child's behavior can escalate into agitation. Her feelings grow more intense, her actions become larger, she upsets other children, and she seems to be losing control. Once she starts to bother others, her problem is no longer her own.

The behavior of a child in the agitated state crosses a boundary and is therefore unacceptable. Her actions may threaten your authority or interfere with your ability to teach; they may destroy other children's opportunities to learn or compromise their safety. Young children are just learning about appropriate and inappropriate behavior, and the concept of boundaries may not be very clear to them. Each person in their world may draw the line in a different place, and some children have few consistent limits in their lives. The WEVAS responses to agitation help children learn about boundaries and limits.

There are two levels of agitated behavior. Children at the first level are beginning to lose control. Their strong emotions confuse their thinking, and they don't know how to handle their feelings or their behavior. However, they're still able to listen to you, and they experience real relief when they know what you expect of them. At the first level of agitation, the issue is educational, and the response is to teach.

The teaching response

A *teaching response* lets a child know that her behavior is unacceptable and teaches her what is acceptable. The first principle is to be positive: The response should tell the child what to do, not what *not* to do. The teaching response should also be polite, respectful, caring, and supportive. It recognizes where the child is coming from and expresses confidence that she can do what you ask, especially if you use empowering language ("I know that you can play with that toy quietly, Vera"). It also states your expectations clearly ("Jeremy, please call my name when you want my attention," "Eric and Sean, it's circle time, so you can sing with us or you can listen quietly").

Using an assertive style like this is more likely to influence the child's behavior (Canter and Canter, 1992). It gets the child's attention, puts your message across, and respects both her needs and yours. It communicates that you have something important to say without putting your relationship in jeopardy. Again, your tone of voice, facial expression, and body language are crucial. Like your words, they must be positive and empowering, not hostile or threatening. When your total message is clear, directive, and supportive, it tells the children what to do in a positive way and gives them the support to actually do it. The key is to offer as much direction and support as each child needs to succeed (Hersey, Blanchard, and Johnson, 2001).

An I-message—a message beginning with the word *I*—can enhance the effect of a teaching response. I-messages tell the child how you feel in the face of her unacceptable behavior. That is, they tell her how her behavior affects you and they allow you to take ownership of your feelings instead of hiding them. Whenever you use an I-message, you are modeling how to identify and express feelings and helping the child develop empathy. But most of all, an I-message places responsibility for changing the behavior squarely on the child, trusting her to respond in a way that takes all parties into account (Ginott, 1956; Gordon, 2000).

Gordon (2000) points out that an I-message puts the person using it in a vulnerable position, and teachers often prefer to seem infallible. It is sometimes easier to hide feelings behind you-messages and blame the child instead. But as Gordon says, I-messages are worth the risk. "Telling a child how you feel is far less threatening than accusing her of causing a bad feeling" (p. 136). Because they require honesty and openness, I-messages foster strong and close relationships.

When a child is agitated, it isn't easy to stay on course—that is, to do what's best for the child and the group. It may take extraordinary effort and focus to keep the goal

Feelings First

I-messages tell children how their behavior affects others and invite them to find solutions to problems (Gordon, 2000). When you're describing unacceptable behavior in an I-message, it is important to avoid labeling and judgmental statements. This is how to construct an I-message:

- *Describe the behavior.* "When you talk during class..."

- *Describe your feelings.* "I get annoyed because..."

- *Describe the effect of the behavior.* "The other children can't hear what I'm saying."

Don't forget that you can use I-messages to convey positive feelings, too.

in view. Some children with challenging behavior are experts at turning the tables and making your intervention seem like the problem. By minimizing their actions or denying that they've done anything, they manage to avoid being held accountable. For example, while you're assigning homework, Karen is talking loudly to Tommy, who's sitting beside her. You say, "Karen, please face forward and listen so you can hear the homework assignment." Karen says, "I was just asking a question. Can't you even ask a question around here?" minimizing the disruption she's caused. Or she says, "I didn't do anything. Why are you always picking on me?" denying involvement altogether. Both these statements suggest that you created the problem, not Karen, and leave you trying to justify your actions or ignoring Karen's remarks and looking as if you agree with her.

A child in an agitated state may also respond to a simple request with questions or statements that divert attention from the task at hand ("Why do we have to do this? It's stupid"). If you answer, you allow the child to take the lead and risk getting lost in the fog, which is why this ploy is called *fogging*.

It is all too easy to feel anger, guilt, or pity and respond emotionally to such tactics. But it's important to stay rational, clear, and focused. One way to handle these situations is to help the child think about her actions. Rather than telling her what to do, ask her *what* questions: "Karen, what are you doing?" Once she's told you, you can remind her about what she should be doing: "What is the rule about listening when the teacher is talking?" Once again, avoid asking *why* questions— her answer is likely to lead you even further astray.

Remember that your request was reasonable and responsible. Listen respectfully to the child's feelings and opinions, tune in to your own reactions, be kind and caring, and keep your goal at the forefront of your mind: "I understand that this feels unfair to you. But I still need you to listen quietly when I'm assigning homework to the class."

If a child is embarrassed or her behavior is meeting an important need, she may not respond to a simple teaching response. You may have better results if you combine it with open communication. Then you can maintain your relationship, help the child to identify the needs that must be considered, and solve the problem together.

Even if the child behaves exactly the same way the next day (and the day after), don't lose heart. Every new situation brings new problems. If the child needs your directions again, give them without anger or resentment. Repetition is normal and essential for young children—they need lots of practice.

The limiting response

At the second level of agitation, the child is feeling antagonistic and she no longer responds to what you're saying or doing. She's trapped in a past script, and she's drawing you into it. Control is the issue here. The WEVAS response, called a *limiting response*, is to help you become aware of the trap the child has laid for you so that you can jolt her into rational decision making and help her escape from this negative cycle (Wood and Long, 1991).

The second level of agitation is a critical stage. The child could either return to a competent state or feel so threatened that she moves into an aggressive state. Your response can determine which way she'll go. When a child moves to the second level of agitation, education is no longer the issue. The issue becomes power, pure and simple. The child doesn't care what you say; she cares that you're trying to influence or control her. Your job is to create a win-win situation and allow the child to change her behavior without losing face or feeling as if she's lost control.

A child at the second level of agitation is very stressed, and she isn't thinking clearly. Driven by intense feelings and negative thoughts, she doesn't listen well, and she says and does things she doesn't mean. She isn't interested in circle time; she thinks it's stupid and you're stupid. Her previous experiences filter her perceptions and govern her behavior, whether they relate to the present situation or not (Wood and Long, 1991). The responses she used in the past may be protective and effective, so when she's calm and competent it might be a good idea to explain to her that you're going to help her learn new behavior. But not now.

It's difficult to get a child out of this trap. If you blurt out a response that confirms the child's expectations, you become part of her cycle, and the inappropriate behavior scripted by her past will probably escalate (Wood and Long, 1991). It's as if she's stuck on a spinning merry-go-round. If you let the child's behavior push your emotional buttons and respond according to her expectations, you make the merry-go-round spin even faster. When you find yourself thinking negatively, you may even feel that the child wants to be punished. But an unexpected response can stop the merry-go-round. Even if it's just for a minute, that may give the child enough time to get off. If you use a limiting response—a planned response that doesn't fit her expectations—to limit her options in a positive way, you can help her to slow down and think about what she's doing. The limiting response forces her to become more rational (see Figure 10.1).

The interrupt

There are two basic limiting responses: the interrupt and the options statement. The *interrupt* is a completely unpredictable response that fits neither the child's past experience nor her present expectations. When Jessica is climbing on the chairs, instead of

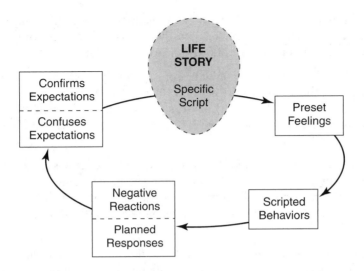

FIGURE 10.1 *Stopping Cycles*
Source: © 2000, WEVAS, Inc. Reproduced with the writen permission of WEVAS, Inc.

telling her to put her feet on the floor (a response that she's expecting), ask her to help you with a puzzle or join you in a game. That gets her off the furniture without eliciting the usual rebellion, and when she's sitting beside you doing the puzzle you can talk to her about the dangers of climbing. This technique is also called *redirection.*

The options statement

The *options statement* provides a child with alternatives. Its intent isn't to teach her how to make good choices but to make her stop and think. Because a child in the second level of agitation is usually looking for a challenge, not a choice, options may surprise her. To consider the options, she has to think, and that act may be enough to move her out of her cycle and allow her to regain some control.

The child is already feeling picked on and doesn't want any direction from you. It is therefore a significant challenge to turn her feelings around enough to return her to a competent state. The way you structure and deliver your options statement will determine whether you can provoke the rational thought that this demands. It is easier when you recognize that a child's behavior is related to her past experiences and perceptions of reality, not to a desire to make you miserable. When you clearly define the options and consequences you're offering, you seem less threatening, which means you're less likely to push the child over the edge. You are simply reminding her of probable outcomes. It's most effective to set limits based on values shared by everyone in the group (for example, everyone should be safe).

WEVAS offers these suggestions for creating an options statement:

- *Think about what you're going to say and how you're going to say it.* The child is being driven by feelings, and her capacity to listen is limited. Your demeanor is contagious. If you're calm, you have a better chance of calming the child and hooking her into a rational decision-making process. Make both the words and delivery of the message calm and nonthreatening by speaking slowly, clearly, and calmly.

- *Cue the child.* Your options statement won't have any effect if the child doesn't hear it. Signal her so she knows you're about to speak. An effective way to do that is to start with her name, followed by a short pause, such as, "Julia . . . it's your decision. . . ." Using pauses makes the child wonder what you're going to say next and helps her to slow down.

- *State the positive first.* The child already thinks this is a control issue, so she doesn't hear much. If you present the positive choice first, she may be able to step back from her feelings and listen to the whole message instead of automatically shutting it out. Perhaps say, "Bethany, you need to make a decision. You can finish your spelling now or do it at home."

- *Be clear, concise, and concrete.* At this level, a child can't listen to a lot of words or abstract concepts. "Sharif, you can sit beside Ollie or next to me, but the rule is that everyone sits down at storytime."

- *Pose choices.* Choices empower the child and give her some control over the situation. Starting with "You decide" or "You have a decision to make" hooks her into thinking about her options. The message is, "You have choices in this situation. Think about them carefully because the choices have consequences. The decision is yours." It's usually enough to offer just two choices.

- *Make the choices realistic.* The child must be able to complete the task. Asking her to choose between tying her shoe herself or having you tie it for her isn't a choice if she doesn't yet know how to tie her shoe.

- *Establish fair and reasonable consequences ahead of time.* In the previous chapter you saw that natural consequences permit children to learn from the natural order of the physical world—for example, if Lola doesn't wear her boots, her feet will get wet. Logical consequences, designed by the teacher, are usually based on the realities of the social world and should relate directly to the unacceptable behavior. For example, if Bethany doesn't finish her spelling in class, she'll have to do it at home.

- *Be sure the consequences are both enforceable and supportable.* Think through the whole range of appropriate consequences before you offer a choice. Remember that if you give a child the option of staying inside, you'll have to stay inside, too! Will that be possible, given the number of children and staff? If the natural consequences of a child's behavior could be either physically or emotionally harmful, you may need to impose logical consequences.

An option statement isn't a threat, as your tone of voice will convey. You just want the child to be aware that her choice will have certain consequences. You may hope that she chooses one option over another, but you must respect her right to choose and experience the consequences of her choice, positive and negative.

It takes time and practice to offer appropriate workable options. It helps to keep the outcome you desire squarely in the front of your mind. For example, if the schedule and the child/teacher ratio require you to go outside with everyone else, the child must come along. Your goal is to get her there in a competent state, and the options you present must enable that to happen: "Lola, you decide. Either you can put on your boots by yourself, or I can help you to put them on." The consequence—that you will help—isn't a punishment or a threat. The child has some control over the situation, and she has to think about what she'll do, which should deescalate her agitation.

Strategies for dealing with the child's response
Following up a limiting response is just as crucial as framing it well—and requires just as much skill and sensitivity. All too often, even when teachers know it's hard for a child, they expect an immediate answer. But there is no rush. Since the purpose of a limiting response is to help the child stop, think, and regain control, let her take her time considering her options. She should feel that this is an opportunity to make a better choice, not a power struggle.

Don't repeat the options statement. The child's actions will tell you what she's decided to do. After a reasonable amount of time, you can assume that she's made a

After you've given a limiting response, the child's actions will tell you what she's decided to do.

choice if she continues to act outside the limits you've set. Tell her again what the consequences will be: "It appears that you have made a choice, so I'm going to help you to put on your boots." Be sure to follow through with the consequences. When a child knows that you mean what you say, she will be much more inclined to pay attention.

It's important to allow her to save face. If she does what you ask, it doesn't matter if she scowls or complains. Saying "This is stupid!" is her way to be cool and preserve her reputation and self-esteem. If you can ignore her remarks and recognize her appropriate actions, you give all the children the message that they can comply and still be safe.

Once again, every child is different, every child has different needs, and knowing the child is the key. Morgan may need more empathy, so instead of simply giving her options, it would be a good idea to let her know that you understand her feelings and respect her need to express her point of view. An effective way to do this is to use several strategies at once. Combining open communication with a teaching response and an options statement tells her that you care, that she has a choice to make, and that you will follow through. If she continues to chat with her neighbor after you've asked her once to work quietly, you can say, "Morgan, I know that this feels unfair to you, and I'd be happy to talk about it later. Right now I need to know that the children around you can get their assignment done, so you have a decision to make: Either you can work quietly or you can find someplace else to work." This combination can be very powerful in enabling a school-age child to return to a competent state. A preschooler will need a shorter message.

The aggressive state: The fire inside

No matter how well you use the WEVAS preventive strategies, there will inevitably be times when a child's behavior becomes aggressive. A child in the aggressive state is out of control, and she doesn't hear or understand anything you say to her. Her behavior is random—even if she's flinging puzzles across the room, her actions aren't really directed at anyone—and her aggression can be both verbal and physical. Reasoning no longer works. She is driven by her emotions and by behavior patterns that worked for her in the past. As WEVAS puts it, she has a fire burning inside her. The fire isn't directed at any specific person, but it will burn anyone who comes too close.

Your goal is to put that fire out or to let it extinguish itself. To do this, you need a plan, and you have to remain calm and collected enough to implement it. Then you can provide the child with the support she needs to return to a competent state. At the same time, you'll be showing the other children that you aren't afraid of intense emotions.

Like gasoline on a fire, words seem to fuel the emotions of a child in the aggressive state. Since talking is out of the question until she's calm, you must use your nonverbal skills to communicate with her and deescalate the behavior. The child is acutely aware of your physical presence, and your body is your most useful tool. If you confront her, put your hands on your hips, or use your body language and size to exert your power and intimidate or threaten her, you will make her feel smaller and more defensive and increase the possibility that she'll become assaultive and lash out at you or at someone smaller when you aren't around. Without giving up your authority, you must communicate openness, caring, and confidence through your relaxed posture, facial expression, and behavior.

The key to this Houdini act is in your head: You must distance yourself psychologically. Whatever the child says or does, don't take it personally. Your emotions can draw you into the struggle, impede your ability to focus on her, and make you less effective. Imagine yourself by the sea or think of the bottom of your feet. These techniques can give you distance and objectivity and help you to relax your face even if your stomach is in knots. If you're mentally in Hawaii, you won't feel nearly so terrified.

This doesn't mean that you ignore her or cut off contact. Rather, it means that you aren't getting hooked into an emotional response that makes it harder for you to be effective. You can remain neutrally involved, giving her attention with your presence, carefully calibrating her behavior and adjusting your actions. Your message to her is that you're not going to respond or join in, but when she's ready to make other choices, you'll be there.

You must also distance yourself physically. When you're using open communication or planned responses, it's better to be at the child's eye level, but with a child in the aggressive state it's important to adjust your position to ensure your own safety and allow the child to feel safe. Because she's responding to your physical presence and isn't rational, she may need much more space than usual. WEVAS suggests a relaxed and

In the aggressive state, the child is driven by his emotions and by behavior patterns that worked for him in the past. Reasoning no longer works.

FIGURE 10.2 *L-Stance*

flexible standing posture that Butchard and Spencler developed with Si-Fu Wes Cameron. Called the centered L-stance (see Figure 10.2), this position is the confident bearing of a person who's in charge of herself, and it sends a message of safety to children who are afraid and a message of stability to children who are out of control.

In the L-stance, you don't face the child directly; instead, you stand sideways so that you don't seem so threatening. What's most important is the position of your shoulders. If they're at right angles to the shoulders of the child (forming an "L"), you appear much less menacing. Your feet are more or less facing in the same direction as your body, though the front one should be turned slightly toward the child at about a 45-degree angle. Keep your feet 12 to 18 inches apart, more if you think there's some danger. Your head is up but not rigidly high, your mouth and eyes are relaxed, your shoulders are dropped but not hunched, your spine is straight, and your knees are slightly bent. For safety's sake, place your weight on the front foot so that you can move out of the way quickly by shifting your weight to your back foot.

Carefully note how your own stance, angle, eye contact, and distance are affecting her, and systematically eliminate any behavior that's feeding the fire. Then let her play out the scene that she started.

In the European American culture, it's natural to make eye contact, but with a child in the aggressive state, eye contact can sometimes ignite the situation, intensify a power struggle, or reinforce a child whose goal is to get your attention. It is therefore a good idea to avoid eye contact when you first enter the L-stance. If you gaze over her shoulder or at the middle of her body, you remove the eye contact without sending a message of fear. Looking elsewhere also helps to keep your face relaxed and your mind clear; and your averted eyes may well surprise the child, interrupt her cycle, and de-escalate her behavior.

Even a child in an aggressive state has to breathe from time to time. During these lulls it's important to figure out whether she's actually calming down—moving back into an agitated or anxious state—or simply out of fuel. You can evaluate her state by slowly bringing your eyes to hers to see if she's ready to begin interaction with you again. Try to gauge whether eye contact actually increases or decreases the aggressive behavior. If it increases or maintains it, look away once more. In this context, eye contact becomes a reward reinforcing calmer behavior, and it tells the child that you are there for her. Her response will tell you whether you have gauged her state accurately.

If you feel that her behavior is deescalating, you can attempt to reason with her. As soon as she seems ready to listen, try a few short, well-chosen words that match her new emotional state: "Jessica, I know this is hard for you." Matching your responses to her new state will help to stabilize her behavior at this level. She's likely to be agitated, so you could use limiting or teaching responses alone or combine them with open communication. In the next lull, you could say, "Jessica, it's lunchtime now, and the markers have to be put away before we can use the table for eating." If she seems ready when she pauses again, you can offer her a choice. "You can put the markers away yourself, or we can do it together."

Mirroring the child's speech helps, too. If you gradually change the tone, volume, speed, and cadence of your voice, you can lead her to a more effective state. But be careful. If you mirror a child in an aggressive state on all dimensions, she may think you're challenging her and become more aggressive.

Acknowledge her feelings. If you can show that you care and understand, she may not feel as much of a need to confront you. At this stage, the words that you use are critical, even the small ones. Instead of *but*, use *and* (which doesn't discount the previous statement); in place of *you*, use *we* (which suggests support); and instead of *should*, use *can* (which implies personal choice). Avoid anything that makes her think that you're challenging or devaluing her. "Jessica, I understand that you're angry and you think these rules are unfair. We can talk about them later so that we both understand them better." This is very different from saying, "You feel that these rules are unfair, but you need to follow them."

Eventually you'll have to debrief (see pages 191–192) and follow through with consequences. But at the height of an aggressive outburst your role is to help the child deescalate and stabilize as quickly as possible. A bonus of this approach is that she learns she can calm herself down.

Just as you rehearsed the children in social skills when they were calm, so you should practice the L-stance in a relaxed environment. Work with your colleagues, coaching, cuing, and supporting one another to become a team.

The assaultive state: Involving the community

Sometimes a child will move from aggressive to assaultive behavior regardless of the strategies you use. Like a child in the aggressive state, a child in the assaultive state has a great deal of energy, but it's no longer random. Even if you aren't the cause of her problem, you or another child have become her target.

When Briana hurls a chair across the room and kicks you in the shins, you must take this behavior very seriously indeed. It will require all the verbal and nonverbal skills you used to deal with a child in the aggressive state, and you must also think of every-one's safety.

To protect the other children and staff, you need a systems response: an emergency plan that involves others. When you're worried about the other children, you can't focus on the child who's out of control. But with a plan in place you can deal with any situation more confidently. As you get to know the children better, you can adapt the plan to suit each child's temperament, needs, and comfort level.

The most effective way to keep the other children safe is to move them out of harm's way. Taking them out of the room not only protects them but also removes the audience—which may allow Briana to calm down more rapidly. A systems response has to be a team effort. With the other staff members in your child-care center or school, figure out a safe place for the children to go and a way to alert the staff that you need help (including a signal such as "Code Red"). Then decide who will do what: who will take responsibility for the other children, who will remove the chairs (or other objects that Briana throws), who will talk to arriving parents. The same person can do more than one task—the point is for every staffer to know exactly what to do. If you're alone with several children, select a responsible child to take the others to the office or to another classroom where there is a supervisor waiting for them. Wherever they go, they should be able to stay until you're ready for them to return. Explain the plan to the children and practice it with them when they're in a competent state. Review the plan periodically to ensure that it's ready to go at a moment's notice.

If the incident began when Briana was with you and you're the one she has a relationship with, it's important for you to stay with her. You are the one who can influence her and calibrate her actions most accurately. If someone else has a better relationship with her, the systems response should alert that person that she's needed. While you wait for her, remain with Briana to keep her focus on you and away from other children and objects. When the other staffer arrives, slowly switch positions with her, one person moving into Briana's line of vision while the other moves out. This is crucial because whoever is in Briana's line of vision becomes her target and allows the other person to escape. Breaking Briana's line of vision also makes it easier for her to deescalate.

You could also intervene in this way if Briana is trying to assault another child and the two are far enough apart. If the other child looks at you, that indicates she wants to get away, and she'll probably respond to your directions. Again, move slowly into Briana's line of vision so the other child can leave safely.

When both children are fighting, you may have to separate them to keep someone from getting hurt. Watch again for the child who looks toward you. She has already moved out of the assaultive state and is no longer focusing all her energy on her target.

Because she's probably trying to figure out how to make a getaway, she's likely to pay attention to your instructions. To actually separate the children, try hockey referee tactics. Be very careful, wait for a lull in the action, then step in and pull them apart.

For you, the principal defenses when you're with a child in the assaultive state are to keep a safe distance and use the L-stance. Do not try to move the child. If you do, her behavior will probably escalate, and you'll put yourself in danger. The only exceptions to this rule are when children are fighting and when a child is in danger (if she's running into the street, you have to act). You can also learn specific strategies and releases to respond to strikes, grabs, chokes, bites, and hair pulling. We won't describe those here; the best way to learn them is in a course or workshop where you can try them out for yourself and benefit from the expertise of a qualified instructor.

Once again, allow this scene to run its full course, interjecting short words and brief eye contact in the lulls as you see the child deescalate. After she's calm, don't insist that she apologize. Asking her to say she's sorry encourages her to say words that she doesn't mean and suggests that it's all right to hurt someone as long as she apologizes afterwards.

What about using restraint?

When a child is dangerously out of control, your instinct may be to restrain her to keep her from hurting herself and others. There are compelling reasons not to do so. In many places, you must get permission from the parents, a physician, or the school or child-care authorities before you can restrain a child. You must also have proper training—used incorrectly, restraint can injure both the child and the adult. Restraint is intrusive and punitive, and it doesn't teach a child to calm herself or to meet her own needs. Some children, particularly those who have been abused, may have extreme escalations in behavior or may suddenly become limp and unresponsive when they're restrained. Others actually like—and seek out—the feeling of deep pressure that they get from being restrained. It is obviously better to teach them to ask for a hug and to hold them when they're behaving appropriately.

Restraint techniques aren't part of WEVAS, although WEVAS recognizes that they may be needed to protect children and adults in some instances. The use of restraint should be part of a comprehensive behavior intervention plan developed by a multidisciplinary team that includes a mental health professional and administered by a teacher trained in restraint techniques.

The open state: A time to debrief and learn

A child who's coming off an aggressive or assaultive state (such as Briana) needs some private time with you. This *debriefing*, as WEVAS calls it, helps her to become competent and face the group with confidence, self-esteem, and a greater understanding of her behavior (Redl and Wineman, 1957; Wood and Long, 1991). Because she's just lived through an emotional crisis, her defenses are down and she's open to new possibilities. This is truly a time to learn, but it is also a time when she feels extremely vulnerable. Unresolved issues from her past may have resurfaced, and she's exhausted from the ordeal she's just experienced. The more emotional energy she expended, the greater the potential for change. For a few minutes to an hour, there is a window for effective debriefing. The timing is tricky. If you debrief too soon, she feels too exposed, but if you wait too long she'll start to rebuild her defenses.

For learning to take place, the child's energy must be dissipated, she must be composed, and she must feel safe, both physically and emotionally (Wood and Long, 1991). Restoring a child to a competent state without conjuring up her defenses is like a dance. Your words and actions can help her rediscover her personal resources—or send her straight back to her armor. Observe her carefully as you gently search for a way to connect with her positive side. If you connect with her defenses instead, back off and try something else.

The gravity of the incident will tell you how much debriefing is required. Sometimes a word or a gesture will suffice, but a debriefing can take as long as half an hour. Once you start, be sure to spend as much time as it takes. This can be a slow and emotional procedure, full of long pauses, and there's nothing you can do to speed it up. You want the child to begin the communication process, and she'll talk when she's ready. If you start to talk before she's prepared to listen, the process may fail, so take your cues from the child.

If she's fidgety and doesn't make eye contact, she's still using these devices to feel comfortable, and it's wise not to draw attention to them. Focus on the incident, ask for details, and ask questions that lead her to think more objectively about what happened. Don't repeat your questions—if she doesn't answer within a reasonable amount of time, move on. Keep on calibrating her, being acutely aware of small changes in her gestures, facial expressions, tone of voice, and body language, and mirror her posture, voice, eye contact, and breathing. When she's ready to engage, she'll probably lean toward you with her arms in an open position.

Remember it is the child who is the focus and the child who needs to do the talking. Accept her wherever she is and, using encouraging statements, help her tap into her strengths and identify her feelings and the basic issues. This takes time, trust, honesty, and respect. Let her remain in control so that she feels competent; your role is to help her use that control to solve the problem. This isn't easy, and she'll need your guidance throughout the process. One way to support her is to use language that empowers her (*we* and *us* offer support and acknowledge her feelings); another is to recognize small victories ("I see that you stopped to think about that").

The child isn't the only one who's vulnerable. Check out your own emotional state, too. This encounter may have stirred up feelings and filters from your own past, or you may have felt that your personal safety was threatened. Because you play an important role in the debriefing process, it's important for you to be centered. If you're feeling wobbly, you also need a debriefing, and it would be better if someone else provided support for the child.

Returning to the group

It's hard for a child to go back to her peers after an experience in the aggressive or assaultive state. Even though Briana is now feeling competent, she's probably also

Picking Up the Pieces

After a serious altercation, staff need debriefing as much as children do. It doesn't have to take place on the same day (you may be too upset), but within a day or two sit down with the team and discuss what happened. Bring everyone up to date, and talk about what went right as well as what went wrong. Was the response quick and effective? Did all the staff members understand their roles and do what they were supposed to do? What should everyone do differently the next time?

Be sure to leave enough time to talk about all the feelings the incident evoked—frustration, powerlessness, anger, sadness, fear. Acknowledging them in a safe place makes it easier to move on (Education Development Center, 1997). This self-care is essential to survival.

embarrassed and more vulnerable than usual, and she needs your help to reenter the group. The other children may be frightened or anxious about having her in their midst again, and they can use your support, too.

Because you want her reentry attempt to succeed, it's sensible for you to make the decision about when she should come back and where she should go. Consider the context carefully. Some children may find it easier to return during a structured time when tasks and roles are clearly defined. Others may need more space, but not as much as recess or gym would provide. As the one who knows her best, you can tell whether she's ready to play with the other children or would do better in a solitary project first. You'll be able to predict that returning to the block corner with Jamie will be a total disaster but drawing with Thau will give her enough time to regroup. Stay with her until she's comfortable. If she isn't ready or doesn't have the support she needs, the slightest frustration will set her off again. Your observations and knowledge will help you determine how long to stick around. If you're feeling overwhelmed by the enormity of the task, ask for help.

The techniques in the WEVAS strategy ask you to recognize the role you play in the child's behavior. It takes a lot of practice to do them consistently and well. Don't worry if you don't master them immediately, but try to become aware of what you're doing and make the effort to improve. Strategies such as looking for a child's anxiety and stating requests positively will eventually become second nature to you, and you'll find yourself using them in the rest of your life, as well!

What Do You Think?

1. In the past you may have thought that you could ignore small things such as thumb-sucking or whining and they would go away. What does WEVAS tell us about these things?

2. Think of a time when you were feeling anxious and someone helped you feel better. What were you feeling and thinking? What did the person say or do that helped you? How did you know that you were starting to feel better?

3. Describe a situation when a child is feeling agitated and develop a teaching response that will enable the child to feel competent.

What are the important elements of a teaching response? When is it appropriate to use it?

4. Do a role-play where one person is the teacher and the other is a child in the second stage of agitation. Using interrupt and option statements, help the child calm down.

5. In pairs, do the L-stance. Look at the illustration on page 188 to check your position. Every detail is important. The person playing the child's role should help you to stand so that you give a message of safety and stability. Practice in front of a mirror at home.

Suggested Reading and Resources

Gordon, T. (1960, 2000). *Parent effectiveness training: The proven program for raising responsible children.* New York: Three Rivers Press.

WEVAS, Inc., 778 Ibister Street, Winnipeg, Manitoba R2Y 1R4, Canada. Email: neil@WEVAS.net or bob@WEVAS.net.

References

Canter, L., & Canter, M. (1992). *Assertive discipline: Behavior management for today's classroom.* Santa Monica, CA: Lee Canter and Associates.

Carkhuff, R. (1987). *The art of helping.* Amherst, MA: Human Resource Development Press.

Education Development Center. (1997). *Supporting children with challenging behaviors: Training guides for the Head Start learning community.* Washington, DC: U.S. Department of Health and Human Services, Head Start Bureau.

Gibb, J. R. (1961). Defensive communication. *The Journal of Communication, 11,* 141–148.

Ginott, H. G. (1956). *Between parent and child.* New York: Avon Books.

Gordon, T. (1970, 2000). *Parent effectiveness training: The proven program for raising responsible children.* New York: Three Rivers Press.

Gordon, T. (1974). *Teacher effectiveness training.* New York: David McKay.

Hersey, P., Blanchard, K. H., & Johnson, D. E. (2001). *Management of organizational behavior: Leading human resources* (8th ed.). Englewood Cliffs, NJ: Prentice-Hall.

Leman, K. (1992). *The birth order book: Why you are the way you are.* New York: Bantam-Dell.

Mehrabian, A. (1972). *Nonverbal communication.* Chicago: Aldine Atherton.

Quinn, M. M., Osher, D., Warger, C. L., Hanley, T. V., Bader, B. D., & Hoffman, C. C. (2000). *Teaching and working with children who have emotional and behavioral challenges.* Longmont, CO: Sopris West.

Redl, F., & Wineman, D. (1957). *The aggressive child.* Glencoe, IL: Free Press.

Tatum, B. D. (1997). *"Why are all the Black kids sitting together in the cafeteria?" and other conversations about race.* New York: Basic Books.

Wood, M. M. (1986). *Developmental therapy in the classroom: Methods for teaching students with emotional or behavioral handicaps.* Austin: Pro-Ed.

Wood, M. M., & Long, N. (1991). *Life space intervention: Talking with children and youth in crisis.* Austin: Pro-Ed.

11

Functional Assessment

Like WEVAS, the strategy of functional assessment requires you to look at the world through the child's eyes. Every challenging behavior can be thought of as a child's solution to a problem and a form of communication. These ideas go back to Plato, who said that a crying baby's behavior serves a function: He is trying to get someone to care for him (Durand, 1990).

This is the underlying principle of functional assessment, a technique developed by behavioral psychologists for understanding a child's challenging behavior—for figuring out what is causing it and what the child is getting from it—and for providing more acceptable behavior that can fulfill those needs instead (O'Neill et al., 1997; Repp, Karsh, Munk, and Dahlquist, 1995). Its goal is to enable you to craft an intervention that works—one that will make the challenging behavior "irrelevant, ineffective, and inefficient" (O'Neill et al., p. 8).

Functional assessment tells us that challenging behavior isn't really as random and unpredictable as it seems. By focusing on the child's immediate environment, the technique of functional assessment helps you understand where the behavior is coming from, why it's happening at a particular time in a particular place (Durand, 1990), the logic behind it, and the function (or functions) it serves for the child (Dunlap and Kern, 1993; Iwata, Dorsey, Slifer, Bauman, and Richman, 1982; O'Neill et al., 1997). Even if the behavior is inappropriate, the function seldom is. Once you understand the function, you can design strategies to help the child achieve his purpose appropriately.

Of course, all of the causes of challenging behavior aren't in the immediate environment, but viewing it from this angle can be extremely helpful. Functional assessment is another powerful strategy to add to your toolbox, especially when you combine it with other methods.

Enter the teacher as detective. When you use functional assessment, you and everyone else who works with the child become a team of sleuths searching together to discover the function of the challenging behavior and solve this case. The key is to see the situation from the child's point of view (Anderson, Albin, Mesaros, Dunlap, and Morelli-Robbins, 1993).

What do you need to know to figure out the function of a behavior?

To do a functional assessment, you must pay very close attention to the context: the environment immediately surrounding the challenging behavior (Carr, 1994). In *Functional Assessment and Program Development for Problem Behavior* (1997), Robert O'Neill and his colleagues put it this way: "Behavior change occurs by changing environments, not [by] trying to change people" (p. 5). The context provides the best clues to understanding why the child is using challenging behavior. Since the ordinary classroom

Power Plus

Devised in the late 1970s and early 1980s in work with persons with developmental disabilities, functional assessment is usually reserved for serious behavior problems (Gable, Quinn, Rutherford, Howell, and Hoffman, 1998). Because it is so effective, it has become federal law, required under the Individuals with Disabilities Education Act (IDEA) Amendments of 1997 whenever behavior interferes with learning or requires disciplinary action (Quinn, Gable, Rutherford, Nelson, and Howell, 1998). The National Association of School Psychologists considers it best professional practice (Miller, Tansy, and Hughes, 1998).

In a study in Illinois, researchers Lynette K. Chandler, Carol M. Dahlquist, Alan C. Repp, and Carol Feltz of Northern Illinois University (1999) trained teams of teachers and others working with preschool children in special education and at-risk classes in the use of functional assessment.

The result? When the teams used this powerful technique to address the challenging behavior of one child in a classroom, the proportion of challenging behavior for the group as a whole was substantially reduced. In addition, the level of active engagement and peer interaction increased, creating a better learning environment for everyone.

environment is a busy and confusing place, filled to the brim with social, cognitive, affective, sensory, and biological factors that influence behavior (Gable et al., 1998; Quinn et al., 1998), functional assessment asks teachers to look at it in a special way. Conducting an *A-B-C analysis* (Bijou, Peterson, and Ault, 1968) can tease out the essential elements and help bring order to chaos (O'Neill et al., 1997).

A stands for *antecedents*—events that take place right before the challenging behavior and seem to trigger it. The research literature mentions demands, requests, difficult tasks, transitions, interruptions, and being left alone (O'Neill et al., 1997). Peers' actions can be antecedents, too—think of teasing, bullying, showing off, coming too close, and exclusion. Andrew throws down his blocks and kicks Liane when you flash the lights and start to sing the clean-up song. The end of free-play and the transition to clean-up time (as indicated by the flashing lights and the clean-up song) are the antecedents.

It is often hard to distinguish between antecedents and their more distant relations—known as *setting events*—that occur before or around the antecedents. Setting events make the child more vulnerable and susceptible to the antecedents and make the challenging behavior more likely (Durand, 1990; Repp et al., 1995). The adults who are present or absent, the number of children in the group, the set-up of the room, the noise level, the lighting, the type of activity, the sequence of activities, and the time of day can all act as setting events. Setting events also include the child's physical or emotional state—being hungry, tired, or sick; being on medication (or not); spending the weekend with the noncustodial parent; hearing parents argue the night before; being forbidden to bring a favorite toy to school; being pushed on the bus; and so on. Setting events are harder to pin down or are just plain unknowable and often depend on information supplied by someone else, such as a mother who remarks that the morning at home was a complete disaster. They may also be difficult or impossible to change.

B stands for *behavior*, which you must be careful to describe so clearly and specifically that anyone who's observing can recognize and measure it (not "Andrew is aggressive" but "Andrew kicks other people") (Durand, 1990; Gable et al., 1998). If the child has several challenging behaviors, describe them all, because you will need to find out if they serve the same or different functions ("Andrew also hits and pushes other people, and sometimes he spits"). Of course you can't observe or measure thoughts or feelings such as sadness or anger—but you can observe and measure crying, yelling, or throwing chairs (Smith, 1993).

C stands for *consequences*—that is, What happens after the challenging behavior? Do you ignore Andrew's behavior and pretend you didn't see it, reprimand him sternly, put him beside you to keep him from hurting someone else, put him in time-out? Do the other children giggle, cry, or move away from him? Any of these responses, positive or negative, may reinforce Andrew's kicking.

Taken together, the A-B-C analysis and the setting events form a pattern that points you toward the function of the challenging behavior. Functional assessment postulates three possible functions:

- *The child gets something* (attention from an adult or a peer, access to an object or an activity, and so on). Whether you reprimand Andrew or keep him beside you, he is getting your attention. Because he's obtaining something he wants, his behavior is being positively reinforced, and it will probably continue.

- *The child avoids or escapes from something* (unwelcome requests, difficult tasks, activities, contacts with particular peers or adults, and the like). Ronnie, who is clumsy at gross-motor activities, pushes his classmates in the gym. You remove him to the sidelines—and he doesn't have to do somersaults or play catch. This response strengthens his behavior and increases the likelihood it will persist.

- *The child changes the level of stimulation.* All people try to maintain their own comfortable level of stimulation, and when they get too much or too little, they act to change it (Karsh, Repp, Dahlquist, and Munk, 1995; Lalli and Goh, 1993; Repp et al., 1995; Repp, Felce, and Barton, 1988). When Jamal has to wait in line to go from the classroom to the bathroom, he begins to poke and push the children around him, and the world instantly becomes more stimulating. Because he is changing the level of stimulation in the environment, his behavior is creating its own reinforcement (Iwata, Vollmer, and Zarcone, 1990).

What about appropriate behavior?

When you're looking at the context, don't forget about the context for appropriate behavior (Dunlap and Kern, 1993; Iwata et al., 1990; O'Neill et al., 1997). It has antecedents, consequences, and setting events, too! Part of planning an effective intervention is knowing how to increase the child's appropriate behaviors, so you'll need to know what engages him, where his talents lie, which peers and teachers he's comfortable with, whether he likes being in structured or unstructured settings, in a small group or with a single playmate. Tuning into his preferences and strengths will enable you to provide him with potent reinforcers for new acceptable behavior.

How do you get the information you need for a functional assessment?

Functional assessment works best when it's a team effort. Everyone who comes into contact with the child—teachers, directors or principals, school psychologists, social workers, teaching assistants, cooks, bus drivers—has something to contribute, and when you pool information and ideas, you are most likely to make links, see patterns, and come up with an effective plan (Gable et al., 1998, 2000). The meetings don't have to be long to help clarify a situation, and if you share your impressions and thoughts frequently, you're more likely to understand one another, no matter what your discipline or background. As a result, you'll probably behave more consistently whenever you're with the child.

Your first task as a team is to come up with a hypothesis—a tentative theory or best guess—about the function of the challenging behavior and the conditions that cause it. Begin with a brainstorming session that will prod memories and stimulate thought. At this point you are trying to come up with as many ideas as possible, no mat-

Difficult tasks, demands, requests, transitions, and interruptions often trigger challenging behavior.

ter how far-fetched. Maybe Andrew wants to get out of clean-up or wants more attention from you or his peers. Maybe Liane or another child is provoking him. Maybe transitions are hard for him and he isn't getting enough warning. Maybe he hasn't had enough time to finish the project he was working on and isn't ready to stop. Maybe there's too much going on and he's overstimulated. As you discuss the situation and gather more facts, you'll be able to narrow your focus and decide exactly what warrants further investigation.

You will need current and accurate data, and the more sources you have, the more accurate the information is likely to be (Dunlap and Kern, 1993; Durand, 1990). One obvious source is your own records. Medical forms, incident reports, daily logs, and children's personal files are no doubt hiding valuable but forgotten nuggets. It's especially important to read carefully through the notes on any previous behavior management plans. Which strategies worked with this child, even for a little while? Which didn't? You want to be sure you don't repeat them!

Interviews are another vital resource. Talk with the family, explain what you're doing, and ask if they will share their considerable knowledge and insight with you. If you're doing an informal functional assessment, you don't need special permission from them the way you would if you were calling in the school psychologist or an outside expert. But of course parents should always know what you're trying to do and why. They have an enormous amount of valuable information to contribute as you begin an assessment, and they can provide lots of useful feedback as it proceeds. They should be full partners in this enterprise.

You can also interview people who've worked with the child in the past, including yourself and others on your team, either individually or as a group (O'Neill et al., 1997). It's tempting to assume that you already know everything you could possibly need to know, but a formal interview actually helps put the information into a structured format—and you may come up with some surprises in the process (Durand, 1990). Take the questions from existing questionnaires (see Suggested Reading at the end of this chapter) or make them up yourself. The idea is to put what you know into a systematic framework.

Ask about the A-B-Cs. Which circumstances almost always surround this child's challenging behavior and which never do (Dunlap and Kern, 1993; O'Neill et al., 1997)? Why do you think the child is behaving this way? This is also a good opportunity to ask about setting events: The child's sleeping and eating habits, allergies, medical conditions, medications, or family problems may all be influencing his behavior in one way or another.

Interviews also help you to fill in the details about previous interventions, especially if you're talking to someone who participated in developing or implementing them.

As you go about your detective work, don't overlook the most obvious source of all: the child himself. Even a 4-year-old may be able to shed some light on how he sees the situation and what causes him to react the way he does. Talk with him in a quiet place at a time when he's feeling calm and good about himself. If your manner, voice, and body language are open, warm, and unthreatening, some very useful information may emerge. Remember to stay away from *why* questions, which make some children feel defensive, and to zero in on his preferences and pleasures as well as his complaints.

Some experts suggest using a behavior rating scale. There are several that can help you deduce the function of the behavior. The Motivational Assessment Scale, developed by V. Mark Durand and Daniel B. Crimmins (1996–2001), for example, is short, easy to use, and available on the internet. A checklist that looks at setting events may also be helpful. You could use the one by W. I. Gardner and his colleagues, which asks parents about what happened the night before the challenging behavior (he "was hurried or rushed more than usual") (Durand, 1990), or you could make a simple, nonintrusive checklist of your own. Be sure to take the family's culture into account as you compose the questions.

All of this knowledge will give you direction as you begin a formal observation and prepare an intervention plan.

Collecting Clues

When you're interviewing people who know the child well, experts (Durand, 1990; Gable et al., 1998; Iwata et al., 1990; O'Neill et al., 1997; Quinn et al., 1998) suggest you ask such questions as these:

- Which of the child's behaviors do you consider challenging, and what do they look like?

- When and where does this behavior occur?

- When and where does the child behave appropriately? Which activities does he enjoy?

- Who is present when the challenging behavior occurs? And who is present when the child is behaving appropriately?

- What activities, events, and interactions take place just before the challenging behavior? Go over the daily routine in your mind. How predictable is the schedule? How much waiting is there? How much choice does the child have? When the routine changes, does it make a difference in his behavior?

- What happens after the challenging behavior? How do you react? How do the other children react? Does the child get something from the behavior, such as your attention or his brother's soccer ball? Does he manage to avoid something, such as putting away his toys or turning off the television? According to Brian Iwata, one of the pioneers of functional assessment, "Parents, teachers, and other caregivers sometimes can describe the functional characteristics of a [child's] behavior problem with uncanny accuracy" (1994, p. 414).

- Can you think of a more acceptable behavior that might replace the challenging behavior?

- What activities does the child find difficult?

- Which approaches work well with him, and which don't? For example, does he prefer his interaction with you to be loud or soft, fast or slow? How much space does he like to have around him? If a particular family member or staff is especially successful with him, what does she do?

- If the child is from a different culture, this behavior may not have the same meaning for the family as it does for you. Is it troubling for them? Why or why not? How would they like you to respond to it?

How do you observe?

By far the best way to learn about a child's behavior is to observe and collect data about it (O'Neill et al., 1997). As the great New York Yankee catcher Yogi Berra once said, "You can observe a lot just by watching."

When you are faced with challenging behavior, there are two major reasons to observe. The first is traditional. Collecting data before, during, and after an intervention allows you to find out precisely what you're dealing with and to reliably measure any change that occurs. The second reason is to enable you to see the relationship between the environment and the challenging behavior more directly (Dunlap and Kern, 1993; Repp et al., 1995)—in other words, to confirm the team's hypothesis about the function of the behavior. Like an interview, an observation may present some startling revelations. For example, you might discover that Andrew's kicks, which seemed to occur dozens of times a day, happen just two or three times, and almost always at morning clean-up. The gap between your perception and the reality may confirm how much the behavior disturbs you and the class, but having the facts will certainly help you intervene more effectively.

Although teachers recognize that observing and recording behavior is crucial to making thoughtful decisions about an individual child, observation often isn't a priority—other things always seem more pressing. Probably it is best to make it part of the daily schedule (Aspen Systems Corporation, n.d.), exactly the way you'd fit in hand washing or storytime.

There's also a logistical problem. When you're actually in the classroom with the children, it may seem next to impossible to observe. Teaching and observing at the same time takes will power, a quick and perceptive eye, and a good memory. Fortunately, it's like any other skill: The more you practice, the easier it will become. Do you remember what it felt like when you were learning to drive? Eventually you don't have to think at all about signaling or braking—you just do them automatically!

A previous experience with a child, or a reputation that precedes him, can sometimes make it difficult to observe accurately and objectively. Teachers tend to see what they expect to see—especially if they're expecting challenging behavior. Self-reflection can help here. Try to identify your biases and preconceived notions and become aware of the words you're using to describe the child's behavior. Instead of saying, "Andrew is angry all the time and jealous of his peers," stick to the bare facts. "Andrew kicked Liane during clean-up" is an accurate description that will eventually lead you to a clearer understanding of the behavior's function and a strategy to deal with it.

Anyone who spends time with the child can participate in the observation process, and others on the team can pitch in as well. The director of the program could arrange for one of your colleagues to observe your group, she could observe herself, or the team could decide to call in a consultant. But outsiders can make you nervous, distract the children, and change the environment. You and the others who are normally with the children are probably the most desirable data collectors (Durand, 1990; Meyer and Evans, 1993; O'Neill et al., 1997).

Using the data you've gathered so far to guide you, select the most promising antecedents, behaviors, and consequences to observe more closely. Choose just two or three target behaviors so that you won't find the job overwhelming, and plan to observe a variety of activities, times, and days. That way, you'll see the full gamut of possibilities and have more opportunities to confirm or disprove your hypotheses (Lalli and Goh, 1993).

Together you and the rest of the team choose to observe Andrew's kicking and hitting. Because you believe that these behaviors usually occur as clean-up begins, you decide to watch particularly closely at that time. In addition, you plan to watch early-morning free-play when he first arrives, structured teacher-directed activities, getting ready to go outside, outdoor play, mealtimes, and transitions. You are especially interested in noticing the amount of attention you pay to him during these activities.

You've hypothesized that the most likely function for Andrew's behavior is that he gets to avoid clean-up. But you're keeping an open mind and looking to see if the function could be that he wants your attention. As you run your program and interact with the children, keep your eyes and ears wide open. This is when you do the serious work of observing—by paying close attention to what happened just before the challenging behavior, who was nearby, and what happened next (Chandler and Dahlquist, 1997). One of the most daunting aspects of this process is watching yourself. You are not merely observing the child's behavior; you are also observing your own.

There are many ways you can record your observations. One is to make a basic A-B-C chart with spaces for the child's name; for the date, time, and place; for the A-B-Cs and setting events; and for your hypothesis about the function of the challenging behavior. We suggest using the functional assessment observation form developed by O'Neill and his colleagues. (For examples of both charts, see Appendices A and B.) You can write directly onto the chart if you keep it on a clipboard stashed in a convenient spot in the classroom. Sometimes it isn't possible to do this right away, so it helps to wear an apron or clothing with pockets and to carry a pen, pad, note cards, or post-its. When you have a moment (at lunch, naptime, the end of the day), make notes of what you saw so that your observations aren't lost or muddled, then transcribe the information onto the chart later. Be sure that all staff who observe record and initial their impressions.

Collect data until a clear pattern emerges and you know whether the team's hypothesis is right or wrong or your collective observations suggest other hypotheses. This usually takes at least 15 to 20 incidents over two to five days (O'Neill et al., 1997). Be careful not to jump to conclusions or to interpret the data prematurely. If you've made a substantial effort and things still aren't clear, perhaps your description of the target behavior isn't specific enough or your personal biases are getting in the way. You may need to find a different way to observe or bring in additional help.

What do you do with all this information?

When you think you have enough data, call the team together for another brainstorming session. It's time to make a plan! To begin, decide which challenging behavior (or behaviors) to tackle first. On this subject the experts disagree. Some say to start with the most severe behavior (Durand, 1990); others prefer to begin with one that's less threatening to the other children and yourself so there isn't so much at stake and your chances of success are higher (Kaplan, 2000; Parrish and Roberts, 1993). It may be best to take on the more difficult behavior later, when everyone is more comfortable with the process.

As you examine your data, you'll probably see some patterns that clarify your hypothesis about the function (or functions) of the behavior (Dunlap and Kern, 1993;

O'Neill et al., 1997). To begin with, you notice with surprise that Andrew frequently kicks or hits during the morning clean-up, but rarely during the afternoon clean-up. What are some differences between morning clean-up and afternoon clean-up, and do they tell you anything about the function of the behavior? Perhaps Andrew isn't trying to get out of clean-up after all.

You find some clues in the transition to clean-up. In the morning, you always flick the lights and sing the clean-up song, and Andrew always kicks or hits another child. But in the afternoon, the assistant teacher, Grace, gives Andrew a special early warning that clean-up is coming before she flicks the lights and sings. Then she goes over to him, gets him started, and makes sure he has something to do, and he doesn't kick or hit. This also gives a hint about the function. Perhaps Andrew wants more attention.

Your observation of the consequences will help clarify this hypothesis. What you see is that when Andrew kicks, you always give him your attention, whether you put him in time-out, sternly remind him of the rules, or keep him by your side to prevent him from hurting someone. As is so often the case with children with challenging behavior, Andrew doesn't care whether the attention he gets from you is positive or negative, as long as he gets your attention. Suddenly you realize that you have inadvertently reinforced his kicking! It appears that the function of the behavior is to get your attention, not to avoid clean-up.

Once you've identified the behavior's possible functions, the next step is to create a strategy that achieves the same purpose for the child (see Figure 11.1). The ultimate objective is to teach him how to get what he wants through appropriate means (Quinn et al., 1998). There are three ways to do this, and you should probably use them all: change the environment, replace the challenging behavior with appropriate behavior, and ignore the challenging behavior (O'Neill et al., 1997).

Change the environment so the child won't need the challenging behavior

This is what O'Neill and his colleagues (1997) mean when they say to make the challenging behavior irrelevant. Once again, prevention is the best method! Begin with the setting events if you can. Andrew's mother has mentioned that he isn't hungry at 6:30 A.M., which is the last chance he has to eat before they leave home in the morning. You realize that Andrew will probably have more self-control if he eats something, and you decide to give him a snack or a cereal you know he likes as soon as he arrives.

The next step is to change the antecedents. This usually involves changing the physical set-up, the program, and/or your approach to the child in order to eliminate opportunities for the challenging behavior to arise. Sometimes this is as simple as informing or reminding the child of what is appropriate before the activity begins. If you're passing around a fragile leaf fossil, for example, explain how to handle it before the children handle it too roughly and it breaks.

Because it is clear that Andrew needs more attention at clean-up, you and the rest of the team decide to give him his own special personal warning and some extra attention a few minutes before clean-up. You also decide to assign specific achievable tasks at clean-up and figure out which task Andrew would like best. You will help him start his job as well as finish it, and you will reinforce his attempts even if they're only close

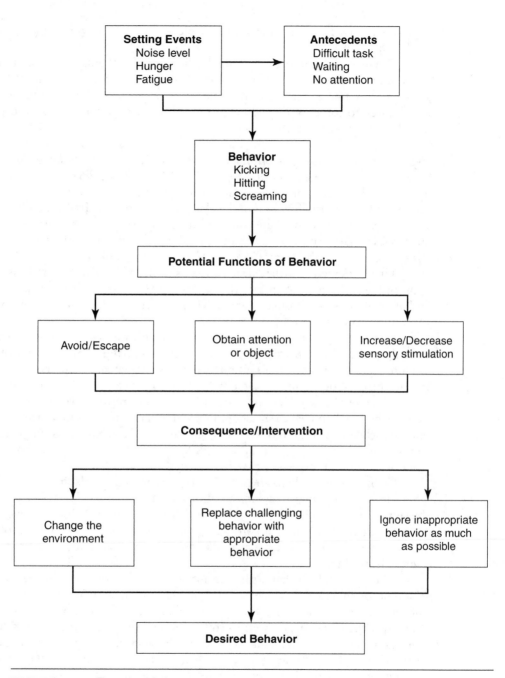

FIGURE 11.1 *Functional Assessment*

approximations. That way, Andrew will achieve his goal of having your attention without hitting.

The team hypothesizes that Jamal, who pushed and poked his neighbor while he was waiting in line, doesn't have enough stimulation. They decide that they will do away with the line entirely and make the transitions more physically active. They ask the children to come to the door and move from activity to activity as birds, squirrels, ants, fish, or other creatures.

Replace the challenging behavior with appropriate behavior that achieves the same outcome for the child more quickly and with less effort

This is one key to the success of functional assessment—and one reason it's so important to understand the function of the challenging behavior. It is not enough to decide what the child must stop doing; you must also know what you want him to do instead—and what will satisfy him because it enables him to easily achieve the same results he got with his challenging behavior (Mace and Roberts, 1993; O'Neill et al., 1997).

This is a cinch with Jamal. Pretending to be an animal during transitions is an appropriate replacement behavior that keeps him stimulated. He is particularly creative and often amuses his classmates with his impersonations. He also receives lots of positive reinforcement from the teachers.

An appropriate replacement behavior for Andrew is less obvious, but you and the team figure out that you are giving him an appropriate replacement behavior by showing him that he can get your attention by participating in clean-up, rather than by kicking or hitting. You decide that you will also try to give him lots of attention at other times when he's behaving appropriately. He seems to respond well to Grace, the assistant teacher, and you agree she should make regular dates to join him at an activity he enjoys, such as puzzles or blocks, where she can be sure to have those important opportunities to give him positive attention. This way, behaving appropriately will get Andrew attention more easily than behaving inappropriately.

Changing antecedents and finding a replacement behavior are both more difficult when the child is trying to avoid something because you need to know why the child doesn't want to participate. Is the task too hard or too boring? Does he have to stay still for too long? Does he think no one will want to be his partner? You will probably have to use a variety of tactics and teach new social or physical skills, even if the child isn't keen to learn them.

The team realizes that it's important not to allow Ronnie to escape entirely from gross-motor activities, because he has difficulty in that area. You suggest that his parents enroll him in a special Saturday swimming program to help him learn to control his body while you focus your efforts on teaching him basic skills. You ask the physical education teacher for advice and start with an easy task, rolling, using a large ball, and sitting close to him so that he will be able to succeed. You immediately encourage all his attempts, no matter how feeble or wild, and someone—staff or peer—plays with him every day. You keep the sessions very short and teach him to ask for breaks so that he'll have an appropriate way to escape when he feels overwhelmed (Iwata et al., 1990). At the same time, you decide to motivate and reinforce him by letting him choose a different kind of activity—one that you know he enjoys, such as drawing—when he's finished

(Repp et al., 1995). You know that gym is going to be hard for him for a long time, and you must continue to support him. One staffer volunteers to find activities that teach body awareness to improve Ronnie's competence and self-esteem so that he has more fun playing and is more willing to try.

Different children lack different skills, so you may need to offer extra help and teach virtually anything—how to hold a pencil or cut with scissors, how to join in or wait your turn, how to share or control your anger, how to hop or throw a ball. "Remember that teaching is among the most powerful behavior management tools at our disposal," O'Neill and his colleagues write (1997, p. 74). In many situations, effectively teaching a new behavior is the best way to reduce a problem behavior.

Start with skills the child can learn quickly and easily—it's important for him to experience as much success as possible as rapidly as possible so that he begins to build self-esteem. Sometimes teachers think that if they wait, the child will learn the skill when he's ready, but in fact he often becomes more convinced that he isn't capable of learning or that the other children don't like him.

As you teach a new skill, give the child lots of opportunities to use it and give yourself many opportunities to reinforce it with words, body language, and activities you know the child really values and enjoys. Respond to every attempt and every approximation, especially in the beginning. To get rid of the old behavior, the new one has to be very successful indeed (Durand, 1990). It's also a good idea to teach these new skills as part of the daily routine—children will learn them more quickly and generalize them

Teaching new skills is one of the best ways to reduce problem behavior.

Prep Time

Children often use challenging behavior to escape from situations they don't have the skills to handle. They may want to avoid feeling frustrated, stupid, or confused, and they may worry that their peers (or the teacher) will make fun of them. In *Beyond Functional Assessment* (2000), Joseph S. Kaplan suggests these questions to ponder as you and the rest of the team decide what to teach and how to teach it:

- Does the child know what's expected of him in this situation? Does he understand it? Are your expectations different from what's required at home?

- Does he know how to do what's expected?

- Does he know when to do what's expected?

- Does he have the self-control to do what's expected?

- Is he aware of his own behavior?

- Seen from the child's point of view, is there more to gain from the challenging behavior or from the appropriate behavior? (It's essential to make the appropriate behavior more rewarding!)

- Are the child's beliefs compatible with the appropriate behavior? For example, does he believe that he's capable of learning and performing the appropriate behavior? Does he believe that he can exert any influence on the situation? Does he believe the new behavior will get him what he wants? Some children may not even try to behave appropriately because they think they have no control over what happens to them.

more readily to other situations if they learn them where they use them (Durand, 1990; Gable et al., 2000).

Ignore the challenging behavior as much as possible
The third way to teach the child how to get what he wants by appropriate means is to ignore the challenging behavior. Psychologists call this process *extinction*, the idea being to show the child that the challenging behavior will not serve the function it used to— it will no longer get him what he wants (Durand, 1990; Mace and Roberts, 1993; O'Neill et al., 1997). This is not as easy as it sounds. It means wading right through the challenging behavior, continuing whatever it is you're doing as if the behavior simply doesn't exist. You may think you're reinforcing his behavior, but according to Durand, the message you're giving the child is, "Your challenging behavior has no effect on us. We'll be happy to give you what you want if you use appropriate behavior" (pp. 148–149).

When you stop reinforcing the challenging behavior, there will probably be an "extinction burst" (Durand, 1990, p. 152)—that is, the behavior will get worse. Don't be discouraged. If you follow your plan and implement your interventions consistently, you should soon see changes. Bear in mind that the child's history will play a role here: The longer he's used his challenging behavior and the more successful it's been for him, the harder it will be to change or eradicate it. Patience is therefore vital (Durand, 1993; O'Neill et al., 1997).

If the function of the behavior is to get your attention, then don't respond: Don't come to his side, speak to him, or look at him. This is easy to do if Andrew pushes Liane but no one is hurt and Liane continues to play. But it's hard to ignore Andrew's challenging behavior if someone is in danger. If Andrew kicks, hits, pushes, or hurts Liane or another child, you can plan to do the next best thing—limit the attention you give him by attending to Liane. Stand between the two children with your back to Andrew and focus on her, eliminating all eye contact and physical contact with Andrew, saying only, "We take care of our friends. Hitting hurts" (Durand, 1990).

When Andrew uses his words or other appropriate means to get what he wants, be sure to give him immediate positive reinforcement. It's possible, however—and especially when you first try this tactic—that his problem behavior will escalate as you continue to ignore him. If he hurts yet another child, respond once more by attending to the other child and reminding him that hitting isn't allowed. It takes time for him to realize that you are serious about this, so it's important to keep at it. If you are consistent, Andrew will discover that his challenging behavior isn't working for him, and it will diminish in force and frequency as time goes by.

This is hard, and you might want to ask another teacher for help. When there are two of you in the classroom, you can remain keenly aware of Andrew without paying obvious attention to him, show him that his behavior doesn't interrupt the normal activity of clean-up, and still be in the right place at the right time. You will feel more confident and ready to act in case you're needed. If this doesn't work and his behavior seems to be escalating, keep everyone safe by using the same emergency plan for dangerous situations you used for WEVAS (see page 190).

On the other hand, if the function is for the child to escape, it's imperative not to let that happen. If Ronnie is screaming uncontrollably because he doesn't want to play with the ball today, hang in there and watch carefully for a pause or an action that you can interpret as a tiny effort or a remote approximation of appropriate behavior. Use your WEVAS techniques and when he stops screaming, even for an instant or just to take a breath, that's your chance to say, "Great, you calmed down." As he regains control, you can tell him what you want him to do. "You choose. You can roll the ball or you can give it to me. Then you can take a break." When he chooses, no matter how badly or angrily he behaves, reinforce him, naming the behavior you want to encourage: "Terrific, you rolled the ball. Take a break. I'll be back soon."

Such situations can be extremely tricky, and they require you to think on your feet and use all of the flexibility and ingenuity at your command. Remember the function of the behavior that you're trying to ignore—in this case Ronnie is trying to escape. The solution often seems silly—he isn't really calm when he takes a breath, and he isn't really rolling the ball when he jams it into your arms—but it's close enough, and it works. He stops screaming, he doesn't feel as if he's escaped, and he doesn't lose face. Furthermore, neither do you. Needless to say, in order to perform such a maneuver, you must stay calm and collected yourself!

When you've figured out the function and carefully considered all three methods for helping the child fulfill his needs appropriately—changing the environment, replacing the challenging behavior with appropriate behavior, and ignoring challenging behaviors as much as possible—you are well on your way. Write down exactly what you want to achieve—your goals and objectives—in measurable terms (Andrew will clean up without hitting; Ronnie will try new skills in the gym), a time frame for reaching them, the methods you've decided to use, and who will be responsible for implementing each intervention. Figure out all the details—what you'll say and do, what materials you'll need, and so on. O'Neill and his colleagues (1997) also recommend including a description of a typical routine and a description of how you'll handle the most difficult situations. Even when you're well prepared, the problem behavior can still occur, and clearly defined procedures ensure that everyone knows what to do and everyone does the same thing. Make sure that all the staff agree and are ready to do their part. To succeed in the long run, an intervention has to be acceptable not only to the child and his family but also to you, the people who will implement it. It has to be consistent with your values, skills, and resources.

Decide how you'll measure your progress and set a date to get together to review it. Will you do another observation? When? One way to measure is to count the occurrences of challenging behavior (which should have diminished). Another is to notice increases in positive behavior, such as when the child

- Initiates private time
- Allows another child to play with him
- Participates in small groups
- Needs the staff less
- Has a friend
- Uses words to ask for help or breaks more often
- Copes better with transitions
- Doesn't hit when he could have (Meyer and Evans, 1993; Schmidt, 1996)

Even very small improvements indicate that you're on the right track.

If you notice no progress at all, you may need to go back to your data to look for a new hypothesis, new strategies, or a totally different slant. You might try to manipulate the antecedents—for example, change your approach to a transition—to see if that changes the child's behavior. Doing a functional assessment is an ongoing, cyclical process in which you are constantly trying things out, getting new information, and revising your strategies.

This chapter has given you a glimpse of how useful families can be when it comes to challenging behavior. In the next chapter we'll look at that topic in more depth.

What Do You Think?

1. "Every challenging behavior can be thought of as a child's solution to a problem and a form of communication." What does this mean to you? Can you remember a time when you or someone you know used challenging behavior to communicate or to solve a problem?

2. How does understanding the function of the behavior affect your attitude toward the child and the child's behavior? In what way does your attitude affect your ability to use an appropriate intervention?

3. In small groups, create and write up a scenario about a child with challenging behavior. Observe the child, record your observations, fill in the Functional Assessment Observation Form on page 263, formulate a hypothesis, and plan an intervention.

Suggested Reading

Artesani, J. (2000). *Understanding the purpose of challenging behavior: A guide to conducting functional assessments.* Upper Saddle River, NJ: Prentice-Hall.

Chandler, L., & Dahlquist, C. M. (2001). *Functional assessment: Strategies to prevent and remediate challenging behavior in school settings.* Upper Saddle River, NJ: Prentice-Hall.

Kaplan, J. S. (2000). *Beyond functional assessment: A social-cognitive approach to the evaluation of behavior problems in children and youth.* Austin: Pro-Ed.

O'Neill, R. E., Horner, R. H., Albin, R. W., Sprague, J. R., Storey, K., & Newton, J. S. (1997). *Functional assessment and program development for problem behavior: A practical handbook.* Pacific Grove, CA: Brooks/Cole.

References

Anderson, J. L., Albin, R. W., Mesaros, R. A., Dunlap, G., & Morelli-Robbins, M. (1993). Issues in providing training to achieve comprehensive behavior support. In J. Reichle & D. P. Wacker (Eds.), *Communicative alternatives to challenging behavior: Integrating assessment and intervention strategies* (pp. 363–406). Baltimore: Paul H. Brookes.

Aspen Systems Corporation. (n.d.). *Training guides for the Head Start learning community. Observing and recording: Tools for decision making.* Washington, DC: U.S. Department of Health and Human Services, Head Start Bureau.

Bijou, S. W., Peterson, R. F., & Ault, M. H. (1968). A method to integrate descriptive and experimental field studies at the level of data and empirical concepts. *Journal of Applied Behavior Analysis, 1,* 175–191.

Carr, E. G. (1994). Emerging themes in the functional analysis of problem behavior. *Journal of Applied Behavior Analysis, 27,* 393–399.

Chandler, L. K., & Dahlquist, C. M. (1997, April). *Confronting the challenge: Using team-based functional assessment and effective intervention strategies to reduce and prevent challenging behavior in young children.* Workshop presented at SpeciaLink Institute on Children's Challenging Behaviours in Child Care, Sydney, Nova Scotia.

Chandler, L. K., Dahlquist, C. M., Repp, A. C., & Feltz, C. (1999). The effects of team-based functional assessment on the behavior of students in classroom settings. *Exceptional Children, 66,* 101–122.

Dunlap, G., & Kern, L. (1993). Assessment and intervention for children within the instructional curriculum. In J. Reichle & D. P. Wacker (Eds.), *Communicative alternatives to challenging behavior: Integrating assessment and intervention strategies* (pp. 177–204). Baltimore: Paul H. Brookes.

Durand, V. M. (1990). *Severe behavior problems: A functional communication training approach.* New York: Guilford.

Durand, V. M. (1993). Functional assessment and functional analysis. In M. D. Smith (Ed.), *Behavior modification for exceptional children and youth* (pp. 38–60). Boston: Andover Medical Publishers.

Durand, V. M., & Crimmins, D. B. (1996–2001). Motivation assessment scale. Retrieved January 28,

2002, from http://www.monacoassociates.com/mas/aboutmas.html.

Gable, R. A., Quinn, M. M., Rutherford, R. B., Jr., Howell, K. W., & Hoffman, C. C. (1998). *Addressing student problem behavior—Part II: Conducting a functional behavioral assessment* (3rd ed.). Washington, DC: Center for Effective Collaboration and Practice. Retrieved February 16, 2002, from http://air-dc.org/cecp/fba/problem behavior2/main2.htm.

Gable, R. A., Quinn, M. M., Rutherford, R. B., Jr., Howell, K. W., & Hoffman, C. C. (2000). *Addressing student problem behavior—Part III: Creating positive behavioral intervention plans and supports.* Washington, DC: Center for Effective Collaboration and Practice. Retrieved February 17, 2002, from http://air-dc.org/cecp/fba/problembehavior3/main3.htm.

Iwata, B. A. (1994). Functional analysis methodology: Some closing comments. *Journal of Applied Behavior Analysis, 27,* 413–418.

Iwata, B. A., Dorsey, M. F., Slifer, K. J., Bauman, K. E., & Richman, G. S. (1982). Toward a functional analysis of self-injury. *Analysis and Intervention in Developmental Disabilities, 2,* 3–20.

Iwata, B. A., Vollmer, T. R., & Zarcone, J. R. (1990). The experimental (functional) analysis of behavior disorders: Methodology, applications, and limitations. In A. C. Repp & N. N. Singh (Eds.), *Perspectives on the use of nonaversive and aversive interventions for persons with developmental disabilities* (pp. 301–330). Sycamore, IL: Sycamore Publishing.

Kaplan, J. S. (2000). *Beyond functional assessment: A social-cognitive approach to the evaluation of behavior problems in children and youth.* Austin: Pro-Ed.

Karsh, K. G., Repp, A. C., Dahlquist, C. M., & Munk, D. (1995). In vivo functional assessment and multi-element interventions for problem behavior of students with disabilities in classroom settings. *Journal of Behavioral Education, 5,* 189–210.

Lalli, J. S., & Goh, H.-L. (1993). Naturalistic observations in community settings. In J. Reichle & D. P. Wacker (Eds.), *Communicative alternatives to challenging behavior: Integrating assessment and intervention strategies* (pp. 11–40). Baltimore: Paul H. Brookes.

Mace, F. C., & Roberts, M. L. (1993). Factors affecting selection of behavior interventions. In J. Reichle & D. P. Wacker (Eds.), *Communicative alternatives to challenging behavior: Integrating assessment and intervention strategies* (pp. 113–134). Baltimore: Paul H. Brookes.

Meyer, L. H., & Evans, I. M. (1993). Meaningful outcomes in behavioral intervention: Evaluating positive approaches to the remediation of challenging behavior. In J. Reichle & D. P. Wacker (Eds.), *Communicative alternatives to challenging behavior: Integrating assessment and intervention strategies* (pp. 407–428). Baltimore: Paul H. Brookes.

Miller, J. A., Tansy, M., & Hughes, T. L. (1998). Functional behavioral assessment: The link between problem behavior and effective intervention in schools. *Current Issues in Education* [On-line], *1*(5).

O'Neill, R. E., Horner, R. H., Albin, R. W., Sprague, J. R., Storey, K., & Newton, J. S. (1997). *Functional assessment and program development for problem behavior: A practical handbook* (2nd ed.). Pacific Grove, CA: Brooks/Cole.

Parrish, J. M., & Roberts, M. L (1993). Interventions based on covariation of desired and inappropriate behavior. In J. Reichle & D. P. Wacker (Eds.), *Communicative alternatives to challenging behavior: Integrating assessment and intervention strategies* (pp. 135–173). Baltimore: Paul H. Brookes.

Quinn, M. M., Gable, R. A., Rutherford, R. B., Nelson, C. M., & Howell, K. W. (1998). *Addressing student problem behavior—Part I: An IEP team's introduction to functional behavior assessment and behavior intervention plans.* Washington, DC: Center for Effective Collaboration and Practice. Retrieved February 16, 2002, from http://ideapractices.org/IDEAresources/depotitem.asp?ResourceId=69.

Repp, A. C., Felce, D., & Barton, L. E. (1988). Basing the treatment of stereotypic and self-injurious behaviors on hypotheses of their causes. *Journal of Applied Behavior Analysis, 21,* 281–289.

Repp, A. C., Karsh, K. G., Munk, D., & Dahlquist, C. M. (1995). Hypothesis-based interventions: A theory of clinical decision-making. In W. T. O'Donohue & L. Krasner (Eds.), *Theories of behavior therapy: Exploring behavior change* (pp. 585–608). Washington, DC: American Psychological Association.

Schmidt, R. (1996, May). *Difficult social behavior problems: A consideration of behaviour teaching strategies.* Workshop presented at the meeting of the Early Childhood Educators of British Columbia, Vancouver.

Smith, M. D. (1993). *Behavior modification for exceptional children and youth.* Boston: Andover Medical Publishers.

12

Working with Families and Other Experts

Even when you know that the causes of challenging behavior are complex, it's sometimes tempting to put all the blame on the child's family. Perhaps they seem too busy to spend any time with their child, argue all the time, or use corporal punishment. Or maybe they just aren't interested in her school experience. Despite their behavior, families are not the enemy. On the contrary: They are on your side. Even though it might not seem that way to you, they love their child and want to help her. Creating a partnership with them is definitely the best strategy.

Connecting with a family is important with any child, but it's especially important where challenging behavior is concerned. It's simply too hard to understand and manage behavior problems effectively in a vacuum. Families know their child best, and their insight and collaboration can be invaluable. They can tell you about their lives and their culture—family roles, origin, support network, patterns of authority—and about such stress factors as illness, divorce, and money problems. They can tell you about the

Home Remedy

> In *To Teach* (1993), William Ayers says, "Parents are a powerful, usually underutilized source of knowledge about youngsters.... We too often dismiss their insights as subjective and overly involved. In fact, the insights of the parents—urgent, invested, passionate, immediate— are exactly what we need" (p. 39).

child's developmental milestones so far, and they can provide information about the nature, frequency, and severity of the challenging behavior at home and in the past as well as the effect that it's having on them. Besides, it's the family's right to know about any problem as soon as you become aware of its existence.

It is essential to try to see things from the parents' point of view and to look for whatever is positive in the family. Even families who are struggling have strengths, competencies, and resources to draw on. If you can make the assumption that they are capable people, they're likely to fulfill your expectations, and together you'll come up with a variety of possible solutions (Education Development Center, 1997).

How do families react to news of challenging behavior?

Families have a strong emotional investment in their children, and they're never really ready to hear about problems, even though they're often acutely aware of them. They may struggle with their child over meals, bath, and bedtime every day; regard a trip to the supermarket as a nightmare; and dread taking her to the playground for fear she will hurt another child—but that doesn't mean they're prepared to hear someone else call her difficult. In *Troubled Families—Problem Children* (1994), psychologists Carolyn Webster-Stratton and Martin Herbert write, "It is not easy for parents to admit that they have a child with behavior problems, a child who is different from other children" (p. 201). Even when families know that their child is having problems in child care or school, it's hard to face this fact and even harder to deal with the many feelings and fears that come with it.

Chances are that a family living with a child with challenging behavior is also living with enormous stress (Webster-Stratton and Herbert, 1994). Home is just not a peaceful or pleasant place to be. Depending on the severity of the child's behavior, parents and siblings may be feeling victimized, insecure, angry, out of control, guilty, depressed, and/or utterly powerless (Webster-Stratton and Herbert, 1994). The child's behavior often causes marital problems because each parent blames the other. And their inability to cope with the challenging behavior may inadvertently increase it. It is far easier to parent a child who's socially competent!

Many parents judge themselves by their child's behavior and feel that others are judging them, too (Webster-Stratton and Herbert, 1994). In their own minds, having a child with behavior problems is a sign that they aren't good parents, and they feel embarrassed, isolated, rejected, and stigmatized by other parents whose children seem perfect. Their own extended family often criticizes the way they discipline the child, making numerous unsupportive suggestions that evoke even more unease and guilt.

Knowing how parents perceive their child's behavior, how they respond to it, and how it affects their lives will help you to understand where the child is coming from—and this knowledge will affect your behavior, as well. The more aware you are of the child's sense of self and the way she communicates her needs, the more equipped you will be to respond to her appropriately—to notice signs of her anxiety, to identify the function of her behavior.

Not all families will be equally willing to collaborate with you on a strategy for addressing challenging behavior. Some will want to be involved in every aspect of their child's life and will quickly throw themselves into each activity. Others won't think that's appropriate—they see a clear separation between what goes on at home and what happens at child care or school. Still others would like to get involved but just don't have the resources: the time, the energy, or the money. A child with challenging behavior devours a family's reserves. Some parents are so overwhelmed that the issue becomes one of survival, a matter of getting from day to day.

An immigrant family may also be struggling with the language and mores of the dominant culture. Being informed about their cultural background will help you understand the options they have and the choices they're making (Lynch and Hanson, 1998). They may believe it's inappropriate to discuss family dynamics or personal problems with a teacher; they may think it's impolite to disagree with you or even to ask questions when they don't understand; they may seem willing to go along with your suggestions when they really have an entirely different view of the situation and prefer their own methods; or they may see you as the expert, while you are trying to create a sense of collaboration, a partnership. Respecting their beliefs is the first step toward communication, but at the same time it's important to help them become aware of their own expertise where their child is concerned.

Lost at Sea

Parents who are living with a child with challenging behavior may feel abandoned by the child's school or child-care setting. One mother told Webster-Stratton and Herbert (1994) about her experience with her son's kindergarten:

> The principal came up to me and said, "Your boy is a very sick boy and is going to need many years of psychoanalytic counseling."—I feel all the teachers knew this and set us up in the school so we couldn't win. I felt everyone else in the kindergarten was on this raft while we were swimming around trying to clutch to get on....
>
> By the end of the school year we started realizing that the kindergarten raft was sailing away, and when they told us not to come back we felt we were left drowning in the water (p. 59).

Source: Carolyn Webster-Stratton and Martha Herbert, *Troubled Families—Problem Children: Working with Parents: A Collaborative Process* (Chichester, England: Wiley, 1994). Copyright John Wiley & Sons Limited. Reproduced with permission.

Although this may be the first time you've broached this subject with the family, it probably isn't the first time someone has informed them about their child's problems. The previous encounters may have been less than ideal, leaving the parents feeling incompetent, helpless, and alienated. Such an experience makes any discussion seem threatening and paves the way for difficulties. On the other hand, if they're hearing about a problem for the first time, they may be devastated or—because no one has contacted them before—consider you the author of the child's problems. They might even be in a state of denial.

Regardless of how the family responds, you cannot allow yourself to become defensive and create a barrier between you. If they feel inadequate and guilty or think that you don't like their child, they will resent you and conclude that you—not the child's behavior—are the problem. They may choose not to share their thoughts or perceptions with you and shut out anything you say so that there will be no real exchange of ideas. This will make it next to impossible to give them the support they need and to coordinate things between you. The bottom line is clear: Responsibility for the success of this venture lies with you, the teacher.

How do you feel?

There may be some anxiety on your side, too. You aren't sure how the family will react to what you have to say, and you might fear they'll hold you responsible for the difficulties the child is having or simply refuse to believe you. If they use very firm—or even physical—discipline at home, and the guidance methods you've learned aren't working with their child, the parents may very well blame you, or feel that you're blaming them. You may also feel angry and upset with the child (Galinsky and Weissbourd, 1992). All of these feelings might spill over into your relationship with the family. It's important

Where They're Coming From

Parents often become defensive when a teacher invites them to discuss their child's challenging behavior. Such a reaction may come from:

* Feeling they should have been told about problems before they became so severe

* Thinking that this didn't happen before so it must be the fault of the teacher or the other children

* Having previous negative experiences with the school about this child or another child

* Having a generally negative attitude toward the center, the school, or the school system

* Living with other family problems that are already creating a lot of stress (Losen and Diament, 1978).

to use your self-reflection skills to become aware of your emotions and take control of them as you proceed.

You probably bring some biases to the table as well. Researchers Susan Kontos and Wilma Wells (1986) found that child-care teachers don't have as high a regard for single parents, families living in poverty, and families of different racial and ethnic groups—"in other words, those who had the greatest pressure to face and the fewest resources to use in doing so" (Galinsky, 1988, p. 8). It's extremely important to refrain from judging families, to get to know them as people, and to learn something about their culture, particularly about the way they raise their children and communicate with others.

If you don't have any children of your own, it may be hard for you to imagine how the family feels. Nonetheless, you share a commitment to helping the child succeed. When you are open and willing to see the child's behavior and the circumstances surrounding it from the family's point of view, when you can recognize that different settings elicit different behaviors as well as different solutions, you've begun to collaborate.

How can colleagues help?

If you're finding it hard to deal with this child's behavior, you might also be feeling very unsure of yourself. Maybe you're even beginning to believe that everything is your fault, especially if you're a new teacher. You might be wondering if you should ask the advice of your director or principal.

Part of the job of the director or principal is to provide you with additional resources, information, and support. It makes good sense to reach out to her or him about any problem you have in the classroom as soon as it becomes a problem. Talking with the director or principal—and with your colleagues—can only enhance your ability to understand and support the child and her family. Although this might be the first time you've encountered a child with challenging behavior, they have no doubt had many such experiences. Some may have taught the child in previous years and have valuable tips to offer. Others can help you figure out how to approach the family. It isn't unreasonable to expect to discuss these problems at a staff meeting.

The problem behavior can be one that's causing trouble for you or the child or simply one that you feel you need to talk about. Any behavior (from not sitting for circle time to hitting someone over the head with a textbook) is fair game. Any feeling (from frustration to bewilderment to anger) is reason enough to seek out a sympathetic ear. Talking may not solve the problem, but it helps to express and clarify what you feel. (Just be sure to do it in a way that safeguards the confidentiality of the child and the family.)

If you don't speak up until you can't face the classroom another day, you've waited too long, and you've made your own job harder and less rewarding. Sometimes people don't ask for help because they fear they'll be judged incompetent or because they think it's necessary to fix any problem by themselves. This is a mistake. No one is omnipotent, and no one is an island. Some children are harder to teach, and everyone needs an outlet and peer support some of the time. Teams are especially important when you're dealing with challenging behavior: People who have different perspectives and skills can help one another come up with creative and effective solutions.

Even though you may be talking about the child's behavior with the director or principal, it is usually better to initially meet with just the parents. Having the director there makes it look to the parents as if you've been discussing their child behind their backs. And with two authority figures present, they're likely to feel intimidated by your collective expertise. Instead, involve the family in the decision to invite the director or principal to a future meeting. Then they'll know why she or he is there and feel comfortable about it. When you bring up the idea, simply say that the director has many years of experience and is well informed about available resources.

How do you arrange a meeting?

If you work in a child-care center, you probably see the family almost every day; if you work in a school setting, you may have met them briefly or not at all. In either case, your first meeting about the child's challenging behavior will establish a new tone and quality for your relationship. What happens there will classify you as either ally or adversary, and that label will influence all of your future contacts. It is important to avoid an expert or authoritarian approach. When you and the parents regard each other as equals, recognize one another's expertise, and acknowledge that differences in opinion are normal, you can use your combined strengths to set goals, make plans, and solve problems. The child, the family, and the program all benefit.

Get in touch with the family as soon as you decide you need to talk with them—if you wait for a regularly scheduled parent-teacher meeting, things may escalate out of control. The best way to make the first contact is by telephone. When you call parents at work, you induce instant panic, so phone them at home where you can set a friendlier tone and take the time you need to choose your words carefully. Since several family members will probably be around, it will also be easier to schedule a meeting time that suits everyone. If the family speaks a different language, find someone to interpret for you.

Begin by introducing yourself, then state the purpose of the call clearly. (It's better not to say vaguely, "I want to talk with you about Jessica," because parents immediately assume the worst.) Instead, stick to the facts and describe exactly what you've noticed: that she's hitting other children and destroying their work. Tell them that you want to talk with them about what you're doing at school and ask their advice about what works at home. Be careful not to accuse or judge them (Galinsky, 1988).

Some parents have been anxiously awaiting this contact, and others may be caught totally off guard, but it's unlikely that any family will have a straightforward response. Feelings—of guilt, anger, disappointment, embarrassment—inevitably surge up, coloring their reaction. In their consternation, they may deny, justify, rationalize, minimize, or even abdicate responsibility: "She's not like that at home," "Maybe she's bored," "She has lots of friends in the neighborhood," "We've just gone through a difficult divorce," "She never listens to us, even when we spank her," "I'm not surprised you called; we don't know what to do at home any more." Even parents who sound like partners on the surface may feel helpless and defensive (Losen and Diament, 1978). Show your concern, and listen carefully to what they are saying and how they are saying it so that when you meet you will be able to help them find ways to support their child.

Talk with them long enough to make it clear that you care about their child and are eager to work with them to help her. You may encounter parents who want to stay on the phone indefinitely and then decide there's nothing further to say, hence no reason to meet. Try not to let things reach this point. Be polite, but point out that it's easier to discuss these matters in person. If everyone has a little time to reflect on the situation, the conversation will be more fruitful.

There should be as little delay as possible between the initial call and your first meeting. Arrange a time that is convenient for everyone—the family, you, and your co-teacher or assistant teacher, if you have one. Be aware that families may not be able to leave their place of employment, and you may have to meet at the end of their work day. Schedule a time to end the meeting as well as a time to begin. Knowing when you have to leave helps everyone stay on topic and keeps parents from being insulted when the meeting is over. Be sure to set aside enough time so that you won't be rushed. In some cultures the family will notice that you're in a hurry and defer to your needs. But they may also feel that you aren't showing respect for them and be insulted or hurt, which will not help the child.

Choose a private space where no one will interrupt, organize enough adult-sized chairs for everyone, and place them so that there are no physical barriers (such as your desk) between you and the family. Remember, you want to convey partnership, not authority. If you're meeting at the center or school at the end of the day, the child will probably be there, so arrange child care for him. If the family doesn't bring the child but you suspect they can't afford a sitter, perhaps the center or school can cover the cost.

In different cultures, different people are responsible for making decisions about the children. In some, men have the say; in others, it is the oldest family member who is in charge; in still others, mothers are key. Before you call, find out which family member to approach first and who else should be present. If the parents are separated or divorced but live in the same city and are both involved in the child's life, ask them both to participate—but tell them ahead of time so they'll be prepared to meet their former partner! This is especially important in cases of joint custody. It is always best if they hear what you have to say directly from you; secondhand information is bound to be distorted. Invite each concerned person individually.

If you don't speak the same language, ask if they would like an interpreter and decide who will be responsible for finding one. It's better not to press an older sibling into service (Lynch, 1998a). Family members may not want to discuss delicate issues in

Let the Good Times Roll

Sometimes when a family has a child with challenging behavior they focus so hard on the problems that they forget the child's positive qualities. It helps when you remind them of her strengths.

If they seem open to ideas from you, suggest that they set aside a few minutes each day to have fun with her. Let them know that if they give her their undivided attention, let her choose the activity and lead the conversation, and show her they like playing with her, they will nourish her self-esteem and point the way to more positive moments together.

the sibling's presence, and the child-interpreter may not wish an outsider to know about sensitive family matters. In addition, being placed in this position alters the child's relationship to her elders and causes problems for both child and parents. On the other hand, the family may not feel comfortable talking with a stranger, and even a member of the same cultural community may pose problems of privacy and confidentiality (Lynch, 1998a). If you have taken on the task of selecting the interpreter, double-check with the family to be sure they're satisfied with your choice (Joe and Malach, 1998). It's a good idea to use a skillful professional who can interpret cultural cues as well as language and let you know what isn't said as well as what is. A first-rate interpreter is a treasure who deserves the very best treatment you can provide (Lynch, 1998a).

Nevertheless, there may still be room for misunderstanding. For example, some concepts seem to defy translation. Eleanor Lynch of San Diego State University describes the problem this way: "Just as English speakers are unable to express the fine distinctions among the kinds of snow that Alaskan Eskimos describe easily, so too is it difficult to explain the nuances of behavior management to someone who has never felt that it was necessary to change a young child's behavior" (Lynch, 1998b, p. 38).

What should happen in a meeting with the family?

First, preparation is essential to success. Decide what you're going to say, and make yourself an agenda with the objectives and the main points you want to cover. Gather your reports, notes, and observation charts together so you don't have to search for things during the meeting. If it's hard for you to put your finger on the child's strengths now that she seems to be interfering with your ability to teach, spend some time going over the days in your mind and making notes so that you have something positive to tell the family. If you're still drawing a blank, do an observation where you look exclusively for appropriate behavior. When parents know that you notice and appreciate their child's assets, they will feel that you believe in her and her ability to behave competently and appropriately.

You should also give some thought to what you're going to wear. Meeting a family calls for a much more formal style than you need to sit on the floor with the children. Dressing up indicates respect, which is important for any family, and especially important for a family from a culture where relationships are formal.

In many cultures, communication is indirect and courtesy is very much valued. Lynch and Hanson (1998, p. 505) suggest using "culturally comfortable" practices such as serving tea, spending a few minutes in polite general conversation before launching into the subject of the meeting, or conducting the meeting in a highly formal way, depending on the culture (Joe and Malach, 1998). If you're using an interpreter, bear in mind that he or she is a go-between, and it's the family you're actually talking with. They are the ones who have to understand you, and they are the ones you have to understand (Lynch, 1998b).

When you meet with the family, you'll need great sensitivity and your very best listening skills. Take some deep breaths to calm your butterflies, and remember that you have important contributions to make: expertise about children, a nonjudgmental ear, and respect for the family's opinions and feelings. Together, you and the family will be stronger than either of you is alone.

Before you talk about problems, let the parents know where their child is succeeding. All families need to hear about their child's strengths: what she does well, who her friends are, what she enjoys.

Then you can talk about the challenging behavior you're observing and the things you need their help with. Be calm, factual, specific, and objective as you describe the skills you're working on with the group, your guidance and encouragement techniques, and your expectations. Tell the family what you see rather than what you think. Ask if they have any information about why this might be happening and any advice to offer. Invite them to share their thoughts and to work with you to develop a plan to solve the problem. Together, brainstorm as many ideas as you can.

Ask the family open-ended questions about the child. What does this behavior mean to them? How does the child behave at home? Is this new behavior, or has she behaved this way before? What have they done about it in the past? What are they doing now? Have there been any new stresses or changes in routine? What was she like as a baby? What works for them? How can you work together? This process will be easier if you've already spent some time trying to understand the family's goals for the child and figuring out how their goals mesh with yours. (Your goals will be important to the family only if they share them.) Do these goals suggest any solutions to the problem?

If they say that their child's behavior is no problem at home, believe them: Not every child with challenging behavior has problems outside a group setting. But it's important to say politely that her behavior is a problem in your class, where she must

Invite parents to share their experience and ideas and to work with you to develop a plan to solve the problem.

share space, toys, and attention. If you work in a child-care center, gently remind them that if the child isn't coping now, she will have a harder time at school, where there are fewer teachers, more children, and many more demands.

Even if they acknowledge that there is a problem, any remarks that sound like criticism of their child may cut them deeply. They are doing their best for her, and they may feel upset, defensive, or angry. These are all normal coping mechanisms. Let them vent their feelings, and give them time to come to terms with what you're saying. Again, try to see things from their perspective rather than passing judgment.

Some parents may already be working with specialists and parent groups and know an enormous amount about appropriate methods for managing their child's problems. Take the opportunity to learn as much from them as you can.

As you talk, be aware of your body language. Keep your arms open, and mirror their message. If they are leaning forward and engaged, you should also be leaning forward and engaged. Be conscious of your eye contact, as well. Are they comfortable with it, or do they seem more at ease if your eyes don't meet theirs? Remember that this can be a cultural issue, and it is important to communicate respect on their terms. Pay attention to the pace, cadence, and tone of their speech, and decide whether it's better to mirror or lead their actions. Their speech, along with their facial expressions and body gestures, will also give you vital clues about their emotions, which can easily sabotage the proceedings. Nothing will get done if the parents are upset or angry. Anxious parents are very much like anxious children, and open communication skills (such as those you learned from WEVAS) should be helpful when you're talking with them.

Active listening will enable you to understand what the parents are saying and demonstrate your respect and interest. Listen carefully to both the surface and the underlying message, and comment on the feelings being expressed with phrases such as "That's frustrating, isn't it?" or "It sounds as if you're feeling upset." Paraphrase what they have said to clarify the meaning and to verify that you've understood their message.

Some teachers are afraid to discuss the problems they're having with a child because they suspect the parents will punish her. Families can make a big difference when they reinforce what you're doing and use strategies at home that you've developed together. But punishment at home is an entirely different story. It won't help, and neither will unrelated consequences, such as forbidding a child to watch a favorite televi-

The Bottom Line

The meaning isn't always on the surface when you discuss problems with a family, so listening is absolutely crucial. First-rate detective work is as important with them as it is with the child.

Ryan has been hitting other children. But when you tell his father that you're trying to help Ryan to control his anger, his father is upset. He wants his son to learn to fight. If you can withhold judgment, listen carefully, and respect his views, the father may tell you why he feels this way. Perhaps he was bullied as a child and doesn't want his son to be victimized as he was. This evidence from Ryan's father will help you to empathize and understand where the child is coming from.

Family Social Skills

Problem solving with families is just like problem solving with children. In her article "Parents and Teacher-Caregivers: Sources of Tension, Sources of Support" (1988), Ellen Galinsky suggests using these six steps:

- Describe the situation as a problem out in front. Avoid accusations or the implication that the source of the problem resides in the personality of the parent or the child.

- Generate multiple solutions. Parents and professionals should both do this, and no one's suggestions should be ignored, put down, or denounced.

- Discuss the pros and cons of each suggestion.

- Come to a consensus about which solutions to try.

- Discuss how you will implement these solutions.

- Agree to meet again to evaluate how these solutions are working so that you can change your approach, if necessary. (p. 11)

sion program because she punched someone at school. It isn't your job to tell parents how to parent, and trying to is almost sure to get you into hot water. Giving unsolicited advice (no matter how useful) can make parents feel their private lives are under attack and give them the impression that you think they're incompetent parents. Instead, tell the family how you handled the situation, and if they bring up the subject, talk with them about what they feel should happen at home. Perhaps they'll recognize that you've dealt with the matter already or be willing to work out a logical and related consequence. You could point out that the most effective consequences are those that follow immediately.

How do you close a meeting?

Once you've generated options together, evaluated them in light of the family's goals for the child, and agreed on a plan, schedule another conference to assess the child's progress. You may have to meet several times to resolve the problem.

Then wrap things up so the parents don't feel cut off. "Our time is almost up. I just want to be sure that we are all clear about what was said and what we've agreed to do next." Be sure to thank the family and leave them with the feeling that they have contributed to the problem-solving process. It's important for them to have a sense of ownership not only of the child and her problems but also of the solutions and the child's potential for success. When they have choices and power, the solutions are more likely to stick.

After the parents leave, record information that will help you to understand and respond to the child's behavior. It's also wise to evaluate the meeting so you can improve communication the next time. Did you say what you felt you needed to say? How was the information received by the family? Did the family feel like an equal partner? What commitments did everyone make? Is the follow-up clear?

*What if you and the family disagree?**

When a conflict arises, first pay attention to what you're feeling (which helps defuse those feelings) and then lock the feelings in a drawer, where you can find them later. If you're going to come out of this situation with a solution everyone can live with, you need an open mind, your reason, and your best eyes and ears. Perhaps your most important goal is to keep the discussion going; resolving differences takes time and communication.

The best thing to do is listen. You don't have to explain your actions, and even when you don't agree with what the family is saying, it's important to accept what they feel. Accepting their feelings is a way to show respect. If they say, "Jessica says you're always picking on her. You aren't fair," stifle your impulse to say that Jessica has it all wrong. It's normal for them to stand up for their child, and there's no point in arguing. Try to hear their feelings and reply, "I can see that she might feel that way. I'll try to reassure her."

When you and the family come from different cultures or backgrounds, it's especially easy to misunderstand and to be misunderstood. As people come to know and understand one another and their cultures, the chances of resolution improve. Or at least everyone's ability to handle disagreement gets better.

Again, it's important to help the parents articulate their goals for the child. It's also useful if you're clear about your own goals and values. If you know what you believe in, it will be easier to hear the family's point of view (Gonzalez-Mena, 1997), even if what they're saying is a criticism of your program.

Some values are nonnegotiable, such as those enshrined in the United Nations Convention on the Rights of the Child. You would never agree, for example, to hit a child, no matter how passionately and persuasively parents argue their case. Nor would you compromise on a matter of racial or gender equality. But other situations aren't quite so clear. You may think initially that you could never change your practice and then come to realize that some changes wouldn't hurt anyone and would make the child much happier. Routines such as eating, sleeping, and toileting might fall into that category—think of how Aki would feel if you lay down beside him at naptime. It's also worth looking seriously at a parent's request for her child to have more holding and nurturing (Chud and Fahlman, 1995). "Culturally responsive caregiving . . . means the willingness to bend, change and revise in order to meet individual needs," says Stacey York in *Roots & Wings* (1991, p. 188).

*This section has been adapted from *Partners in Quality, vol. 2/ Relationships* © CCCF 1999, written by Barbara Kaiser and Judy Sklar Rasminsky, based on the research papers of the Partners in Quality Project. With permission from Canadian Child Care Federation, 201-383 Parkdale Avenue, Ottawa, Ontario, K1Y 4R4.

From there, it's a matter of dialogue, negotiation, problem solving, and compromise, always keeping the best interests of the child in the front of your mind. You may reach a solution; you may agree to disagree. Either way is all right if you keep communication open and treat one another with respect. It's better for the child if you and the family are running down the same road in the same direction, but don't despair if that doesn't happen. Work to keep a dialogue going between you and in the meantime concentrate on the child. What she learns from you will stay with her.

How do you handle challenging behavior when the parent is present?

When parents and teachers are in the same room—as in a family resource program or a cooperative preschool or when the parent is helping out on field trips or picking up or delivering the child—everyone gets slightly confused about who's in charge. Problem behaviors that have largely disappeared may reemerge if the child hasn't generalized the behavior she learned at school to the home setting. This can take time and may not happen at all if there are no changes within the family. Parents are often the last people to benefit from positive changes in their child's behavior.

Probably the best procedure is to hesitate for a moment to see if the parents will step in. But don't wait too long. If they don't act, use the chance to model an appropriate response. If they take over, you will have a golden opportunity to see them interact with their child—and no matter what you think of their behavior, you'll have to let it go. You simply cannot criticize them in front of the child and other parents. If necessary, you can do some damage control and say the things you believe the child needs to hear. Later, create a private moment with the parents and talk to them about what you saw. Don't judge or criticize, but ask how they felt about what happened, and tell them what you do and how the child responds to it.

What should you say to the parents of the other children?

Whenever a child in your class has been hurt by another child and requires first aid, you must tell your supervisor, director, or principal and complete an incident report right away.

As soon as the family of the injured child arrive, let them know exactly what happened without mentioning the name of the child who was responsible. Even though the children tell their families what's going on, it is important for you to protect everyone's privacy. Be prepared for an angry reaction, either on the spot or after they've seen the bruise. They may accuse you of not watching or demand that the other child leave the program, and they may not hear any explanation you offer. Just stay as calm and understanding as you can. In a day or two, either you or the director or principal can talk to them privately about the school's plans for handling the situation.

Even the families of children who aren't directly involved may become upset, protest, gossip, or contact the program's board of directors or the PTA. Some may instruct their children not to play with the child who behaves aggressively. Explain that you are watching carefully, keeping everyone safe, and teaching the children to defend themselves with words—a skill they need on the playground and in life.

If families want more information or wish to discuss a child who isn't theirs, refer them to the director or principal. It is your ethical obligation to be discreet in both your professional and private lives, even when you need to share your feelings with fellow staff members. Don't talk in public places or mention last names. You never know whom you'll run into or who will be sitting behind you in a crowded restaurant or movie theater. This is an important part of being a professional and showing respect for children and families.

What about getting expert advice?

At a certain point it may be time to call in the experts. Together with your supervisor, director, or principal, assess what services are available to assist you. If there isn't a psychologist, social worker, or school counselor on staff, there may be one who works with the center or school from time to time. Your school may have a special team to help you out, or you may belong to a professional association or support group. If not, see whether an outside mental health consultant can observe you and the children. The consultant can't understand the child without your help. Tell her what you've seen during your observations, any patterns you've discovered in the child's behavior, and any strategies that work (even if they work only part of the time!).

Don't forget that you will need parental consent, but because you've been working with the family and including them in the decisions, this shouldn't be a problem. When you ask the parents' permission, be sure to mention how useful it can be to have another pair of eyes with a fresh point of view. At the same time, make it clear that the consultant will be watching you and the other children as well as their child. Having this information should make it easier for the parents to agree.

Another approach is to ask the school or child-care center to organize a workshop that will give the whole staff some special in-service training. This enables everyone to learn new skills, share in the process, and get vital peer support.

Remember that asking for help is not a sign of weakness; rather, it is a sign of wisdom. You are trying to solve your problem by thinking creatively and acquiring new skills. You have to trust your professional judgment—your knowledge of developmental norms, the instinct you've developed by working with children, your awareness of how a particular child is pushing your buttons. The crucial thing is to act *long* before you feel yourself approaching the breaking point. It may take months for help to arrive, and a burned-out adult is not capable of dealing objectively with either the child or the challenging behavior. At that point you'll barely hear the advice of an expert consultant, let alone follow it.

What if the child needs more help?

After you've had expert help at the center or school and nothing is working, you and the director or principal may decide to suggest that the family get outside help for the child. Timing is critical. If you and the family haven't had several discussions about the child's behavior and you haven't thoroughly investigated possible solutions within your classroom, it will be difficult to get their support. They may not believe that extra help is necessary, and they probably won't follow through. They may even decide to look for another center or school where the teachers "care more" about the children, although this option is probably just delaying the inevitable. Within a matter of months, the family will find itself having the same conversation with the director or principal there.

You and the director or principal will need extensive preparation for this conversation with the family. There is tons of information to gather if you are going to give them really helpful, meaningful advice. Specifics of all kinds are a must. Because in most cases the family will have to make their own decisions and appointments, you want to tell them as much as you can about how the system works and the resources that are available, including an up-to-date list of names and numbers that you have checked out ahead of time.

To start with, you must be familiar with what the community offers: hospital services, clinics, private practitioners, alternative schools and programs, local and state social service organizations, resource and referral agencies. If you think their child might have a medical problem, such as hearing loss, recommend that the parents take her to see their pediatrician or family physician. But for other problems they will probably be better off at the local hospital's developmental clinic or a community agency that can call on a range of specialists. School and Head Start programs may also have

The family will need information about how to contact outside experts, what services they offer, and what the cost may be.

their own social workers or family workers who can help. The family will need information about what the services are, who uses them, and what kind of help a speech therapist, occupational therapist, psychiatrist, or special school can provide. They will need to know where to go, how to make the initial contact, what the cost may be, how to apply for financial assistance, and how to interpret test results. To minimize their frustration, find out about waiting lists, too. If you can, try to match the family with a service or personality that will meet their needs best (Losen and Diament, 1978). You should be able to count on your supervisor for help with all of these issues.

Raising the matter with the family will require the most extraordinary delicacy on your part. Even though you've had several difficult talks with them, this will probably be the hardest. Don't try to impose your values, and be sure to separate the child from the behavior. Be specific about why you still have strong concerns. Remind them of strategies you've tried, and explain that you think it's important for the child's long-term development to get help for her. Tell them again how much you appreciate their collaboration.

This message will hit families hard. It is serious stuff, and it is much harder to accept than merely "having trouble" in school. They may not even hear what you have to say, so be sure to impress on them that they can call you later with their questions.

Reassurance is definitely required. Some families may find the idea of referral to a specialist totally alien and see it as a rejection and a form of stigmatization. They may have fears about what this step might mean for their child and themselves, and they may need emotional support. They may also be worrying about the cost and length of the treatment (Losen and Diament, 1978) and wondering how they can possibly fit it into their already overburdened lives. In addition, their culture may consider it inappropriate to discuss family problems with a stranger. They might feel more comfortable if you offer to accompany them yourself.

Find out if the family has worked with professionals before and how they felt about that experience. Your job will be an easy one if they consider it time well spent. But if they had a negative experience, they may be quite reluctant to try again. Ask about what problems they had, and try to help them to find a service or person that you know has a different approach.

Getting an assessment for a preschool-age child can be very difficult. Because she is growing and changing so quickly and the range of normal is so wide, some problems, such as attention deficit disorder, can't be accurately diagnosed until a child is 5 or 6 years old, and professionals are reluctant to give her a label she may keep for years.

A letter from you with a detailed description of the behavior will help. Ask the family's permission to write it, and put the original and a copy for them into an unsealed envelope so that they can read it and decide whether they want to deliver it. If you would like feedback from the specialist, ask the family to authorize him or her to release information to you—although they may prefer to report the findings to you themselves.

It is possible that the family will reject the idea of outside intervention. This is their right, and their decision doesn't imply that they don't love their child—only that they aren't ready or that their view of the situation is different from yours.

What about asking a child with challenging behavior to leave?

If you are at the end of your rope, ask your supervisor or principal for help. An administrator's bag of tricks may include hiring additional staff for part of the day, pitching in at critical times, giving you a couple of hours (or days) of leave, or setting up support sessions for the whole staff. If you've been discussing the situation with the director and your colleagues all along, they will understand your request and willingly pick up the slack. They, too, want what's best for the child. Burn-out is a legitimate complaint, and you may be eligible for short-term disability.

It is only when a child becomes a real danger to herself or others—and when you've exhausted every technique that you and the experts can devise—that exclusion becomes thinkable. Sometimes asking the parents to withdraw the child from the program may be the spur that helps them get the intervention the child needs, but you should never use this possibility as a rationalization for making such a decision.

Handing the child over to another adult is rarely a viable solution. Unless the program can afford to hire another person, a move like this usually requires too much juggling of people and schedules. There is also another important consideration: Attachment is critical in child development. You spend many hours a day with this child, and it's important for her long-term development (and particularly her ability to trust) for her to know that she can trust you, that you can take care of her, and that she can't destroy you. Sending her away doesn't teach anything positive. Rather, it is the ultimate destroyer of self-esteem because it says in neon lights, "I don't want you here," confirming the child's most negative self-image.

Being asked not to return also tells a school-age child that you think she's bad—which means she must be *really* bad. When she goes to another school, she brings along that sense of who she is and feels more comfortable trying to show everyone how bad she is rather than showing them (or herself) that the previous school made a mistake.

Teachers have a responsibility to teach every child in their class (and no child is truly unteachable).

What Do You Think?

1. In this chapter we've mentioned some of the people and organizations that help the families of children with challenging behavior: hospital services, clinics, private practitioners, alternative schools and programs, local and state social service organizations, resource and referral agencies, speech therapists, occupational therapists, psychiatrists. There are probably some of these in your neighborhood. Compile a list of them; describe what each of them does; get the name, title, and phone number of a person to contact at each; and get a brochure, flyer, business card, or some other written information that would be useful to a family.

2. With a classmate, role-play a parent-teacher meeting with one person being the teacher and the other(s) the parent(s) of a child with challenging behavior. Evaluate the meeting. What were some of the difficulties for the teacher? For the parents? How did you deal

with their response? What would you do differently? Conduct a follow-up meeting to iron out some of the problems that arose.

3. Reverse roles and do the previous exercise again.

Suggested Reading

Galinsky, E. (1988). Parents and teacher-caregivers: Sources of tension, sources of support. *Young Children, 43,* 4–12.

Greenberg, P. (1988). Ideas that work with young children: Avoiding "me against you" discipline. *Young Children, 44,* 24–29.

Webster-Stratton, C., & Herbert, M. (1994). *Troubled families—Problem children: Working with parents: A collaborative process.* Chichester, England: Wiley.

References

Ayers, W. (1993). *To teach: The journey of a teacher.* New York: Teachers College Press.

Chud, G., & Fahlman, R. (1995). *Honouring diversity within child care and early education: An instructors guide.* Victoria: British Columbia Ministry of Skills, Training, and Labour and the Centre for Curriculum and Professional Development.

Education Development Center. (1997). *Supporting children with challenging behaviors: Relationships are key: Training guides for the Head Start learning community.* Washington, DC: U.S. Department of Health and Human Services, Head Start Bureau.

Galinsky, E. (1988). Parents and teacher-caregivers: Sources of tension, sources of support. *Young Children, 43,* 4–12.

Galinsky, E., & Weissbourd, B. (1992). Family-centered child care. In B. Spodek & O. Saracho (Eds.), *Issues in child care: Yearbook in early childhood education, Vol. 3* (pp. 47–65). New York: Teachers College Press.

Gonzalez-Mena, J. (1997). *Multicultural issues in child care.* Mountain View, CA: Mayfield.

Joe, J. R., & Malach, R. S. (1998). Families with Native American roots. In E. W. Lynch & M. J. Hanson (Eds.), *Developing cross-cultural competence: A guide for working with children and their families* (pp. 127–164). Baltimore: Paul H. Brookes.

Kaiser, B., & Rasminsky, J. S. (1999). *Partners in quality 2: Relationships.* Ottawa, Ontario: Canadian Child Care Federation.

Kontos, S., & Wells, W. (1986). Attitudes of caregivers and the day care experiences of families. *Early Childhood Research Quarterly, 1,* 47–67.

Losen, S., & Diament, B. (1978). *Parent conferences in the schools: Procedures for developing effective partnership.* Boston: Allyn and Bacon.

Lynch, E. W. (1998a). Conceptual framework: From culture shock to cultural learning. In E. W. Lynch & M. J. Hanson (Eds.), *Developing cross-cultural competence: A guide for working with children and their families* (pp. 23–45). Baltimore: Paul H. Brookes.

Lynch, E. W. (1998b). Developing cross-cultural competence. In E. W. Lynch & M. J. Hanson (Eds.), *Developing cross-cultural competence: A guide for working with children and their families* (pp. 47–86). Baltimore: Paul H. Brookes.

Lynch, E. W., & Hanson, M. J. (1998). Steps in the right direction: Implications for interventionists. In E. W. Lynch & M. J. Hanson (Eds.), *Developing cross-cultural competence: A guide for working with children and their families* (pp. 491–512). Baltimore: Paul H. Brookes.

Webster-Stratton, C., & Herbert, M. (1994). *Troubled families—Problem children: Working with parents: A collaborative process.* Chichester, England: Wiley.

13

Bullying

Bullying has probably existed forever, but few researchers took it seriously until 1982, when newspapers in Norway reported that three boys, ages 10 to 14, had committed suicide after being bullied by their peers. The news shocked the country, and in the fall of 1983, Norway's Ministry of Education launched a nationwide program against bullying in primary and junior schools (Olweus, 1991, 1993). Since then, interest in the subject has gradually spread throughout Europe, Ireland, and the British Isles into Japan, Australia, New Zealand, Canada, and the United States (Olweus, 1993; Smith et al., 1999).

What is bullying?

Bullying is a special form of aggressive behavior. The world's leading authority on bullying, Dan Olweus, who designed the Norwegian intervention program, defines it this way: "A person is being bullied when he or she is exposed, repeatedly and over time, to negative actions on the part of one or more other persons" (Olweus, 1991, 1993). What differentiates bullying from other aggressive acts is that the child who bullies intends to

231

harm, there is more than one incident, and an imbalance of power makes it hard for the child who's being bullied to defend himself. This difference in power can be physical—the child who bullies can be older, bigger, stronger; or several children can gang up on a single child. It can also be psychological, which is harder to see but just as potent—the child who bullies can have more social status or a sharper tongue, for instance. According to English criminologist David Farrington, in a bullying situation the child who is victimized feels oppressed (Rigby, 2001b) and experiences pain, humiliation, and distress (Beane, 1999; Pepler and Craig, n.d.).

There are several kinds of bullying:

• *Physical* bullying is the easiest to identify: Hitting, kicking, shoving, and destroying property are probably what most of us envisage when we think of bullying. Physical bullying is more common among boys (Nansel et al., 2001).

• *Verbal* bullying includes name-calling, insulting, mocking, threatening, taunting, teasing, and making racist and sexist comments. When does teasing cross the line and turn into bullying? Not everyone agrees, but researchers at Educational Equity Concepts in New York and the Wellesley College Center for Research on Women in Massachusetts (Froschl, Sprung, and Mullin-Rindler, 1998) see it as part of a continuum of intentionally hurtful behavior, different only in degree. In a study of bullying in the midwest, Ronald Oliver, John H. Hoover, and R. J. Hazler (1994) found that children are confused about teasing: They said it was done in fun, but they also ranked it as the most frequent bullying behavior. Verbal abuse is the most common form of bullying for children of both sexes, even young ones (Kochenderfer and Ladd, 1996; Nansel et al., 2001).

• *Relational or psychological* bullying uses relationships to control or harm another person (Crick, Casas, and Ku, 1999; Crick et al., 2001)—excluding him from the group or events, talking behind his back, spreading rumors, or telling lies about him. According to Nicki Crick and her colleagues at the University of Minnesota, relational bullying deprives children of the opportunity to be close to and accepted by their peers—needs that are important for their well-being and development (Crick et al., 2001). Girls are more likely to use, and to become the targets of, relational bullying (Crick et al., 1999; Crick and Grotpeter, 1995).

Making faces and gesturing can also be bullying, although they don't fit neatly into a category.

The experts also classify bullying as *direct*, which is when the child doing the bullying attacks openly so the child who's being victimized knows who he is (Olweus, 1993), or *indirect*, which is when the child doing the bullying tries to inflict harm without revealing his intention (Alsaker and Valkanover, 2001). Physical bullying is usually direct, but verbal and relational bullying can be either direct or indirect. Most preschoolers don't yet have the social skills to bully indirectly, so their bullying tends to be direct ("I'm going to cut off your mother's head") (Crick et al., 2001; Crick et al., 1999). Older children are more subtle and their methods can be more indirect, as when a group of third-graders never seems to find enough space at their lunch table for Aisha. Because indirect bullying is harder to observe, less is known about it (Smith and Sharp, 1994).

The difference in power can be physical—the child who bullies can be older, bigger, stronger; or several children can gang up on a single child.

In fact, bullying usually takes place out of the view of grown-ups. Children who bully choose venues where adults are scarce: Playgrounds are a favorite spot, along with corridors, bathrooms, and locker rooms. When Wendy Craig and Debra J. Pepler (1997) videotaped and recorded bullying on Toronto playgrounds, they saw teachers intervene in only 4 percent of bullying incidents, although 75 percent said they always responded. And children who bully make it very clear that neither the onlookers nor the children who are victimized are to divulge what happened. This tactic is strikingly successful: Children who are targeted seldom tell either their parents or their teachers (Pepler and Craig, n.d.; Smith and Sharp, 1994).

Bullying is not a reaction to academic failure (Olweus, 1993), and in Scandinavia it isn't even related to the family's socioeconomic status. There is not yet enough data to say the same for the United States (Olweus, Limber, and Mihalic, 1999).

How common is bullying?

Bullying happens everywhere (Mellor, 1993), whether the school or the classroom is large or small, urban or rural (Olweus, 1993). Most children experience it at some time during their school careers (Juvonen and Graham, 2001) and fortunately it is minor and fleeting for the majority (Pepler and Craig, n.d.).

The first large-scale study of bullying in the United States—a representative sample of more than 15,000 children in grades 6 to 10 in public and private schools all over the country—revealed that 8.8 percent of children bully others frequently (once a week or more) and 8.4 percent are bullied frequently. Almost 30 percent of children are frequently or moderately involved in bullying—13 percent bully others, 10.6 percent are targeted, and 6.3 percent both bully others and are targeted themselves (Nansel et al., 2001). These rates are considerably higher than those found in Olweus's large Norwegian study, where 15 percent were involved "now and then," 2 percent bullied others, and 3 percent were targets once a week or more (Olweus, 1991). Canadian and American statistics are similar, and Craig and Pepler's (1997) videotapes captured a bullying act on Toronto playgrounds every seven minutes.

Studies in Europe have found that bullying declines steadily after grade 2, but in the United States it seems to increase after grade 3, peak during grades 5 to 8, and diminish after grade 10 (Hoover and Oliver, 1996; Nansel et al., 2001). The few small studies done on bullying among young children show that it starts as early as preschool (Crick et al., 1999), that 10 to 18 percent of children are targets, and 17 percent bully others (Alsaker and Valkanover, 2001; Crick et al., 1999). One study that followed children from kindergarten to grade 3 determined that 4 percent were persistently victimized (Ladd and Ladd, 2001).

Some children never stop bullying, though we call their handiwork by different names in adult life—such as harassment, wife abuse, child abuse, racism, and sexism (Pepler and Craig, n.d.; Smith, Cowie, and Sharp, 1994).

Who are the children who bully others?

By definition, a child who uses bullying behavior is strong and chooses to dominate weak children. Several risk factors might dispose him to behave this way. To begin with, he may have an impulsive temperament, a tendency to be hot-headed, problems with attention and hyperactivity, and a low tolerance for frustration. If the child who bullies is a boy, he may be physically strong and good at sports and fighting (Olweus, 1993).

It's likely that the child acquired a positive attitude toward violence at home, where he probably viewed close up how effective it can be. He may have been bullied himself, or he may have observed his parents or siblings bully others (Sharp and Smith, 1994). Olweus (1993) found that the families of children who bully often use power-assertive child-rearing methods, such as physical punishment and violent emotional outbursts. The families also tend to be permissive—they don't set clear limits or prohibit aggressive behavior. And they are usually cold and indifferent toward their child, which increases his risk of aggressive behavior. As a result, he has a strong need to dominate others, to get his own way, and to be in control, and he isn't interested in negotiating, cooperating, or accepting anyone else's ideas (Hoover and Hazler, 1991; Olweus, 1993; Rigby, 1998). Pepler and Craig (n.d.) point out that he's learned some important lessons—that those with power can be aggressive, and that power and aggression can help bring him dominance and status.

Unlike children who use aggressive behavior indiscriminately, children who bully are generally well liked and surrounded by friends and supporters, although their popularity decreases in their midteens (Olweus, 1993; Rigby, 1998). They may try out their tactics on several targets before settling on one who doesn't resist (Perry et al., 1992). Because they choose carefully and use force swiftly and unemotionally to get what they want (Perry et al., 1992), their behavior elicits little negative reaction and seems to be an acceptable way to achieve social success (Hoover and Hazler, 1991). Children who bully have little empathy and don't worry about the pain or discomfort they cause (Olweus, 1993). On the contrary, they may even enjoy it (Rigby, 2001b).

In fact, children who use bullying behavior feel quite comfortable with themselves. They tend to be outgoing and self-confident and feel little anxiety or insecurity. It is a myth that they lack social skills and self-esteem (Olweus, 1991, 1993). In elementary school, their grades are average, but they have trouble following the rules and tend to behave aggressively and defiantly toward adults (Olweus, 1993).

Children who bully are at risk for a whole host of problems as they grow older (Olweus, 1991; Pepler and Craig, 2000):

- Aggressive behavior

- Alcohol and drug abuse

- Delinquency, gang involvement, and vandalism

- Sexual harassment and dating aggression

- Academic problems and school dropout

- Peer rejection

They may also suffer from mental health problems, such as conduct disorder, depression, and anxiety (Olweus, 1991; Pepler and Craig, 2000). Children who use relational bullying also face risks as they grow older: They are likely to be lonely, depressed, rejected, and have little self-esteem (Crick, Casas, and Mosher, 1997).

Olweus (1993) found that by the age of 24 about 60 percent of the boys who had bullied others in grades 6 to 9 had been convicted of a criminal offense, and 35 to 40

Feeling Blue

Mark G. Borg (1998) of the University of Malta asked about 2,000 primary school children what they felt after they had been bullied. They said they felt

- Angry (34 percent)

- Vengeful (33 percent)

- Self-pity (44 percent)

- Indifferent (24 percent)

- Helpless (28 percent)

Boys tended to feel more vengeful; girls tended to feel more self-pity.

percent had three or more convictions. Among boys who didn't bully and weren't harassed, the rate was only 10 percent.

Who are the targets of bullying?

It is no fun to be on the receiving end of bullying. The immediate effects—physical injury, humiliation, helplessness, rejection, unhappiness—are painful enough, but the knowledge that all this will soon be repeated multiplies the distress. Children who are harassed experience fear, anxiety, insecurity, oppression, inability to concentrate in class, headaches, stomach aches, and nightmares. It is not surprising that they want to avoid school (Kochenderfer and Ladd, 1996). Being bullied has a devastating effect on self-esteem. It's hard for a child to stop thinking that he deserves whatever he gets (Boivin, Hymel, and Hodges, 2001; Olweus et al., 1999; Rigby, 2001b; Wilczenski et al., 1994).

How does a child become the target of bullying? What makes him vulnerable? As with the child who engages in bullying, part of the explanation is temperament. Olweus (1993) found that most children who are harassed are what he terms "passive victims": "cautious, sensitive, quiet, withdrawn, passive, submissive and shy . . . anxious, insecure, unhappy, and distressed" (p. 57). Instead of standing up for themselves when they're insulted or attacked, they cry or run away, sending a clear signal that they are easy marks. And because children who are targeted usually have poor social skills, spend a lot of time alone, and have few or no friends, the child doing the bullying knows that no one will come to their defense (Egan and Perry, 1998; Hodges, Boivin, Vitaro, and Bukowski, 1999; Perry, Hodges, and Egan, 2001).

Children who are bullied might also be physically weak (Perry et al., 2001) and have what Olweus (1993) calls "body anxiety": They're poorly coordinated, afraid of being hurt, and weak at sports and fights. They are always the last ones chosen for a team.

They often have a history of insecure attachment, trouble separating from their parents, and a fear of exploring their surroundings. Their parents tend to keep them under close control, overprotecting them, manipulating their thoughts and feelings, or using coercive and power-assertive discipline. These tactics all threaten the development of the child's sense of self, undermine his confidence, and batter his self-esteem (Perry et al., 2001).

Are children who are harassed different in other ways? In two studies, Olweus (1993) found that boys who are bullied are no more likely to have physical differences—to be overweight, to wear glasses, or to speak with an accent, for instance. But other researchers dispute his findings, or at least wonder whether they apply to more heterogeneous societies. American psychologists David G. Perry, Ernest V. E. Hodges, and Susan K. Egan (2001) point out that physical differences seem to incite teasing, which can cause distress and a loss of self-esteem, and which may in turn put a child at risk of harassment. In a survey in the midwest, researchers found that the top reason for being bullied was "just didn't fit in" (Hoover and Oliver, 1996). And a study in Sheffield, England, showed that two-thirds of children with special needs were bullied, compared

Early Signs

To find out how children take on the role of victim, psychologists David Schwartz, Kenneth A. Dodge, and John D. Coie (1993) ran a series of experimental play groups of first- and third-grade boys who didn't know each other.

In the early sessions, some boys were unassertive. They started fewer conversations, spent more time in parallel play, and didn't try to tell their peers what to do. When others approached them aggressively and in rough-and-tumble play, they submitted, rewarding their attackers.

This behavior marked them as potential targets. In later sessions, the other members of the group treated them more and more negatively, coercively, and aggressively.

with only 25 percent of their mainstream peers (Whitney, Smith, and Thompson, 1994).

Not all children who are harassed are passive. Perhaps 10 to 20 percent fight back and even egg on their abusers. Dubbed "provocative" victims by Olweus (1993), who first identified them, they are also called "aggressive" or "bully victims."

They have much in common with both children who bully and targeted children who don't fight back. Like children who bully, they have trouble concentrating, and they're likely to be impulsive and hyperactive. They also try to dominate others, and their behavior is often aggressive and antisocial (Olweus, 1993). Like children who are targeted and don't fight back, they are anxious, depressed, rejected, and lonely. Lacking social skills, they have few friends (Perry et al., 2001; Perry et al., 1992; Schwartz, Proctor, and Chen, 2001). They are also physically weak and have the same body anxiety as children who respond passively to harassment (Olweus, 1993).

But perhaps their most prominent quality is their volatility. Because they can't regulate their emotions, they lose their tempers, overreact, argue, and fight about all kinds of things, and they almost invariably lose. For this reason, David G. Perry, Louise C. Perry, and Elizabeth Kennedy (1992) call them "ineffectual aggressors" (pp. 320, 323). Their lack of self-control also means they have trouble in school (Schwartz et al.,

Cultureless Shock

Are children bullied because of their ethnicity or culture? A study in the Netherlands found no more victimization among Moroccan, Turkish, and Surinamese immigrant boys than among their native Dutch peers (Junger, 1990). In a survey of 15,000 U.S. students, about 3 percent of boys and girls reported being harassed once a week or more because of their race or religion, and about 8 percent were belittled at least once a week because of their looks or speech (Nansel et al., 2001).

2001). With this irritating, provocative behavior, they manage to elicit negative reactions from just about everyone (Olweus, 1993).

It is no surprise that children who combine aggressive behavior with being victimized usually come from a harsh environment where the parenting is hostile and punitive and there is a lot of conflict and violence. In one study, 38 percent of the boys who emerged as "aggressive victims" had been physically abused (Schwartz, Dodge, Pettit, and Bates, 1997).

In the long run, there is risk for any child who is bullied. When Olweus (1993, 2001) followed up a subgroup who'd been bullied in grades 6 through 9, he found that at the age of 23, they were more depressed and had lower self-esteem than their non-victimized peers. The Australian bullying expert Ken Rigby (2001a) found that high levels of peer victimization "correlated positively with high levels of mental and physical distress three years later" (p. 322). In his study, the students who were bullied were more likely to be anxious, depressed, socially dysfunctional, and physically unwell. They were also more prone to thinking about suicide.

In later life, children who've been the targets of relational bullying face risks above and beyond those encountered by the targets of physical bullying. They are even more depressed, lonely, anxious, and rejected (Crick et al., 1999; Crick et al., 2001).

Who are the bystanders?

Bullying is a group activity, situated in a social context that influences both the appearance of bullying and the response to it. In Olweus's studies, 60 to 80 percent of the children who were harassed reported that more than one person had bullied them (Olweus et al., 1999), and the hard evidence of Craig and Pepler's cameras (1997) showed that peers were involved in 85 percent of bullying incidents. In fact, bullying lasts longer when more peers are present (O'Connell, Pepler, and Craig, 1999), and when they don't intervene, bullying becomes increasingly acceptable. The result is a harsher, less empathetic social climate that fosters more bullying (Olweus et al., 1999).

An audience is the lifeblood of a child who bullies. The bystanders' reactions—their active assistance, comments, and laughter—encourage, reinforce, and even incite his behavior (Slaby, 1997). In the Toronto schoolyard study, peers joined in with words or actions 21 percent of the time in each bullying episode (O'Connell et al., 1999). Even

The Bitter Fruit of Bullying

Children who are the targets of bullying are at risk for aggressive behavior. They may respond to a perceived threat by retaliating or striking preemptively (Slaby, 1997).

According to a recent survey (Anderson et al., 2001), students who killed their fellow students and teachers in schools between 1994 and 1999 were twice as likely to have been bullied by their peers as those they killed. The authors suggest that the students who turned on their classmates may well have been at particularly high risk—among the 10 to 20 percent who both bully and are victimized by bullying.

children who observe quietly are lending support to the bullying behavior by sending the message that they condone it (O'Connell et al., 1999). The same playground study found that peers were silent witnesses 54 percent of the time during each bullying incident. Children stood up for the child being bullied just 11 percent of the time, and when they did they often made a difference (Pepler and Craig, 2000).

Research in Finland by psychologist Christina Salmivalli and her colleagues (1999, 2001) has shown that during bullying episodes children take on different roles, depending on their individual dispositions and what the group expects of them. In addition to bullying and being victimized, they play the following parts:

- *Assistants* help and join the child who is doing the bullying. In a study of these roles in 7- to 10-year-olds in England, Jon Sutton and Peter K. Smith (1999) found that 7.3 percent of children acted as assistants.

- *Reinforcers* come to see what's going on and encourage bullying behavior by laughing and commenting on the action. Sutton and Smith (1999) found that 5.7 percent took on this role.

- *Outsiders* stay away and don't take sides, but their silence permits bullying. Almost 12 percent fit this description in Sutton and Smith's study (1999).

- *Defenders* side with the targeted child, comfort him, and try to stop the bullying. In the Sutton and Smith study (1999), 27.5 percent of children came to the defense of the child under attack. Defenders are more likely to be self-confident, popular, and well liked by their peers.

Enablers

British bullying experts Helen Cowie and Sonia Sharp (1994) describe two powerful ways that children support bullying:

> First, pupils can passively support the bullying behaviour by ignoring it or by remaining silent. These pupils can maintain the victim's role by avoiding the bullied pupil(s) or by not inviting them to join their social group. They can socially reinforce the pupils who are doing the bullying by co-operating with them, being friendly towards them or by not saying anything to them about the bullying behaviour. They can even help to enhance the reputation of the bullying pupil by gossiping about bullying incidents.
>
> Second, pupils can support bullying behaviour in a much more active way. They can do this by: verbally encouraging the behaviour; preventing the pupil being bullied from escaping the situation; shielding the situation from adult view; acting as "look out" or warning the pupils who are bullying that an adult is approaching; generally assisting the pupil to bully by holding the pupil being bullied, or holding coats or bags; directing the bullying behaviour, e.g., "Go on, put her bag down the toilet!"; acting as a messenger for the pupils who are bullying; laughing or smiling at the bullying behaviour; writing graffiti confirming the role of the pupil as victim or bully; refusing to give information about the situation even when asked. (p. 89)

In other words, almost 40 percent of the children, including those who were doing the bullying, took a pro-bullying stance. Among older children these numbers are higher (Salmivalli, 2001).

Paradoxically, 83 percent of the children in a large Canadian survey reported that bullying made them feel either "a bit" or "quite" unpleasant (O'Connell et al., 1999). Clearly, there is a gap between children's attitudes and their behavior. Why do bystanders behave the way they do? First of all, they may be attracted by the aggression, which excites and arouses them. As Pepler and Craig (2000) put it, "Peers are the audience for the theater of bullying" (p. 9). They may also fear the child who bullies and realize that if they try to defend the child who's been targeted, they will put their own safety at risk (O'Connell et al., 1999).

There are also group and social learning processes at work, Olweus (1993) and others (O'Connell et al., 1999) explain:

- *Social contagion.* Research has shown that when children (or adults) see someone acting aggressively, they tend to act more aggressively themselves. This effect increases when the observers have a high opinion of the aggressor. The child who bullies is a model of aggressive behavior, and the admiring assistants and reinforcers follow his lead. Olweus (1993) says these followers are likely to be anxious, insecure, and dependent, and siding with the child who's doing the bullying boosts their social status and protects them from harassment in the future.

- *Weakening of the controls against aggressive behavior.* Children's inhibition against aggressive behavior becomes loosened when they see it has no negative consequences and that it gets rewarded by a turn on the swing or a prime seat at the table. Children who see aggressive behavior rewarded may also become desensitized to violence. So far there is no direct research about this phenomenon where bullying is concerned, but it is well established for television violence.

- *Diffusion of individual responsibility.* When several people are involved, each of them feels less guilt and responsibility.

- *Cognitive changes in perception of the victimized child.* Success enhances the reputation of the child who bullies as a protector, but the more harassment a child who's targeted endures, the more his peers come to regard him as weird, worthless, and deserving of abuse (Olweus, 1993). In their midwestern study (1994), Oliver, Hoover, and Hazler found that many students thought that bullying "teaches about behavior unacceptable to the group" (p. 15). In a study of students in grades 6 and 7 (Graham and Juvonen, 2001), two-thirds thought the child being bullied was responsible for his own harassment. Because most of them believed that the child who was victimized could control his behavior, they were angry, more likely to reject him, and unwilling to come to his aid. Just 25 percent thought the bullying was due to factors beyond his control, such as his being younger or weaker than the child who bullied him or the school's having a lot of tough kids. In general, people who blame uncontrollable circumstances are more sympathetic and willing to help. Students may also blame the targeted child because it's difficult to function in life if one believes that things are random and unjust.

It's far less threatening to take the view that the world is a just place and people get what they deserve (Wilczenski et al., 1994).

• *Role stabilization.* Once a child assumes a role in a group, it's hard to change it. The other members of the group expect him to behave in a way that's appropriate to his role, and the child begins to define himself this way as well (Salmivalli, 1999).

Last but not least, children don't intervene to help a child who's being harassed because they don't understand the process of bullying and don't know how to counteract it (O'Connell et al., 1999).

How can teachers combat bullying?

Bullying is a learned behavior and it can be unlearned and even prevented. It isn't easy to eliminate it entirely, but even finding ways to cut down on its frequency or duration can make a difference in a child's ability to cope (Ladd and Ladd, 2001).

Olweus advocates a whole-school approach, where all the people in the environment—administrators, teachers, children, parents, assistants, bus drivers, lunch supervisors, counselors, nurses, clerical staff—become attuned to bullying and undertake to fight it. This is the method the Norwegian government used so successfully in its

You might ask the child who bullies to take the role of a child who's been victimized in a role-play with puppets.

national bullying intervention between 1983 and 1985. According to an evaluation of 2,500 elementary and junior high school students in Bergen (Olweus, 1993, 2001), bullying of all kinds decreased by half or more among boys and girls across all grades studied. There was a substantial improvement in the school's social climate. Students reported that they had more positive social relationships and a more positive attitude toward school and schoolwork, and there was more order and discipline. Other forms of antisocial behavior—vandalism, fighting, theft, truancy—also declined. The effects were cumulative, better after the second year than the first.

Replications of the intervention in the United States, England, and Germany produced less spectacular but similar results (Olweus, 2001; Olweus et al., 1999). In both the original program and the replications, the more aspects that the teacher and class implemented, the better the outcome.

Other researchers agree that a systemic approach is essential (Rigby, 1998; Sharp and Thompson, 1994). When everyone is doing the same things, the anti-bullying message and its underlying values come through loud and clear, and there's more back-up for any effort at prevention and intervention that children and staff undertake (Sharp and Thompson, 1994).

The goal of the whole-school approach is to restructure the environment so there are fewer opportunities and rewards for bullying and more reinforcement for positive behavior (Olweus, 1993, 2001; Olweus et al., 1999; Sharp and Thompson, 1994). The idea is to change the social context so that bullying is less effective and children understand that it is not acceptable under any circumstances. They also know that adults are

The Lion's Many Roars

Quit It! A Teacher's Guide on Teasing and Bullying for Use with Students in Grades K–3 (1998) includes a unit on the concept of courage. Merle Froschl, Barbara Sprung, and Nancy Mullin-Rindler write:

- It takes courage not to "follow the crowd," especially at this young age when belonging is so important. If we can help students find their own inner strength in the early grades they will be better prepared to resist the peer pressure that becomes so intense in adolescence.

- It takes courage to disagree with someone and risk that they might not be your friend.

- It takes courage to go against the social norm and break down barriers to friendships between girls and boys. . . .

- It takes courage to perform acts of kindness, especially when they involve overcoming a barrier or standing up for someone who is often a target of teasing or bullying. There are many factors that influence how easy or difficult it is to be courageous: your age; size; how popular you are; and whether you are a boy or a girl.

- It takes courage to control your own emotions and not lash out. (p. 67) behind them 100 percent—that they will intervene consistently, protect them, believe their reports, and fully support their efforts to stop it.

It's best to work on the level of the whole school (as well as with the parents, each class, and each child). But if your school or child-care center doesn't already have a bullying policy, you can still introduce one in your own classroom. Be aware that the process will take time and that when you first begin, the problem may appear to get worse before it gets better (Pepler and Craig, 2000). Much of what is suggested here has been discussed in previous chapters of this book, so you are already well on your way.

Committed and well-informed adults hold the key to the success of any anti-bullying project. A teacher's enthusiasm, along with the belief that she or he can actually change things, is crucial to success (Rigby, 1998). The power imbalance that's inherent in bullying makes it impossible for children to fight it by themselves, and adult inaction equals tacit approval: It has been known for decades that the presence of passive adults increases children's aggressive behavior (Siegel and Kohn, 1959).

Adults have some familiar and effective tools to bring to this enterprise. Probably the most important are their warm and involved relationships with the children, firm limits on unacceptable behavior, close monitoring and supervision, models of the positive use of power and problem solving, and a cooperative classroom climate (Olweus, 1993).

To set limits, clear rules against bullying are vital, and the best way to create them is to involve the whole class. (See page 133 for a discussion of class rules.) Olweus suggests three:

- Don't bully other children.

- Help children who are bullied.

- Include children who are left out. (1993, p. 117)

There is a great deal for children to discuss as they draw up their rules. They need to talk about what bullying is—a difficult and complicated topic—as well as why rules are important and what they can do to make the class safer.

Regular class meetings on the subject of bullying are also essential. Used in combination with rules, they bring about larger reductions in bullying (Olweus, 1993). In other words, the subject of bullying should be an ongoing, integral part of the curriculum, and again there is lots to mull over. Power, empathy, peer pressure, courage, prosocial behavior, the difference between accidental and on purpose, the difference between tattling to get someone into trouble and telling to get someone out of trouble, the line between teasing and bullying, how it feels to be unwelcome—all of these topics kindle interesting discussion, and they can all be expanded and reinforced with age-appropriate books, drawings, and role-plays. Children can begin to deal with these ideas as soon as any bullying behavior appears.

To increase awareness of bullying, children could create bullying maps that indicate spots in the school where they feel unsafe, and teachers can set up a box to receive anonymous reports of bullying. You could also use some of this meeting time to teach and practice social skills (see pages 136–152).

Good supervision during less structured times of the day and in areas such as the playground, lunchroom, bathrooms, and hallways can reduce bullying considerably. Researchers have found that there is less aggressive behavior when children play organized, noncompetitive games, and a Rhode Island program that dedicated an area to noncompetitive games significantly decreased both playground and classroom bullying (Froschl et al., 1998).

It's also important to involve parents even before there is a problem. The more they know about bullying and the class rules, the more support they can give you and the more successful your policy will be. Probably the easiest way to do this is to invite them to a meeting where you show a video about bullying, present your policy and the important facts about bullying, and encourage them to discuss the topic. It's especially important to let them know about the bystanders' role so that they can discuss it with their children at home. For the same reason, it's important for them to understand the difference between tattling and telling to protect someone. In addition, some parents might want to talk about what their child and his friends could do to help someone who's being harassed or excluded (Olweus, 1993).

Roughing It

Teachers sometimes find it hard to distinguish between bullying (or fighting) and rough-and-tumble play, when children chase, wrestle, restrain, and hit one another for fun. Rough-and-tumble play is a normal activity that at one time probably helped to develop fighting skills and now perhaps plays a part in working out the dominance relationships in a group (Berk, 2000). English bullying expert Michael Boulton (1994) offers these tips on how to tell rough-and-tumble play from serious aggressive behavior:

- *Facial and verbal expression.* In rough-and-tumble play, children usually laugh and smile. When they fight for real, they frown, stare, grimace, cry, and get red in the face.

- *Outcome.* Children continue to play together after rough-and-tumble play, but after a real fight they separate.

- *Self-handicapping.* In a play fight, a stronger or older child may let his opponent pin or catch him. This doesn't happen in a serious fight.

- *Restraint.* In playful fighting, the contact between children is relatively gentle. When children are really fighting, they go all out.

- *Role reversals.* In rough-and-tumble play, children alternate roles—for example, they take turns chasing and being chased. This doesn't usually happen in a fight.

- *Number of partners.* Lots of children—10 or more—can participate in rough-and-tumble play. Usually just 2 fight when it's serious.

- *Onlookers.* Spectators aren't interested in play fighting, but a serious fight or bullying usually draws a crowd.

One very effective way to encourage parents to attend a parent-teacher evening—and to inform them about bullying—is to use drama. If the whole class participates in writing and putting on a play about bullying, the children can invite their parents to a performance and discussion afterwards, and most parents will probably attend. The creation process, which requires the children to do lots of role-plays and lots of thinking about the issue, teaches them a great deal about how destructive bullying is and how they can avoid, prevent, and deal with it. Be careful not to cast a child who bullies in a bullying role or a child who is victimized in a role where he's harassed so you don't inadvertently reinforce them.

What helps children cope with bullying?

Researchers have singled out some protective factors and strategies that enable children to avoid bullying altogether, to respond to it in ways that deter future attacks, and to cope so that it doesn't overwhelm them. Physical strength and intelligence both lend a child some protection (Smith, Shu, and Madsen, 2001), but there are other useful qualities that teachers can help children to acquire more easily.

- *Self-esteem* is an excellent shield against bullying. Children who have high self-esteem refuse to tolerate bullying and defend themselves assertively and effectively (Egan and Perry, 1998). To help build self-esteem, it is important to encourage and reinforce children's strengths—to pay attention to their potential, help them develop it, and give them lots of opportunities to feel proud of their accomplishments. It is also helpful to catch them being good. Both children who bully and children who are victimized need ways to feel good about themselves if they're ever going to kick the bullying habit (Rigby, 1998).

- *Assertiveness skills* seem especially important. Bullying experts have found that assertiveness training is an effective way to reduce bullying because when children respond assertively, the child doing the bullying will stop or move on. Assertiveness training can also help children gain control, confidence, and self-esteem. In the training groups in Sheffield (Sharp and Cowie, 1994), children learned to make assertive statements, resist manipulation and threats, respond to name-calling, leave a bullying situation, enlist support from bystanders, boost their own self-esteem, and remain calm in a stressful situation. Assertiveness training isn't just for children who are harassed. Salmivalli (1999) notes that being assertive can help the children who are the bully's assistants and reinforcers to resist peer pressure and refrain from bullying. It can even encourage them to try to stop it. Changing the attitudes and behavior of the associates of the child who bullies may help to change him, too.

- *Social skills* that help a child to become a valued member of a group seem to give him some immunity to bullying. These include sharing, taking turns, friendliness, and having a sense of humor (Egan and Perry, 1998; Perry et al., 2001). Activities that encourage empathy and teach problem solving, group entry, and anger management skills all help to foster friendships, which can prevent and reduce bullying. When you're working on empathy, it's important to remind children of their own uneasy feelings about bullying and to help them to practice tuning into them (O'Connell et al., 1999). The *Quit It!* curriculum (Froschl et al., 1998) suggests some natural subjects for lessons on problem solving: children's options in a bullying situation. Walking away to avoid confrontation, diverting the attention of the child who bullies to diffuse the situation, negotiating to resolve a conflict, asserting yourself, seeking adult help to protect yourself—all of these subjects readily lend themselves to discussion, role-play, and puppet play.

• *Cooperation skills*, honed in a cooperative social context, are also crucial. Children who bully and children who are victimized tend to be less cooperative—children who bully because they have little empathy, and children who are victimized because they're often introverted and less accepted by their peers—but because children who cooperate are happier and more popular, this is a valuable skill for building friendship and preventing bullying (Rigby, 1998).

• *A friend* can be a "powerful buffer" against harassment, research shows. In one study (Boivin et al., 2001), having a best friend significantly reduced the likelihood of being victimized over a one-year period. Another study (Kochenderfer and Ladd, 1997) found that an effective strategy for 5-year-olds was to have a friend help them out. And a third (Hodges et al., 1999) found that children who have a best friend suffer from fewer emotional and behavioral problems after they've been bullied. But researchers have also observed that the quality of the friendship is critical. A weak friend who can't protect a child against bullying may actually increase the risk of harassment (Hodges et al., 1999).

• *Thinking that he has some control (having an internal locus of control)*—as opposed to feeling that something immutable in his character makes him a target—helps a child to look for ways to change and cope. For example, he may be more likely to seek help or use positive self-talk, rather than feeling helpless or depressed (Graham and Juvonen, 2001; Ladd and Ladd, 2001).

• *Telling a teacher* is a successful strategy for 5- and 6-year-olds, one study found, whereas walking away and fighting back don't work (Kochenderfer and Ladd, 1997). For older children it is more effective to ignore bullying (Smith et al., 2001). However, even if this an effective tactic, it is important for children of all ages to tell an adult about bullying, whether they do it in person or through anonymous means, such as putting notes in boxes set up in various places around the school to report bullying.

• *Help children to map bullying hot-spots* like bathrooms and secluded areas on the playground. If they are aware that they're in danger, they can avoid this territory, go with a friend, or stay within a reasonable distance of a teacher's watchful eye.

As this list makes plain, there's a lot that teachers can do to bolster resilience and head off bullying. Many of the factors and strategies we've just mentioned are described in more detail in Chapter 8, pages 136–152. Role-playing and rehearsal are absolutely essential for learning them all.

How do you respond to bullying?

Despite your best efforts to prevent it, bullying may still arise. At some point before it does, take some time to understand your own feelings on the subject. If you bullied other children (or were bullied yourself) when you were a child, your feelings may be very strong, and it's important to understand and separate them from what the children themselves are experiencing. These emotions may make it hard for you to remain open to how the child is really feeling as well as to keep your cool, and when you're dealing with a bullying situation a nonthreatening tone of voice and body language are essential. You can use the WEVAS techniques—such as concentrating on the soles of your feet—to help you stay in control (see pages 186–189).

When you encounter bullying in a person, it's crucial to respond immediately. Probably the best plan is to do just what you'd do with any other act of aggression in your classroom—go to the child who's being bullied, let him know you're there to support him, and help him to respond assertively (Sharp and Cowie, 1994). Doing this allows you to state the rules without giving attention directly to the child who's doing the bullying. At the same time, ask the bystanders to leave. They are no doubt encouraging him and intimidating the child who is being victimized.

When you talk with a child who's been bullying others, stay away from power-assertive language and methods. They are sure to backfire.

Later in the day, follow up with an activity for the whole group—for example, read a book about bullying and talk about what bullying is and how it makes children feel. You might even ask the child who is doing the bullying to take the role of a targeted child in a role-play. Ask the children to draw pictures and write their own stories about bullying. Working with the whole group increases the power of the intervention and provides all the children with opportunities to learn about the impact of bullying and how to respond to it.

Be sure to sensitize the children to the role of the bystanders. Explain that they probably don't realize it, but when they're present, even if all they're doing is watching, they are actually supporting the child who bullies. Discuss what they can do instead—walk away, tell the child who's bullying to stop, tell the teacher, include the child who's left out.

At the same time, talk with them about how grown-ups can help in a bullying situation—that secrecy helps the child who bullies, and that teachers and parents need to talk to each other and work together to protect children. Explain that this is why you will call their parents any time bullying is suspected.

Olweus (1993) says to hold private "serious talks" with both the child who did the bullying and the child who's been harassed soon after you learn about the bullying. Although there are pros and cons to talking with either child first, if you start with the child who bullied, he can't accuse the victimized child of tattling on him. If a group of children is participating, arrange to see them individually, one right after the other, so they won't have a chance to cook up a common response or use the group as a power source. The discussion doesn't need to be long, and it shouldn't be an interrogation. If a child feels you're cross-examining him, he will just clam up.

When you're talking with a child who bullies, you aren't trying to intimidate or disempower him, so stay away from language and methods such as hostility, aggression, sarcasm, threats, and humiliation. They are sure to backfire, providing a justification for more bullying and inspiring the invention of more covert ways to bully (Sharp and Cowie, 1994; Sharp, Cowie, and Smith, 1994). Instead, sit at his level in a quiet spot and remind him of the rules. (Even if you have no anti-bullying rules, you should have rules about respecting, taking care of, or not hurting others.) Stick to *what*, *when*, and *where* questions, and talk with him about how his behavior is affecting others, including the bystanders. Be sure to let him have his say. Tell him that bullying is serious and you'll be contacting his parents because they will want to work with you to help him stop this behavior.

Should there be consequences? The experts think so, but they disagree about what they should be. Pepler and Craig (2000, p. 19) favor "formative" consequences, which teach empathy, awareness, and social skills; send the message that bullying is unacceptable; and hold children responsible for their behavior. Formative consequences are logical. They help a child who behaves in a cruel way to learn to treat others with more kindness and to make amends for his mean behavior. This approach enables children who bully to "turn their negative power and dominance into positive leadership" (p. 19).

Rigby (1998), who works with older children, believes that penalties don't deter children with serious bullying problems; instead, he comes down on the side of a

Learning Opportunity

Pepler and Craig (2000) believe that consequences should help children who bully to learn skills and acquire insight. Here are some suggestions:

- Read stories about bullying and talk about how bullying makes people feel.

- Do a role-play with the teacher where the child who bullies takes the part of the child who's victimized.

- Observe and report on acts of kindness around the school and in the community.

Pepler and Craig suggest encouraging the child who bullies "to identify the link between power (or strength) and kindness. It is important for [him] to view prosocial behaviour as worthwhile, valid, and consistent with positive leadership" (p. 20).

respectful, humanistic approach based on the desire to understand, not blame, the child who bullies, the child who's been bullied, or the bystanders. He proposes listening carefully, establishing two-way communication, and using a technique such as the No Blame Approach developed by George Robinson and Barbara Maines in England (1994, 1997) or the Method of Shared Concern created by Anatol Pikas in Sweden (1989). As the names imply, these procedures don't blame anyone, aim to arouse the empathic concern of the child who bullies for the child who's being harassed, try to help children break away from a bullying group by speaking with them one on one, and focus on what can be done to resolve the problem (Smith, Cowie et al., 1994). Although the methods were written for children age 9 and older, these principles apply to younger children, too.

Punishment will not lead to a lasting change in bullying behavior any more than it does with other inappropriate behavior. It may even provoke more serious attacks. Children need your help to learn alternative skills and means of communicating and achieving their goals. Robinson and Maines (1994) put it this way: "It is only by the development of 'higher values,' such as empathy, consideration, and unselfishness, that the bully is likely to relinquish her behavior and function differently in a social setting. If the preventative policy depends on policing the environment, forbidding the behavior, encouraging the victims, and punishing the perpetrators, then no lasting change can be expected."

When you talk with the child who's been victimized, tell him that he has the right to feel safe, and make it clear that you will support and protect him (Pepler and Craig, 2000). Find out what happened by using open-ended questions, and be careful not to suggest that the bullying is his fault or that he deserves it in any way. Together, explore ideas for improving the situation. You might remind him of assertive responses, suggest that he avoid certain areas of the school or center where the bullying is more likely to occur, or help him figure out which child could go with him so

Bullying Straight Talk

Here are some of the things you might say to a child who bullies:

- Jamie isn't feeling very good about being in our class right now. Why do you think he's having such a hard time?

- What do you think we can do to make him feel better?

- What makes you feel happy? What can you do to make Jamie feel happier?

Just as it is in the No Blame Approach and the Method of Shared Concern, the goal here is to get the child to feel some empathy for the child who's being harassed and to help solve the problem with an idea of his own ("I'll ask him to sit with me" or "I'll tell Will to leave him alone"). Encourage and accept any positive suggestion he makes, and above all, don't accuse him, blame him, or argue with him.

that he'll feel safer and not so alone (Pepler and Craig, 2000). Reassure him that you'll be there to help him put these ideas into action. If he seems to be a child who provokes bullying, talk to him about how his behavior might be placing him in the role of a target. Try to understand the reasons behind the provocative behavior, and together try to generate ideas for changing it. For example, he may feel that if he teases or taunts, it gives him some control over the situation. What else could he do to get some control? Reassure him the same way you would reassure any other child who's been targeted—let him know that you're there to protect him and that you're going to work with him to help him change his behavior.

It's also important to tell the child who's been targeted that you're going to speak to his family. Explain that they will want to do everything they can to help and that it is safer if they know what's going on. If he doesn't want you to tell his parents, talk with him for as long as you can to encourage him to accept the idea, but eventually you will have to go ahead without his permission. On the other hand, you can make it clear that you won't proceed with any action plan unless you have his consent. It may take some time, but it's essential if you're going to keep his trust.

In your follow-up activity with the whole group later in the day, be sure to include activities addressed to the child who's been bullied, such as a discussion of why it's important to tell someone who can help you, role-plays of assertive responses, and work on problem-solving skills.

Consult with your director or principal right away—she or he will almost certainly have useful suggestions. Call the parents of the children involved, and set up appointments to see them as soon as possible. Continue to monitor the children carefully, and redouble your efforts to teach social skills, especially assertiveness, cooperation, and empathy.

What do you do if you don't see the bullying?

If a child tells you that he (or someone else) is being bullied and you don't actually see an incident yourself, your instinct might be to wait to intervene until you've witnessed the bullying with your own eyes. This response seems logical, but it can be very tricky. Children do not make up tales about being harassed (Pepler and Craig, 2000), and telling a teacher can be difficult and risky, even for a child who isn't the target. If the child who's doing the bullying knows, his friends may rally around him and the bullying may escalate and spread to the defender. It is therefore extremely important for you to be open to what the child is saying. Tell him that he was right to come to you and that you believe him. Now that you know what's going on, you will be able protect him (or the child who's being bullied) and help him to protect himself. If the targeted child has come to you in person, reassure him that you will keep him safe, and let him know that you'll need to contact his parents because they need to know, too. If a defender has come, assure him that you won't tell anyone who gave you the information.

You may never know exactly what happened because it's hard to gather the facts and each child has his own perspective, but in the end that isn't really important. What's important is knowing that bullying has occurred and exactly which children were involved—the child or children who bullied, the child or children who were targeted, and the bystanders. It is also useful to know where and when the bullying is taking place so that you can move immediately to prevent it.

That is your next step—to prevent further incidents by keeping a very close eye on the children involved, especially at the times and places where the child who's a target is at risk. If there are corners of the room that you can't see, rearrange the furniture. If children are going into the cloakroom or bathroom without an adult, change the schedule so that you or someone else is there to supervise. If you manage to see a bullying episode, you will have enough information to proceed—and again it's important for you to intervene at once.

But if your new vigilance deters the child who bullies, you will see nothing at all. You won't know whether he has actually stopped bullying or whether he's devised new subterranean strategies. If the targeted child is still in danger, he may not have enough courage or trust to talk to you again, and if he does, the child who bullies may accuse him of tattling and intensify his bullying. On the other hand, if you take the initiative and approach the child who bullies yourself, he'll probably deny any involvement and suspect the child who's been victimized anyway. All of this makes for a huge quagmire.

You cannot let this situation continue for more than a day or two because you won't be able to protect the child who is under attack. If you are already using an anti-bullying program, bring it out again and continue to work with the whole group using discussion and role-plays. Another solution is to make an opportunity to talk with the child who's doing the bullying in the general and nonthreatening way we just described, not accusing or blaming him but trying to elicit some empathy for the target and one concrete idea about how he personally could improve the life of the child who's being victimized. Remind him that when there is a bullying issue, it's your job to call the parents of any children who may be involved. Be sure to keep your tone of voice neutral.

Guiding Principles

Peter K. Smith, Helen Cowie, and Sonia Sharp (1994), who directed the Sheffield bullying intervention, suggest that schools and teachers use four principles to guide them when they're working with students involved in bullying:

- Focus on solving the problem . . . ;

- Encourage the pupils themselves to propose solutions to the problem;

- Employ assertive styles of communication rather than aggression or passivity;

- . . . Ensure that other steps are taken to deal with the problem on a long term basis. (p. 212)

You aren't threatening or punishing him; you are doing what grown-ups do in order to keep children safe.

Again, discuss the problem with your director or principal, and arrange to see both sets of parents.

How can you work with the parents of children involved in bullying?

When there's bullying among the children in your classroom, it's imperative to tell the parents (Pepler and Craig, 2000). Olweus's Bergen study (1993) showed that parents wanted to know about bullying problems when their child was involved, even if the teacher "merely suspected bullying was taking place" (p. 95). Because of the difficulty of establishing the facts in a bullying situation, it makes sense to talk to the parents whenever bullying makes an appearance, even if you merely suspect that a particular child is participating. It's always best for the child when teachers and parents work together, and families are a very important part of the solution. As soon as you discover that the problem exists and have spoken with the children involved, arrange to meet separately with each set of parents (see Chapter 12).

Whether their child is doing the bullying or being harassed, parents may know nothing about the bullying. One study showed that just 62 percent of victimized children and 48 percent of children who bully tell a parent (Pepler and Craig, 2000), usually their mother (Rigby, 1998). It's humiliating to tell, and this step is often a last resort for a child who's being bullied (Rigby, 1998). He may be afraid to tell his parents because he's worried that they'll interfere and make the problem worse. You might discover that the parents feel a sense of relief when you first approach them. The news that you're bringing may answer some of their questions, such as why their child doesn't want to take the school bus, stay at school for lunch, or go to school at all. But once they've processed the information, they're likely to feel angry, embarrassed, and helpless.

They'll blame you and the school and wonder why no one is providing adequate supervision. They'll want action right away, and they might also want retribution (Pepler and Craig, 2000).

On the other hand, it is entirely conceivable that you will learn about the bullying problem from an irate, stressed, and worried parent. Since bullying is an underground activity, you may not see it yourself, and the children certainly won't rush to tell you. In one study, just 47 percent of primary school students confided in their teachers (Ziegler and Pepler, 1993). The fact that you don't know about the situation will make it impossible to offer useful feedback or propose a solution on the spot—and once again, the parents will be angry and see your lack of knowledge as the result of your poor supervision. They will probably also take their child's version of events as gospel, down to the last detail.

Under these circumstances, your primary job is to listen. It's essential not to become defensive, as difficult as that may be. Let the parents know that you're very glad they've told you about the situation, and assure them that you take the matter seriously and will make it a priority. Although bullying requires immediate attention, you will need some time to investigate, just as you did when one of the children reported a bullying incident that you hadn't seen. Arrange for a meeting as soon as you are ready. Discuss your intentions with the parents and listen to what they have to say. Their input is important and should be included in your plans.

If you haven't seen the bullying yourself but learned about it from a child or another adult—or "merely suspect" that it's going on—tell the parents that it's the policy to talk to them whenever there's a suspicion of bullying. Let them know that the research shows that children rarely fabricate stories about being bullied and that you're not accusing or punishing their child, but that it's your job to follow through for the sake of all the children involved. Tell them how important it is for you to work with them. Their cooperation and support will make any intervention you undertake much more effective.

Although you'll meet separately with the parents of the children involved, with both families it's important to keep three strategies firmly in the front of your mind:

* Let the parents know that you care about their child and are trying to help him.

* Avoid blame and arguments at all costs—nothing will sabotage your efforts more quickly. Listen to the parents' concerns and try to see things from their perspective, but don't get hooked, even if they attack you.

* Remember that you are presenting a problem to be solved, and the best way to solve it is with their collaboration. Having parents play an active role in the development of a strategy will reduce their feelings of anger, anxiety, or helplessness and provide their child with the parental support he needs. Parents can help you identify the child's strengths, and they can figure out strategies to reinforce your efforts at home.

In other ways, these two conversations—one with each set of parents—may be quite different. The parents of the child who's bullying may deny there's a problem or see bullying as a normal part of growing up. Be understanding but firm. The issue is not whether bullying is acceptable or whether their child is bullying other children; the purpose of the meeting is to find common ground and develop a strategy to help change their child's behavior. Describe the school's policy (and yours!) of creating a safe and caring environment for all children (Pepler and Craig, 2000). Tell them briefly what their child has done, and be sure to make clear that it is his behavior that is unacceptable, not the child himself. At the same time, tell them what your expectations are and the actions you've taken so far. Remember to talk about the child's positive side as well. It's also a good idea to try to establish a shared concern for the child who was targeted. Listen to their ideas, and work together to develop a plan. Try to project a sense of optimism—all parents ultimately want their child to succeed (Beane, 1999).

The parents of the child who's been harassed may feel accused of being overprotective, and they may be feeling guilty or embarrassed that their child doesn't stand up for himself and appears to be an easy target. If they were harassed when they were young, their feelings will probably be magnified. And they will probably still be very angry that you've let their child be hurt (Pepler and Craig, 2000). Your response can either increase or decrease their anxiety about an already stressful situation. Listen to their concerns and be understanding. Explain the bullying policy in your school or

Wise Words for Parents

You probably don't want to tell parents how to parent, but you could offer them the following tips from the Scottish Council for Research in Education (1999):

- Be patient—make time to listen to your child.
- Ask questions but do it sensitively—don't interrogate.
- Show your child that you care.
- Be careful not to say or do anything which could make an already anxious or lonely child feel even more alone.
- Do not take any action before you discuss with your child what you could do, and what he or she could do. It may take a little longer for you to agree on the best course of action than if the decision is taken by the adult alone, but this is time well spent. But make sure you do something.
- Do not make promises you can't keep. It is very important that your child knows that he or she can trust you. . . .
- And remember that if you discover that a child is in serious danger, whether that danger comes from an adult or another child, you must act even if the child wants you to do nothing.
- Tell your child that he or she has done the right thing by talking about what has happened [and] that bullying is wrong.

classroom, and let them know what you've done and what you intend to do to support and protect their child and to educate all the children about bullying. Then talk about what you can do together to keep the child from becoming a target in the future. Encourage them to continue advocating for their child—but remember that he should have a say in any plan that either of you develops.

Let both sets of parents know that you will stay in touch by phone and that they're welcome to call you or come back if they continue to be concerned.

What Do You Think?

1. How has your past experience influenced your attitudes about children who bully, children who are victimized, and bystanders?

2. It is important to reinforce young children's learning about bullying with literature. Find appropriate stories to read and discuss with a particular age group. Explain why your selections will provide useful information and how they will strengthen what you are teaching.

3. How does what you learned in the preven-

tion chapters (Chapters 7 and 8) relate to what you now know about bullying?

4. Why do you think that the rates of bullying in the United States and Canada are so much higher than in Scandinavia?

5. Which behavior do you think is the hardest to change—behavior of children who bully, behavior of children who are victimized, or behavior of bystanders? Why?

Suggested Reading and Resources

Committee for Children. (2001). *Steps to Respect*. A school-based program to reduce bullying. Committee for Children, 568 First Avenue South, Suite 600, Seattle, WA 98104–2804; phone 800–634–4449; http://www.cfchildren.org/violence.htm.

Olweus, D. (1994). *Bullying at school: What we know and what we can do*. Malden, MA: Blackwell.

Pepler, D. J., & Craig, W. (2000). *Making a difference in bullying*. Toronto: LaMarsh Centre for Research

on Violence and Conflict Resolution, York University, Report No. 60. http://www.yorku.ca/lamarsh/articles.htm.

Rigby, K. (2001). *What is bullying? Defining bullying: A new look at an old concept*. http://www.education.unisa.edu.as/bullying/define.html.

School Violence Resource Center. http://www.svrc.net/PDF/Bullying.htm.

References

Alsaker, F. D., & Valkanover, S. (2001). Early diagnosis and prevention of victimization in kindergarten. In J. Juvonen & S. Graham (Eds.), *Peer harassment in school: The plight of the vulnerable and victimized* (pp. 175–195). New York: Guilford.

Anderson, M., Kaufman, J., Simon, T. R., Barrios, L., Paulozzi, L., Ryan, G., et al. (2001). School-associated violent deaths in the United States,

1994–1999. *Journal of the American Medical Association, 286*, 2695–2702.

Beane, A. L. (1999). *The bully free classroom: Over 100 tips and strategies for teachers K-8*. Minneapolis: Free Spirit .

Berk, L. E. (2000). *Child development* (5th ed.). Boston: Allyn and Bacon.

Boivin, M., Hymel, S., & Hodges, E. V. E. (2001). Toward a process view of peer rejection and harassment. In J. Juvonen & S. Graham (Eds.), *Peer harassment in school: The plight of the vulnerable and victimized* (pp. 265–289). New York: Guilford.

Borg, M. G. (1998). The emotional reactions of school bullies and their victims. *Educational Psychology, 18*, 433–444.

Boulton, M. (1994). How to prevent and respond to bullying behaviour in the junior/middle school playground. In S. Sharp & P. K. Smith (Eds.), *Tackling bullying in your school: A practical handbook for teachers* (pp. 103–132). New York: Routledge.

Cowie, H., & Sharp, S. (1994). Tackling bullying through the curriculum. In P. K. Smith & S. Sharp (Eds.), *School bullying: Insights and perspectives* (pp. 84–107). New York: Routledge.

Craig, W. M., & Pepler, D. J. (1997). Observations of bullying and victimization in the school yard. *Canadian Journal of School Psychology, 13*, 41–60.

Crick, N. R., Casas, J. F., & Ku, H.-C. (1999). Relational and physical forms of peer victimization in preschool. *Developmental Psychology, 35*, 376–385.

Crick, N. R., Casas, J. F., & Mosher, M. (1997). Relational and overt aggression in preschool. *Developmental Psychology, 33*, 579–588.

Crick, N. R., & Grotpeter, J. K. (1995). Relational aggression, gender, and social-psychological adjustment. *Child Development, 66*, 710–722.

Crick, N. R., Nelson, D. A., Morales, J. R., Cullerton, C., Casas, J. F., & Hickman, S. E. (2001). In J. Juvonen & S. Graham (Eds.), *Peer harassment in school: The plight of the vulnerable and victimized* (pp. 196–214). New York: Guilford.

Egan, S. K., & Perry, P. G. (1998). Does low self-regard invite victimization? *Developmental Psychology, 34*, 299–309.

Froschl, M., Sprung, B., & Mullin-Rindler, N., with Stein, N., & Gropper, N. (1998). *Quit it! A teacher's guide on teasing and bullying for use with students in grades K-3*. Washington, DC: NEA Professional Library.

Graham, S., & Juvonen, J. (2001). An attributional approach to peer victimization. In J. Juvonen & S. Graham (Eds.), *Peer harassment in school: The plight of the vulnerable and victimized* (pp. 49–72). New York: Guilford.

Hodges, E. V. E., Boivin, M., Vitaro, F., & Bukowski, W. M. (1999). The power of friendship: Protection against an escalating cycle of peer victimization. *Developmental Psychology, 35*, 94–101.

Hoover, J., & Hazler, R. J. (1991). Bullies and victims. *Elementary School Guidance and Counseling, 25*, 212–219.

Hoover, J. H., & Oliver, R. (1996). *The bullying prevention handbook: A guide for principals, teachers, and counselors*. Bloomington, IN: National Educational Service.

Junger, M. (1990). Intergroup bullying and racial harassment in the Netherlands. *Sociology and Social Research, 74*, 65–72.

Juvonen, J., & Graham, S. (2001). Preface. In J. Juvonen & S. Graham (Eds.), *Peer harassment in school: The plight of the vulnerable and victimized* (pp. xiii–xvi). New York: Guilford.

Kochenderfer, B. J., & Ladd, G. W. (1996). Peer victimization: Manifestations and relations to school adjustment in kindergarten. *Journal of School Psychology, 34*, 267–283.

Kochenderfer, B. J., & Ladd, G. W. (1997). Victimized children's responses to peers' aggression: Behaviors associated with reduced versus continued victimization. *Development and Psychopathology, 9*, 59–73.

Ladd, B. K., & Ladd, G. W. (2001). Variations in peer victimization: Relations to children's maladjustment. In J. Juvonen & S. Graham (Eds.), *Peer harassment in school: The plight of the vulnerable and victimized* (pp. 25–48). New York: Guilford.

Mellor, A. (1993). *Finding out about bullying*. Scottish Council for Research in Education. Retrieved November 12, 2001, from http://scre.ac.uk/spotlight/spotlight43.html.

Nansel, T. R., Overpeck, M., Pilla, R. S., Ruan, J., Simons-Morton, B., & Scheidt, P. (2001). Bullying behaviors among US youth: Prevalence and association with psychosocial adjustment. *Journal of the American Medical Association, 285*, 2094–2100.

O'Connell, P., Pepler, D., & Craig, W. (1999). Peer involvement in bullying: Insights and challenges for intervention. *Journal of Adolescence, 22*, 437–452.

Oliver, R. O., Hoover, J. H., & Hazler, R. J. (1994). The perceived roles of bullying in small-town Midwestern schools. *Journal of Counseling and Development, 72*, 416–420.

Olweus, D. (1991). Bully/victim problems among schoolchildren: Basic facts and effects of a school-based intervention program. In D. J. Pepler & K. H. Rubin (Eds.), *The development and treatment of childhood aggression* (pp. 411–448). Hillsdale, NJ: Erlbaum.

Olweus, D. (1993). *Bullying at school: What we know and what we can do*. Malden, MA: Blackwell.

Olweus, D. (2001). Peer harassment: A critical analysis and some important issues. In J. Juvonen & S. Graham (Eds.), *Peer harassment in school: The plight of the vulnerable and victimized* (pp. 3–20). New York: Guilford.

Olweus, D., Limber, S., & Mihalic, S. F. (1999). History and description of the Bullying Prevention Program. Excerpted from *Blueprints for violence prevention: Book 9, Bullying Prevention Program*. Boulder, CO: Center for the Study and Prevention of Violence. Retrieved November 3, 2001, from http://www.colorado.edu/cspv/blueprints/model/chapt/BullyExec.htm.

Pepler, D. J., & Craig, W. (2000). *Making a difference in bullying.* Toronto, Ontario: LaMarsh Centre for Research on Violence and Conflict Resolution, York University, Report No. 60. Retrieved February 1, 2002, from http://www.yorku.ca/lamarsh/articles.htm.

Pepler, D. J., & Craig, W. (n.d.). *Making a difference in bullying: Understanding and strategies for practitioners.* Toronto, Ontario: LaMarsh Centre for Research on Violence and Conflict Resolution, York University. Retrieved February 1, 2002, from http://www.yorku.ca/lamarsh/ articles. htm.

Perry, D. G., Hodges, E. V. E., & Egan, S. K. (2001). Determinants of chronic victimization by peers: A review and new model of family influence. In J. Juvonen & S. Graham (Eds.), *Peer harassment in school: The plight of the vulnerable and victimized* (pp. 73–104). New York: Guilford.

Perry, D. G., Perry, L. C., & Kennedy, E. (1992). Conflict and the development of antisocial behavior. In C. U. Shantz & W. W. Hartup (Eds.), *Conflict in child and adolescent development* (pp. 301–329). New York: Cambridge University Press.

Pikas, A. (1989). The common concern method for the treatment of mobbing. In E. Roland & E. Munthe (Eds.), *Bullying: An international perspective* (pp. 91–104). London: Fulton.

Rigby, K. (1998). *Bullying in schools and what to do about it.* Markham, Ontario: Pembroke.

Rigby, K. (2001a). Health consequences of bullying and its prevention in schools. In J. Juvonen & S. Graham (Eds.), *Peer harassment in school: The plight of the vulnerable and victimized* (pp. 310–331). New York: Guilford.

Rigby, K. (2001b). *What is bullying? Defining bullying: A new look at an old concept.* Retrieved November 28, 2001, from www.education.unisa.edu.au/bullying/define.html.

Robinson, G., & Maines, B. (1994). *The no blame approach to bullying.* Summary of a paper presented at a meeting of the British Association for the Advancement of Science. Retrieved November 12, 2001, from http://www.globalideasbank.org/BI/BI–9.HTML.

Robinson, G., & Maines, B. (1997). *Crying for help: The no blame approach to bullying.* Bristol: Lucky Duck.

Salmivalli, C. (1999). Participant role approach to school bullying: Implications for interventions. *Journal of Adolescence, 22,* 453–459.

Salmivalli, C. (2001). Group view on victimization: Empirical findings and their implications. In J. Juvonen & S. Graham (Eds.), *Peer harassment in school: The plight of the vulnerable and victimized* (pp. 398–419). New York: Guilford.

Schwartz, D., Dodge, K. A., & Coie, J. D. (1993). The emergence of chronic peer victimization in boys' play groups. *Child Development, 64,* 1755–1772.

Schwartz, D., Dodge, K. A., Pettit, G. S., & Bates, J. E. (1997). The early socialization of aggressive victims of bullying. *Child Development, 68,* 665–675.

Schwartz, D., Proctor, L. J., & Chen, D. H. (2001). The aggressive victim of bullying: Emotional and behavioral dysregulation as a pathway to victimization by peers. In J. Juvonen & S. Graham (Eds.), *Peer harassment in school: The plight of the vulnerable and victimized* (pp. 147–174). New York: Guilford.

Scottish Council for Research in Education. (1999). *Let's stop bullying: Advice for parents and families.* Retrieved January 31, 2002, from http://www.scotland.gov.uk/library2/doc04/lsbp-00.htm.

Sharp, S., & Cowie, H. (1994). Empowering pupils to take positive action against bullying. In P. K. Smith & S. Sharp (Eds.), *School bullying: Insights and perspectives* (pp. 57–83). New York: Routledge.

Sharp, S., Cowie, H., & Smith, P. K. (1994). How to respond to bullying behaviour. In S. Sharp & P. K. Smith (Eds.), *Tackling bullying in your school: A practical handbook for teachers* (pp. 79–101). New York: Routledge.

Sharp, S., & Smith, P. K. (1994). Understanding bullying. In S. Sharp & P. K. Smith (Eds.), *Tackling bullying in your school: A practical handbook for teachers* (pp. 1–6). New York: Routledge.

Sharp, S., & Thompson, D. (1994). The role of whole-school policies in tackling bullying behaviour in schools. In P. K. Smith & S. Sharp (Eds.), *School bullying: Insights and perspectives* (pp. 57–83). New York: Routledge.

Siegel, A. E., & Kohn, L. G. (1959). Permissiveness, permission, and aggression: The effects of adult presence or absence on aggression in children's play. *Child Development, 36,* 131–141.

Slaby, R. G. (1997). Psychological mediators of violence in urban youth. In J. McCord (Ed.), *Violence and childhood in the inner city* (pp. 171–206). New York: Cambridge University Press.

Smith, P. K., Cowie, H., & Sharp, S. (1994). Working directly with pupils involved in bullying situations. In P. K. Smith & S. Sharp (Eds.), *School bullying: Insights and perspectives* (pp. 193–212). New York: Routledge.

Smith, P. K., Morita, Y., Junger-Tas, J., Olweus, D., Catalano, R., & Slee, P. (Eds.) (1999). *The nature of school bullying: A cross-national perspective.* New York: Routledge.

Smith, P. K., & Sharp, S. (1994). The problem of school bullying. In P. K. Smith & S. Sharp (Eds.), *School bullying: Insights and perspectives* (pp. 1–29). New York: Routledge.

Smith, P. K., Shu, S., & Madsen, K. (2001). Characteristics of victims of school bullying: Developmental changes in coping strategies and skills. In J. Juvonen & S. Graham (Eds.), *Peer harassment in school: The plight of the vulnerable and victimized* (pp. 332–351). New York: Guilford.

Sutton, J., & Smith, P. K. (1999). Bullying as a group process: An adaptation of the participant role approach. *Aggressive Behavior, 25,* 97–111.

Whitney, I., Smith, P. K., & Thompson, D. (1994). Bullying and children with special educational needs. In P. K. Smith & S. Sharp (Eds.), *School bullying: Insights and perspectives* (pp. 213–240). New York: Routledge.

Wilczenski, F. L., Steegmann, R., Braun, M., Feeley, F., Griffin, J., Horowitz, T., et al. (1994). *Promoting "fair play": Interventions for children as victims and victimizers.* Workshop presented at the meeting of the National Association of School Psychologists, Seattle. (ERIC Document No. ED380744).

Ziegler, S., & Pepler, D. (1993). Bullying at school: Pervasive and persistent. *Orbit, 24,* 29–31.

Appendix A

The Functional Assessment Observation Form [*]

Understanding the functional assessment observation form

Robert O'Neill and his colleagues have developed a chart for recording observations for a functional assessment. The functional assessment observation form is organized around what the authors call "problem behavior events." An event could be one challenging behavior that lasts for mere seconds (Andrew kicks Liane) or an incident that includes several challenging behaviors (kicking, screaming, shouting) and continues for some time. The event starts when the first problem behavior begins and ends when three minutes have passed without any problem behaviors.

The functional assessment observation form indicates:

- The number of events of problem behavior

- The problem behaviors that occur together

- The times when the problem behaviors are most and least likely to occur

- The antecedent events

- Your perception of the function of the behavior

- The actual consequences

You'll find two copies of this form following this explanation. There is one form filled out for an observation of Andrew's behavior in Chapter 11, and there is a blank one for you to use later. The form's eight sections are as follows:

---

[*]Explanation and chart adapted from *Functional Assessment and Program Development for Problem Behavior: A Practical Handbook*, 2nd edition, by R. E. O'Neill, R. H. Horner, R. W. Albin, J. R. Sprague, K. Storey, and J. S. Newton. © 1997. Reprinted with permission of Wadsworth, an imprint of the Wadsworth Group, a division of Thomson Learning. Fax 800–730–2215.

A. At the top, write the child's name and the dates of the observation. You can use this form to record observations over one day or several.

B. In the column on the extreme left, indicate the time of day or the times of specific activities ("9:00–9:20 Circle Time" or "10:00–10:45 Math"). The intervals can be different sizes if, for example, you suspect there will much more challenging behavior at circle time than at nap time.

C. List the behaviors you want to observe (those you identified in your team's discussions and interviews) in the section labeled "Behaviors." Note each behavior separately so that you can figure out which ones occur together.

D. Just under the date, there is a space to put the antecedents that immediately precede the challenging behaviors. Again, your interviews will tell you what these are likely to be. The most common—demands/requests, difficult tasks, transitions, interruptions, and lack of attention—are already listed. If you suspect other antecedents are involved, write them into the empty slots. Some likely possibilities are a particular activity, task, or setting event (such as noise) or a peer or an adult whose presence seems related to the behavior.

E. The next group of columns is for your perception of the behavior's function. What purpose does it serve for the child? Does he get something, avoid or escape something, or change the level of stimulation? Why do you think he behaved this way? Again, the functions most often found in the literature are already listed, and there is space for you to add functions that you identified in interviews and discussions.

F. The next section is for consequences. What follows the behavior? When you're setting up the chart, fill in the diagonal blanks with the consequences that actually seem to occur most often. Do you ignore the behavior, redirect the child, or put him in time-out? Does he get the tricycle? Do the other children laugh? Observing the consequences will help you see exactly what the child is getting from his behavior and provide more evidence of its function. For example, if you're using time-out when the child wants to avoid an activity, the consequence is actually reinforcing the problem behavior.

G. The last column on the right is for comments or initials. Be sure to initial the form so you'll know that you were observing during this time period even if there were no behaviors to record.

H. Finally, the bottom rows, "Events" and "Date," enable you to keep track of the number of events and the days on which you observed them. We'll explain how in the next section.

Using the functional assessment observation form

The first time a problem behavior occurs, write *1* in the appropriate box in the "Behavior" column at the right time of day. As you continue to observe that behavior, continue across the form writing *1* in the appropriate boxes for the antecedents, functions, and consequences. Finally cross off the number *1* in the "Events" row at the bottom. When the second behavior occurs, write *2* in the appropriate boxes across the form, then cross off *2* in the Events row, and so on.

At the end of the day, draw a line after the last number you crossed off in the "Events" row and write the date beneath it. This will show you how many incidents occurred that day and allow you to compare the frequency of events over time.

You can also use this form to observe and record appropriate behaviors. But it probably makes more sense to do that on a chart dedicated to that purpose. Spending several days observing only appropriate behaviors could provide some very interesting ideas for your intervention plan.

You should always assist a child who needs your help, even when you're observing.

A Name: *Andrew*

Starting Date: *Oct. 10 (Mon)*   **Ending Date:** *Oct. 12, 2001*

C Behaviors **D** Antecedents **E** Possible Functions **F** Consequences **G**

B Time	Kicking	Hitting	Demand/Request	Difficult Task	Transition	Interruption	No Attention	Child too close	Child teases	Attention	Desired Item/Activity	More/Less Stimulation	Demand/Request	Activity (Clean-up)	Person	Don't know	Time-out	Reprimand	Stays with teacher	Ignore	Comments/Initials
8–8:45 Free play	2, 10	1, 9, 15		2	10	9, 15	1	1		9, 15			2, 10, 16,17	1	1	10, 17		1, 9, 15			
8:45–9 Clean-up		3, 16, 17				3, 16, 17				3								2, 16	3		
9:30–10:15 Structured activity		4,5, 11, 18	4, 11, 18	5									4, 11, 18			5, 18	5, 18	4, 11			
10:15–11 Outside (Clean-up)	19 /12	6		/12		19 /	19 /	19 /6	19 /6	19 /			/12	6				6, 19 /12			
12–12:30 Lunch	13	13					13	13	13					13	13	13	13				M10/10 M10/12
2:45–3:15 Circle	7						7	7		7						7	7				M10/11 Grace does Circle G10/12
3:15–4 Free play	8, 14	8, 14				8	8	14	14	8				14	14		14			8	Grace arrives G10/10 G10/12
4–4:15 Clean-up																					G10/10 G10/11 G10/12
H Totals	5	15	3	3	3	6	3	3	3	6			8	4	4	6	9	4	1	1	

H Events: 1 2 3 4 5 6 7 8 | 9 10 11 12 13 14 15 | 16 17 18 19 20 21 22 23 24 25

Date: Oct. 10 | Oct. 11 | Oct. 12

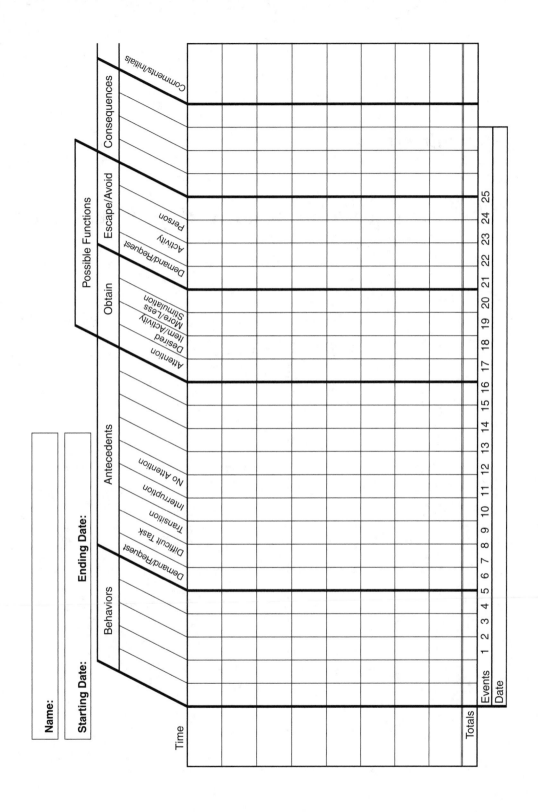

Name:

Starting Date:

Ending Date:

	Behaviors							Antecedents												Possible Functions									Consequences					
								Demand/Request	Difficult Task	Transition	Interruption	No Attention								Attention	Desired Item/Activity	More/Less Stimulation		Demand/Request	Activity	Person						Comments/Initials
Time																																	

Events	1	2	3	4	5	6	7	8	9	10	11	12	13	14	15	16	17	18	19	20	21	22	23	24	25
Date																									

Totals

263

The Functional Assessment A-B-C Chart

Child's Name: _____ Date: _____ M T W Th F

Time/ Activity	Antecedent	Behavior	Consequence	Perceived Function

Setting Events:

Appendix C

The Division for Early Childhood of the Council for Exceptional Children

Position Statement on Interventions for Challenging Behavior*

Many young children engage in challenging behavior in the course of early development. The majority of these children respond to developmentally appropriate management techniques.

Every parent, including parents of young children with disabilities, wants his or her child to attend schools, child care centers, or community-based programs that are nurturing and safe. Many young children engage in challenging behavior at various times during their early development. Typically, this behavior is short-term and decreases with age and use of appropriate guidance strategies. However, for some children these incidences of challenging behavior may become more consistent despite increased adult vigilance and use of appropriate guidance strategies. For these children, the challenging behavior may result in injury to themselves or others, cause damage to the physical environment, interfere with the acquisition of new skills, and/or socially isolate the child (Doss & Reichle, 1991). Additional intervention efforts may by required for these children.

*Adopted April 1998, reaffirmed June 2001. Endorsed by the National Association for the Education of Young Children. *Note:* Permission to reproduce this DEC Position Statement is not required.

DEC believes strongly that many types of services and intervention strategies are available to address challenging behavior.

Given the developmental nature of most challenging behavior, we believe that there is a vast array of supplemental services that can be added to the home and education environment to increase the likelihood that children will learn appropriate behavior. A variety of intervention strategies can be implemented with either formal or informal support. Services and strategies could include, but are not limited to: (a) designing environments and activities to prevent challenging behavior and to help all children develop appropriate behavior; (b) utilizing effective behavioral interventions that are positive and address both form and function of a young child's challenging behavior; (c) adopting curricular modification and accommodation strategies designed to help young children learn behaviors appropriate to their settings; and (d) providing external consultation and technical assistance or additional staff support. In addition, all professionals who work with children in implementing IEPs or IFSPs must have opportunities to acquire knowledge and skills necessary for effective implementation of prevention and intervention programs.

DEC believes strongly that families play a critical role in designing and carrying out effective interventions for challenging behavior.

Given the family-focused nature of early childhood education, we acknowledge the critical role that families play in addressing challenging behavior. Often times, challenging behavior occurs across places, people and time, thus families are critical members of the intervention team. A coordinated effort between family members and professionals is needed to assure that interventions are effective and efficient and address both child and family needs and strengths. All decisions regarding the identification of a challenging behavior, possible interventions, placement, and ongoing evaluation must be made in accordance with the family through the IEP, IFSP, or other team decision-making processes.

Reference

Doss, L. S., & Reichle, J. (1991). Replacing excess behavior with an initial communicative repertoire. In J. Reichle, J. York, & J. Sigafoos (Eds.), *Implementing augmentative and alternative communication: Strategies for learners with severe disabilities.* Baltimore, MD: Paul H. Brookes.

Index

A-B-C analysis, 197, 203, 260–263, 264
Abuse, 39, 64 (*see also* Substance abuse)
  emotional, 62, 232
  and hostility in children, 15
  physical, 15, 35, 36, 38, 39–40, 62, 63, 64, 139, 142, 191, 234, 235, 238
Activities for groups, 133–134, 135
Activity level as a character trait, 25
Adaptability as a character trait, 25
Adler, A., 157
Adrenocortical system, 147
Affective aggression, 15
African American culture, 85, 86, 92, 93–95
Aggression (*see also* Aggressive behavior):
  affective, 15
  cognitive script model, 14
  vs. conflict, 16
  defined, 13
  developmentally appropriate, 10–11
  early onset, 13
  frustration-aggression theory, 14
  and gender, 34–35
  hostile, 15
  instrumental, 15
  late onset, 13
  and moral understanding, 16
  and physical space, 112
  proactive, 15
  reactive, 15
  relational, 15
  social information processing model, 14
  social learning theory, 14
  and stress, 16
Aggressive behavior, 10, 115, 118, 130
  and brain development, 66
  and culture, 17–18
  discouraging, 130
  and poverty, 17

  and social information processing, 14–15
Aggressive state, 186–189
Aggressor effect, 42
Agitation, 179–186
Alcohol during pregnancy, 30
Alcohol-related neurodevelopmental disorder (ARND), 30, 113, 143
Andersen, K., 33, 109, 119, 145, 161, 163
Anderson, E., 94
Anger management, 147–149, 169, 171, 245
Anxiety, 63, 137, 175, 177–179, 235, 236, 237
  in catastrophic events, 40, 125, 126
  in teacher, 72, 216
Approach or withdrawal as a character trait, 25
Asian Pacific culture, 85, 86, 96–98
Assertiveness, 16, 27, 98, 137, 143, 149–152, 180, 236, 237, 245, 247, 249, 250, 252
Assessment (*see* Functional assessment)
Attachment, 141
Attention deficit disorder (ADD), 28–29
Attention deficit hyperactivity disorder (ADHD), 28–29, 113
Attention span as a character trait, 25
Autonomy of resilient children, 53
Ayers, W., 71, 74, 76, 83, 97, 214

Balaban, N., 72, 77
Bandura, A., 14
Behavior, challenging (*see* Challenging behavior)
Behaviorist theory, 157, 159, 167, 170, 195
Benard, B., 52, 53, 54
Bernhard, J. K., 82, 84, 86, 90
Biological risk factors, 23–35 (*see also* Environmental risk factors)
  ADD/ADHD, 28–29
  gender, 34–35

genes, 23–24
language and cognition disorders, 32–34
malnutrition, 32
pregnancy/birth complications, 29–30
substance abuse during pregnancy, 30–31
temperament, 24–28
Body language, 179 (*see also* Nonverbal communication)
Boulton, M., 244
Brain, diagram of, 66
Brain development, 58–67
and abuse, 64
and aggressive behavior, 66
and cortisol, 62–64
critical periods, 60–62
early caregiving, effects of, 61–64
and environment, 59
experience-dependent, 61
experience-expectant, 60
forming attachments, 62
IQ, 62
nerve cells, 59–61
neurotransmitters, 65
and posttraumatic stress disorder, 64
sensitive periods, 60–62
and stress, 62–64
synapses, 59
Bredekamp, S., xi-xii, 88, 111
Bronfenbrenner, U., 80
Bullying:
bystanders, 238–241, 248
children who bully, 234–236
coping with, 245–246
and culture, 237
defined, 231
direct, 232
early signs, 237
enablers, 239
frequency of, 233
group processes in, 240–241
indirect, 232
involving parents, 244
physical, 232
relational, 232
responding to, 247–252
risk factors, 234
targets of, 236–238
verbal, 232
whole-school approach, 241–245

Butchard, N., 174, 188
Bystander effect, 43

Catastrophic events, 40–42, 123–126, 135
Challenging behavior:
appropriateness of, 10
defined, 9
function of, 195–196, 197–198
outgrowing, 11
and positive reinforcement, 163–165
prevention of, 105–126, 129–152, 174, 177–179, 204–208
risks in school, 12
Chandler, L. K., 196
Chess, S., 24, 25, 26, 27
Child care, 43–44, 88–90 (*see also* Early care and education)
Child-rearing practices, 28, 76, 80, 84, 85, 98, 99, 234
Chud, G., 80, 82, 83, 84, 86, 87, 90, 96, 224
Classroom space (*see* Physical space)
Clean-up, 96, 111, 116, 120, 121
Cocaine during pregnancy, 31
Cognition disorders, 32–34
Cognitive script model, 14
Coie, J. D., 6, 10, 11, 12, 13, 16, 18, 32, 35, 36, 40, 136, 137, 148, 149, 237
Colleagues, working with, 217–218
Coloroso, B., 165
Columbine High School, 5, 42
Communication:
and culture, 86
nonverbal, 4, 86, 95, 99, 150, 159, 164, 186, 190
with parents, 79–82, 126, 213–225
techniques, 178–179
Community, 130–136
African American, 94
and language, 132
and resilience, 54–56
Conflict vs. aggression, 16
Conflict resolution, 146–147
Confucian heritage, 96
Consequences:
and bullying, 248–249
and functional assessment, 197
natural and logical, 165–167, 184, 223
Cooperation skills, and bullying, 246
Cooperative games, 133–135

Cortisol, 62, 63, 66
Cowie, H., 234, 239, 245, 247, 248, 249, 252
Crack during pregnancy, 31
Craig, W., 10, 34, 35, 232, 233, 234, 235, 238, 239, 240, 243, 248, 249, 250, 251, 252, 253, 254
Critical periods:
    for social/emotional behavior, 61–62
    for visual system, 60
Cultural diversity (*see* Culture)
Culture:
    African American, 93–95
    and aggressive behavior, 17–18
    Asian Pacific American, 96–98
    and assertiveness, 150
    and behavior, 91
    of child care and school, 88
    and communication, 86
    Confucian heritage, 96
    defined, 82
    and emotional regulation, 142
    high-context, 85, 86
    identifying, 87
    and identity, 83, 84
    inner city, 94
    involuntary minorities, 92
    low-context, 85, 86
    Latino, 92, 95–96
    Middle Eastern American, 98–100
    multiple, 90
    Muslim, 98, 99, 100
    Native American, 96, 97
    and physical space, 111
    and self-esteem, 85
    and time-out, 95
    and transition, 90–91
    voluntary minorities, 92

Dahlquist, C. M., 196
Davidson, R. J., 65, 66, 67, 68
Dawson, G., 29, 67
Deater-Deckard, K., 94
Debriefing after aggressive or assaultive behavior, 191–193
Depression:
    in children, 11, 39, 42, 170, 235, 237, 238, 246
    in mothers, 29, 35, 63, 67, 214

Derman-Sparks, L., 87
Developmentally appropriate practice, 88
Dewey, J., 74
Distractibility:
    as a character trait, 25
    as a feature in ADD/ADHD, 28
Diversity (*see* Culture)
Dodge, K. A., 6, 10, 11, 13, 14, 15, 16, 18, 32, 35, 36, 38, 40, 94, 146, 147, 149, 237, 238
Domestic violence, 39
Donahue, J. J., 36
Dreikurs, R., 165
Durand, V. M., 195, 196, 197, 199, 200, 201, 203, 207–209

Early care and education, 136, 167 (*see also* Child care)
Ebonics, 93
Electroencephalography (EEG), 58, 67
Emotional punishment, 171
Emotional regulation, 65, 67, 141–143
Empathy, 23, 40, 52, 86, 98, 135, 141–143, 149, 151, 152, 171, 180, 235, 238, 243, 245, 246, 248, 249, 250
Encouragement, 162–163
Environment:
    and brain development, 59–61
    and temperament, 26, 27
Environmental risk factors, 35–44 (*see also* Biological risk factors)
    abuse and neglect, 39
    child care, 43–44
    family, 35–37
    lead-based paint, 37
    parenting style, 35–37
    poverty, 37–38
    turbulent times, 40–42
    violence, 38–40
    violent media, 42–43
Eron, L. D., 6, 17, 36, 42, 106
European American culture, 27, 28, 34, 85, 86, 87, 88, 90, 92, 95, 98, 111, 115, 142, 150, 161, 189
Exclusion from group, 134
Executive functions, defined, 33–34
Extinction, 208–209
Eye contact, 73, 86, 95, 96, 150, 188, 191, 192, 209, 222

Fahlman, R., 83, 84, 86, 87, 90, 96, 224
Family (*see also* Parents):
  and culture, 82, 215
  collaborating with, 79–82, 213–216
  disagreement with, 224
  meeting with, 218–222
  of other students, 225
  and risk factors, 35–37
  reaction of, 214
Family-centered approach, 80
Family-systems theory, 80
Farrington, D. P., 35, 232
Feltz, C., 196
Fetal alcohol syndrome (FAS), 30,
  113, 143
Flexibility and prevention, 107
Fogging, defined, 181
Friendship, 55, 62, 94, 99, 111, 133, 134,
  138–139, 236, 237, 245, 246
Froebel, F., 115
Frontal lobe, 66, 143
Froschl, M., 232, 242, 244, 246
Frustration-aggression theory, 14
Functional assessment, 195–210
  antecedents, 197
  collecting data, 201–203
  consequences, 197
  defined, 195
  diagram, 205
  extinction, 208
  function of behavior, 196–198
  interviewing, 200
  Motivational Assessment Scale, 200
  observing, 201–203
  replacement behavior, 206
  setting events, 197

Galinsky, E., 82, 216, 217, 218, 223
Garbarino, J., 51, 52, 53, 54, 56
Gender, 34–35
  and Muslim culture, 100
Genes, 23–24, 26, 28, 59, 65
Goleman, D., 130, 131, 142, 143, 144, 147,
  170
Gonzalez-Mena, J., 76, 84, 86, 87, 90, 94, 95,
  146, 159, 161, 165, 168, 170, 171, 224
Gopnik, A., 61, 62, 71, 142
Gordon, T., 178, 179, 180–181
Greene, R. W., 32, 33, 109, 146, 166

Greenman, J., 40, 109, 123, 135
Greenough, W. T., 59, 60, 61
Group entry, 145–146
Group projects, 133–134
Guidance techniques (*see* Consequences;
  Positive reinforcement; Punishment;
  Time-out)
Gunnar, M. R., 63, 64, 66

Hall, E. T., 82–83, 85
Hallowell, E. M., 28
Hanson, M. J., 82, 215
Harlow, H., 61
Harlow, M., 61
Harris, J. R., 131–132
Hazler, R. J., 232, 234, 235, 240
Head injuries, 40
Hearing loss, 113
Herbert, M., 12, 37, 142, 159, 160, 162, 163,
  166, 167, 214, 215
Heritability of temperament, 26
Heroin during pregnancy, 31
High-context culture, 85, 86
Hobbes, T., 14
Hoover, J., 232, 234, 235, 236, 240
Hostile aggression, 15
Hubel, D., 60, 61
Huesmann, L. R., 36
Hyperactivity as a feature of ADD/ADHD,
  29

Identity and culture, 83, 84
I-messages, 180, 181
Immigrant minorities, 92
Impulse control, 143–145
Impulsivity as a feature of ADD/ADHD, 28
Inattention as a feature of ADD/ADHD,
  28
Increased appetite effect, 43
Individualized support, 107–109
Individuals with Disabilities Education Act
  (IDEA), 196
Inner cities (U.S.), 16, 38, 94
Instrumental aggression, 15
Intensity of reaction as a character trait, 25
Interrupt as a limiting response, 182–183
Involuntary minorities, 92
IQ, 30, 37, 62
Iwata, B., 196, 198, 201, 206

Kagan, J., 26, 27, 28
Kaplan, J. s., 203, 208
Katz, L. G., 108
Kuhl, P. K., 61, 62, 71, 142
Kurcinka, M. S., 25

Language:
    and community, 132–133
    delays, 32
    disorders, 32–34
Latino culture, 85, 86, 92, 95–96
Lead-based paint in environment, 37
Levin, D. E., 42, 117, 124
Limiting response, 182–183
Logical consequences, 165–167
Long, N., 182, 191, 192
Low-context culture, 85, 86
L-stance, 188, 189
Lynch, E. W., 76, 82, 83, 85, 86, 215, 219, 220

Maccoby, E., 16, 34
Magnetic resonance imaging (fMRI), 58
Maines, B., 249
Malnutrition, 32
Marijuana during pregnancy, 31
Maslow, A., 158
Materials, selection of, 116–117
McClellan, D. E., 108, 130, 133, 134, 135, 139, 167, 168
Media violence, 42–43, 117
Meltzoff, A. N., 61, 62, 71, 142
Methadone during pregnancy, 31
Mild cognitive impairments, 33
Mirroring, 179, 189, 192
Mischel, W., 143
Moffitt, T. E., 12, 32–33, 34, 35
Mood as a character trait, 25
Motivational Assessment Scale, 200
Motor delays, 32
Muslim culture, 98, 99, 100

Nagin, D. S., 137
Native American culture, 96, 97
Natural consequences, 165
Negative self-image, 163–164
Nerve cells and effect of experience, 60–61
Neuropsychological damage, 29
Neurotransmitters:

    and aggression, 65
    and brain development, 65
    dopamine, 65
    emotional regulation, 65
    norepinephrine, 65
    and Prozac, 65
    serotonin, 65
    vasopressin, 65
Nicotine and pregnancy, 31
Nonverbal communication, 4, 86, 95, 99, 150, 159, 164, 186, 190
Nonverbal learning disabilities, 33
Nonverbal positive reinforcement, 159, 164

Observation, 145, 158–159, 160, 175
Obsessive-compulsive disorder, 59
Obstetrical problems, 29
Occipital lobe, 66
Ogbu, J. U., 92
Olds, D., 29, 31
Oliver, R., 232, 234, 236, 240
Olweus, D., 131, 149, 231, 232, 234, 235, 236, 237, 238, 240, 242, 243, 244, 248, 252
O'Neill, R. E., 195, 196, 197, 198, 200, 201, 203, 204, 206, 207, 209, 210, 259
Open-ended activities, 135
Open-ended questions, 178
Operant conditioning, 159
Opportunity factors, 50 (*see also* Protective factors)
Optimism of resilient children, 53
Options statement as a limiting response, 182
Orbitofrontal cortex, 66

Paley, V. G., 134
Paraphrasing children's messages, 178–179
Parenting style and risk factors, 35–37
Parents (*see also* Family):
    and bullying, 252–255
    communication with, 79–82, 126, 213–225
    guidance from, 109
Parietal lobe, 66
Patterson, G. R., 36, 149
Peer partners, 134, 139
Peer rejection, 12, 15, 16, 34, 51, 92, 106, 134, 136, 139, 145, 146, 147, 149, 163, 178, 235, 236, 237, 238, 240

Pepler, D. J., 10, 12, 14, 34, 35, 106, 232, 233, 234, 235, 238, 239, 240, 243, 248, 249, 250, 251, 252, 253, 254
Perinatal trauma, 29
Persistence as a character trait, 25
Phillips, C. B., 91
Physical aggression, 10, 34
Physical punishment, 94, 171, 234
Physical space:
  and aggression, 109, 112
  and culture, 111
  crowding, 111–113
  designating areas, 110
  level of stimulation, 113
  open spaces, 110
  personal space, 99, 111
  and prevention, 109–114
Piaget, J., 88
Pikas, A., 249
Play:
  and catastrophic events, 124–125
  competitive, 116–117, 120, 135
  cooperative, 109, 115, 130–131, 133–134
  and physical space, 109–114
  rough-and-tumble, 34, 130, 244
  and social context, 130
  structured, 114–116
  as therapy, 124–125
  violent, 117, 124–125
Plomin, R., 26
Positive reinforcement, 159–167, 206, 207
  of approximations of desired behavior, 161, 207
  as a consequence, 165–167
  nonverbal, 159, 164
  praise vs. encouragement, 162–163
  provoking challenging behavior, 163–165
  rewards, 160
  verbal, 159
Positron emission tomography (PET), 58
Posttraumatic stress disorder, 29, 39, 64
Poverty and risk factors, 37
Praise, 162–163
Prefrontal cortex, 66
Pregnancy, complications of, 29–32
  obstetrical problems, 29
  perinatal trauma, 29
  premature birth, 29
  stress, 29
  substance abuse, 30–31

Prevention of challenging behavior, 105–126, 129–152, 174, 177–179, 204–208
  effectiveness of, 106–107
  flexibility, 107–109
  meeting children's needs, 107
  and physical space 109–114, 129–152
  and supervision, 116
  and teacher's program, 114–126
Proactive aggression, 15
Proactive assertive behavior, 151
Problem solving, 30, 33, 34, 40, 53, 130, 131, 135, 146–147, 151, 223, 225, 243, 245, 250
  skills of resilient children, 53
Professional help, 226–229
Program:
  activities, 118–120
  choices, 114–116
  circle, 114, 119–120
  clean-up, 121
  materials, 116–117
  play, 124–125
  routines, 122, 125
  structure, 114–116
  transitions, 120–122
Projects for groups, 133–134, 135
Prosocial behavior, fostering, 26, 43, 114, 130–135, 137, 140, 243, 249
Protective factors, 50–55
Prozac, 65
Punishment, 167–171
  and bullying, 248–249
  emotional, 171
  problems with, 170
  time-out, 167–169

Racial discrimination, 38
Ratey, J. J., 28
Reactive aggression, 15
Reactive assertive behavior, 151
Redirection as a limiting response, 183
Reframing children's statements, 179
Refugees, 92
Regularity as a character trait, 25
Rejection (*see* Peer rejection)
Relational aggression, 15
Relational bullying, 232
Religious faith and resilience of child, 54

Repp, A. C., 195, 196, 197, 198, 202, 207
Resilience of child, 50–56
Restraint, 191
Responsiveness as a character trait, 25
Rhythmicity as a character trait, 25
Rigby, K., 232, 234, 235, 236, 238, 242, 243, 245, 246, 248, 252
Risk factors (*see* Biological risk factors; Environmental risk factors)
Robinson, G., 249
Rogers, C., 157
Rogers, F., 135
Role modeling, 14, 36, 38, 53, 54, 56, 62, 71, 97, 130–131, 132, 135, 137, 139, 140, 141, 144, 180, 225, 240, 243
Role-playing, 133, 134, 140, 141, 144, 146, 151, 243, 246, 248, 249, 250
Rough-and-tumble play, 34, 130, 244
Routines, maintaining, 122, 125
Rutter, M., 23, 24, 50, 51, 52, 53, 55, 62
Rules and policies, 133, 243

Salmivalli, C., 239, 240, 241, 245
Schwartz, D., 237, 238
Self-control skills, 143–145
Self-esteem of resilient children, 53
    and bullying, 245
    and culture, 85
    low, 28, 51
Self-image, negative, 163–164
Self-reflection, 74–77
Sensitive periods (*see* Critical periods)
Sensory integration, 33
September 11, 2001, xii, 5, 40, 123, 125, 135
Serbin, L. A., 12, 35
Serotonin, 65
Serotonin-transporter gene, 65
Sharifzadeh, V.-S., 98–99, 100
Sharp, S., 232, 233, 234, 239, 242, 245, 247, 248, 252
Sibling interaction, 12
Skinner, B. F., 170
Slaby, R. G., 6, 7, 11, 14, 15, 34, 35, 42, 106, 113, 114, 115, 117, 130, 135, 139, 144, 146, 150, 151, 162, 167, 169, 238
Smith, P. K., 231, 232, 233, 234, 237, 239, 245, 246, 248, 249, 252
Smith, R., 51–52, 53
Social competence of resilient children, 52
Social context:

activities, 133–134
creating, 129–136
defined, 129
group projects, 133–134
rules and policies, 133
teacher's role in, 130
Social information processing, 14–15, 136, 147
Social learning process and bullying, 240
Social learning theory, 14, 157, 159, 167
Social skills:
    anger management, 147–149, 169, 171, 245
    assertiveness, 16, 27, 98, 137, 143, 149–152, 180, 236, 237, 245, 247, 249, 250, 252
    and bullying, 245
    conflict resolution, 146
    emotional regulation, 141–143
    empathy, 23, 40, 52, 86, 98, 135, 141–143, 149, 151, 152, 171, 180, 235, 238, 243, 245, 246, 248, 249, 250
    friendship, 138
    group entry, 145–146
    importance of, 136
    impulse control, 143–145
    inclusion, 139
    learning, 137–139
    peers, 139
    problem solving, 30, 33, 34, 40, 53, 130, 131, 135, 146–147, 151, 223, 225, 243, 245, 250
    teaching, 136–151
Spencler, R., 174, 188
Stress, 29, 124
    and aggression, 16
    and hormones, 16, 62–64
    and pregnancy, 29
Substance abuse:
    and pregnancy, 30–31
    risk for, 12, 13, 51
Suomi, S., 65
Supervision, 36, 38, 53, 94, 99, 109, 116, 118, 135, 190, 243, 244, 251, 253
Synapses, 59

Tatum, B. D., 87, 92, 178
Teaching response, 180
Teasing, 13, 171, 232, 236, 242, 250
Television, 40, 42–43, 117, 126

Temperament, 23, 24–28, 37, 40, 56, 68, 81,
        83, 111, 113–114, 116, 120, 158, 234,
        236
    and culture, 28
    and cortisol, 64
    and emotional regulation, 141
    and environment, 26, 27
    heritability of, 26
    of teacher, 71, 73
    traits, 25
Temporal lobe, 66
Thomas, A., 24, 25, 26, 27
Time away, 169
Time-out, 95, 167–169
Tobacco during pregnancy, 31
Transitions, 120–122
    and culture, 89
Tremblay, R. E., 6, 10, 11, 12, 18, 34, 35, 36,
        137, 139
Turecki, S., 25, 26

U.S. culture and aggressive behavior, 17

Validating children's messages, 178–179
Verbal reinforcement, 159
Victim effect, 42–43
Video games, 42
Violence, 38–40, 94, 117
    programs for prevention, 131, 152–153
Violent media, 42–43, 117
Vision, 60–61

Voice tone, 179
Voluntary minorities, 92

Webster-Stratton, C., 11, 12, 36, 37, 142,
        159, 160, 162, 163, 166, 167, 214, 215
Weissbourd, M., 82, 216
Werner, E. E., 50, 51–52, 53, 54, 55, 56
WEVAS (Working Effectively with Violent
        and Aggressive States), 174–194, 204,
        247
    aggressive state, 186–189
    agitated state, 179–186
    anxious state, 175, 177–179
    assaultive state, 190–191
    calibration, 175
    debriefing, 191–192
    interrupt, 182
    limiting response, 182–185
    model, 176
    open state, 191–192
    options statement, 182, 183–185
    restraint, 191
    returning to group, 192
    teaching response, 180–182
Whole-school approach, 6, 241, 243
Wiesel, T., 60, 61
Withdrawal as character trait, 25
Wood, M. M., 178, 182, 191, 192

Yoshikawa, H., 6, 23, 39